Auo

£30—

£14—
As seen

INDIA

British-Indian campaigns in Britain
for Indian reforms, justice & freedom
1831 — 1947

India in 1857

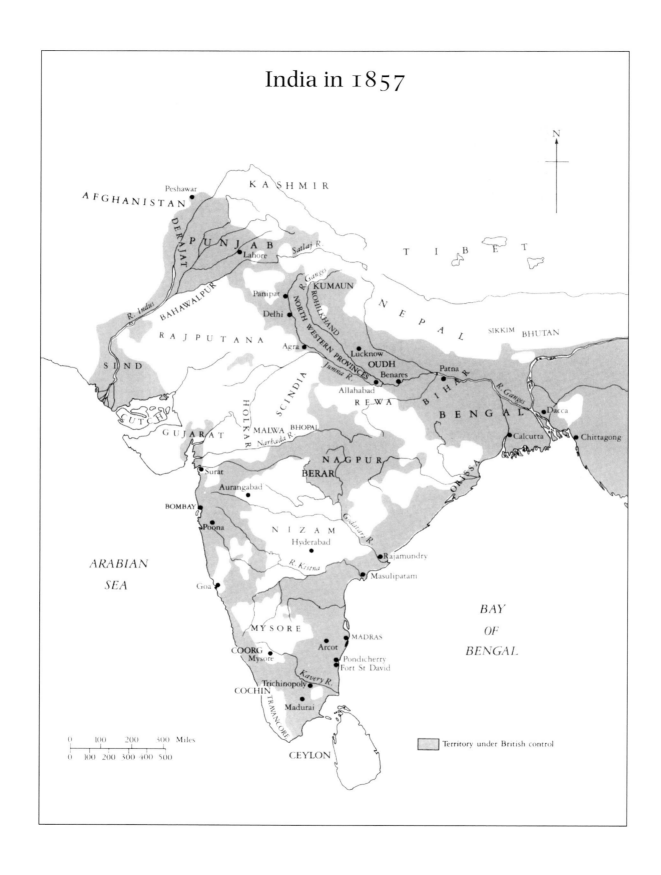

AFGHANISTAN

Peshawar

KASHMIR

DERAJAT

PUNJAB

Lahore

Satlaj R.

R. Ganges

KUMAUN

N E P A L

TIBET

SIKKIM BHUTAN

R. Indus

BAHAWALPUR

Panipat

ROHILKHAND

Delhi

NORTH WESTERN PROVINCES

RAJPUTANA

Agra

Lucknow

OUDH

Benares

Patna

BIHAR

R. Ganges

Dacca

SIND

Jumna R.

Allahabad

REWA

BENGAL

SCINDIA

HOLKAR

MALWA BHOPAL

Narbada R.

CUTCH

GUJARAT

Calcutta

Chittagong

Surat

NAGPUR

BERAR

ORISSA

Aurangabad

BOMBAY

Godavari R.

Poona

N I Z A M

Hyderabad

Rajamundry

ARABIAN

SEA

R. Krisna

Masulipatam

Goa

BAY

OF

BENGAL

MYSORE

Arcot

MADRAS

COORG

Mysore

Pondicherry

Fort St David

Kavery R.

Trichinopoly

COCHIN

TRAVANCORE

Madurai

CEYLON

0   100   200   300 Miles

0   100 200 300 400 500

Territory under British control

KUSOOM VADGAMA

INDIA

....

British-Indian campaigns in Britain
for Indian reforms, justice & freedom
1831 — 1947

Published in the Golden Jubilee year
of India's Independence

BANYAN TREE PUBLISHING

LONDON

British Library Cataloguing in Publication Data:
A catalogue record for this book is available
from the British Library

ISBN 0-9531630-0-8

Published in the UK in 1997 by
Banyan Tree Publishing
808 Finchley Road
London NW11 6XL

1 3 5 7 9 8 6 4 2

Set in Photina
Designed and produced by
Pardoe Blacker Publishing Limited
Lingfield · Surrey

Typeset by The Studio, London
Printed in Britain by
Bookcraft (Bath) Limited

Contents

To
MY MOTHER
AND THE MEMORY
OF MY FATHER
for all their love
and
affection

Foreword

KUSOOM VADGAMA is an author of exceptional quality. She is an earnest, careful and diligent researcher. She is gifted with a remarkable clarity of thought and lucidity of expression. She has India and its heritage in her heart. Her earlier book *India in Britain* received widespread praise. I found in it a mirror reflection of the pageant of India in Britain.

Through this remarkable book which is an engaging narrative of the Indo-British encounter and engagement and is in a sense a sequel to her earlier book, Kusoom Vadgama has rendered a yeoman service to the understanding of the more positive aspects of Indo-British relations. This is the story of the British friends of India, not the story of the Empire. With her characteristic equanimity and objectivity, she celebrates the contributions of those who battled for the larger cause of freedom and gives credit where it is due. She pays homage of remembrance to British scholars, administrators, statesmen and many others who made common cause with those who struggled for fairness, justice and freedom. Here is a panoramic view of Indo-British relationship in perspective. The vignettes and episodes in this book represent an aspect of Britain which we in India applaud and appreciate. To give an accolade to those who saw India as a civilisation and who saw the freedom struggle of India as a legitimate imperative during the colonial period imparts a golden touch to the celebration of 50 years of our Independence and is an abiding contribution to Indo-British friendship which has entered a new phase of partnership.

LM Singhvi
HIGH COMMISSIONER

Preface

THE INDO-BRITISH RELATIONSHIP is richly textured and has shown itself to be remarkably durable. Following India's independence, London and New Delhi, while bound by the Commonwealth connections, may have drifted away politically due to the cross-currents of the Cold War; but the bonds between the Indian and British peoples were strengthened in a variety of ways, not least by the growing Indian presence within British shores. This includes the vast majority of East African Asians who look to India for their ethnic and cultural roots.

The great Indian novel, the small Indian take-away, the posh Indian restaurant, Bhangra and the classical dance, pop music and the classical *raaga*, Bollywood and its cinematic counterpoints, Satyajit Ray, Ritwick Ghatak, Shyam Benegal and their line, the Indian corner shop and the fashion boutique, all have woven fresh patterns in a relationship that moves confidently into the new millennium.

The best British values during the Raj clearly fell on fertile ground in what is now the Republic of India: democracy, the rule of law, the concept of a civil society, not forgetting the English language, are an integral part of Indian life. 'Without the British, India would not have been complete', said Tagore. For its part, India marked the British as no other dominion or colony ever did.

The post-imperial chapters in the Indo-British story promise to be every bit as interesting as the earlier ones. In Britain, people of Indian origin sit in the House of Lords and in the House of Commons; Indians excel in business, the professions and in education. Temples, mosques and gurdwaras lend colour and vitality to the pluralism of the British social and cultural landscape. The Indian work ethic is simply another manifestation of the Victorian work ethic and is proving just as fruitful.

In the Golden Jubilee Year of Indian independence it is right that those Britons who laboured for Indian causes are remembered. This book is a personal tribute to their memory. It is a dedication also to Indo-British fellowship.

Acknowledgements

NOTHING HAS GIVEN ME as much pleasure as working on this book since October 1996 when I first thought of the subject. It has been a most stimulating and delightful experience tracing the history of India's struggle for freedom and the realisation that it all started in Britain and with British help.

I have had the good fortune of having Dr Premen Addy, visiting tutor at Kellog College, Oxford, as editorial adviser, to whom I owe a very special debt of gratitude, first and foremost. I have relied heavily on his sound judgement and enormous knowledge of history and have welcomed his valuable additions and alterations to the text of the book. He has carried out his job with great care and generosity, which is deeply appreciated.

My special thanks to Azim Husain, one of India's most senior and distinguished diplomats, for his sustained interest in the publication of this book.

I am most grateful to Michele Cornish for her superb and ready assistance at all times.

I must now express my sincere thanks to the patient understanding and supply of archival material by the army of librarians and their assistants, without whose help this book would not have been possible. I am grateful for their courtesy and willingness to help. It is a great pleasure to put on record my indebtedness to each and every one of them and am delighted to have this opportunity of expressing my thanks to: Jill Kelsey, Assistant Registrar, The Royal Collection Trust, Windsor Castle; Terence Pepper, Curator, Photographic Collection, National Portrait Gallery; James Kilvington, Bernard Horrocks, Jennifer Cozens and Paul Cox, the Picture Library, National Portrait Gallery; Anne L Lewis, Reference Librarian of the Library of Congress, Washington DC; William J Walsh of National Archives and Record Administration, Maryland, USA; I A Baxter, David Blake and Rod Hamilton of the Oriental and India Office Collection, the British Library; T R Padfield and Nicholas Coney of the Public Record Office; Sylvia Carlyle, Peter Daniels and Tabitha Driver, Assistant Librarians, Quakers, Religious Society of Friends in Britain; Jane Newton, Assistant Director, the Centre for the Study of Cartoons and Caricature, University of Kent at Canterbury; David J Johnson, Clerk of the Records, Record Office, House of Lords; Sarah Priddy of Public Information Office, House of Commons; the Main Reading Room, Social Policy Information Service and the Newspaper Library of the British Library; *The Daily Telegraph*.

I am deeply indebted to Tim Robinson, Producer, and Clare Ragsdale, Researcher, both of BBC 2 TV, Arts Department, for making it possible for me to have access to the recently released Indian Political Intelligence files, at the Oriental and India Office Collection, of the British Library. My thanks to Graham Shaw for his help in finding some of those files at my request at very short notice.

To those whose names I have inadvertently omitted, I must of course apologise.

While every care has been taken to ensure exactness of details and information, I can only apologise if there are any inaccuracies or insufficient details on events or individuals: often it has not been possible to obtain precise or reliable facts.

Quotes taken from journals are reproduced faithfully in their original style which may appear unfamiliar by today's standard.

India in Britain

INDIA IS BOTH COUNTRY AND CIVILISATION. In the opening years of the eighteenth century they were fast approaching their nadir. The last of the great Mughals, Aurangzeb, who ruled from 1658 to 1707, sought to remake India in his own orthodox Sunni image, the exercise ending in ultimate disaster. Marathas, Sikhs and Jats resisted his attempts to chasten them into a common Islamic shape. The result was war and repression. The effort drained the imperial exchequer and reduced the country to a listing hulk, a prey to Hobbesian anarchy within and a temptation to predators from without, once the old Emperor had departed the scene.

Northern India was traumatised in turn by the Persian Nadir Shah and the Afghan Ahmed Shah Abdali. The Marathas were unable, eventually, to become a unifying national force; nor, subsequently, were the Sikhs any more successful. India, as the historian Jadunath Sarkar remarked, was truly spent. Science and scientific inquiry had long been buried under theological dogma and the cultural horizons of the people had shrunk, leaving them with little coherent sense of their past.

When the British East India Company established its dominion in Bengal in the middle of the eighteenth century, it did so initially through further plunder, resulting in a famine of appalling scale and devastation (1770). However, with the beginnings of stable government under Warren Hastings (1772–85), the life of the mind showed movement after the long night. With the Governor-General's encouragement, a Company servant, Charles Wilkins, attained a scholarly command of Sanskrit and produced the first English translation of the *Gita* in 1785.

Hastings pronounced the *Gita* as 'a performance of great originality, of a sublimity of conception, reasoning and diction almost unequalled...' Of the corpus of such Sanskrit works, he proclaimed with astonishing prescience: 'These will survive when the British dominion in India shall have long ceased to exist, and when the sources which it once yielded of wealth and power are lost to remembrance'.

A distinguished line of British Indologists, William Jones, Charles Wilkins, Horace Hayman Wilson, William Carey, James Fergusson, Henry Thomas Colebrooke, James Prinsep, Alexander Cunningham, Brian Houghton Hodgson and teams of scholar administrators such as Monstuart Elphinstone, John Malcom, Thomas Munro, Col. James Tod, Charles Metcalfe and others of the genre, in rediscovering India's classical past and settling the country, awakened the Indian people to the magnificence of their lost heritage. From this was to spring Indian self-awareness and cultural pride: seedbeds of an emerging political identity. In Britain the study of Sanskrit became a rigorous academic discipline. The Boden professorship was set up at Oxford and similar chairs were established over time at the universities of Cambridge, London and Edinburgh.

It was at Oxford that the Anglo-German, Professor Max Muller (1823–1900), undertook his magisterial and pioneering work on the *Rig-Veda*, thereby establishing his reputation as the greatest Western Indologist of the century and earning the admiration and gratitude of Indian Sanskritists and the country's educated class.

Raja Radhakanta Deb (1783–1867), once the orthodox Hindu adversary of the liberal Raja Rammohun Roy, editor of a new Sanskrit encyclopaedia and dictionary and a patron of Sanskrit scholarship, on receiving the first volume of the *Rig-Veda*, wrote a letter of appreciation to Max Muller in which he said: 'Your labours will furnish the Vaidik Pandits with a complete collection of the holy Samhita of the first Veda, only a detached portion of which are to be found in the possession of a few of them'.

When Max Muller's second volume reached him, Radhakanta Deb was moved to pay the author this eloquent tribute: 'By successfully embarking on such an arduous undertaking, you have done to the Hindus an inestimable benefit, supplying them with a correct and superb edition of their holy scriptures. Accept therefore my most grateful and sincere thanks, which, in common with my countrymen, I owe to you.'

Swami Vivekananda (1863–1902), the prophet of the reforming neo-Hindu revivalist movement, wrote: 'The *Rig-Veda*, upon which nobody could set his eyes as a whole, has now been beautifully printed, and can be read by the general public, as a result of an enormous expenditure on the part of the East India Company and the years of labour by the Professor.'

Max Muller's Indian biographer Nirad Chaudhuri quotes Vivekananda as saying of him: 'There are a number of great souls in the West who undoubtedly are well-wishers of India, but I am not aware of one in Europe who is a greater well-wisher. He is not only a well-wisher, but also a deep believer in Indian philosophy and religion... Though all through life he has lived with and steeped himself in ancient Sanskrit literature, the India of the Professor's imagination is not simply that which resounded with chanting of the Vedas... he also is ever alert to whatever in the way of new developments is happening in every corner of India and keeps himself well posted about them.'

Max Muller, who never visited India, met with a number of eminent Indians in Britain, including the charismatic religious reformer Keshub Chandra Sen (1838–1884), in whose work he took a special interest, and Swami Vivekananda himself. Earlier in life, as a young student in Paris, Max Muller had encountered Prince Dwarkanath Tagore, grandfather of Rabindranath Tagore, and held a series of absorbing conversations with him about Indian culture.

If Hastings created one enduring tradition in the Indo-British relationship, his prosecutor Edmund Burke left the legacy of another: the moral and political accountability of rulers and the scrutiny of their abuses of power under due process. The British Marxist historian Victor Kiernan writes: 'Hastings was the first Governor-General of India, in an age when conquest and empire stood for not much more than plunder and rapine; the fact that he could be made to stand trial before Britain's highest court on charges of high crimes and misdemeanours, even if in the end unsuccessfully, left an indelible impression. It was a salutary warning to all his successors and their subordinates; it did much to make British rule, with all its sins of omission and commission, on the whole a rule of law, for which its Indian subjects could feel some respect'.

Yet, the adversaries, Hastings and Burke, were joined in admiration and regard for India and the Indian peoples, unlike such maligners as the utilitarian James Hill and the evangelical Charles Grant. Their confrontations entered the public domain through pamphlets, books and newspapers, reflecting in part contemporary Britain, where issues of

Rabindranath Tagore (1861–1941) India's greatest renaissance man. First came to Britain in 1877. Bengali poet, novelist, short story writer, essayist, dramatist, philosopher, educationalist, painter and founder of Shantiniketan (abode of peace), an institute of Indian Arts and Literature at Calcutta 1901, agricultural school, 1914 and International University, 1921; Nobel Prize for literature *Gitanjali* (Song Offering) 1913, the first Asian to be so honoured. Knighted in 1915, an honour which he resigned in 1919 as a protest after the Jallianwalla Bagh massacre in Amritsar in 1919. Bestowed the title 'Mahatma' (Great Soul) on Gandhi; composed Indian national anthem – long before Independence in 1947; officially accepted in 1948 by the new Cabinet.

Swami Vivekananda (1863–1902)
Navendra Datta, later to become Swami Vivekananda, carried the message of India across the whole world; he attended the Chicago Parliament of Religions in 1893 where his speeches electrified the audience; he was made to speak last to keep the public from leaving the hall. Deeply impressed Max Muller during his visit to Europe; addressed the Congress of History of Religions in Paris in 1900.

the moment were discussed in the press with vigour and, frequently, with considerable spite as well.

James Hickey founded the weekly *Bengal Gazette* in 1780, but the journal was closed down in 1782 following its irreverant attacks on Hastings. However, Hastings, understanding the need for an organ sympathetic to the government, founded the *India Gazette*. Over the next century and a half, newspapers, with their British and Indian owners, battled for the public ear, some seeking to justify the colonial enterprise, others pointing to its injustices and excesses. It was a paradox of British rule that, while press freedom was curtailed, from time to time, at the margins, it was never extinguished at the centre of public life.

The Canadian scholar Milton Israel in his study of the Indian press notes: 'A totalitarian regime might have prevented nationalist leaders from achieving such notoriety, and suppressed as well news reports of embarassing events. But the British government of India lacked absolute power. It could and did control at the margin, but in the main the communications system was extraordinarily free to use propaganda on behalf of the mission (as long as the attacks were not associated with violence).'

The role of the press in the nationalist movement underlined, in his words, 'the extraordinary syncretic nature of the Indo-British encounter and the colonial political culture that would provide the foundations of the modern Indian state'.

The first great figure of modern India, Raja Rammohun Roy (1772–1833), argued powerfully for press freedom against the government's repressive Press Ordinance of 1823. He had started a Bengali paper, *Sangbad Kaumudi* (1821), and another in Persian called *Mirat-ul-Akhbar* in 1822, both based in Calcutta. Earlier, the Baptist missionary William Carey founded the first Bengali-language newspaper *Samachar Darpan* (1818), as did Fardunjee Marzaban the *Bombay Samachar* in 1822. These papers thought aloud for India.

Raja Rammohun Roy, polymath, social reformer and educationist, also Arnold Toynbee's foremost Herodian, was the outstanding voice of his generation in the Indo-British encounter, the first in what became a long and distinguished line. As a visitor to Britain in 1831, he understood the true significance of the much discussed Reform Bill and its possible consequences for the future of British representative democracy and for the evolution of a new India under a more enlightened British dispensation.

On a visit to Manchester the humble folk of this newly industralising city turned out to greet him in their hundreds, as they were to do with Mahatma Gandhi a century later. Rammohun Roy argued strongly for the Reform Bill and was answered enthusiastically with shouts of 'The King and Reform for ever'.

Viewing India from London in 1853, that fierce critic of British imperialism and all other imperialisms, Karl Marx, detected through the smouldering ruins of the British conquest and its numerous brutalities, the earliest dawn of India's regeneration. He remarked: 'The political unity of India, more consolidated, and extending farther than it ever did under the Great Moguls, was the first condition of its regeneration. That unity, imposed by the British sword, will now be strengthened and perpetuated by the electric telegraph. The native army, organised and trained by the British drill-sergeant, was the *sine qua non* of Indian self-emancipation, and of India ceasing to be the prey of the first foreign intruder. The free press, introduced for the first time into

Asiatic society, and managed principally by the common offspring of Hindus and Europeans, is a new and powerful agent of reconstruction.'

'Can you make a European society with India's religion?', Vivekananda asked, to which he gave his own confident reply: 'I believe it is possible and must be.' During one of his several journeys to Europe the Swami, addressing an English audience, exclaimed: 'No one ever landed on English soil with more hatred for the race than I did for the English... There is none among you... who loves the English people more than I do now.' They were a 'nation of heroes: the true Ksatriyas!... there is a deep spring of feeling in the English heart. If you know how to reach it, he is your friend for ever... They have solved the secret of obedience without slavish cringing (great freedom with great law-abidingness'.

In a conversation with the French traveller Jacquemont, some twenty-five years before Marx, Raja Rammohun Roy had said that India needed peace above all else after the turmoil that had preceded British rule. The Pax Britannica, he felt, would create a middle class which, in the next hundred years or so, would lead India to freedom. From their different standpoints Roy and Marx, it would appear, reached broadly similar conclusions on India's likely future.

Over the next century and more, until Indian independence finally arrived, many eminent Britons, and others less eminent, contributed in diverse ways to India's cause in word and deed, whether it was in Parliament, in newspapers, pamphlets or through active organisations on the ground and public meetings – and all manner of work permitted in a democratic society. The issues on which they fought must be judged by time and circumstance; each carried a different measure of significance but their combined weight helped tilt the balance of British opinion in India's favour.

In speaking out for India these British men and women frequently braved the cold hostility of their government and the prejudice and wrath of jingoist diehards of whom, in the nineteenth century, there were a good number. Consider, for example, this veiled broadside at the founder of the Indian National Congress, Allan Octavian Hume, by Lepel Griffin in the pages of the *Fortnightly Review* (1892, Vol. 51): 'The Indian National Congress is no more representative of India than a Socialist meeting is representative of England. Its Frankenstein was an Englishman whom a speaker in the House [of Commons] asserted would have been hanged or shot as a traitor under any less mild rule than our own...'

BRITISH SUPPORT FOR INDIA'S CAUSE

In her Proclamation of 1858, Queen Victoria promised that all her subjects in India, British and Indian, would be treated equally. In reality, her pledge was never honoured. There was always one law for the British or Europeans and another for the Indians. Even the Indian Criminal Procedure Code gave an Englishmen twelve times the advantage over an Indian criminal.

For ordinary law-abiding Indians who had no say in the government of their own country, who were allowed a meagre share in the privilege of Empire, it was a constant struggle for rights and respectability for the next nine decades.

Remarkably, India's campaign for justice and self-rule was given much needed and much appreciated support by a formidable and fairminded section of the British public both in India and in Britain.

Queen Victoria
When the Queen assumed responsibility for the government of India, she and the Prince Consort were determined that her Indian subjects should be well governed. In his journal the Prince Consort wrote that the Queen was 'a female sovereign who speaks to more than a hundred millions of Eastern people on assuming the direct government over them... giving them pledges which her future reign is to redeem... Such a document [the proclamation signed on 2 August 1858] should breath feelings of generosity, benevolence and religious toleration...

This book is a chronicle of their admirable and noble efforts for India's cause. Their campaigns were conducted in a spirit of comradeship and selflessness. By their involvement in the movement they made it clear that Britain spoke with many voices, of which the Government was only one. For these British friends the Indian cause was just as dear to them as it was to most Indians. In helping the cause of Indian freedom, they were building a bridge between the British and Indian peoples, ensuring that the association between Britain and India would endure. For them, justice and morality were indivisible. What was rightfully given to the people of Britain had also to be given to the people of India.

The first Britisher to promote India's profile in Parliament and outside, was John Dickinson who founded the Indian Reform Society in 1853. To him must go the credit of creating an awareness that India needed serious and special attention, and the laws that governed it needed to be reformed. He was the forerunner in the movement in Britain for India's freedom. He was followed by Sir William Wedderburn, one of the great allies of the Indian people. Sir William, together with Dadabhai Naoroji, brought the Indian question to the attention of the British public. They argued on India's behalf with the British Government. As members of Parliament they had the ear of the country's legislators. But Wedderburn and Naoroji were not alone. There were others in Britain who contributed nobly and selflessly to India's cause.

One of the ablest Congress representatives in the Parliament was Charles Bradlaugh who had a chequered political career, and was an associate and supporter of Annie Besant's work. He constantly spoke on Indian affairs and wrote the annual reports of the Indian National Congress. In order to create an awareness of its work in Britain, Bradlaugh distributed countless pamphlets to those interested in the relations between Britain and India. To his dying day, he continued to work for the cause so dear to his heart.

Sir William Wedderburn, however, played a pivotal role for India in the nineteenth century. He commands a special place in the story of India's freedom. His influence in the counsels of the Indian National Congress and its British Committee and its journal *India* contributed greatly to their success.

In his address as the President of the Indian National Congress in 1889, Wedderburn explained that the Indian Civil Service was a sort of hereditary calling in his family. His father was in India for 30 years. He himself went to India in 1860 and stayed there for 27 years. He was able to detect at first hand, an undercurrent of unrest in the Indian population, that required understanding and sympathy. When he returned to Britain, one of his first undertakings was to establish the Indian Parliamentary Committee, the idea being to create a more powerful body than the British Committee of the Indian National Congress, of which he was chairman. He wished to make the House of Commons more sensitive and responsive to Indian issues. He invited W C Caine, Naoroji and others, to a dinner in 1893 to discuss his project, and the Committee passed a resolution 'for the purpose of promoting combined and well-directed action among those interested in Indian affairs'.

There was hardly any meeting or committee, public or private, official or unofficial, concerned with India that Sir William Wedderburn was not involved with. He shepherded India's cause through modest gatherings to mass meetings all over the country, thereby making it an issue the Government could not ignore. Wedderburn was a master at public relations, doing the right thing at the right time for the right reasons.

Sir William Wedderburn Bt (1838–1918)
Judge, Bombay High Court (1885), Chairman, Governing Body of Deccan Education Society (1884–87), Member of Parliament (1893–1900). A distinguished member of the Indian Civil Service. After retirement from the ICS he took a leading part in the foundation of the Indian National Congress and attended its first session in 1885. President of the Congress in 1899 and 1910; helped maintain the Congress organ *India*; Chairman of the India Parliamentary Committee. Remained a steadfast supporter of the Indian National Congress until his death.

Sir William Wedderburn. *It must be acknowledged with gratitude that people like Sir William Wedderburn showed a readiness to understand and appreciate India's point of view and initiated and extended their patronage and support to it.*

Wedderburn saw his work in England just as important as the work he had done in India. The British and Indian founders of the Congress took it upon themselves to form a pressure group in England to lobby Parliament and the India Office. AO Hume was convinced that the natural function of the Congress in Britain was to become an agitational force. Wedderburn described its purpose as 'awakening the British people to the consciousness of the wisdom and justice of the present administration'. He had the valuable support of the first President of the Indian National Congress, WC Bonnerjee, who spent his time between England and India.

Wedderburn was deeply distressed by India's sufferings. Whether it was its financial drain or the political and social injustices meted out by his own people. He lived in Gloucester and for as long as his health permitted, he never missed an opportunity of attending India-related meetings in London or elsewhere in the country. His devotion to India's cause was its principal force in Britain. Wedderburn was a natural leader, an inspiration to others. India's debt to him was a notable one.

He was elected the President of the Indian National Congress in 1889 and in 1910. On the eve of his departure to India as President-elect of the Congress Session in India in 1889, a farewell luncheon was held for him at the National Liberal Club in London, attended by over 70 guests and journalists, among whom were Dadabhai Naoroji and Sir William Hunter. The luncheon was reported in detail by over a dozen British national newspapers. In his speech Wedderburn said: 'Vast masses of India are altogether unrepresented. They have no voice in the management of their own affairs. Now they have found a voice in the Indian National Congress through which to address the people of England.

A kindred spirit was Joshua C Wedgwood who shared Wedderburn's passionate commitment to justice for India. In fact, the public was hardly aware of the true range of his services to the country and its people.

Wedgwood enjoyed liberty and freedom and desired that the Indian people also enjoy the same blessings. His life's work was aimed at building an association between Britain and India based on the free will of their peoples. From the time he entered Parliament in 1906, he wasted no time in protesting against the injustices of British imperial rule in India. He argued vigorously for civil and constitutional liberties for Indians in their own country.

During the First World War, Wedgwood fought alongside Indian soldiers in some of the worst battles in Belgium and Gallipoli. He was deeply moved by their loyalty to the British Crown and was deeply affected by the ungenerous treatment many of then received when they returned to India. Wedgwood was on the side of the nationalist leader Lala Lajpat Rai, when the British authority took away his passport. His long battle with the Home Office finally ended in the release of the document.

George Yule was the first Briton to be the President of the Indian National Congress at Allahabad in 1888. He was a non-official Englishman who supported and sympathised with the people of India. He was on the British Committee of the Indian National Congress and its journal *India*, which was a forum for discussion of Indian affairs in Britain. Also on the committee were J E Ellis; W S B McLaren, MP; Sir William Wedderburn, Chairman; W S Caine, MP; William Digby, CIE, Secretary; and Dadabhai Naoroji. William Digby was also the first editor of *India* – first published in London in 1890 – and wrote *Prosperous British India*.

AO Hume, the force behind the establishment of the Indian National Congress in 1885, became its first and the longest serving Secretary from 1885 to 1908. His views on India were so forceful and radical that reactionary diehards dubbed him the assassin of the British Empire. Hume saw the Congress as the blue print for a parliament. Wedderburn regarded the Indian National Congress as 'the direct result of the noblest efforts of the British statesmen, the rational and healthy fruit of higher education and free institutions' acquired by the people of India.

Wedderburn who took over the presidency of the Indian National Congress from George Yule, said in his Presidential address: 'For whom should I work if not for the people? Born of the people, trusted by the people, I will die for the people'.

Although she never visited India, Florence Nightingale had a long-standing interest in India's medical and social conditions. At a public meeting in Norwich in 1873, she read out a paper on the health situation in India. Following the establishment of the Indian National Congress in December 1855, she wrote to Allan Octavian Hume, welcoming the 'birth of a new nationality' on the eve of its first meeting in Bombay.

George Yule
The first Englishman to become the President of the Indian National Congress, in 1888. Member of the British Committee of the Indian National Congress.

Sir William Hunter said: 'The history of India has yet to be written and when it is truly written, Englishmen will learn that the present movement is the inevitable result of causes which we ourselves let into motion. I believe this political movement in India is an indestructible part of the great awakening in India which is showing itself not only in the intellectual progress of the Indian people, but in India's commercial development and in many signs of new national life.

DADABHAI NAOROJI

The early history of the campaign for India's rights was intertwined with the life and work of Dadabhai Naoroji. No one of his generation did more for Indian emancipation. A venerable and revered figure in Britain and in India, Naoroji was the moral prophet of Indian nationalism in the nineteenth century. He worked tirelessly as author, pamphleteer, agitator, public speaker and parliamentarian for India and her people. For much of his life Naoroji lived in Britain. He was an Indian voice that engaged simultaneously with the British government and the British

Dadabhai Naoroji (1825–1917)
Founder of Indian Society 1865, later to become East India Association; in 1882 launched in India the *Voice of India*: the only object was to present to the British public a fair hearing and justice for India. Naoroji funded this monthly journal and bore losses until it was incorporated with *Indian Spectator* in 1890. This was an act of supreme dedication to secure India's voice in Britain in order to make the British understand and sympathise with the deep sense of injustice inflicted upon the people of India. Founder of Bombay Presidency Association 1885 'for the promotion and advocacy of the public interest of India'. Founder member of the Indian National Congress. President of the Indian National Congress 1886, 1893, 1906. Founder member of journal *India* 1890; British English Committee of the Indian National Congress 1890. First Indian member of British Parliament 1892; first Indian member of Welby Commission 1897; first Indian Professor at British university; author of *Poverty and Un-British Rule in India*.

Dadabhai Naoroji. *'The story of a life so noble and yet so simple needs no introduction from me or anybody else. May it be an inspiration to the reader even as Dadabhai living was to me'.*
M K GANDHI, 19 October 1938

public. To both he argued forcefully for Indian aspirations. In this great endeavour he received the unstinting support and encouragement of his British friends, who were as much committed to India's cause. Support also came from the Indian students in England and political agitators from India, and members of various Indian delegations visiting Britain.

Naoroji was the voice of India in the British Parliament from 1892 and 1895 when he was elected as Liberal member from Finsbury Central, London. His success received acclaim and attention, some of it in Britain being racially hostile.

Outside Parliament, Naoroji's relentless campaign for India continued apace. His national speaking tours came to be known as the 'platform-campaigns'. He demanded withdrawal of discriminatory laws in India and argued passionately for self-government for India.

Naoroji had come to Britain in 1855 to join the Indian business firm of CAMA, the first in the country. On 10 December 1865 he founded the first Indian organisation in Britain, the London Indian Society. When membership was opened to the British, it changed its name to the East India Association. By the time the Indian National Congress came into being in 1885 Naoroji, Hume, Wedderburn, Bonnerjee, Gokhale, Tilak and many others had become effective partners, both in Britain and in India. Naoroji also wrote a book, *Poverty and un-British rule in India*, blaming the British for draining India's wealth (the 'drain theory').

Naoroji, with Hume, Wedderburn, Caine, Ellis, Digby and others, launched *India* in 1890 as the official voice of the Indian National Congress and its British Committee. Apart from being the first Indian MP at Westminster, Naoroji scored another two firsts: he was the first Indian professor at a British university, teaching Gujarati at the London University, and became the first Indian to be appointed a member of a Royal Commission, the Welby Commission, which was set up to apportion imperial military expenditure between Britain and India.

Naoroji had always said that, 'the desire of my life is to serve the people.' This he did with honour and distinction. Not surprisingly, the Indian National Congress elected him President three times, in 1886, 1893 and 1906.

Naoroji's voice was never stilled. He even sent a message to Queen Victoria on her Diamond Jubilee in 1897, pleading India's case in a most courteous manner. In his letter of 5 February, he wrote:

The most striking consequence of the utter violation of her Majesty's most sacred pledges and of Acts and Resolutions of Parliament, are the extreme impoverishment of the people of British India and the infliction upon them of all the scourges of the world, war, pestilence and famine. May I hope to look forward to a beneficial change in the present great occasion of Her Majesty's reign?

In the same year Dinshaw Wacha and G K Gokhale, in Britain as delegates of the Indian National Congress, joined in Naoroji's 'platform campaign' throughout the United Kingdom. At a meeting in 1898, Naoroji also drew attention to the harsh treatment suffered by Indians in South Africa.

When Naoroji was voted out of Parliament in the 1895 General Election another Indian, M M Bhownagree, replaced him as Conservative and Unionist Party MP, representing Bethnal Green in East London. No two individuals could be so different in personal make-up and outlook. His election provoked serious misgiving in India and his Anglo-Indianism was received unfavourably. However, he had supported Naoroji in his election to Parliament in 1892 and, like him, fought for the rights of

Indians in South Africa. He was also one of the moving spirits behind the establishment of the Imperial Institute in London (now the Commonwealth Institute), which was set up in 1893, as a memorial to Queen Victoria's Golden Jubilee. Bhownagree and Naoroji were both defeated in the 1906 general election.

At the time of Naoroji's appointment to the membership of the Welby Commission, in 1897, there was a widespread desire in Britain and in India that he should be honoured with a knighthood. Naoroji found the idea embarrassing and he discouraged those who sought thus to honour him. Some years later, the Shah of Iran wished to decorate Naoroji and conveyed his intentions through Bhownagree. Naoroji replied: 'I fully and deeply appreciate the great compliment which I should feel in receiving it. But as the prevailing sentiment in my mind at present is not to have any personal decoration, I think it will be as well for me to keep to this sentiment. I repeat that I feel the compliment and honour most deeply and gratefully.'

Mr Naoroji in his old age

Following his retirement from active politics, calls to honour him were often repeated, but Naoroji refused to allow his name to go forward. Even the persuasion of his life-long friend Sir William Wedderburn who wanted him knighted, failed to move him. He kept faith with his principles to the end.

Naoroji finally left Britain for India in 1907. In his retirement, his interest in India's future never flagged. It was 30 years after his death on 30 June 1917 that India became a free nation.

*   *   *

India's struggle for self-rule did not lose momentum with Naoroji's death. Mohandâs Karamchand Gandhi, an admirer of Dadabhai Naoroji, because of the untimely death of Gopal Krishna Gokhale, became Naoroji's true heir and successor.

When Gandhi was asked during his civil-disobedience campaign, if he thought Naoroji would approve of his tactics, his reply was 'yes'.

The third Indian to take his seat in the British Parliament was Shapurji Saklatvala. He represented Battersea North, London, for the Labour Party in 1922. He left the Labour Party and was re-elected in 1924 as the Communist member. Saklatvala was a strong critic of the Indian National Congress and Gandhi's approach to Indian freedom. He was a man who believed in violent class struggle and had no time for *ahimsa*.

Shapurji Saklatvala's ovation in Parliament was notable both for its content and form. A passionate man, who had witnessed Indian contribution to the British war effort, he was incensed at the British Government's ungenerous and brutal response in the aftermath of the conflict, notably at Jalianwalla Baag. His speeches were fiery and fearless and often landed him in trouble and gaol. He was imprisoned following his May Day speech in Hyde Park in 1926.

INDIANS IN PARLIAMENT

Dadabhai Naoroji has been hailed as one of the pioneer nation builders of modern India, and as the Grand Old Man of India. At the centenary of his election to the House of Commons, celebrated in 1992 with a special dinner at the House of Lords, he was called the Icon of Indian Nationalism.

By any standards, Naoroji was an extraordinary patriot, truly great and noble, a man who captured the spirit and imagination of India as

Uday Shankar (1900–1977)
Dancer, choreographer; studied at JJ
School of Art, Bombay, and Royal College
of Arts, London, 1920; teamed with
Russian ballet dancer Anna Pavlova to
play Krishna to her Radha; both toured
Europe and America.

Prince Ranjitsinhji

no figure of his generation did. He was the first Indian to take his seat
in the British Parliament, but he did so for India. A full and detailed
description of Naoroji's work is beyond the scope of this book, but a
selection of events from his political life convey something of his heroic
stature. He dedicated his all to the service of India.

SIR SATYENDRA PRASSANO SINHA KC

The Indian contribution to British politics was not limited to the three
members of the House of Commons. In 1919 SP Sinha became the first
Indian hereditary peer – and to date the only Indian to be so honoured
– and took his place on the Liberal benches in the House of Lords.

Lord Sinha's goal was self-government for India and he made various speeches on the subject. He participated in the Peace Conference at
Versailles as a member of the British delegation and represented the
India Office as Under-Secretary of State. He is the only non-Briton ever
to have been a member of a British government.

But life transcends politics. In the world of literature, the artist
William Rothenstein introduced Rabindranath Tagore's English ren-
dering of his *Gitanjali* to WB Yeats who read it with considerable
enthusiasm and organised a soiree (at the Trocadero restaurant in
London for his fellow poet from India. Among those present at the
meeting were distinguished Britons like EB Havell, HB Nevinson,
HG Wells and R Vaughan Williams. Responding to their warm welcome, Tagore replied: 'I have not the power adequately to express my
gratitude for the great honour you have done me. This is one of the
proudest moments of my life... I cannot do more than assure you that
the unfailing kindness with which I have been greeted in England has
moved me more than I can tell. I have learned that, though our
tongues are different and our habits dissimilar, at the bottom our
hearts are one.'

In mathematics the partnership between GH Hardy, a distinguished
Fellow of Trinity College, Cambridge, and Srinivas Ramanujan, the
obscure clerk from Madras, whom he befriended and whose genius he discovered, also occurred at about this time. Indian science was to develop
a special relationship with Cambridge: JC Bose, PC Mahalanobis,
S Chandrasekhar, Vikram Sarabhai and Homi Bhabha, among others,
established their reputations there; while PMS Blackett, a Cambridge
Nobel laureate, became one of Jawaharlal Nehru's counsellors in the
making of independent India's science policy. Nehru himself had studied for the Natural Sciences Tripos at Trinity College, Cambridge.

Two seminal names in Indian philosophy, SN Dasgupta and Sarvepalli
Radhakrishnan, taught respectively at Cambridge and Oxford; and a
galaxy of Indian political and legal luminaries, from Mahatma Gandhi to
Mohammad Ali Jinnah, were products of the Inns of Court in London.

In the performing arts there was the great Indian dancer Uday
Shankar who visited Britain with his troupe and in later years his
younger brother Ravi Shankar, the sitar maestro, who popularised
Indian classical music in the West. In sporting endeavour, Prince
Ranjitsinhji captured the imagination of the English cricketing public
with his magical batsmanship. It was AG Gardiner who referred to him as
'the prince of a little state, but the king of a great game'. He concluded:
'I think it is undeniable that as a batsman the Indian will live as the
supreme exponent of the Englishman's game... It is the Jam Saheb's

service that, through his genius for the English game, he has familiarised the English people with the idea of an Indian as a man of like affections with ourselves, and with capacities beyond ours in directions supposed to be peculiarly our own... his name will live in the hearts of hundreds of thousands of British people, to whom he had given happy days and happy memories.'

On 6 August 1912, Gopal Krishna Gokhale, among the truly great figures of Indian nationalism, speaking at a memorial meeting for Allan Octavian Hume at Caxton Hall in London, paid a moving tribute to the man who, more than any other, was responsible for the formation of the Indian National Congress.

The First World War was a defining moment in Indo-British relations. British repression in its aftermath, culminating in the Jallianwala Bagh atrocity, and Mahatma Gandhi's civil disobedience movements, transformed Congress into a mass party, where before it had been a party of middle-class lawyers and professionals. Most of the old British friends of India had died, among them William Wedderburn, but new faces were coming to the fore.

The remarkable Annie Besant was, however, no debutante in public life. She had worked heart and soul for India in India and was elected President of the Indian National Congress in 1917. Her acceptance speech was an oratorical and political *tour de force*, which thrills even now. She declared with ringing voice:

Today when India stands erect, no suppliant people, but a nation, self-conscious, self-respecting, determined to be free; when she stretches out her hand to Britain and offers friendship not subservience, cooperation not obedience; today let me, Western born but in spirit Eastern, cradled in England but Indian by choice and adoption, stand as the symbol of union between Great Britain and India, a union of hearts and free choice, not of compulsion...

Mrs Besant had set up her Home Rule for India League in 1912. Ten years later its name was changed to the Commonwealth of India League, which sought Dominion status for India. It was little more than a debating society for Indian students and British sympathisers of India. In 1928 Krishna Menon was elected its Joint Secretary with James Harley. In 1930 Krishna Menon became its General Secretary and gave the name India League to the 28-year-old organisation.

The India League placed Purna Swaraj (total independence) at the top of its agenda, and in so doing it broke with Mrs Besant's Commonwealth of India League.

At different levels the Round Table Movement and the India Conciliation Group, which contained such close friends of Gandhi as CF Andrews, HSL Polak, Agatha Harrison, and Horace Alexander, worked for India in their different ways.

The India League was a more radical voice than its previous incarnations and inducted into its ranks some of the most eminent British personalities of the time, including Harold Laski, the socialist political theorist, and the philosopher Bertrand Russell who served a spell as its Chairman. The present President of the India League is the former Labour leader, Michael Foot. Through these groups, Quakers, churchmen, humanists, socialists, Liberals, and Communists (albeit with a different agenda from the rest) all joined the struggle for India's freedom.

Shortly after the Second World War, a British Parliamentary delegation toured India. One of its members, Reginald Sorensen, said: 'I want the two countries, Britain and India, to be friends and there can be no

Agatha Harrison (1885–1954)
University Welfare Tutor, London School of Economics 1917–1920; visited India with Royal Commission on India 1929; invited by Gandhi to be his representative as mediator and conciliator in London in 1931; Secretary of the Indian Conciliation Group 1950; took interest in India League activities after the Indian Conciliation Group ceased operation in 1950.

Michael Foot (Born 1913)
Journalist, author and politician. President of Oxford Union 1933; Assistant editor of *Tribune* 1937–1938; managing director of *Tribune* 1948–1952 and 1955–1956; Labour MP; supported Indian cause in Britain; Chairman of India League 1985–, President of Indian National Congress Celebrations Committee, UK, 1985.

durable friendship save on the basis of mutual respect. I pray the day will come when the hand of friendship shall be stretched out from India to England and from England to India. From both points of view, I believe, it must be accepted that British rule must end.' And end it did 'at the stroke of the midnight hour' on 15 August 1947 when, in Jawaharlal Nehru's memorable words, India kept its 'tryst with destiny' and awoke 'to life and freedom'.

The shade of Lord Macaulay would have nodded in approval, for he had said in a speech to Parliament on 10 July 1833:

The destinies of our Indian empire are covered in darkness... The laws which regulate its growth and its decay are still unknown to us. It may be that the public mind of India may expand under our system till it has outgrown that system; that by good government we may educate our subjects into a capacity for better government; that, having become instructed in European knowledge, they may, in some future age, demand European institutions. Whether such a day will ever come I know not. But never will I attempt to avert or retard it. Whenever it comes, it will be the proudest moment in English history.

Twenty years after India's freedom, Sorensen wrote:

... India has become a free and sovereign state in equality with Britain in the Commonwealth and with all other nations. Her destiny... is in her own hands and those of us who played even a fragmentary part to achieve this can appreciate both the tragedy within the struggle and the majesty of the achievement.

PERSONAL

Indian immigration to East Africa was at its peak between 1890 and 1914. Their social and economic conditions in the new country of abode changed dramatically, but their status as second-class citizens did not. The Europeans, who exhibited uninhibited racial superiority over all other ethnic groups in East Africa, enjoyed unlimited privileges and, as a consequence, created deep resentment in the rest of the society.

The Europeans lived in exclusively white areas, had their own schools, libraries and sports clubs. Demands by the Indians for political and economic equality were disregarded. Their only area of contact with the Indians was in the business and legal areas.

Indian Independence Day in Nairobi, Kenya, where I lived, began with a 5000-strong dawn procession in drizzle through the city. It had started from the Desai Memorial Hall and returned there in time for the flag hoisting ceremony performed by Mr S G Amin, the President of the East African National Congress, established in 1914. In the afternoon another flag-hoisting ceremony was organised by one of the most influential and active women's associations, the Bhagini Samaj. Similar ceremonies took place in Mombasa, Nakuru, Thika, Dar-es-Salaam, Zanzibar and Kampala. It was a great and historic day for the Indian community in East Africa, but it did not change their lives; they were still subjects of the British Empire.

Mr Gladstone speaking from the Opposition benches in the House of Commons.

CHAPTER 1

Parliamentary debates and the public campaigns

THE BRITISH CROWN ASSUMED DIRECT RESPONSIBILITY over India from the East India Company, following the revolt of 1857. Since 1784 Parliament had only supervised the activities of the East India Company through the Board of Control. In 1858, the India Office was established in Whitehall. The Secretary of State for India became a Cabinet post.

Just as India was the subject of debate in Parliament, Parliament itself became a discussion point for its dealing of Indian affairs.

On 24 December 1872, Lord William Hay considered that 'India in Parliament' was an important enough subject for a special lecture he delivered at Queen Street Hall in Edinburgh, to the members of the Philosophical Institution. The large attendance reflected the interest of the general public in the subject, just 14 years into the British Raj.

Hay began by quoting the Earl of Chatham who had said: 'Indian affairs are, according to the ideas of greatness, the most important of all our concerns', and continued:

If there be any truth in those words, I need make no apology for the subject of my address this evening. Evidence is not wanting that our Indian fellow-subjects are greatly dissatisfied with the manner in which Parliament has interpreted its duties towards them since 1858, a year for ever to be remembered in the history of India. Parliament (and I employ the word in its widest sense as including the Crown, the House of Peers, and the House of Commons) cannot afford to be unpopular in India. Whatever may be said to the contrary, our rule there rests as little on mere force as any in the world. If Parliament be misrepresented, let the misrepresentation be exposed. If, on the other hand, there be some fire to account for the smoke, let measures be forthwith taken for its extinguishment. The allegation is, then, that Parliament is ignorant of, and therefore indifferent to, the affairs of our Eastern dominions, and has failed to fulfil towards them the responsibilities and obligations which it voluntarily imposed upon itself. Let us first endeavour to ascertain the nature and extent of those obligations and responsibilities, and for this purpose let me ask your attention for one moment to the document from which they were mainly to be gathered. I refer to that Magna Carta of India, the proclamation through the medium of which it was in 1858 announced to its millions of inhabitants 'that the territories in the East, hitherto under the government of the East India Company, in trust for Her Majesty, should in future be governed by, and in the name of, Her Majesty.' Now the promises which this proclamation contained are in substance as follows: First, it promised to give full force to the broad principle contained in the words 'We' (that is, Her Majesty) 'hold ourselves bound to the natives of India by the same obligations of duty which bind us to all our other subjects.' Second, to maintain scrupulously all treaties and engagements made by the East India Company with its princes, and to respect their rights, dignity, and honour. Third, to abstain from any extensions of territory. Fourth, not to interfere with the religious belief or worship of the natives. Fifth, to employ them as far as possible in the public service. Sixth, to respect the feelings of attachment with which they regard their lands; and lastly, in framing and administering the law, to pay due regard to their ancient rights, usages, and customs. No more important communication was ever made by one nation to another; and we cannot be surprised that our fellow-subjects in India should watch with jealous interest the manner of its fulfilment. It must be evident to those who are acquainted with our system of government that Parliament cannot be regarded as having undertaken to administer the affairs of India in the sense that it administers the affairs of these islands. It did not undertake to make laws for India, or to administer directly its finances, or control the Executive in the manner and to the extent that this duty is discharged in regard to Great Britain. What Parliament undertook to do was to see that the promises contained in Her Majesty's Proclamation should be strictly performed. It undertook by the exercise of efficient supervision over the Indian Executive to supply, as far as possible, the place of popular institutions. If it could not make its laws, it undertook to see that legislation was conducted on sound principles. If it abstained from determining what taxes should be levied, it certainly engaged to protect the natives against the imposition of unnecessary and unsuitable fiscal burdens. In one word Parliament constituted itself the great court of appeal for India, and therefore the guardian and protector of the rights and interests of our Indian fellow-subjects. But I fear that the pages of Hansard will be searched in vain for any signs of serious interest in the great empire which has been so strangely committed to our keeping. Look at the annual presentation of the accounts, involving over one hundred millions of money – the latest possible day chosen for their submission, the Secretary of State rising to address empty benches, the emptiest being the one usually crowded with Her Majesty's advisers – the discouragement offered to independent members. These unsatisfactory features repeat themselves year after year. The sight, it must be confessed, is not edifying, nor is it creditable to Parliamentary government. It is not one which can be repeated without greatly lowering us in the estimation of our Indian brethren. We have not been engaged in educating them for the last hundred years and more without having taught them many lessons, and among others, that great power is not given to nations without corresponding duties to be performed; the neglect of which is a crime no less than a reproach...

Having drawn your attention to some of the consequences of the unfortunate lethargy and indifference of Parliament, I will venture to make some suggestions, the adoption of which would, I think, to some extent prevent their occurrence. First, it is indispensable that a day should be fixed for the introduction of the Indian Budget; a day probably one early in the session would be most convenient when the attendance of members could be assured. Moreover, everything should be done to encourage independent members to take part in the discussion, even if so doing were to involve the curtailment of the generally somewhat exuberant Ministerial statement which it is the fashion to make. No one has placed in clearer light the heavy responsibilities of Great Britain in respect to India than our Premier. 'What,' asked he in 1858, 'what else do you want by the changes that you wish to introduce into the Indian Government? You want, or at least I, for my own part, want to bring public opinion to bear upon Indian affairs. I want to see the people of England more sensible than they have hitherto been of the enormous responsibility they have contracted with regard to India.' Surely the way to accomplish so worthy an object is not to shunt the whole subject of India to the end of the session...

If I have criticised somewhat severely the lethargy of Parliament, and the feverish activity of the Government of India, I have done so because I sincerely believe those criticisms to be deserved. The difficulties of governing India, always great, have increased tenfold since 1858. The suppression of the mutiny left a widespread feeling of irritation against the British authorities, while the cost of the war and of the large European force it was necessary to maintain rendered increased taxation unavoidable...

Every day it becomes more evident that if the connection between the two countries is to be lasting and beneficial it must be on the condition that they are administered upon identical principles.

I would remind you that, though I have in the course of my observations invariably referred to Parliament as the body accountable for the performance of this nation's duties towards India, the real responsibility is, after all with us, the members of a great commonwealth, of which Parliament is but the servant.

Let us show that we are ourselves conscious of the great task before us, no less a one than the regeneration of one-seventh of the human race.

The lecture was listened to throughout with close attention; and, at its close, a cordial vote of thanks was given to Lord William Hay.

(From *The Asiatic*, 24 December 1872)

British influence in the affairs of India was constantly debated by politicians, of whom only a minority paid serious attention to the subject.

*   *   *

The first distinguished Indian presence in Britain was that of Raja Rammohun Roy, polymath and social reformer, who visited the country during the movement for the 1832 Reform Bill whose significance, not least for India, he appreciated and which he therefore vigorously supported.

It was believed by the representatives of the emerging Indian middle class that if Indian grievances were ventilated in Britain, British public opinion, driven by a sense of fairplay, would help in redressing them.

Raja Rammohun Roy (1772–1833)
The inaugurator of the modern age in India, and considered 'the greatest Indian of his age'. The origin of all progressive and emancipation movements in India can be traced to Raja Rammohun Roy, the pioneer of modern education, promoter of freedom of speech and press, possibly the first exponent of comparative religion.

Raja Rammohun Roy was the first Indian to come to England on an official visit. He arrived in 1831 on a mission of complaints to the British Government regarding the renewal of the East India Company's charter. He particularly wanted to be in Parliament for the debates on the Reform Bill, the Factory Act, the Act of Abolition of Slavery. Due to a mishap and misdirection of the hotel he was staying at, he was too late for the debates. Rammohun Roy had a select committee meeting at the House of Lords in March 1832 dealing with the issue of tax on salt in India. He died in Bristol and there is a monument where he was buried.

The Graphic of 17 March 1888, under the heading 'India in the House of Commons', said that 'the announcement of an Indian debate caused the majority of members to fly from the House, leaving the discussion to be carried on by a body of veteran Qui-hys, aided by Mr Bright and one or two other amateur enthusiasts'.

The first Indian voice to be heard in the British Parliament was that of Dadabhai Naoroji. He was elected to the House of Commons in 1892 from Finsbury Central, London, winning his seat by a majority of five votes. Naoroji was, and remains, the most influential and active Indian in Britain during the second half of the nineteenth century. He personified the culture and spirit of the new India: he worked tirelessly on India's behalf, made speeches and wrote articles in the press on the subject of Britain's unjust economic exploitation of India. His stay in Britain between 1855 and 1907 was interrupted by visits to India to participate in the deliberations of the Indian National Congress.

By the time he took his seat in Parliament, Naoroji was well versed in the act of making Britain see the logic and justice of India's cause. He was tactful, persuasive and, most importantly, a brilliant organiser. He was at the heart of the formation of the Indian National Congress, the London Indian Society and the East India Association. Naoroji was also the first Indian to be appointed to the Royal Commission on Indian Expenditure. He made his maiden speech in the House on 8 August 1892 at the age of 67, and showed that none of his progressive instincts and vision were dimmed.

Naoroji had an unequalled devotion to the interest of India. He was beyond any doubt one of the very few men of any age or country, the salt of humanity, who age almost perfect. He was India's greatest patriot of the last century.

John Bright (1811–1889)
Liberal politician. Friend of India. Member of Parliament. Suggested that Government of India be made a department of British Government, 1853; proposed decentralisation in India 1858 and 1879.

Dadabhai Naoroji

The debate on Indian Council Cotton Duties in the House of Commons. Dadabhai Naoroji is the central figure.

In his Maiden speech in the House of Commons in August 1892, Dadabhai Naoroji said:

It may be considered rather rash and unwise on my part to stand before this House so immediately after my admission here; and my only excuse is that I am under a certain necessity to do so. My election for an English constituency is a unique event. For the first time during more than a century of settled British rule an Indian is admitted into this House as a Member for an English constituency. That, as I have said, is a unique event in the history of India, and, I may also venture to say, in the history of the British Empire. I desire to say a few words in analysis of this great and wonderful phenomenon. The spirit of the British rule, the instinct of British justice and generosity, from the very commencement, when Parliament seriously took the matter of Indian policy into its hands, about the beginning of this century, decided that India was to be governed on the lines of British freedom and justice. Steps were taken without any hesitation to introduce Western education, civilisation, and political institutions in that country; and the result was that, aided by a noble and grand language, in which the youth of that country began to be educated, a great movement of political life – I may say new life – was infused into a land which had been decaying for centuries. The British rulers of the country endowed it with all their own most important privileges. A few days ago, Sir, you demanded from the Throne the privileges which belong to the people, including freedom of speech, for which they have fought and shed their blood. That freedom of speech you have given to us, and it enables Indians to stand before you and represent in clear and open language any desire they have felt. By conferring those privileges you have prepared for this final result of an Indian standing before you in this House, becoming a Member of the great Imperial Parliament of the British Empire, and being able to express his views openly and fearlessly before you. The glory and credit of this great event (by which India is thrilled from one end to the other) of the new life, the joy, the ecstasy of India at the present moment, is all your own; it is the spirit of British institutions and the love of justice and freedom in British instincts which has produced this extraordinary result, and I stand here in the name of India to thank the British people that they have made it at all possible for an Indian to occupy this position, and to speak freely in the English language of any grievance which India may be suffering under, with the conviction that, though he stands alone, with only one vote, whenever he is able to bring forward any aspiration, and is supported by just and proper reasons, he will find a large number of other Members from both sides of the House ready to support him and give him the justice he asks. This is the conviction which permeates the whole thinking and educated classes of India. It is that conviction that enables us to work on day after day, without dismay, for the removal of a grievance. The question now being discussed before the House will come up from time to time in practical shape, and I shall then be able to express my humble views upon them as a Representative of the English constituency of Central Finsbury. The moral force to which the right hon. Gentleman the Member for Midlothian (Mr W E Gladstone) referred is the golden link by which India is held to the British Power. So long as India is satisfied with the justice and honour of Britain so long will her Indian Empire last, and I have not the least doubt that, though our progress may be slow and we may at times meet with disappointments, if we persevere, whatever justice we ask in reason we shall get. I thank you, Sir, for allowing me to say these few words, and the House for so indulgently listening to me, and I hope that the connection between England and India which forms five-sixths of the British Empire may continue long with benefit to both countries.

* * *

In an unusual act of protest outside Parliament, aimed at it, was a 'brief and respectful appeal' to the House of Commons from Mr G K Gokhale, in July 1906. In a response to a report in the *Daily News* of 19 July on a debate on India he stated:

The situation in India was serious enough before the Liberal party came into power in December last, and it has since been further aggravated by the continued and persistent exercise of coercion by the authorities in Eastern Bengal. In this country, on the other hand, one sees signs on all sides of a new awakening, and the question is whether India is to be permitted to share in this general advance, or whether she alone is to be kept out of it. Friday's debate will answer this question, and I think there should be no difficulty in understanding the frame of mind in which my countrymen are awaiting it.

The position is this: A foreign bureaucracy, whose members live in the country only long enough to earn their pensions, governs India, uninfluenced by Indian public opinion, and uncontrolled in practice by any higher authority. As a result, Indian interests are systematically subordinated to the interests of the Army, the European services, and the European capitalists. The steady and continuous rise in the death-rate of the country and the miserable pittance spent on elementary education should be sufficient to satisfy any impartial mind as to the low place occupied by the interests of the people on the

Government slate. Our death-rate, according to the *Statistical Abstract for British India* (a Parliamentary publication) was under 25 per thousand in 1882–84. It rose to 30 per thousand in 1892–94 (before recent famines or plague appeared on the scene), and it is 35 per thousand today. As regards elementary education, the Government of India spends on it only about £200,000 out of State funds, as against 21 millions spent on the Army and about four millions paid in salaries to Europeans in civil employ; only one child out of eight is at school, and one village out of five has a school house. Your Parliamentary grant to elementary education, it is interesting to note, is 16 millions for the current year.

Now, there is only one remedy for this state of things. It is to redeem the pledges given to the people of India by the Sovereign and the Parliament of this country, and associate them steadily more and more with the management of their own affairs, till eventually India becomes an integral and self-governing part of this Empire. The practical steps by which this result is attained will necessarily have to be a matter of continued compromise between conflicting views. But as regards the necessity of moving forwards, I hope there will be no difference of opinion among those who represent the forces of democracy in this country, and I earnestly trust that this will be made amply clear by Friday's debate.

At present we in India are moving in a vicious circle. The bureaucracy wants to keep the educated classes out of the government of the country till the masses have been qualified by education to take an intelligent part in public affairs. No steps, however, are taken to push on mass education, and there is no chance of such steps being taken till we have a larger voice in our own government.

The officials, again, constantly speak as though the responsibility for redeeming England's plighted word is ours and not theirs. They formulate no proposals of their own, and confine themselves merely to picking holes in what we urge. Their most favourite plea for inaction is that the people are not yet qualified for any substantial measure of self-government. Mr Gladstone once observed: 'It is liberty alone which fits men for liberty. This proposition, like every other in politics, has its bounds, but it is safer than the counter-doctrine, Wait till they are fit.' The officials in India, however, do not recognise the wisdom of this observation.

Issues of far-reaching importance depend on Friday's debate. For the first time in the history of British rule, a truly democratic House of Commons will deal with the subject of the government of India. The present House, the present Ministry, the present Secretary of State, all have stimulated a new hope in my country. India stands expectant, and I fervently trust that she will not be disappointed.

There were 196 members of the Indian Parliamentary Committee at that time.

Amongst a variety of debates in the House, the subject of Indian students was a fairly regular topic. Their living as well as conditions of education were under constant scrutiny and reform as was on 14 July 1910.

HOUSE OF COMMONS · INDIAN STUDENTS IN BRITAIN

SIR MARK STEWARD asked the Under Secretary of State for India if he was aware that parents in India, and many interested in Indian students, desired that there should be more adequate machinery in London and at the university than at present existed for guiding and advising Indian students in this country, and, if so, if he would say what action he proposed to take in the matter.

MR MONTAGUE: The Secretary of State has established an Advisory Committee in London, of which Lord Ampthill is chairman, and a Bureau of Information for Indian students under the charge of a specially qualified educational advisor. The hon. member will find full information on the subject in my predecessor's Budget Statement of August 5 of last year, and I propose to make a statement on the present position in my Budget Statement. *(India, 22 July 1910)*

Often the issues were a little out of the ordinary as was the case of Savarkar on 18 July 1910:

THE ALLEGED ESCAPE OF SAVARKAR

MR JOHN WARD asked the Secretary of State for Foreign Affairs whether the Indian prisoner Savarkar, while being carried to India for trial on charges of sedition and treason, escaped from the ship while calling at Marseilles; whether he was recaptured and brought back to custody by the French police; and whether he had made any communication to the French Government upon the subject.

MR CHURCHILL (who replied) said: I understand that the prisoner made an attempt to escape while the ship was at Marseilles, but was stopped by aid of the French police. No occasion has arisen for communicating with the French Government on the subject.   (*India*, 22 July 1910)

This was followed by the regular mix of politics in India and Indian politics in Britain.

*　　*　　*

Once in a while parliamentary debates were brought to the notice of *India* via other newspaper reports of the proceedings; with a comment of its own, the journal reproduced the reporting of the debates as it did on 9 April 1909:

'HOME RULE FOR INDIA' · A YELLOW NIGHTMARE

In order that our Indian readers may gain an idea of the methods of that London 'Yellow Press' which is forever seeking to impress public opinion in England with the enormities of Indian journalism, we reproduce textually from the columns of the *Daily Express* of Friday last (April 2), the entire report which it thought fit to give of the preceding day's debate in the Commons on the second reading of the Indian Councils Bill. The matter purports to emanate from 'Our Parliamentary Representative,'and is headed, 'House of Commons, Thursday':

A curry of the recent debates in the Lords was served up in the Commons tonight on the motion for the second reading of the Indian Councils Bill with the addition of pro-seditionist chutney. Messers Keir Hardie, Mackarness, O'Grady and Co sat ready to urge a far greater measure of Home Rule for India than this Bill provides. The Government is apparently determined to throw down another gauntlet to the Lords. It was announced that they are going to insist on reinserting Clause 3, providing for the establishment of provincial councils. This the Lords deleted on the ground that it gave too much Home Rule power.

Lord Percy, for the Unionists, criticised the giving of too much representative power on the Indian Councils to Eastern peoples not prepared for Western form of government.

Mr Asquith took the various objections voiced by Lord Percy, and contended that the Indian people ought to have some voice in their affairs. 'This reform,' he said, 'is only the legitimate development, the introduction, of the elective element.' (*Loud cheers from the pre-seditionists*) Lord Percy had complained, said Mr Asquith, that the fact that behind their acts was the veto of the Viceroy would tend to a feeling of irresponsibility in the councils. 'That,' said the Prime Minister, has always been stated in reply to any power of veto (*Liberal groans*) the exercise of which creates a considerable amount of irritation. (*Mocking Unionist cheers*) But still we go on (*Unionist laughter and cheers*) but I don't say how long it will last.' (*Still louder Unionist cheers*)

Mr Balfour was sceptical about the benefits of the Bill. 'I cannot help feeling much misgiving,' he said, 'that the Government has been mistaken in initiating this policy, and I must, on behalf of myself and the Opposition, disclaim all responsibility for the step taken or the consequences which are likely to follow.'

James Keir Hardie
One of the founders of the Labour Party in Britain and the first Labour candidate for Parliament. He represented Merthyr Tydfil from 1900 to 1915.

Mr Keir Hardie (Socialist Member for Merthyr Tydfil) referred to a speech of Mr J Hicks, the Tariff Reform member for North-West Manchester. Mr Hardie declared that Mr Hicks had referred to the Hindu native press thus: 'In one column they accept these reforms, and in another they support sedition.' 'I can conceive no Indian journal,' said Mr Keir Hardie, 'descending to the same low level of scurrility as papers of the type of the *Daily Express*, and the journalistic supporters of the Unionist members generally.'

The bill was read a second time without the division, and was referred to Committee of the whole House. The House rose at 11.20.

Of course the subject matter had to be important enough for *India* to take it from another paper, rather than make its own reporting, for not what happened in the House but how it was seen by those with an unsympathetic view of Indian affairs.

While the subject of India was being tossed about inside Parliament, those outside were keener to score points for and against the Liberal or Conservative parties. The newspapers were never slow in endorsing the policies of their favoured political party. What was good for a party was not always good for India. Indian policy, as far as repressive laws were concerned, was viewed with disfavour and distaste by many members of the Parliament. On 7 October 1910 *India*, quoting *The Hindu of Madras*, stated that 'what is required under present conditions is a system of government in which the interest and will of the people must largely preponderate and in which sympathetic provision must be made for reaching their higher form of development in the near future.'

The only road along which Indian reforms could proceed was through Westminster. Often the debates in Parliament tackled the issues head on but none generated as much heat as did the subject of Indian Home Rule demands. A taste of the views expressed was reported in *India* on 30 November 1917.

IMPERIAL PARLIAMENT

SPECIAL REPORT FOR INDIA OF ALL PARLIAMENTARY
PROCEEDINGS RELATING TO INDIA
THURSDAY, NOVEMBER 22 · HOUSE OF COMMONS

HOME RULE LEAGUE AND 'YOUNG INDIA'

COMMANDER WEDGWOOD asked the Chancellor of the Exchequer whether he was aware that charges had been made by the Home Secretary against an Hon. Member of this House of supporting a publication which advocated assassination as a political weapon in India; whether he was aware that the charge was unsupported by any evidence but was made to discredit the Indian Home Rule movement in the interest of the Anglo-Indian irreconcilables, contrary to the wishes of the India Office, by a Home Secretary insufficiently acquainted with the gravity of Indian politics; and whether he would allot time to have this charge against the honour of a Member of this House discussed.

MR BONAR LAW: I cannot agree with the suggestions contained in this question, nor do I think it necessary to give a special opportunity for the discussion of the subject.

COMMANDER WEDGWOOD: Am I to understand that a charge of such gravity can be made against a Member of this House by the Home Secretary without any further proceedings being taken and without any opportunity being given of showing that it was without a shadow of foundation?

MR BONAR LAW: I have read the question and the answer, and I have not drawn that inference from it. After the answer which I have given, perhaps the Hon. Member would address his question to the Home Secretary.

COMMANDER WEDGWOOD asked the Secretary of State for the Home Department if he would state on what date the Home Office or police intimated to the India Office their desire to have the office of the India Home Rule League raided; whether the India Office concurred verbally or in writing; in view of his accusation against a Member of this House, would he lay Papers showing the responsibility of both the India Office and the police for the raid and for the assassin charge.

COMMANDER WEDGWOOD also asked the Secretary of State for the Home Department whether he would indicate the passages in the book *Young India*, by Lajpat Rai, with an introduction by the honourable Member for Newcastle-under-Lyme, which he held to advocate assassination; whether he read these passages before making the charge or whether he was merely stating the opinion of Sir Archibald Bodkin; whether the idea of the raid on the Indian Home Rule League originated with the Home Office, the police or the India Office; whether the India Office recommended the Home Office or the police to raid the offices of the Home Rule for India League; whether he was cognisant and approving of the raid before it took place; and whether he would indicate the passages in the book *Young India*, by Lajpat Rai, and having an introduction written by the honourable Member for Newcastle-under-Lyme, which recommended assassination.

and the debate went on and on...

The Times reported the proceedings in Parliament regularly but occasionally brought the debate into its editorial columns with a decisive opinion of its own on a topic, as was the case on 17 April 1924:

THE DEBATE ON INDIA

Tuesday night's debate in the House of Commons on India had two good results. In the first place, the House made a movement towards reasserting its legal and authoritative position in regard to the conduct of India policy. In the second place, the debate elicited a definite statement of the attitude of the Government towards the present difficult situation. It is necessary that the British Parliament should take a close and continuous interest in India. It is more than ever necessary now, when in India itself a complicated Parliamentary system has been set up for which the British Parliament is responsible and on the results of which it will ultimately be called upon to take a decision...

That the House on Tuesday showed signs of uneasiness is all to the good. Anxiety about India is widespread, and if unclarified it may have a debilitating effect. The position is that the Reforms Act is not working well...

The question of how India is to be governed is again raised in an acute form and demands earnest attention in this country. The demand is put forward by Indian politicians that the Act of 1919 should be extended without delay. They want a round-table inquiry that would put the reforms in the melting-pot...

There may be, and there are, many conflicting opinions as to the merits and the demerits of the Reforms Act. The important fact is that it is law and that the term of its preliminary operation is fixed by the British Parliament...

An inquiry is being conducted by the Government of India within the terms of the Act, and opportunity is being given to consult responsible Indians. This, at any rate, is firm ground, and the necessity now is to remain steadfast on what firm ground there is. To be pushed by irresolution into the shifting sands of an endless and ruinous controversy would be a misfortune both for Great Britain and for India.

*   *   *

As well as being the centre of debate and the law-making body, Parliament was often the venue for visiting delegates from India. British hospitality extended only as far as providing luncheons or receptions: meeting demands from the delegates of self-rule was decidedly out. However, these high profile discussions were not for exchanging

Lala Lajpat Rai (1856–1928)
Took a leading part in organising relief of community distress of all kinds. Joined Indian National Congress in 1888. Member of the Congress deputation to England (1905). Deported to Burma for Sedition (1907); to escape political harassment he spent eight years in America where he ran a paper called *The Young India*, 1915. President of the special Congress Session in 1920 that adopted the programme of non-cooperation. Author of *Unhappy India*, *Arya Samaj*, etc. While leading a demonstration in Lahore in 1928 he was hit by a police baton and died from his injuries. Wrote foreword for Josiah C Wedgwood's book: *The Man and His Word*.

codes of etiquette. They simply re-emphasised Britain's determination to make no concessions to India's demands and India's will to make no retreat. On 12 May 1927, the President of the Indian Legislative Assembly, Mr V J Patel, with other members of the Empire Parliament, was a guest at a luncheon of the United Kingdom branch of the Empire Parliamentary Association at the House of Commons. *The Times* of 13 May 1927 reported:

PARLIAMENTS OF EMPIRE
MR McCORMACK ON LOANS TARIFF POLICY

Mr Amery presided, and in proposing the health of the visitors said Mr McCormack [Premier of Queensland] was in this country to deal with a problem which in the natural course of events presented itself to young as well as to old countries, where to find the 'needful'. In Mr Patel they had the first Speaker of the Indian Parliament. It was hoped before long to have a conference in which all the other Parliaments of Empire might take part. Since a good many years would intervene between the present day and the general election (*Laughter*), he hoped it might not be impossible to find the opportunity for such a conference...

POWERS OF INDIAN LEGISLATURE

Mr Patel said the Indian branch of the association had affiliated with the British branch in the free spirit of comradeship and honourable co-operation. Given the requisite goodwill and mutual confidence, the intercourse among the members of the various legislatures ought to lead to the happiest results.

The Central Legislature in India was not yet the sovereign body as Parliament was in the United Kingdom. Their franchise would have to be generously extended to bring the Indian Parliament, if he might so call it, in line with the various self-governing countries within this vast combination of races and creeds, but he hoped that the advent of that devoutly wished-for consummation would be largely celebrated by the fraternal and friendly intercourse between the members of the various constituent units of the Empire Parliamentary Association. The association furnished in the very heart of the Empire a central place where the representatives of its branches could meet and freely discuss not merely the technique of parliamentary procedure, but the larger question of broadening and widening the basis of freedom. Since the Indian branch was inaugurated last year, a number of Indian members had visited the country and had testified to the usefulness of the association, and they were also glad to welcome in India some of the British members during the last cold weather. Apart from the great value of the exchange of personal visits, the publications of the association enabled them to follow with intelligent interest the proposals for legislation and the views of the representatives of different parties in other legislatures which had to deal with similar problems to theirs. As time went on and they received that full measure of self-government, to which they were intently looking forward, and which he believed was, or, at any rate ought to be, the aim of all parties here, the importance of the association as the focus of all parliamentary experience and legislative wisdom would steadily grow. (*Cheers*)

He hoped that before long the Legislature in India, with its power and status largely extended, would have the pleasure of welcoming to Delhi the representatives of all the parliamentary bodies within the British Commonwealth to a joint discussion of problems common to all. He believed that brief visits of a month or two would do more to bring to the minds of all the realisation of needs and difficulties than years spent on reading books written about each other by authors who, with all their learning and labour, might be ill equipped for the task owing to the absence of a sympathetic insight into their affairs. For that reason he was consulting the Speaker, as joint president of the United Kingdom branch, and also with Sir Howard D'Egville, as to the prospects of a visit here from some members of the British Parliament. He was convinced that the association had a great mission before it no less than that of uniting together the different units of world-wide organisation. It would have failed in its purpose if its activities did not tend in the direction of increasing, however indirectly, the bounds of freedom in all parts of the Empire.

PUBLIC CAMPAIGNS

The first ever all-Indian public meeting in England took place on 10 December 1865 at 4 Pall Mall Place, London. It was the London Indian Society meeting, chaired by its founder Dadabhai Naoroji. In a booklet the minutes of the event were put on record that clearly illustrate the dissatisfaction of unjust British rule in India. The meeting was specially organised to discuss the Indian Civil Service examinations and its discriminatory rules, following information received by the British Indian Association of Calcutta. Amongst the speakers was WC Bonnerjee who addressed the group of young Indian students.

Naoroji made a very long speech, going into details of British prejudice against accepting Indians on the Civil Service Roll.

For WC Bonnerjee, there was no other subject of greater importance to discuss:

We ought to make our business (duty) to watch the conduct of the authorities. If we saw reason to be dissatisfied with any part of the Government of India, we should put it before the British public and urge our cause accordingly to the rules of the British constitution with consideration, justice and fairplay. All English statesmen, who have taken part in Indian politics, have agreed to say that we are entitled to 'Good Government' and you will mark that the words are employed unconditionally. We are entitled to unconditional Government, and I have no doubt that the English Government is really desirous of giving it to us. We do not ask for one law for the Anglo-Indian civilians and another for the Indians. What we want is that both should be governed by the same laws.

WC Bonnerjee (1844–1906)
Studied Law at Middle Temple. Fourth Indian to be called to the Bar in England in 1867. Founder member of the Indian National Congress and its first President 1885. Successful lawyer; had chambers in Lincoln's Inn Fields. Settled in England in 1902 and continued to promote the cause of India until his death in London. With Dadabhai Naoroji started the London India Society in 1865. Cremated at Golders Green Crematorium, London.

Three years after the London Indian Society meeting, Dadabhai Naoroji organised another gathering of British and Indian members of the London Association. He felt that it was 'necessary to have a clear understanding about the duties and work of the Association in India and in this country'. His comments are recorded in a special booklet, *On the duties of Local Associations in connection with London Association*, with a view to making Indian subjects popular among the British public and to bring India near to the 'minds of England'. He urged the members of the Association to put before the public, through its journals, the results of their experiences in India. It was his hope that the British members of the Association would make an effort of reading Indian topics in the papers, adding:

We sometimes find it difficult to make the Government see at once the justice of our cause, or seeing the justice, to believe that a reasonable portion of the community are prepared for the measure, but for all such cases it would be simply a question of time. We have only to persevere, and I am satisfied that the English are both willing and desirous to do India justice.

*   *   *

Keshub Chandra Sen, who joined the Brahmo Samaj in 1857, came to England in 1870 on an evangelical lecture tour. Within his missionary work he found the time and opportunity to present India's case before the British public. The people of India, he said, expected 'fairness, justice and humanity' from Britain. As a representative of the Indian people, he pointed to the:

Keshub Chandra Sen (1838–1884)
Religious and social reformer; joined the Brahmo Samaj started by Raja Rammohun Roy. Visited England in 1870 and gave more than 70 lectures and talks; was well received, among others, by Queen Victoria. One daughter married Maharajah of Mayurbhanj and another married Maharajah of Cooch Behar.

many serious defects in the administrative machinery which have to be rectified, many just grievances of the people to be redressed, many instances of injustice and oppression whose recurrence should be prevented by more humane legislation, many scandals which have to be removed. For these you are responsible and I trust you will not neglect to give India all she wants and which she has a right to demand from you.

Mr Sen spoke at a meeting of the East India Association on 13 May 1870 at the Guildhall, Bath, on the subject of 'England's duties towards India', to a large and appreciative audience.

Proud of our nationality, we shall ask you to give us all the good things you have in England but not your corruption. In your Parliament you generally introduce Indian subjects for discussion at the end of the session when the honourable members have been fatigued and exhausted by their labours. You should not treat India as though it were a country peopled with savages. An awful and tremendous power vests in your hands and if you like you can abuse it and revel in most ignoble and shocking triumphs or you can use your prerogatives rightly and in a Christian-like manner.

On 17 June 1870 Sen addressed a meeting at Temperance Hall, Leicester, on 'Indian reforms'. The audience comprised members of all sects and parties. On the platform were representatives of various religious denominations and political creeds.

Mr Sen began by referring to the religious conditions of India, before returning to the subject of his lecture. He expressed the hope that the British people would study and understand the situation in India. 'Unfortunately in this country there are very few who cared to pay much attention to the affairs of India,' he observed reprovingly. He added that the days for maltreating his countrymen and denying them justice were gone.

Mr Sen visited Bristol on 9 September 1870 for the inauguration of the Bristol Indian Association, before returning to India.

*   *   *

Politics apart, the other subject that occupied the minds of Indians and their British sympathisers was famine. While its cause was attributed to negligence by the British administration, the concern expressed in Britain showed that there was no complacency there.

On 11 December 1877 a huge public meeting was held in Manchester by the Manchester Indian Association in the city's Town Hall. The Mayor was in the chair and the speakers were the Rt. Hon. John Bright MP and Sir Arthur Cotton KCSL.

*   *   *

India, a monthly magazine, was first published in London in February 1890. The man behind the journal was Mr William Digby, once the Secretary of the National Liberal Club. *India* was deemed necessary to provide a digest of reliable information on Indian affairs.

THE CONGRESS IN BRITAIN

THE CAMPAIGN FOR EDUCATING THE BRITISH PEOPLE ON INDIAN QUESTIONS

PUBLIC MEETINGS HELD IN LONDON AND THE PROVINCES

Apart from the information they contain, the speeches themselves are of so able a character, and were delivered with so much intense conviction that they entice the reader who once begins their perusal to follow on, column after column, until he reaches the end. The reason for this lies not only in the excellence of the speeches themselves; it arises largely from the goodness of the cause advocated. India and England alike will benefit by the adoption of the reforms urged. The good which is behind this movement makes the things said on its behalf instinct with power and living force. *India*, 25 April 1890

The first public meeting reported by *India* was at Manchester in March 1890. It was addressed by Mr C Bradlaugh MP on the subject of the *Indian National Congress*. In his first sentence he made it clear that he was not there to defend the Congress and its activities, but to justify them: he was not there to apologise but to plead for it. He added that according to certain people 'there was some nonsensical talk of national movement in India because there was no Indian nation'. That, however, according to him was a mere quibble of words. In his view, what the Congress sought to do was not to shake the Empire but make it better and firmer. 'The Indian question would come before us more and more. It ought not to be and could not be neglected.'

The first public meeting convened under the auspices of the British Committee of the Indian National Congress in Britain, was held at the Forrester's Hall, London in April 1890. The object of the meeting was to highlight the workings of the Indian Councils in India. The meeting was chaired by Sir William Wedderburn. At this first meeting Mr Surendra Nath Bannerjee, a visiting delegate from India, was also present.

MR W DIGBY (the Secretary of the Committee) read letters of apology and expressive of sympathy with the objects of the meeting from those unable to attend.

The Chairman, SIR WILLIAM WEDDERBURN said: Ladies and Gentlemen, under the ancient Roman Empire the humblest citizen had a right to appeal unto Caesar. In India you have an Empire with a population double that of the Roman Empire, and those millions of your unrepresented fellow-citizens desire now TO APPEAL UNTO CAESAR, THAT IS TO THE SOVEREIGN BRITISH PEOPLE. (*Cheers*) Hitherto, it has been the complaint that the people of India were dumb; but now, happily, they have found a voice through the Indian National Congress. (*Cheers*) That Congress has sent delegates to England, men of ripe experience, men who are trusted by the people and are acquainted with the needs of the people; men who can speak eloquently because they speak from the heart. (*Cheers*) Formerly, as I have said, the millions of India were dumb, and we may ask, how is it that they have now found a voice? The answer is this, because you have given them education, not only the education of schools, but the education of Colleges and Universities. When Lord Macaulay was advocating this great boon for the Indian people, this extension of the higher education that we ourselves enjoy, he said to Parliament: 'It would be a base policy to keep people ignorant in order to keep them docile.' He felt that we must have TRUST IN THE PEOPLE OF INDIA as we have trust in the people of England. (*Cheers*) Gentlemen, that was a noble policy, and it has been splendidly justified by the results, for the people of England have thereby gained the gratitude and the attachment of the whole educated class, who are the leaders of the people of India. . .

It appears to me most suitable that on this happy occasion the first meeting addressed should be one among those metropolitan constituencies which have shown so kindly and so practical a sympathy towards India, which sent to Parliament Professor Fawcett, the first English member for India (*Cheers*) and which, I hope will also send to Parliament my friend, Mr Naoroji, as the first Indian member for India. (*Loud cheers*) It appears to me that PRACTICAL SYMPATHY LIKE THAT EXHIBITS A TRUE IMPERIAL INSTINCT, and that this is the true method to consolidate our Indian Empire and to promote the progress of the human race. I need hardly ask for my friend Mr Surendra Nath Banerjee, a

Charles Bradlaugh (1833–1891)
Social reformer and MP; refused, as an unbeliever, to take his oath of allegiance on the Bible; ejected from the House several times by force. Published numerous leaflets, and from 1874 to 1885 was a close associate of Mrs Annie Besant.

patient and sympathetic hearing, because I am sure you will give it to him. I have now the pleasure to introduce him to deliver an address to you this evening.

MR SURENDRA NATH BANERJEE: Sir William Wedderburn, Ladies and Gentlemen, I appear before you, commissioned by the Indian National Congress to lay our grievances and to appeal to you for redress. I confess that I feel myself unequal to the magnitude of the task, and the greatness of the trust which has been reposed in me, but I am supported and encouraged by the conviction which is deep in me, that feeble as the advocate may be, great is the cause which he has the honour to represent (*Cheers*) and that the claims for liberty and justice on the part of two hundred millions of human beings, whose destinies an all-wise Providence has entrusted to your care, cannot but appeal with irresistible force to the deepest instincts of the English people...

The redemption of sacred pledges which have been uttered in your name and in your behalf by the Parliament of this country, and by the ruling authorities of India – PLEDGES AND PROMISES which I regret to say, up to this moment REMAIN INADEQUATELY REDEEMED, and, I ask you, finally – and this forms the most important part of my appeal to you – to extend to us in part, at least, those representative institutions, which have followed in the path of English power and civilisation, and which, wherever they have been established, have inaugurated a new era of peace, prosperity and happiness to the peoples concerned. (*Cheers*) It is with some measure of confidence that I appeal to you in respect to this matter, for you have already done the people of India the great honour of nominating one of the most distinguished of our countrymen as a Liberal candidate for representation in Parliament. (*Cheers*) Mr Dadabhai Naoroji has won for himself, by his devoted public services extending through the period of a lifetime, the esteem, the confidence and the admiration of all classes of the Indian community, and he has set before us, the men of a younger generation, an ideal, a lofty ideal, of public duty which it is impossible for us ever to hope to attain to. I only trust that you may lead him to victory (*Cheers*) and that it will be possible for him primarily to serve his constituents, and, in the next place, to serve the voiceless and unrepresented millions in India. (*Cheers*)

At the end of the meeting a resolution was moved:

That this meeting authorises the Chairman to sign a petition for presentation to the House of Commons, praying the House to allow for the insertion in the Indian Councils Bill, of a section permitting the election of one-half of the members of the Supreme and Provincial Legislative Councils, and of a large increase in the number of the members of the respective Councils.

The resolution was carried unanimously. A vote of thanks to the Chairman, proposed by Mr Naoroji and seconded by Mr Chintamon, brought the proceedings to a close.

*   *   *

Mr Surendra Nath Banerjee was one of the delegates of the Indian National Congress visiting England. He delivered an address on the Indian National Congress programme to a public meeting assembled in the hall of the Eleusis Club, Chelsea, and reported in *India*:

At the end of the session, a resolution was moved: 'That this public meeting having heard Mr Surendra Nath, a statement of the desire of the Indian people to be granted some share in the making of the law by which they are governed, do heartily approve the object, and would urge on the authorities that this claim should be admitted and accepted. That a copy of this resolution be forwarded to Her Majesty's Secretary of State for India, and to the public press.'

Mr Surendra Nath Banerjee was an eloquent public speaker. *India* of 23 May 1890 proudly presented a profile of him, with a likeness, during his short stay in England:

It is a misfortune that, in at least every large town in the United Kingdom, the people of this country have not had an opportunity of hearing with what force and appropriateness the English language can be spoken by an Indian Subject of the Queen.

The following observations tell of the impression he left on his British audience:

(1) A workman and democrat [in the Eleusis Club] – 'It gives me, a workman and democrat, sincere pleasure to see that India is taking such action that will, I feel sure, end in their demands being granted.'
(2) *South Wales Daily News* – 'It may surely be now admitted that India has at last found a voice in Cardiff.'
(3) *Taunton Echo* – 'When I heard Mr Banerjee speak, I was surprised, startled, electrified.'

Before his return to India, *Weekly Despatch* of London interviewed Mr Surendra Nath Banerjee. An extract was published in *India* of June 1890. It describes precisely and to the point his mission in England and India's demands:

CORRESPONDENT: You have come as a delegate from the Indian National Congress. May I inquire what is the nature of your mission?

MR BANERJEE: The Indian National Congress, ever since it had its first meeting at Bombay, in 1885, has been pressing for the introduction of the representative element in the constitution of the Indian Government. Nothing has been done in this direction, and it thinks that the time has come when the reform can no longer be postponed with advantage to the country or the Government. Accordingly, at the last session of Congress, several of us were appointed as delegates to come over to this country to appeal to the English constituencies.

CORRESPONDENT: What is the precise nature of the reforms you suggest?

MR BANERJEE: We have what are called Legislative Councils – bodies which impose taxes and make the laws. The members are all nominated by the Government. They are sham councils altogether. It would be the same thing as if your Parliament was to consist exclusively of members appointed by Lord Salisbury under the advice of Mr Balfour. We want to reconstitute these councils upon a partially elective basis; but the sovereign power will remain where it is at present vested, viz., in the Executive Government of the country. We say that half the members should be elected, the other half will continue to be nominated as before; and the president will be either the Viceroy or one of the provincial governors, as the case may be, and further, the Executive Government will have reserved to it the right of vetoing any decision of the council, if such a step should be considered necessary in the public interests, recording, of course, the reason for such a step. The councils will thus be purely consultative in their character, with this departure from the present system, that the people will have the right of electing their own representatives instead of the Government doing it for them.

CORRESPONDENT: How many meetings have you held since you have been in this country?

MR BANERJEE: I have been here now for little more than six weeks, and I have addressed twenty meetings in different parts of the country. We have had a very successful campaign in the West of England, including Wales; and everywhere we have been received with the utmost cordiality. The provincial Press has been especially sympathetic in its attitude.

CORRESPONDENT: Do you appeal to any particular party with a view to get what you want?

MR BANERJEE: No, we bind ourselves to no parties, but appeal to the sense of fairness and justice to all parties. Our meetings have hitherto been organised upon a non-party basis but I am bound to say that the sympathy we have received has chiefly come from the Liberal party as a party, though no doubt many Conservatives are with us in this movement.

As a journal for the discussion of Indian affairs, *India*, from the first year of its publication, was true to its promises. No sooner did the Indian National Congress delegation come to London than a request was made for them to meet Mr Gladstone, the great Victorian Liberal Prime Minister. Mr Gladstone expressed his ready willingness to receive the Congress delegates, consisting of Mr Hume. Mr Banerjee, Mr Mudholkar and Mr Digby. He was said to be 'glad' to see them and grant an interview, and saw them on 12 June in his private room in the House of Commons.

GLADSTONE ADDRESSING HOUSE OF COMMONS

William Ewart Gladstone
(1809–1898)
Liberal politician and Prime Minister 1868–74, 1880–5, 1886 and 1892–4, (when Naoroji was elected the first Indian Member of Parliament).

Mr Banerjee spoke of the thirty or more meetings he and others had addressed in various parts of England and Scotland, respecting which Mr Gladstone asked a number of questions. Before, however, this phase of the movement was discussed fully, Mr Hume explained to Mr Gladstone the Congress position and what were its proposals, particularly in regard to the Muhammadan opposition. This latter, indeed, Mr Gladstone himself brought to the front, characteristically seizing upon the central point of the Reform movement so far as it may affect the proceedings in Parliament. Mr Hume was able to give Mr Gladstone most assuring information on this point, while it was pressed upon him that there was no ethnographical difference between Hindus and Muhammadans, that there was little likelihood of any serious troubles existing between them.

'I, congratulate you, gentlemen,' said Mr Gladstone, 'on the interest which is taken in your subject. I do not consider the political tone of the present day is anything like so good as it was in the past, not so good as it was forty or fifty years ago. But, even then, consider what would have been thought of a proposal to grant, in however mild a degree, representative institutions to India.'

Mr Digby then described, in brief terms, Mr Goschen's attempt to associate agitators for Indian reform with Irish-American Leaguers, and the complete failure which had attended his efforts.

Mr Gladstone's comment on his review of the situation was as follows: 'Well, it seems you must be prepared to wait a little longer for realization of your hopes. You will have to wait a while.'

Agreement with this was expressed, and it was remarked that postponement was the only thing feared; the cause was a winning one, and must certainly succeed.

We are informed that the deputation brought away with them from the interview an impression that Mr Gladstone will take part in the second reading debate. All readers of this journal we are sure, will hope the impression may prove a correct one. (*India*, 21 June 1890)

*　　*　　*

Within just four months of its publication, *India* made quite an impact on contemporary British journals. They advised their own readers that those who wished to know what was going on in India, should see *India*. The journals praised *India's* editor as having proved that 'the ignorance of some English journals on Indian matters is still stupendous'.

Sir Madhava Rao's Seventy-six Reasons in Favour of Native-Indian Rule, tempered by British over-lordship, published in our last issue, has excited unusual interest in the Anglo-Indian circles in this country. From officials and non-officials alike we have received testimony on this point. One good friend of the Indian people, who is by no means a Congress-wallah, thus expresses himself on the subject: 'British Lordship is good for India – provided it does not go beyond over-lordship (except perhaps in certain localities such as the presidency towns, which are of our own peculiar creation. It is not good beyond this, because it then tends to root out native institutions, and substitute for them those of another civilisation, the growth of other physical, social and historical circumstances. That this is inevitable we have been warned by the history of art, and also scholastic education in India. Now the Congress as it is, is a volunteer organisation, as our educational system was at first, before the introduction of the English political system into India. This abstractly, is one of the very worst results of English administration in India; and consequently, as the Congress is actually developing, this is already becoming manifest to me. On the other hand, if the Congress limited itself to the revival of native institutions – if it made Sir Madhava Rao's Seventy-six Reasons the seventy-six planks of its platform – its work would at once assume a beneficiary aspect, and it would have the prayers and blessings of every sympathetic Englishman.' The spirit of these observations is most commendable. We are not, however, at all sure that it would be good policy to accept the advice given. Indeed British administration has made a return to Native-Indian modes of rule in the British Provinces impossible. For good or evil, Western civilisation, Western methods of rule, have become a part of Indian policy. These things are working into the very warp and woof of Indian daily life and experience. There is no going back. The only wise course is to go forward. Those who stop progress are contending with an irresistible force and, by damming what otherwise would be a peaceful and fertilising stream, are inviting calamity. Their invitation is certain to be accepted.   (*India*, 4 July 1890)

*   *   *

The Indian National Congress delegation visiting England in 1890 had addressed numerous public meetings during their stay, which were reported in *India*. What added to their serious business-like dealings with the public, as well as with the Committee in England, were the publication of minutes of their own private meetings. *India* published extracts of one such set of minutes of a meeting of the British Committee of the Congress on 4 July 1890:

THE PUBLIC MEETINGS ON BEHALF OF INDIAN
REFORM IN GREAT BRITAIN

The meetings of the summer campaign held in various parts of the United Kingdom having come to an end, the Committee wishes to place on record its senses of their great value in bringing the question of Indian reform before the British public. On the whole, the meetings have been well attended, and in every case the audiences manifested great interest in the reform proposals of the Congress and were enthusiastic in favour of the resolutions submitted, such resolutions in every instance having been adopted and petitions sent to the House of Commons praying for the acceptance of the Congress scheme of Council reform.

The Committee desires further to express its high appreciation of the services rendered by the gentlemen delegated by the Congress in December last who have visited England, namely, Surendra Nath Banerjee, R N Mudholkar, A O Hume, and Eardley Norton; and also to Dadabhai Naoroji and to Syed Ali Imam, resident in England, all of whom have addressed several meetings; particularly does it desire to recognise Mr Surendra Nath Banerjee's prolonged and able services; he attended all the meetings and succeeded, by his powerful oratory, in exciting an unusual degree of interest among his audiences.

Having regard to the number of questions before the British electorate, the Committee feels it must remark that the work of educating public opinion has only been begun, and that prolonged effort will be required to bring the Congress proposals adequately before the constituencies.

RESOLVED: That a copy of this minute be forwarded to the Joint-General Secretary of the Congress in India for circulation to the respective Standing Congress Committees, and that a copy be sent to each of the gentlemen named therein.

*   *   *

The social side of the visit of the Indian National Congress delegation was just as important as was their public appearances. After the end of the Congress's summer campaign of meetings and on the eve of Mr Surendranath Nath Banerjee's departure from London, Mr E C Schwann MP and Mrs Schwann gave an At Home in honour of the Indian delegates. *India* reproduced a detailed account of the function on 4 July 1890, quoting from the London Letter of the correspondent of another Indian journal:

AN INDIAN NATIONAL CONGRESS
RECEPTION IN LONDON

Tuesday night's function was of a social-political character. Mr E C Schwann MP, and Mrs Schwann gave a dinner-party to the delegates and held a reception in their honour afterwards. The house occupied by the Schwanns is in Prince's Gardens. It is a large one and recently been redecorated throughout, fitted up with the electric light and adorned in the latest and most admired manner. A prettier place for such a gathering could hardly have been imagined and no better one could have been desired. When to these pleasant surroundings were added the most charming and cordial hospitality of the host and hostess your readers will realise that the Delegates from India have every reason to be gratified with the attention shown them. Mr Schwann's dinner-party suffered somewhat from the excitement in the House of Commons, consequent on Mr Labouchere having moved the adjournment of the House to discuss the proposals for public business which Mr Smith had announced. A very pleasant party assembled nevertheless, as will be seen from the list of those who sat down, which list I herewith append:

Rt. Hon. J Stansfeld MP; W S B Mclaren MP; H Asquith QC, MP; F A Channing MP; Prof. Stuart MP; F Schwann; Surendra Nath Banerjee; R N Mudholkar; Dadabhai Naoroji; Eardley Norton; Geo. Yule; Wm. Digby CIE; J Keble (Bradford); A J Holland and Sidney A Chalk.

The reception afterwards was very crowded. A large number of members of Parliament attended and not a few members of the fashionable world. Titles were not numerous, but many distinguished people were present. Mr Gladstone was, unfortunately, unable to attend, although he had stated he much wished to be present. His daughter-in-law Mrs Henry Gladstone was giving a party that evening, and herself taking a part in the entertainment of her guests. Front-bench men were represented by Mr Childers, Mr Stansfeld, and Mr Mundella. The main body of the party was there, in all shades of Liberal opinion. Shortly after dinner, Mr Schwann mounted a chair, formally introduced the delegates to the assembly, and stated what were the objects of the Congress which the delegates had visited this country to expound. After this, first Mr Surendra Nath Banerjee and then Mr Mudholkar, addressed the assembly for a quarter of an hour each.

R N Mudholkar

The speeches of the host and the main guests were also reported:

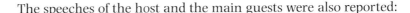

MR SCHWANN: I will ask our friends to say a few words to us. We have some idea of the object of their visit. It is to interpret to the English people, by meetings held throughout the United Kingdom, wishes of the great Indian people. I think the special point to which they desire to direct attention is the necessity for the representation of the people in the Legislative Council. I believe our friends from India would be satisfied if half the Council were elected by the Indian people. I do not know whether that is an irreducible minimum or not. You will hear Mr Banerjee and Mr Mudholkar, messengers from the Indian people, and they will no doubt give us a very accurate idea of what their wishes are. At the same time I believe that most of those in this room at any rate will agree that each people is the best judge of its own needs and requirements, and it is impossible for the most superior people to interpret the wants and wishes of the two hundred millions of India. We know that with regard to a neighbouring island some of us are stirring for great reforms in the government of the country. India is fifty-five times as great as Ireland, and I think we shall all feel that it is not an exaggerated wish on the part of the Indian people to desire to have a voice and hearing in the Indian Councils by direct representatives. The fact is, with regard to many of the conclusions come to by the great Indian National Congress held in recent years, though at first its recommendations were received with demur and criticism by the official mind, many of them have been promptly adopted and carried out. It appears, therefore, that the representatives of the Indian people who meet in the great National Council are able to make suggestions which are of advantage to the Government and to the people of India. I think all who are present will hope, having met the gentlemen who have come to give us the ideas that animated our fellow subjects in India, that they will be inspired to pursue the course upon which they have entered. You will I am sure give them a patient hearing. I have myself had the pleasure of hearing them in one of their great meetings, and I can only say that more accomplished orators you will have great difficulty in meeting. I will first call upon Mr Banerjee, Principal of the Ripon College in Calcutta, to address you.

MR SURENDRA NATH BANERJEE: Ladies and gentlemen, my first difficulty is that I am on a chair. I am accustomed to stand upon a platform and to move about a little, but here I am cabined, cribbed and confined within the limits of the chair. But my first words will be words of acknowledgement for the hospitality of our kind host and hostess, Mr and Mrs Schwann, and what is still more for the opportunity they have afforded us of meeting so many distinguished persons and talking in an informal way on a subject which is so near and dear to us. But the feeling which Mr and Mrs Schwann have shown in this matter represents really the universal British feeling on the subject. (*Hear, Hear*) We have addressed as many as thirty meetings in different parts of the country...

Ladies and gentlemen, we shall go home (I am going tomorrow) with a message of joy and hope. We shall tell our countrymen there when we go back, that whatever may be their feeling of dissatisfaction with the Government of the country, the great heart of the English people is sympathetically disposed towards them; that there is abundance of justice and abundance of desire on the part of the English people to give them the justice that they demand and to which they are fairly entitled...

Ladies and gentlemen, with your permission I would repeat the words, the memorable historic words which Sir Charles Metcalfe made use of. A deputation waited upon him in Calcutta, and in reply to that deputation he said, 'It cannot be that we are destined by an Almighty Providence to be here in India for the purpose only of collecting taxes and paying deficits; we are here for a higher and nobler purpose altogether, namely, to pour into the East the knowledge, culture, enlightenment and civilisation of the West.' That was said in 1835...

A despotic government may be a very good form of government in the early stages of civilisation, but it becomes a curse and crime after a certain stage (*Hear, hear*), and I am afraid that that stage has fairly been reached at the present moment...

We believe in our cause, we believe that persistency in constitutional agitation will culminate in the triumph of the cause, and above all we believe in the sense of justice and the sense of liberty of the English people. We shall, therefore, continue this agitation and with your help and under God's providence we are bound to win in the noblest contest that has ever warmed the hearts or inspired the energies of men. (*Cheers*)

MR MUDHOLKAR: Ladies and gentlemen, my friend has, it is true, expressed his obligations to our kind host and hostess, but according to our Eastern ideas I think I should be guilty of a grave dereliction of duty if I also did not express the gratitude I feel for the cordial reception which our kind host and hostess have given us tonight. Indeed, throughout our whole tour in England, which has extended over a very considerable part of the country, we have met not only with sympathy, but I may say with warm friendship from English men and English women. That is a sort of thing that we are not accustomed very much to meet in India. There are some of our friends here, I need not name them, who have seen them and who I am sure endorse what I say. Of course there are exceptions, and very good exceptions; but I am speaking of the general rule. It is, therefore, natural when we find English ladies and gentlemen so very kind and warm to us that we should feel the honour all the more. My friend has already told you something of the nature of the demands which we are urging upon the attention of the English people. Those demands may be thus shortly stated. We wish the British Government to carry out the policy which itself laid down years ago, viz., that of associating the people in the government of the country.

*   *   *

Subscribers to *India* were able to receive their copies in India from all the large cities, such as Bombay, Calcutta, Madras, Central Province, North West Province and Lucknow. Members of the Indian National Congress, on reading *India* of 23 October 1891 may have been more than interested in the report, 'The Congress Gathering in England' which it published as a copy of the minutes of the meeting of the British Committee of the Indian National Congress held on 13 October:

THE CONGRESS GATHERING IN ENGLAND

On the notice given by Mr Bannerjee, who was unable to be present, that the question as to whether it would not be advisable for the Congress to meet in England next year, be re-considered, a long and careful consideration of the whole matter followed.

On the motion of Mr Caine, seconded by Mr Dadabhai Naoroji, it was resolved: That the resolution passed at the last meeting of this Committee, recommending the postponement of the proposed meeting of the Congress in England next year, be affirmed;

At the same time the Committee think it desirable that no other session of the Congress, after that of December, 1891, be held until the Congress has assembled in England; and

Recommended to the Nagpur Congress that Resolution XI of the last year be re-affirmed, the early summer of 1893 being substituted for 1892;

Further resolved: That a Reception Committee be formed to raise funds for the entertainment of one hundred delegates to the Congress of 1893 in England for one month; and

That a formal letter of invitation, signed by the Chairman and the Secretary of this Committee, be forwarded to the Joint General Secretary of the Congress, for presentation to the Congress at Nagpur in December next.

The resolution of the preceding meeting of the Committee which has been affirmed was in the following terms:

That in view of the certainty of the General Election taking place during 1892, and the uncertainty of the time during the year when the Queen may dissolve Parliament, the British Committee of the Indian National Congress advise that the meeting of the Congress proposed to be held in London next year be postponed: but they urged upon the Standing Congress Committees the importance of sending a number of delegates to England able to advocate the claims of the people of India before the electors of the United Kingdom pending and during the Election contest.'

Probably, in regard to no matter which has come before them have the Committee given so much serious thought and careful deliberation as to the assembling of the Congress in England. Not even in India has the fact been so strongly realised as it has been by Sir W Wedderburn and his colleagues that the Congress cause will make but little progress until the aims and objects of Indian reformers are brought under the immediate cognisance of the British electorate.

On 27 November 1891, *India* reminded its readers of the visit of the 1885 Indian National Congress delegates to England. They were Messrs Manomoham Ghose, Rai Bahdur Salem Ramaswamy Mudaliyar and Narayana Ganesh Chandavarkar, who had arrived on the eve of the General Elections, a most timely visit that attracted the right kind of attention for being in the right place at the right time. By comparison, the 1890 visit of another delegation from the Indian National Congress was not as successful:

THE INDIAN DELEGATES TO BRITAIN IN 1885

Their mission attracted special attention, chiefly because it synchronised with the excitement and high endeavour which characterise an appeal to the English people to elect a new Parliament. Its surprising success was, also, in no small measure, due to the fact that the delegates (with one or two exceptions) attended Liberal meetings only. An opposite course was adopted in 1890, when Mr Surendra Nath Banerjee and Mr Mudholkar were in England: that course was not so successful. In nineteen cases out of twenty, Conservatives refused to have anything to do with the meetings, while, not being convened by the local Liberal Association, not a few Liberals did not feel called upon to exert themselves. After the formal banning of the Congress Party by Captain Middleton, on behalf of the Central Conservative Organisation, to say nothing of the ridicule and contempt poured on the movement by the Conservative press, Indian Reformers have no resource but to ally themselves with the Liberals and take advantage of the enormous Liberal gatherings sure to be held in every large town to promulgate the Congress programme. Assuming that this will be unreservedly done by the delegates, and that they will visit England at a time when the great meetings are held, it is safe to say that the triumph and success of 1892 will be even greater than were those of 1885. The success achieved six years ago was of significant and striking character, so much so that the new campaign ought to be entered upon with courage and confidence. Indian questions are better understood now than they were in 1885. By the Tory press, of course, the delegates were received with insult and slander. But, they did not repay railing with railing. As a rule, they treated, with deserved contempt, the foolish and untrue things said of them. Of the campaign, as a whole, the *Pall Mall Gazette* said: 'It is only the barest justice to say that the representatives of the Indian educated class have conducted their campaign, amid disgraceful insults and slanders, with a dignity and magnanimity which is itself one of the best possible testimonies to the justice of their appeal.'

THE WORK DONE

The gentlemen constituting the deputation were: Mr N G Chandavarkar LLB of Bombay; Mr Salem Ramaswamy Mudaliyar of Madras and Mr Manomohun Ghose MA of Calcutta. The last-named, who was in England, was by telegraph, desired by two of the Bengal Associations to become their representative. Early in October the whole of the delegates arrived in England. On the 12th of that month a meeting of friends interested in the objects of the delegation was held at the National Liberal Club, London. A consultation took place between those present as to the best way in which the objects in view could be obtained. It was unanimously agreed that the *modus operandi* should be three-fold in its character:
  1. By the delegates addressing public meetings in the metropolis and in different parts of the country;
  2. By arranging, in concert with Liberal electors, for test questions to be put to every candidate for Parliament; and
  3. By the circulation of leaflets, including a manifesto from the people of India to the electors of Great Britain and Ireland.

The meeting unanimously resolved itself into a committee, with power to add to its number, to be called 'The Indian Delegates' Committee'. The committee being purely consultative and advisory – the financial arrangements were made in Bombay. Only two meetings were held. Most valuable counsel was given by Professor WA Hunter MP, Mr W Martin Wood, Mr F W Chesson, Colonel Osborn, Mr J Seymour Keay and others.

The novel campaign upon which the delegates entered was carried through with ability, with devotion and with courage of high order, and at the same time with so much acceptance as to win the most cordial approval of those English men and English women who were so fortunate as to hear the speeches and to make the acquaintance of the delegates.

Public meetings were held in London and in many of the great towns in England and Scotland. Several were either presided over or attended by some of the most notable of the Liberal statesmen, e.g., the Right Hon. John Bright MP, the Right Hon. J Chamberlain MP, the Right Hon. Sir Charles Dilke, Bart MP, and others. Interviews of a cordial and satisfactory character were obtained with the statesmen named, with the ex-Viceroy (the Marquis of Ripon KG), with the Secretary of State for India Lord Randolph Churchill MP and with many others, both Liberal and Conservative. Though owing to circumstances arising out of the principles inspiring the respective parties, meetings were more frequently held under the auspices of leading Liberals than in connection with Conservatives, the delegates in no way formally associated themselves with either of the two great parties.

The personal impressions made by the delegates on the English folk with whom they became acquainted were of the most gratifying character, and were such as to heighten the respect in which able and cultured Indians are held by their British fellow-subjects. Both politically and socially nothing was left to be desired either in the zeal or in the aptness with which your representatives performed their arduous and important duties. Their campaign was short; into the few weeks at their disposal they crowded much work and accomplished great things on behalf of their country.

*   *   *

Delegates at the 1885 Indian National Congress were well received in England. At their farewell breakfast at the National Liberal Club, the chairman, Dr Hunter MP, was happy to state that during their stay in England, one of the delegates, Mr N Chandavarkar, had addressed eighteen meetings to around a total of twenty-six thousand people, which he called an entirely successful mission. Dr Hunter's remarks were reported by *India* on 27 November 1891:

BREAKFAST TO THE INDIAN DELEGATES

The CHAIRMAN, Dr Hunter: They had not visited England for the object which some had ascribed to them (viz., to introduce a new element into our elections of forcing candidates on the British electors solely for Indian reasons, without any reference to home questions. Their object was to create an interest at home in Indian affairs, and in that they had been entirely successful, as the meetings which they had held in London, Birmingham, Manchester and as far north as Aberdeen had testified. They would never forget the reception they had met with everywhere; their utterances had met with such a response as he believed they never anticipated. He, of course, regretted that their friend Mr Lalmohun Ghose had not been successful at Deptford. He hoped that his want of success might not be misunderstood by the people of India. The Conservative party required every seat they could possibly obtain, and he did not think they could complain that they had not allowed Mr Ghose to take the seat at Deptford.

One of the delegates, Mr Lalmohun Ghose, resident in England, was the first Indian to stand for a Parliamentary seat, Deptford, in the general election. Dr Hunter expressed regret that Mr Ghose was not successful, and said that:

The defeat of Mr Ghose did not depend upon Mr Ghose or upon India, but had simply reference to the Liberal party. That contest had demonstrated two things – first, that an English constituency was willing to sacrifice its predilections for an English candidate in order to give a native of India an opportunity to bring forward in the Legislature the grievances of his country; and second, that a native of India could make of himself master of those home questions in which they were all interested.

The delegation left England and their friends with good spirits and earnestly hoped that the work which had been so well begun would continue.

*   *   *

A large part of *India* of 28 October, 1898 was devoted to the report of an important meeting at Westminster Town Hall on 26 October. It was jointly organised by the British Committee of the Indian National Congress and the Westminster Liberal Club to hear speeches on the subject of the 'Misgovernment of India and the reversal of the wise policy of Lord Lawrence and Lord Ripon'. Sir W Wedderburn MP presided and among those on the platform were Mr WC Bonnerjee (of Calcutta), Mrs and Miss Bonnerjee, Mr WA Chambers, Editor of the *Bombay Champion*, the Hon Mark Napier, Mr Dadabhai Naoroji, Mr Romesh C Dutt CIE, Mr GS Ross, Mr HS Khalil, Mr W Martin Wood and Mr AG Symonds.

THE CHAIRMAN, in opening the proceedings, said: We have upon this platform this evening two gentlemen, one an Indian and the other an Englishman who wish to speak to you on behalf of poor, unhappy, suffering India. Less than fifteen years ago India was peaceful and prosperous. (*Hear, hear*) Under the wise and sympathetic rule of Lord Ripon – (*Cheers*) – we had in our great dependency a contented people, friendly neighbours beyond the frontier, and a full public treasury. (*Hear, hear*) Taxation was reduced; by a wise system of local self-government the people were given a voice in the management of their domestic affairs; and when Lord Ripon left India on the completion of his term of office, the people in all parts rose as one man to testify their gratitude to and affection for him. (*Cheers*) I was myself present in Bombay on that memorable occasion, and I shall never forget that spontaneous burst of popular feeling. (*Cheers*) The city of Bombay – the second city of the Empire, for it comes next to London – was decorated from end to end, and for three days the vast population of 800,000 inhabitants made holiday and swarmed in the streets... All that Lord Ripon did was to carry out good British methods honestly and fearlessly. (*Cheers*) He administered India in that spirit of justice and sympathy which is declared in the Queen's gracious Proclamation of 1858, which is ordained in our Acts of Parliament, and which is I believe approved by you, ladies and gentlemen, and by the great body of the British people. (*Cheers*) Now, I grieve to say all this happy condition of things has been changed. The wise and humane policy of Lord Lawrence and Lord Ripon has been deliberately reversed, and what is known as the 'forwarded' policy has been adopted, a policy of aggression abroad and repression at home. Now what have been the results of that reversal of the accepted British policy? Instead of peace beyond the frontier we have had an unjust, foolish and disastrous war; instead of a full treasury and reduced taxation we have increased burdens with exhausted resources and threatened insolvency; instead of prosperity within our borders we have a people dying from hunger and disease; and instead of contentment we have misery and unrest. To crown all and to make matters worse we have the suppression of free speech, police terrorism, and imprisonment without trial. (*Shame*) Now I would ask, who are the people responsible for the disastrous change in the condition of affairs in India? Surely the responsibility lies on those authorities in England and in India who within the last few years have changed the whole spirit of our Indian administration... I am not able to speak of recent important events in India from personal experience, but I am glad to be able to introduce to you two gentlemen who have recently come from India and who are thoroughly well qualified to tell you the facts. First I will introduce to you my friend Mr Bonnerjee. He is a barrister with very large – perhaps I should not be wrong if I said the largest – practice in Calcutta. He also has occupied an important official position as Standing Counsel to the Government of India, and as a member of the Bengal Legislative Council. I feel sure that when you have heard him you will be assured that the British Government in India has no better friends in India than the educated Indians, among whom he is one of the most trusted leaders. (*Loud cheers*)

MR BONNERJEE: I am indebted to you, Sir William for the kind manner in which you have introduced me to the audience, and to the audience for the cordiality with which they have received me. I have no claim to stand before you tonight except that, as a native of India, I am deeply interested in the welfare of that country. (*Hear, hear*) I have studied closely Indian politics for a considerable number of years, and I have been from its very inception one of the persons who have taken part in the organisation and in the carrying on of that assembly of educated Indians which the Marquis of Dufferin and Ava so epigrammatically but incorrectly described as a microscopic minority of the Indian people – the organisation which is known by the name of the Indian National Congress. (*Hear, hear*) My claims do not go any further; but such as they are you will, I trust, favour me with your attention for a few minutes while I place before you the cause of my country. (*Cheers*) I think, sir, I should best discharge the duty which the organisers of this meeting have entrusted to me by reading at the outset the resolution which I am called upon to move. It is as follows: 'That this meeting deeply deplores the suffering condition of the Indian people, and protests against the reversal of the wise policy of Lord Lawrence and Lord Ripon which gave peace and contentment to India; especially it condemns the repressive legislation which has recently been passed by the Indian Government, and trusts that it will be repealed at the earliest opportunity'. Leaving 'the suffering condition of the Indian people' for a moment, I will deal with the protest 'against the reversal of the wise policy of Lord Lawrence and Lord Ripon'. What was the policy of Lord Lawrence? It was peace with our neighbours, happiness, contentment, and progress on the part of the people.

It has always seemed to me that there are two bogies which affect the imagination of English statesmen, both in India and in this country. One has been in existence for very many years – for over half a century. It is the bogey that Russia is going to invade India and displace English power there. That that is a bogey there can be no doubt. (*Hear, hear*) Russia has to think of many things before she can come to India. (*Hear, hear*) India now is not what she was when the East India Company first went there. The Pagoda tree has been cut down and has disappeared, and today India is as poor, to use a vulgarism, 'as a church mouse'. Consequently Russia will never get anything there at all, even if she were foolhardy enough to try to go there. That is one bogey which has been in existence for very many years. The other bogey which has taken possession of the minds of our statesmen – our statesmen so-called – in the India Office at the present moment is that of sedition. . .

It is apparently in existence only in the minds of the so-called statesmen who believe in it, Yet somehow it does not strike the mind of these gentlemen that if there really were any sedition in India it would tell greatly against their competency to rule the country, for remember India has been ruled by England certainly from before the year 1793, or over a century, and if after the lapse of such a period of time England has not been able to win the attachment and affection of the Indian people, then England ought not to be there. (*Hear, hear*). . .

Our rulers do not attempt to understand the people of India, and they pass laws which are unintelligible to them and which become a source of very great discontent. Sedition in India means not that the Government is to be upset, but that one must not speak at all disrespectfully of the powers that be. If you say that the Government of India as at present constituted is not wise, or strong, or able to govern, you would be held up as a seditious man. (*Shame*). . . The one thing in this new law of sedition to which everybody with a reasonable turn of mind objects is that intention has no lot or part in it. However innocent the intention may be, however willing one may be that the connexion between India and England should exist for ever, if you say anything which might bring the Government of India into discredit you are a seditious individual and may be liable to be transported for life. (*Shame*) Is life worth living under these conditions in India? (*Cries of no*) I agree with my friends. I say emphatically that it is not. (*Cheers*) In addition to this sedition law we have, as you have pointed out, sir, got spies; we have got persons dogging the footsteps of those supposed to be seditious. To speak the honest truth, last year in India, according to the people at large, was a year in which there was a reign of terror. Were our great and glorious leader alive and at the head of affairs, such a

Bill as Lord George Hamilton's would never have been passed. (*Cheers*) Were he alive now and likely in a short time to have the direction of affairs the Bill would be repealed at once. But, unfortunately for India, unfortunatley for the great British Empire, Mr Gladstone is no more. Let us hope that his mantle has fallen upon some worthy successor, and let us hope that when the Liberal party come back to power they will take up the case of India (*Cheers*) – and will not rest until this obnoxious, this unecessary, this irritating measure is wiped out of the statute book. (*Cheers*) If that is done the Indian people will be able to breathe, but if it is not done I do not know what the consequences may be. The resolution goes on to deplore the suffering condition of the Indian people...

The people deserve your sympathy, but they desire something more. They desire your assistance to become free from the trammels of this legislation which has been imposed upon them. Every man amongst you who has a vote to return a member to the House of Commons is indirectly responsible for the government of India – the proper government of India – and I appeal to you all to consider the question of India a little more carefully than you are in the habit of doing. (*Hear, hear*) I appeal to you all to take the circumstances of India into your consideration and to do what you can to bind the Indian people to you by silken cords, and to make them happy and contented by doing all you can to ameliorate their condition. (*Loud cheers*)

THE CHAIRMAN next introduced Mr WA Chambers, a civil engineer who went to India in 1890, who had interested himself in public matters there, and was the only European who had ever secured the confidence of the people to the extent of being elected by them, in a contested election, a member of a municipality. He was also the Editor of the *Bombay Champion* and, above all, he had kept himself free from class prejudices and had had the courage and patriotism to look at things with an impartial and unprejudiced eye. (*Cheers*)

MR CHAMBERS: Mr Bonnerjee devoted the latter part of his speech to a criticism of the Sedition Law in India; but he did not tell you, as I will tell you, that he may deliver a seditious speech in England for which on his return to India he may be brought before the court of justice and charged under the law. He did not tell you either, as I will tell you, that I can deliver as many seditious speeches as I like in England, and there is no court in India which can try me, I being an Englishman and he being an Indian. (*Shame.*) That one fact is one, I think, sufficient to condemn the present methods of British administration in India, and to excite your commiseration. (*Hear, hear*)

If you constantly tell the Indian people that they are seditious you will end by making them so, and that would be a most serious disaster for this country. Treat them as people like yourselves, as members of the British Empire. Let them have part and share in that empire of which they are as proud as yourselves. They like to feel that they are under the protection of your fleet and your army; that they are part of the empire. But if they feel that their part of the empire is that of Cinderella, that you are going to all the balls and having all the fun (*Laughter*) – they may fall into a sulky mood, and possibly in time become 'sedition mongers'. I want you to play the part of the fairy godmother to Cinderella, to enable her to shake off her rags and let her share the enjoyments which fall to your lot. (*Loud cheers*)

THE CHAIRMAN then read amid cheers the following letter from Mr A O Hume:

'The Chalet, 4, Kingswood Road, Upper Norwood. S. E. October 25, 1898.

'My dear Sir William, – I regret much that the state of my health still prevents my taking part in public meetings. I need not say how entirely I am in sympathy with the object of this coming meeting, which I understand to be to endeavour to draw public attention to the fact that all the troubles by which India has been recently beset are mainly due to the complete change of policy which has characterised the administration of that country the past twelve or thirteen years...

Never were the people of India more prosperous, more loyal to their Queen-Empress, more happy and contented than when some fourteen years ago Lord Ripon's auspicious reign closed amid expressions of national gratitude and love, such as no other ruler of India ever secured.

Allan Octavian Hume ICS
(1829–1912)
Educated at Haileybury. Went to India in 1860. Indian Civil Servant and ornithologist; joined Bengal Civil Service 1849; CB for services in Indian Mutiny 1860. Convinced that united action of responsible friends of India was necessary to counteract the dangerous current of opinions in the country and to turn them into positive channels of communication. Took initiative in organising and establishing the Indian National Congress in 1885, and became its first and longest serving General Secretary. Prepared a scheme for the redemption of agricultural indebtedness and village Panchayats; declined offer of Lieutenant-Governorship; collaborated in standard work on Indian game birds. Helped maintain the Congress organ *India* in England.

And now, look at India! A more unhappy land can hardly be found, and I fear none whose people are more thoroughly, are more righteously, dissatisfied with their rulers. And why? Because since Lord Ripon's time that evil policy of aggression abroad and repression at home, which Lord Ripon's liberal instincts revolted from, has become dominant in all later rulers' reigns, because they have given us ceaseless and unjust wars in lieu of peace; reckless and iniquitous military extravagance in lieu of economy; reactionary measures which recall some of the worst features of Russian despotism in lieu of reform, and setting aside Lord Ripon's unshaken, and, as the result proved, righteous trust in the people, have allowed suspicion and distrust of that people to reign supreme in their minds.

You do well to try again and again to fix public attention on those facts, for thus far it seems as though, for us English, history for ever vainly writes her warnings upon the wall of time. I have grown old and weary in urging on my fellow countrymen the inevitable consequences of this wrong doing; but so surely as there is a divinity who shapes all mortal ends, who requites, slowly it may be but surely, all good and evil doing whether of individuals or nations, so surely shall poor England in some darkest hour of danger and distress have meted to her full retribution for all the wrongs done and now doing in her name to the people of India – a people the most loveable in the world, who need only fair play, justice and kindly trust to figure a generation hence as the premier bulwark of the Empire of which, if our present policy is persisted in, they must some day become the subverters.

In the whole history of the world I know of nothing sadder than the dull apathy in regard to this vital issue which continues to prevail here. May it be your happier lot – I have toiled in vain – to awaken some real interest in this, which if rightly understood is the most momentous question that England has ever had to decide.

The welfare, the destiny of nearly three hundred millions of people, and the persistence in the coming century of Great Britain as a first-class power are both involved.

Yours very sincerely,

A. O. Hume

*   *   *

While the 14th Indian National Congress was meeting in Madras, India, in December 1898, the London Indian Society held the annual conference of all Indians resident in the United Kingdom, at the Westminster Town Hall. A large Indian community of all religions and professions as well as a considerable sprinkling of English ladies and gentlemen, received with acclamation the venerable and revered President, Dadabhai Naoroji. The 30 December 1898 issue of *India* reported that:

It was very gratifying to observe the increasing interest in Indian affairs manifested by the English visitors, many of whom supported the various resolutions in emphatic yet well-weighted terms. Again there was heard a warlike note from some of the younger Indians, a not unnatural manifestation indeed, though not altogether politic; but it ought to serve the very important purpose of suggesting to the authorities some keener sense of the gross impolicy of exasperating men who wish nothing better than reasonably fair treatment for their countrymen and their country. It was impossible for any unbiased mind to listen to the arguments urged by the speakers without being moved to profound sympathy, and without being amazed that policy should be so perverse as to create such grounds of complaint and to labour to repress instead of endeavouring to conciliate.

Mr Naoroji moved the first resolution from the chair. The first basis represents a claim that Mr Naoroji has urged so consistently and steadily that the British public can hardly fail to be ashamed that the demand still remains unsatisfied. It is the claim of fulfilment of 'the oft declared and pledged policy of the British people, through Acts and resolutions of Parliament and Proclamations of Her Majesty the Queen, to treat Indians as British subject in this country.'...

The second basis of the resolution is the distinguished 'loyalty, heroism and soldierly qualities' of the Indians engaged 'in the recent war beyond the frontier and in all preceding wars'. 'In all preceding wars' observe, as well as in the recent campaigns. This is a point that is too often forgotten by Englishmen. They ought to remember that for every Englishman with Clive in the decisive battle of Plassey, there were two Sepoys. And so it has been all the way down the centuries of Indian conquest. The British Empire in India has been raised on the blood and bones and money of Indians in a very literal fashion. Mr Mahtab Singh drove home the point effectively. On these two solid bases, then, the resolution demands 'that Indians should be allowed commissions and command in the Indian army in the same manner and through the same methods as are open to Englishmen, by competition and training, and by promotion for distinguished ability and gallantry in the field'. Possibly enough, as one speaker remarked, Englishmen may dislike to serve under the command of Indian Officers. But it is part of the price we must pay for our Imperial boast if our Imperialism is to be anything but the pinchbeck article which Mr Asquith scorned and repudiated...

The second resolution is especially opportune. By it the Conference 'deplores all legislation restricting self-government in India, urges the Government to withdraw the Calcutta Municipality Bill now before the Bengal Council, and affirms the principle that the extension of popular rights and the trust and confidence in the people is the surest foundation of British rule in India.'...

Why should India not be dealt with in this matter on a like footing with the colonies? As Mr Dutt properly pointed out, it is through the full grant of self-government, 'the greatest of English privileges,' that the colonial empire is both prosperous and loyal.

Mr Bipin Chandra Pal moved the third resolution. This 'condemns the new Sedition Law of India,' and sets forth five most mischievous consequences necessarily flowing from that ill-advised legislation. This odious law creates invidious distinctions between classes; it fetters freedom of discussion of Indian measures by menaces that reach the outspoken Indian even in other countries; it represses unworthily the long-established liberty of the Press; it places in the hands of the magistrates, heads of the police, dangerous powers over the editors of newspapers, tending to professional deterioration and even to personal demoralisation under the menace of a demand for security for good behaviour or in the alternative, imprisonment with hard labour 'without trial for any specific offence'; and it is 'based on suspicion and distrust against the people, and is thereby calculated to alienate the people and weaken the foundation of the British Empire in the East'. The law is supplemented in practice by an extra-legal, if not positively illegal, institution of 'Press Committees,' which the Government of Bombay at least seems ashamed to own, for it throws the odium on the local collector. Mr Justin MacCarthy once wrote very clear-sightedly:

'You must have the voice of India; you must know what its populations wish for themselves, and claim for themselves; and, till you hear the voice speaking to you directly, as people unto people, you cannot possibly hope to govern with stability and with safety a great country like India. You cannot control India except by the consent of various populations whom this Empire undertakes to govern. That is what we want. We want to win the consent of the different populations, to instil in the confidence in our intelligence, in our goodwill, in our anxiety to make them happy and prosperous; and when we have attained that consent, and can act on and with that consent, then, and not by any possibility till then, can we make a stable and permanent Imperial State.'

But if you gag the voice of the people at every turn, how are you to obtain that necessary basis for your 'stable and permanent Imperial State?' This Conference will demonstrate not only the loyalty of the Indians but also how severely their loyalty is tried by our blind and deaf authorities in Calcutta and at Westminster. The situation will be profitably pondered by all who wish to see assured the stability and permanence of the British Indian Empire.

SIR W WEDDERBURN ON INDIAN POLICY
LECTURE AT THE NEW REFORM CLUB

A most interesting and enthusiastic meeting took place at the New Reform Club, Adelphi Terrace, Strand, London in December 1902. It was held in connection with the League of Liberals against Aggression and Militarism and the invitation to Liberals evidently had some effect, for the lecture hall was filled with an attentive and sympathetic audience to hear Sir William Wedderburn deliver a lecture on Indian Policy.

SIR W WEDDERBURN, who was received with cheers said: Mr John Stuart Mill, in his book on *Representative Government*, has an instructive chapter regarding 'The Government of Dependencies by a Free State'. Under this heading he discusses the case of India; and specifies certain unavoidable evils from which she suffers by reason of her foreign rule; showing that a subject people profits little by the fact that its masters are themselves a free democracy. As he puts it, the despotism of 20 million foreigners is not necessarily better than the despotism of one home-bred autocrat. Poor India has had experience of both kinds of despotisms; first under Native despots; and now, under the British people. We ourselves are now the '*de facto*' despots; and the immediate practical question is: What can be done to minimise the unavoidable evils of our foreign rule, and to develop whatever good is possible?...

The problem is a grave one, affecting as it does one-sixth of the human race. But unfortunately the people of this country have never properly realised their responsibility as proprietors of so vast a national joint-stock concern.

MR W C BONNERJEE entirely agreed with all that had been said by Sir W Wedderburn. If he dared to open new ground he was afraid his remarks would not be palatable to an English audience. (*A voice: 'let us have it.'*) His view was that the sympathy which was supposed to be shown by the English people towards Indians was nothing but a delusion and a sham. (*Hear, hear, and No, No!*) There was no sincerity in it at all. English people met together to hear Indian topics discussed, passed a resolution that India ought to be properly treated, and then went home, and directly their heads touched the pillows they forget all about India and become absorbed in domestic affairs. He did not say that was unnatural; it was quite the contrary, but why should they pretend to take an interest in India. Englishmen were bound hand and foot to certain persons who were called their agents, were satisfied with everything they told them, and if a Native Indian got up and told a different story they would remark that the Natives of India were accustomed to draw long bow and they say things which were not absolutely accurate. Englishmen forgot that they were the rulers of nearly 300 millions of human beings. (*Hear, hear*) If England could not discharge the duties that her responsibility threw upon her she ought to say so openly and retire from India, leaving the Indians to shift for themselves. Say what they would India was not governed in the interest of the people in India, but in the interests of the middle class and aristocratic class of this country. . .

He was afraid he had said many things which were not palatable, but he held that the time had gone by when 'mealy-mouth' speeches were any good. . .

He hoped that in discovering the Colonies Mr Chamberlain would not lose sight of India, because after all it was from India that they got the Imperial idea, that India which at one time was called the brightest jewel in the crown of England. . .

The only form of representation which at present obtained was that in the legislative councils of the Viceroy and the Governors there were a certain number of members who were proposed by different representative bodies equivalent to the county councils, chambers of commerce and universities. . .

The suggestion that there should be a Parliamentary Committee for India was a excellent one.

*　　*　　*

One of the most brilliant speeches made by Dadabhai Naoroji on his return from India in December 1902 was at the Newington Reform Club, Walworth, London. It was reported in *India* of 5 December 1902:

MR DADABHAI NAOROJI ON INDIA

Mr NAOROJI, who was cordially greeted, said he proposed to speak specially of the system of government in India. He did not wish to blame any official or any single individual, but to deal with the defence made by Anglo-Indians. The present system of government in India was not in accordance with the Acts of Parliament or proclamations made by the Queen, or the pledges which the British people were bound to carry out. One of the arguments put forward in defence of the system was that the British prevented the different peoples of India from plundering each other. That was only a half truth; the whole truth was that they prevented the different peoples from plundering each other in order that they themselves might plunder all. (*Cheers*) Then they were told that the British had introduced security of property and security of life, for which Indians ought to be very grateful. Yes, they had introduced security of property, but in order that they might carry it away with perfect security. As to the security of life it was said that the old oriental despots used to kill thousands and thousands and harass the people. If that was so the British Government with great ingenuity and scientific precision was killing millions by famines and plagues, and starving scores of millions. It was acknowledged that the old despots were butchers and struck with violence. The whole world was horrified, and particularly Anglo-Indians were horrified at their deeds. But the Anglo-Indians, or the British, were like clever surgeons who, with the sharpest scalpel, cut the very heart, and drew every drop of blood without leaving a scar. Then it was said that the British introduced law and order which India never previously possessed, as if India never existed before they went to India, or Indians were not thousands of years ago, when the British were wandering in forests like savages without clothes, at the height of their civilisation; when they had a government with law and order that Englishmen would not be sorry to possess. What was the whole truth of the matter? Law and order were vitally important and necessary to the existence of Englishmen in India. That was the reason why they were so anxious for law and order, for without it Englishmen could not stay there one week. He did not blame Anglo-Indians for that, but at the same time he asked what benefit the people of India received. Their portion of law and order was the utmost wretchedness in which they were compelled to live and die. During the last famine over a million of people died, and it was only such occurrences which drew the attention to the English people to the condition of Indian people. But they had no idea of the normal condition of the people. . .

English people said, because they had saved Indians from plunder and violence, they should hold them as slaves and seize their property. If it was monstrous for a man who had saved a man's life to claim his property and make him a slave, then it was monstrous for the British to keep Indians as helots and slaves under their heels. (*Cheers*) The beauty of it all was that the British claimed the Indians' gratitude, held their property, and kept them slaves without having risked a single farthing of their own. The British Empire was built up entirely at the cost of the Indians. The Army that fought for them was the Indian Army. The European army of those days was not one-tenth of the Indian Army which fought and bled, and if any gratitude was due from one to the other it was due from the British to the Indians. (*Cheers*) The only gratitude India received was that her people were kept as slaves, and their property was carried away. They were sometimes told that if the English left India, Russia would come in, and that it would be bad thing for the Indians. Let that be granted. But because the Russians would be bad was that a justification for the English to be bad also? . . .

The question for them to consider was whether they were ruling India according to the promises and pledges given, according to the policy which the whole British people in the name of the sovereign and by Acts of Parliament had laid down. No, they were entirely going upon one principle, and that was to plunder the Indians as much as they could, or, to use the words of Lord Salisbury, to bleed Indians. Lord Curzon said that India was the pivot of the British Empire, and that if India was lost the sun of the British Empire would set. And yet Lord Curzon and all the authorities, the Secretary of State, the British Government, and the Government of India acted on the principle of taking the utmost they could out of India and treating the people as slaves. . .

It was true that in the history of India she had been invaded and her people treated with violence and oppression, but when those invasions occurred the invaders went away, and the wounds caused by the plundering healed up. Germany conquered France and made her pay a very heavy penalty, but when that was paid the wound healed and France was now as wealthy as ever. But in India the British came as foreign invaders and did not carry away so many millions and leave the country, but they remained and bled the country to the tune of nearly 30 millions every year. Could any country in the world stand that? If England were subjected to any such process by France, for instance, her condition in a year or so would be a poverty-stricken one. . .

In 1833 an Act was passed in which it was clearly laid down that the people of India should be able to enter the service of the Crown on the same level as any British subject, without reference to class, creed or colour. That Act of Parliament still existed, for it had not been repealed, but it had been more honoured in the breach than in the observance. Not the slightest step was taken to give effect to the Act. If they read the speeches made on that occasion by Lord Macaulay and Lord Lansdowne they would find that the reasons given for that Act were that it was righteous and true, and most in consonance with the honour and justice of the British name. Those were speeches of giants and men of righteousness, but the East India Company and their successors gave no effect to the Act. Then came the Mutiny, which was all British work. The people remained loyal; it was only the British Army, which was treated so badly, that created the Mutiny. After it was suppressed English people were very angry about the horrible massacres which took place, although the horrible massacres of Indians were never reported. Because of the mutiny of the army they had no right to punish the whole people. The cost of the Mutiny – some 40 millions – was borne by India, although the fault lay with the British. After the Mutiny the British people acted in the way in which British instincts of justice and honour led them, and in the name of the Queen proclamations were issued which emphasised and confirmed the Act of 1833, promising that Indians should be treated like all her Majesty's subjects. That was the very reason why Indians allowed the English to become their rulers – because they desired to raise themselves to the position of British citizenship. On the occasion of the Jubilee the Queen repeated the promises of that proclamation. When she took the title of Empress the Viceroy at the great Durbar at Delhi proclaimed that in honour and justice the British Government must give Indians the rights of citizenship. But these were all empty hollow words, and Indians today were as much the slaves of the old system as they had been from the middle of the eighteenth century, when England first obtained any political power in India. In the early days the treatment of the people was such that the Court of Directors on the one hand, and the Viceroy on the other, complained in the most bitter terms that the people then under the control of the British were oppressed in a manner the like of which had never been seen in any country or in any age. Then the system was more open and violent, now it was less violent and open, but it was concealed and unseen, and at the same time was of twenty times greater force than in the early days. Indians were often called partners in the British Empire, but it was an extraordinary kind of partnership, for the Indians had to find all the money, while the English took all the profit. . .

Mr Naoroji concluded by appealing to the whole British people to ask themselves whether they had done their duty towards India or whether their servants had carried out the policy sanctioned by Parliament. Was it not their duty as human beings, as the great civilising people who claimed to have advanced the world, to look to it that the British name might not be fouled by the betrayal of trust of their servants? (*Cheers*)

*   *   *

Mr J M Parikh, Barrister-at-Law, was a member of the British Committee of the Indian National Congress. He gave a series of lectures, sixteen in all, during the winter of 1902. *India* of 5 December 1902 published extracts of some of Mr Parikhs speeches:

Mr J M Parikh lectured before the Literary and Debating Society of the Inns of Court Mission on Wednesday, November 5, 1902 on 'Is the Government of India responsible to anyone?' Mr Parikh divided his question into two parts: (a) Is the Government of India responsible to the tax-payer? (b) Is the Government of India responsible in practice to the Home Government? After reviewing the constitution of the Indian Government Mr Parikh answered both his questions in the negative. He then addressed himself to the economic aspect of the question and the economic results of the present system. A discussion followed. Mr Parikh in his reply defined his position thus: 'We want British rule, but the time has come when Indian experts ought to have a voice in Indian Government'.

On November 9 a most interesting address was given by Mr Parikh to the members of the Peel Institute. The Friends' Meeting House, Clerkenwell, where the meetings are held, was filled with an audience of men, mostly young, of the artisan class who listened with intense interest to Mr Parikh's lucid explanation of the grievances and disabilities to which Native Indians are subjected. Mr Parikh's visit to the 'Pleasant Sunday Afternoon' meeting had (writes a local correspondent) been looked forward to with pleasure on account of the favourable impression made by him on the occasion of his lecture to the Peel

Debating Society. Lectures of this character are doing a great deal to dispel the mist of ignorance which obscure the knowledge of the English people as to the real state of Indian affairs. At the close of the meeting Mr Councillor Geo. M Gillett proposed a vote of thanks to Mr Parikh, which was most heartily accorded by the crowded meeting.

On November 11, at a public meeting held in the large hall attached to the Paddington Radical Club, a lecture was delivered by Mr J M Parikh on 'The Condition of India'. His remarks were heard with great interest and endorsed by Englishmen in the audience, who spoke from personal experience as residents in the country. The following resolution, proposed by Mrs Bracey-Wright, one of the Hon. Secretaries to the Metropolitan Radical Federation, was adopted unanimously, and ordered to be sent to the Premier, the Secretary of State for India, and the leader of the Opposition: 'That this meeting is of opinion that the excessive and increasing taxation of the impoverished people of India, without due representation, is unjust; that its effect is disastrous, and until the people themselves are given a full share in the government of the country these evil conditions are likely to continue.'

Mr Parikh lectured to the New Southgate Debating Society on 'India' on November 13. Dealing specially with the economic causes of the poverty of India, he sketched the history of the British conquest, and showed how the action of the East India Company had almost destroyed the old manufacturing industries, and had compelled ninety per cent of the inhabitants to depend upon agriculture. He showed that the cause of the famines, which have now become chronic, is not failure of the rain supply and deficiency of crops, but the constant drain from India to Great Britain of thirty millions a year in charges for which India has no economic return. The whole cost of the acquisition of India had been borne by that country, and the size of the army maintained there was regulated by Imperial considerations. Mr Parikh argued therefore that a large part of the cost of the Indian Army, together with all home charges, should be borne by the Imperial Exchequer. The lecture was received with utmost interest, and the opinions expressed in it were generally supported in the discussion which followed.

A public meeting was held in the large hall of the Hammersmith Club on November 25, and was largely attended, when Mr Parikh gave a most interesting lecture on 'The Pressing Needs of India'. After the lecture several questions were asked and satisfactorily answered. We hope (the secretary writes) to have further addresses at some future date.

The foregoing reports are extracts from appreciative accounts kindly forwarded to us by officials of the various societies addressed by Mr Parikh.

*   *   *

Mr WC Bonnerjee, the first President of the Indian National Congress (1885) divided his time between India and England. He was always in the public eye at meetings in England on affairs of India and in great demand as a speaker. A public meeting was held at Westbourne Park Sunday Afternoon Conference for discussion on 'Britain's responsibility to India' which Mr Bonnerjee was invited to address. Mr J Wallis Chapman presided. *India*, in its issue of 16 January 1903, published a report of the meeting:

THE CHAIRMAN, in opening the proceedings, declared that the responsibilities of Britain towards India were three- or four-fold. There was the duty of the stronger to help the weaker. It should be remembered that the Indians stood in a very different position from that of Australians and the Canadians. They were a conquered people, and therefore in respect of India this country had to face the responsibility of maintaining its system of government whether it be for good or for ill. Finally, it must be borne in mind that the people of India had practically no voice in the management of their own affairs, and that cast a still greater responsibility on Great Britain. (*Hear, hear*)

MR BONNERJEE, who was received with much applause, said that before it was possible for them to realise the responsibilities of this country towards India it was necessary for them to understand the problems connected with India and they were many. Time was short, and he could not hope to place them exhaustively before those assembled. He proposed therefore to devote his remarks to three fallacies which have taken a deep hold in the public mind. The first was that India ought never to be made a party question, that she should stand outside party politics, and should be dealt with upon her own merits, independently of whether the advocacy of her claims came from a Chamberlain or a Bannerman. The second fallacy for which Sir Henry Fowler was responsible was that every member of the House of Commons was a member for India. The third fallacy was that the people of India along with the other peoples of the East were so fond of show that they might almost be said to be children, whose loyalty was to be inspired by processions of elephants with all sorts of gay decorations, bearing upon their backs in howdahs the Viceroy and the King's brother. These fallacies had done an immense deal of mischief. Take the first. When India was in the hands of the East India Company it was quite proper that she should be outside party politics. The East India Company was, so to speak, a buffer between the Crown on the one hand and India on the other, and the experience of the last half century had shown that India was better governed by the Company than she had been by the Crown. When India passed from the Company into the hands of the nation a Secretary of State for India was created, and was given a seat in the Cabinet. That brought her within the region of party politics, for all knew that the Cabinet had its power at the will of the majority of the members of the House of Commons and of the electors of the country, and whenever Indian questions were debated in Parliament, however incorrect the version of facts given by the Secretary of State, his view was supported by the party to which he belonged – the majority, that was to say, of the House of Commons, which kept the Government in power. Were it possible for Indian topics to be dealt with their merits independently of party considerations he would say, by all manner of means, let India stand outside the range of party politics, but he did not think that that was possible under the existing system of party government. On all questions which cropped up in Parliament there were divergent views, and therefore they must not delude themselves into the belief that India was not a party question. Indeed, there were a great many advantages to be gained by treating her as a party question, for it enabled the opponents of a Government to expose the weak points of its policy, and thus to arouse the nation to a sense of its responsibilities.

The next fallacy was that every MP was a member for India. If that were so they had at the present time a very large number of members for India, but unfortunately they were blissfully ignorant of the needs and necessities of their Indian constituents. In regard to their British constituents they were made to realise their responsibilities; they had to meet them face to face; they were subjected to heckling, and they were compelled at intervals to give an account of their stewardship. But to lay down the principle that they were all responsible for the welfare of India was in fact to take the whole subject of India out of their consideration: what was everybody's business was nobody's business. If they could only have a few men returned directly by India to the British House of Commons they would have a great deal more justice done them than they obtained at present. Whether they would become a second Ireland in giving trouble to the Government of the day he could not say.

Now he came to the third fallacy. It had been a kind of traditional belief in this country ever since the reign of Queen Elizabeth I, when the rich people in the East, by vieing with one another in the display of their wealth, aroused the cupidity of European nations, that the Natives were to be dominated by gorgeous display. But when they came to consider the religions of the people and the kind of lives they led they saw at once that gorgeous display was very far from their nature. It did not go beyond their eyes. It never found a lodgment in their hearts, it never met their commendation among them; and this applied equally to Mahomedans and Hindus. As for the latter, they considered this world to be no real world at all; they looked on it as a phenomenal world, behind which there was another world which would not pass away. To say that such a people were fond of show, and that the only way to arouse their loyalty was to give gorgeous shows at tremendous expense was to put forward a most fatuous view. Again in the case of Mahomedans, their very religion was against it; it prohibited them even instrumental music in their services. They wanted nothing to appeal to their senses except moral truths, which went right down into their hearts. Simplicity was the dominating feature of the life of the Mahomedan as it was also in the case of the Hindu, and therefore it was extremely wrong to suggest that they must be fed with gorgeous displays.

Now let them consider for a moment whether the Government of India by England was a responsible Government; if so to whom was it responsible? It was conceded that the Government owed no responsibility to the people over whom it was placed. Apparently they were to be treated like children; they were to be allowed to have freedom to express their opinions in their newspapers; they were to be properly treated no doubt, but they were so immature in their opinions, they were so ignorant with regard to their own material interests; they were, in fact, so ignorant generally that no heed should be paid to what they said, but were to be governed according to the tender mercies of the Government. The Governors of the various Presidencies and the Commissioners in India were responsible to the Viceroy, who was responsible to the Secretary of State, who in turn was supposed to be responsible to Parliament. But was he really so? Consider what occurred when the Indian Budget comes on for consideration. When the Indian Budget came to be discussed in the House of Commons so acute was the responsibility felt to be that it sometimes happened that the only persons present in the House were the hon. member who was speaking and Mr Speaker himself. He had himself seen such a state of things when Sir Roper Lethbridge happened to be the member who was addressing the Chair. Now in his view the first responsibility which Great Britain owed to India was to convert what was now a farce into a reality, namely, the responsibility of the Secretary of State to Parliament – or, in other words, to the inhabitants of Britain. Unless that was done the Government of India would continue to be at the mercy of the Secretary of State. No doubt the people of this country were pleased with the descriptions which had been telegraphed at such great expense to this country of the Delhi Durbar, with a view to conveying an idea of the British power in India. But let them for a moment consider the amount that had been expended on that show – which the Natives looked upon as a useless show, which, having pleased the eye for a moment, was quickly forgotten. As one of his own countrymen had described it, it was not an Imperial durbar at all: it was simply a 'Curzonoration.' (*Laughter*) In the Budget a quarter of million sterling had, he believed,been set apart to cover the expense, but the accounts which had reached him and other people went to show that the expenditure would not be less than £750,000. But suppose they put it at only half a million. What good had it done; for whose benefit had it been incurred? Was it to impress the Oriental mind with the power of Great Britain? If so, then the rule of Great Britain in India for a hundred years had been a failure, supposing that the people of India still required to be convinced of the prowess of Great Britain in order to ensure their loyalty. If Great Britain in that time had failed to win the affection and loyalty of the people she was not likely now to secure it by a mere expenditure of half a million in gorgeous display. No, the durbar was not arranged for the benefit of the people of India; neither was it got up for the benefit of the people of this country, because only a few privileged friends of Lord Curzon were present, and surely they did not require to be impressed with the great power, wealth, and organisation of Great Britain. For whose benefit, then, was it got up? Was it not with the view of making an impression upon continental nations as to the power of Great Britain? Was it not, in other words, a game of brag, the same as has been going on for the last few years. Was it not saying to them in effect 'Look at the splendid possessions we have in the East; look what splendid shows we are able to give to the people: we are far superior to you in every way?' But, could Great Britain honestly say to continental nations that that show had increased the material prosperity of the people of India; that it had made them more contented and more loyal subjects of the Crown? England was a Christian country. She professed to possess a better religion than that of the people of India, but if that were so, was it a teaching of the religion that they should spend money on these empty vanities? If it were, then, all he could say was that the people of India had better remain adherents of the religion which descended to them from their forefathers. In conclusion, he submitted that the duty of every British citizen towards India was to impress upon every candidate for Parliamentary honours the desirability of carefully studying the subject of India. If every elector were to insist on hearing from his member how he had fulfilled his responsibility towards India, the grievances of that empire – and they were many – would soon be redressed. But unfortunately the average British citizen knew little about the needs of India. The public here were not aware that one result of the policy pursued in India had been to destroy its great silk and cotton fabric manufactures, and to drive the operatives engaged in them on to the soil for a living, so that when scarcity arose they died off in millions like insects. Famine in India was not caused solely by drought. If scarcity occurs in one district there was an abundance of food for all produced in another, but the difficulty was one of money.

A very interesting discussion followed. Some of the speakers dissented from the view that India was better governed by the East India Company than by the Crown, but Mr Bonnerjee contended that inasmuch as the Company's charters had to be subjected to Parliamentary criticism and renewal from time to time there was always a wholesome check upon its operations and reforms had to be introduced whether the Company liked them or not. One speaker contended that it was under the Company that the policy was initiated which eventually destroyed Indian industries and drove the people to the land. What was wanted was better provision against famine and not mere political reforms. Mr Bonnerjee replied that the East India Company's hands were forced by Parliament, as regards the manufactures, and that political reforms were absolutely necessary, in addition to better provision against famines.

Mr W C Bonnerjee (Liberal Candidate for the Walthamstow Division of Essex) addressed a crowded meeting at the Norwood Congregational Church, West Derby Road, Liverpool on 18 October 1903 on the subject of 'To whom is the Government of India responsible?' A full report of the meeting appeared in *India* of 23 October 1903.

MR W C BONNERJEE AT LIVERPOOL
'TO WHOM IS THE GOVERNMENT OF INDIA RESPONSIBLE?'

MR BONNERJEE, who was warmly received, said: By mysterious dispensation of Providence the destinies of the Indian people have now been in the hands of the British people for over a century and a half. Britain in consequence owes a great responsibility to the Indian people as regards their well-being, happiness, and contentment in this world. This responsibility must be approached and undertaken in Mr Gladstone's spirit, that is, with a deep feeling of religion. In this house your Pleasant Sunday Afternoons have almost invariably been spent in listening to addresses from a purely religious point of view. I am fully alive to this fact; nevertheless, I think the subject to which I draw your attention this afternoon is one which has religion on its dominant side. One of the noblest precepts to be found in the New Testament is, 'Do unto others as you wish they should do unto you', and in the light of that precept I desire that you should act towards India. The question with which I start is: 'To whom is the Government of India responsible?' and my answer to it is: 'In reality, to none'. Statesmen of the parties who have held sway in India have been unanimous in laying it down as a rule of their government, and acting upon this rule, that the voice of the people of the country should have no influence in their

Council. They are to be ruled with justice and equity, but they are to have no hand in pointing out effectively how this policy of justice and equity is to be achieved. Most of you are, no doubt, aware that there are three Executive Councils in India; namely, the Council of the Viceroy, and the Councils of the Governors of Bombay and Madras, in addition to the Council of the Secretary of State for India in London. But no single Native of India has ever found a place in any of these Councils. And, mind you, these Executive Councils lay down the policy and in reality govern the country. There are, besides these Executive Councils, the Viceroy's Legislative Council, and the Legislative Councils of the Governors of Bombay and Madras and the Lieutenant Governors of Bengal, the United Provinces of Agra and Oudh, of the Punjab and of Burma. In these Councils Natives of India have been members, partly by the direct nomination of the Government, and partly by the nomination of Government based upon representation of various public bodies, as regards the minor Legislative Councils, and the recommendation of non-official members of the Local Councils as regards the Viceroy's Legislative Council. These members have the privilege of interpolating the Government on question of policy, debating measures brought before the Councils, and of criticising Budget proposals laid before them. But they have no power to move any resolutions on the Budget proposals, and they are always in such a minority that the Government are in a position to carry any measure they choose. A striking example of this was given a short time ago, when in the Bombay Legislative Council, the Government having carried a measure against the unanimous voice of all the Native members, these in a body left the Council chamber as a protest against the high-handedness of the Government. The opinion of Englishmen resident in the country also has no influence upon its rulers, and the latter avowedly do not consider themselves responsible to them. The Government of India in India is under the Secretary of State for India in England, but as most of the measures intended to be carried out in India are concerted with him in the first instance, the responsibility for them is as much his as theirs. He seldom, if ever, consults the Cabinet, of which he is a member, as regards these measures, and if any objection is taken by anybody, either in the House of Commons or elsewhere, with regard to them he is supported by the full strength of the party in power...

When the East India Company had sway over India they had to come to Parliament from time to time to obtain a renewal of their Charter, and this renewal was never granted without a thorough enquiry being made into the government of the country for the previous twenty years, and not even then, until the Company had pledged themselves to carry out reforms recommended by the Enquiring Committee. The Company, then, were responsible, in the real sense of the term, to Parliament, and Parliament was jealous in maintaining its supremacy over the Company. This state of things has altogether ceased to exist. There has been no enquiry into the government of India since the memorable month of November, 1858, when our late Queen was proclaimed the direct ruler of India. Even in a matter such as the periodical famines, which have devastated the country, the appeal of the people of India, backed by earnest men and women of all parties in this country, for enquiry as to the condition of the people, not in India generally, but in some selected places, has been rejected, and the famine policy of the Government is now being carried on without any such enquiry. Now, in these circumstances, what is the duty of Christian men and women in this country towards India? In the first place, they should remember that the Government of that country is carried on in their name and on their behalf, and that the blame for the misgovernment of the country falls on them, while the praise for any act of good government goes to the credit of the statesman who achieves it. It is quite true that the people of this country have no direct hand in the selection or appointment of either the Secretary of State for India, or the Viceroy, or any of the local Governors. But these are appointed by persons at the head of the party whom the suffrages of the electors place in the position of power. And the duty which is incumbent upon these electors is to give thought to the 250 millions of human beings whom Providence has placed under their control, and so to elect representatives who will endeavour to do their duty to the Indian fellow-subjects. An irresponsible Government cannot, in the nature of things, be a good Government. It is with Governments as with individuals. Every individual owes a responsibility to the community, the father to the children, the children to the father, the family to the community, the community to the body politic, owe responsibility of no common degree, on to the other. Individuals who consider themselves irresponsible almost invariably turn out to be indifferent citizens, and add to the number of the criminal class. Governments which consider themselves irresponsible similarly turn out to be bad Governments... I appeal to you all most fervently to do all that in you lies to bring about a just appreciation of the responsibility that lies on this country as the ruler of India.

At the conclusion of the address, which was frequently applauded, the Rev. Thomas Yates said they were extremely obliged to Mr Bonnerjee for coming to Liverpool to give the lecture to which they had just listened with so much interest and instruction. He trusted that what Mr Bonnerjee had said would remain with them, and be an incentive to them to carry out the duty they owed to their fellow-subjects in India.

*   *   *

Mr Donald Smeaton CSI, formerly a member of the Viceroy's Council, delivered lectures on 'A Future for India' in Edinburgh, Stirlingshire and in Fifeshire, in Scotland in February 1904. *India* followed Mr Smeaton and gave the following report on his speeches:

A FUTURE FOR INDIA

REMARKABLE LECTURE BY MR DONALD SMEATON

'SIMPLIFY MACHINERY AND REDUCE EXPENDITURE'

A SCHEME FOR AN INDIAN PARLIAMENT

MR DONALD SMEATON said: From whatever point of view India is considered, whether from its great past in centuries while our little islands were in heathen darkness, from its teeming population of one-fifth of the entire human race, or from its remarkable awakening within the last few years, it presents a problem at once the most profound and the most interesting in the history of the world. Nor is the spectacle of Great Britain's almost invisible hand directing India's destiny less marvellous. Here are two little Western islands governing a vast Eastern continent 6,000 miles away, with a population of 300 millions; and not merely – as in some of the Crown Colonies – directing and overlooking lines of general policy, but controlling the intimate relations of man and man; moulding for good or evil the character of every man, woman and child. The Continental Governments, in administering their small dependencies, attempt no such task as we undertake in India. They leave the people to work out their future in their own way, interfering as little as possible in internal affairs or domestic polity. Our Government in India, whatever its faults may be – and they are many and grave – has, till within the last three or four years, at least aimed at what it has, from time to time, considered to be for the benefit of the people... Its positive or constructive measures have, for the most part, been well intentioned and sincere on the whole. Their effect has not always – in fact, I may say not often – been for the ultimate well-being of the people. But cast your thoughts for a moment far back into remote ages. Is it not strange – passing strange – to think that while yet the British people – now the Pioneers of Western civilisation in the East – were a nation of savages, India was a busy hive of civilisation, a centre of the highest and most dignified human thought and speculative philosophy, a treasure-house of beautiful romantic literature, the cradle of delicate and useful industries, the very birthplace, it may even be said, of modern language, the home of great warriors, statesmen and prophets? While yet Europe was in the grip of degraded heathendom, India was giving voice to Divine Revelation by the lips of the holy

Rishis in pre-Vedic times; and long centuries before our Saviour appeared on earth some of His gracious words were anticipated – perhaps even foretold – by the holy Buddha, the Light of Asia, who arose, like Christ, to purge and purify the Pharisaism of the then debased Hindu faith...

The Mutiny was the great catastrophe but brought her into the world before her time; and it is Great Britain which has, without any foresight or intention, given shape to her destiny since then. For weal or woe, we have committed India irrevocably to a form of development which must determine her future among the nations. How, in what form, and when that future will emerge it is hard to say; but we are in a position to survey the difficulties to be encountered, and to devise the best means of overcoming them...

There are two Bills now before the Council of Calcutta – both of them the offspring of a Russianising Viceroy. The Official Secrets Bill, otherwise the Press Gagging Bill and the Universities Bill, which Lord Curzon is now, as I write, trying to force on India, the one to prevent the Native Press, under penalties of imprisonment and fine, from obtaining and publishing any news save what is doled out to it; the other to make education more expensive, destroy private colleges and convert the Universities into mere Government departments – these iniquitous Bills would never have seen the light if the Viceroy had had to face free representative assembly...

I doubt not the Press Gagging Bill and the Universities Bill have been introduced and will eventually be passed under threat, or at least an implied threat, of the penalty of resignation which this omnipotent ex-Under Secretary of State is empowered to impose. Finally, as if to crown the farce, 'No resolution may be moved, nor may the Council be divided, in respect of any financial discussion or of the answer to any question; and questions must be submitted beforehand to the Viceroy, who may disallow them if he thinks fit!': Could any sham be hollower than this? And yet the British people are deluded into believing that we are doing our duty to India! The sham must be removed, and the reality take its place. The reforms therefore – or, rather, perhaps I should say the rough outline of the reforms – for which I ask your strenuous support are as follows:

First. Alter the name of 'Legislative Council of India' to 'Indian Parliament'!
Second. Increase the number of representatives in this Parliament from 22 to 60.
Third. Constitute this body of 60 members thus:
(i)   The five members of the Executive Council, i.e. the Cabinet, of whom one shall be an Indian.
(ii) One European and two Indians from each of the 13 principal provinces, excluding the Andaman Islands, which are a Convict Settlement i.e., 39 in all.
(iii) One member from each of the five principal Chambers of Commerce.
(iv) One member from each of the five Universities.
(v)   One practitioner from each of the five High or Chief Courts.
(vi) One Feudatory Chief.
Fourth. The representatives of the thirteen provinces to be elected by delegates or electoral colleges of the various districts of their provinces, these delegates to be subject to a voting qualification similar to that required in some of the Crown Colonies, but probably higher; the other representatives to be elected by their respective bodies. The Feudatory Chief to be appointed by the Viceroy.
Fifth. The Indian Parliament, as thus constituted, to run for five years, after which to be dissolved and new members to be elected.
Sixth. The Parliamentary season to be sixth months from October to March, and to hold its sessions in Calcutta, and under no circumstances in Simla. The recent scandalous introduction of the 'Official Secrets Bill' in a hole and corner Council meeting in the Himalayas should not be forgotten.
Seventh. The Indian Parliament to have control by debate and division over all taxation, all expenditure, all legislation; and to have the right to challenge the acts of the Executive.

Eighth. Seeing that under present circumstances an adverse vote could not turn out the Government in India, the control of the Indian Parliament to be exercised as follows:

(a) Where a division has resulted in an adverse vote, the question at issue to be referred to the British Parliament for decision.

(b) The Secretary of State for India to have no independent powers except such as the British Parliament may delegate to him.

(c) The Secretary of State's Council to be abolished; it survives only as a costly sham.

(d) The Secretary of State's salary to be borne on the British Estimates, thereby enabling any of his acts to be challenged in the House of Commons, and a division taken

(e) In lieu of Secretary of State's Council, each Indian province (excluding the Andamans) to elect an agent in London to represent its affairs and to be entitled to be heard at the Bar of the House of Commons.

These suggested reforms would place India in a position midway between a self-governing Colony and a Crown Colony; and I venture to think that her representative assembly would prove itself even more competent than those of any Crown Colony, and quite as loyal to the Crown.

The essence of the whole matter is this: India's representation in the House of Commons is useless; it has been proved so. Public meetings and resolutions, complaints and talking, are useless; they have been proved so. The movement for reform must begin in India itself. Indian representatives in the House of Commons are powerless. The Secretary of State's voice is all-powerful; the Indian member speaks in vain to a listless score or less of the House, and he is over-borne. What is required is a representative assembly in India which can at any time raise a specific issue in the House of Commons on which a division must be taken. When a British Government knows that an adverse vote in the House on an Indian question can turn it out of office, it will be careful and scrupulous in its dealing with India. This very rough and tentative sketch of reforms which I have given is, of course, imperfect, and necessarily faulty in detail. But I am convinced that the principle is not only sound, but that its recognition is urgently necessary if we desire, as we all do, to knit India firmly to the Empire, and to ward off the peril which I declare, with a conviction based on a thirty years intimate knowledge and experience, is at present time – and has been for the last three or four years – threatening its foundations in the East.

* * *

India published a special report on illustrated lectures by Mr J M Parikh, Barrister-at-Law, and Mr J C Mukherji under the auspices of the Newington Reform Club at the Club-House in Hampton Street on 25 November 1904. The subject was 'India'.

DEFECTS OF BRITISH RULE IN INDIA
LECTURE BY MR PARIKH AND MR MUKERJI

MR PARIKH said he proposed that night to try and describe what in past days had been the conditions under which the millions of our fellow-subjects in India had lived, and to show their lot at the present time. The statement made by Edmund Burke, one of the greatest of Liberal leaders, 125 years ago, to the effect that the administration of the country was governed solely in the interests of the Englishmen, who took everything they could out of the country, was equally applicable today, and inasmuch as Burke took a prominent part in the impeachment and trial of Warren Hastings, the first Governor-General of India, he would like to see the rise of another Burke today to impeach Lord Curzon. Burke made his charge in the days of existence of the old East India Company. That Company existed solely for gain, and possibly a good illustration of its method of rule was provided by the Chartered Company of South Africa today. The effect of such rule was a continuously increasing drain of the wealth of the country. In 1837–38 that annual drain was estimated at two and a quarter millions. About that time an Act of Parliament was passed with a view of giving Native Indians a share in the government of their own country; it provided that they were not to be disqualified for office by reason of their religion, colour, place of birth, or descent. But the Act proved to be a dead letter, and although the promise was reiterated in 1858, and on subsequent occasions, it had never been operative; it had simply been made and repeated in order to hoodwink the public. What became of the revenues of India? The principal source was the land revenue, which produced just over seventeen millions sterling annually, and more than this was expended on the maintenance and charges of the India Office. Why was India treated differently from the Colonies? Neither Mr Chamberlain nor any other Colonial Minister would dare to call upon the Colonies to contribute towards the upkeep of the Colonial Office, and it was simply because the Indians had no voice in the government of their own country that they were subjected to this injustice.

*   *   *

In August 1905, the Liberals of Kettering assembled in the grounds of Mr and Mrs Loake to hear addresses from Mr F A Channing MP and Mr Lajpat Rai, delegate of the Indian National Congress. *India* described the event on 18 August 1905 .

LIBERAL GARDEN PARTY AT KETTERING
SPEECHES OF MR CHANNING MP AND MR LAJPAT RAI

MR CHANNING, who met with an enthusiastic reception, expressed his regret that his friend Sir William Wedderburn was unable to be present, but offered a cordial welcome to the Indian delegates. He did not think they could exaggerate the importance of grasping for themselves and spreading the knowledge among others of the question of India. It they looked into it only a little way from an Indian standpoint they would see at once that it was not a favourite question with Mr Chamberlain. India was perhaps one of the most wonderful examples of the success of Free Trade. India was one of the great obstacles which stood, fortunately, in Mr Chamberlain's way. The success of Free Trade in India had been so stupendous that it had practically converted even the most Tory rulers to a unanimous determination that whatever else was done India should not be swept into Mr Chamberlain's net...

MR LAJPAT RAI, who was greeted very cordially, said he must, in the first place, pay a sincere homage to the memory of that great and good man who for several years so successfully represented their neighbours in Parliament, and manfully fought the battles of the unrepresented millions of India – Charles Bradlaugh. Turning to the system and methods of government that rule in India, Mr Lajpat Rai said that as they were accustomed to see the bright side of the English rule, which is so frequently and profusely painted by Anglo-Indians who can never see its shortcomings, he would, with their permission, confine his remarks to the dark side of that rule. It was always an unpleasant task to find fault with the doings of men in whom one's audience is interested, and who, in a way, derive their power and authority from the latter. But, then, this was the only tribunal to which aggrieved people like the Indians could appeal, and from which they could demand that justice which is withheld from them by those in immediate authority over them in their own country. It was the system the Indians attacked. What they pressed for was such a change in the system and methods of government in India as might remove the existing anomalies, and might tend to strengthen the ties of fellow-feeling and brotherhood between Indians and Englishmen. This they asked for because they were convinced that the good of England also requires the same reform. No foreign rule could ever be very safe and secure, at least for any great length of time, unless it was based upon the affections of the people, and unless the people were so well treated as to be justified in identifying themselves with the rulers. This, however, could not be achieved until the ruling class were prepared to merge themselves in the people, give up the special and anomalous privileges which they enjoyed, put an end to all class distinctions as such, and unless they treated the people as fellow subjects of a common Sovereign power, and as fellow citizens of a common empire. So long as there was a ruling class in India distinct from and quite independent of the people, so long Englishmen in India must be considered as aliens and their rule as unnatural and tyrannical...

Whether on the hills, on holiday and health resorts, in courts of justice, on railways, in markets or in Municipal Corporations, everywhere a Native of India met with evidences of an Englishman's arrogance and racial pride. It was no wonder that, under the circumstances, Indians are very much dissatisfied with the Government of India and that there was a great deal of discontent. Was it not a fact that just now every Indian who has a grain of self-respect in him, from the ruling chief down to the lowest rayat, is unhappy and miserable? Princes of royal blood, whose ancestors had enjoyed sovereign powers for centuries past, and who could trace their authority to a period of history when the English had not yet stepped into civilisation, were at this minute made to feel the humility of their present position by the insolent behaviour of petty British agents, and the assumption of a haughty and over-bearing attitude on the part of Viceroys and Governors...

There was one thing he would like to make clear before sitting down; namely, that in demanding reforms in the system of government in India, they were not for anything that patriotic Englishmen could not entertain. In fact, they based their claims on the solid rock of the mutual good of both countries. What they urged was that the present methods of administering the affairs of India are undermining the stability of British Government in India. As patriotic Indians, they were interested in seeing that their country should continue to enjoy that peace which it was the privilege of the British to establish, and that it should be also happy and prosperous at the same time. It was the desire of the Indians to enjoy the same amount of political freedom as the other parties of this self-governing Empire do, and in asking for that they knew they were making a demand the granting of which would rebound to the credit and glory of Britain, and would be sure to benefit all parties concerned.

MR PARMESHWAR LALL said that India, from being one of the richest when the British first went there, had sunk to one of the poorest countries in the world. The average income of the whole nation was estimated at 3d. a day. Their manufactures had died, and the famines that were perpetual now in India were not so a short time ago. What they asked the English was to let them try and govern themselves.

*　　*　　*

Lala Lajpat Rai and Mr G K Gokhale, the Indian National Congress delegates, spent a busy time in England in 1905 addressing meetings all over the country. With them, whenever possible, went Sir Henry Cotton and Sir William Wedderburn, as they did for a meeting in Manchester in October 1905 and reported in *India* of 18 October. The meeting was chaired by Mr Schwann.

THE CONGRESS DELEGATES

INDIA AND THE BRITISH ELECTORS

IMPORTANT PUBLIC MEETINGS

SPEECHES BY MR GOKHALE, MR LAJPAT RAI,
SIR HENRY COTTON AND SIR W WEDDERBURN
(CHAIR: MR SCHWANN)

MR GOKHALE, on rising to address the meeting, was received with great enthusiasm. He spoke first (according to the *Manchester Guardian* report) of the appreciation of the Indian people for the sympathetic interest which Mr

Schwann (the Chairman) had for so many years taken in their affairs. 'If the faith of my countrymen in your sense of justice and love of fair play is still alive in spite of many disappointments and many discouragements, it is due to the fact that there are among you, men like Mr Schwann, who place righteousness above everything else.' (*Cheers*) Explaining his mission in England, he said he had come on behalf of the Indian National Congress to arouse the sympathetic interest of the electors of this country in the affairs of India. 'Never, in my opinion,' he said, 'was there greater need of your paying attention to the affairs of that great dependency. The country is at this moment seething with discontent from one end to the other. . .'

A resolution thanking Mr Gokhale and Sir W Wedderburn and expressing the conviction that the British people should interest themselves actively in the prosperity of their Indian fellow-subjects and give careful consideration to their pressing need and legitimate aspiration, was carried unanimously and acknowledged by Mr Gokhale.

*　　*　　*

At many of the public meetings the majority of speakers were understandably British. They became the voice of India. The size of the audiences reflected their success. These public meetings were held on a regular basis, sometimes once a week. The Hoxton Liberal and Radical Association at Shoreditch Town Hall in October 1905 which *India* reported on 13 October. The chair was taken by the President, Mr S H Verinder, supported by Mr Henry Ward, the Liberal Parliamentary Candidate for the division, Mr C R Reddy of Madras and others.

SIR HENRY COTTON AT HOXTON

SIR HENRY COTTON, who was warmly received, said he was glad to see so considerable an audience assembled to hear addresses on India. It was a symptom of the happiest augury when the British people showed an interest in the affairs of that great country. Englishmen could do much to familiarise themselves with the conditions of things in India. It would be impossible for them to master the details of administration, which must be left in the hands of those officials who devoted their lives to the work, and who, he was glad to be able to say, conscientiously and faithfully endeavoured, as a rule, to discharge their duty. But they could do much to acquaint themselves with Indian affairs, and, above all, they could acquire a knowledge of those great principles which should guide Englishmen in administering those affairs, and insist upon wise, liberal, and sympathetic principles being followed by the officials employed in India. (*Hear, hear*). . .'

Sir Henry then proceeded to describe the founding of the Indian National Congress as one of the results of this advancement. He described its character, its aims and its works. He cited some of the resolutions which had been passed by the last Congress, over which he had the honour to preside, and the immense amount of interest which was evoked amongst the Indians themselves by its work. . .

The only way in which they could rule and control a country like India was by adopting a policy of sympathy, of friendliness, of kindness with the people of that country. (*Loud cheers*). . .

MR HENRY WARD, LCC, moved the following resolutions:
(1) That this meeting desires to express its cordial sympathy with the aspirations of the people of India, as represented by the Indian National Congress, for a steadily increasing measure of self-government. It recognises in such a policy the only effective way to the increased prosperity of the people, without which the ravages of famine and plague cannot be checked, and the contentment and happiness of the people ensured. The meeting is further of the opinion that for enabling Parliament to discharge more satisfactorily its responsibility in regard to the government of India, periodical Parliamentary enquiries into the condi-

Sir Henry John Stedman Cotton (1845–1915)
Member of the Indian Civil Service, served in the Bengal Civil Service 1867; Chief Commissioner of Assam 1896–1906; President of Indian National Congress 1906; Member of Parliament 1909–1910; Author of *New Indian or India in Transition* and *Indian and Home Memories.*

tion of India should be revived, and the salary of the Secretary of State for India should be placed on the British estimates.

(2) That this meeting urges the Liberal leaders, when in power, to select for the offices of Viceroy of India and Secretary of State for India, men prepared fearlessly to apply sound Liberal principles in the administration of India.

(3) That the preceding resolutions be forwarded to Earl Spencer KG, and Sir Henry Campbell-Bannerman MP, the leaders of the Liberal party in Parliament, and that the first resolution be sent to the Prime Minister, to Lord Lansdowne and the Secretary of State for India; and also to the Viceroy of India, and the Governors of Bombay and Madras.

*　　*　　*

Mr G K Gokhale addressed a public meeting at Sheffield in 1905. Among those present were Sir W Wedderburn and Mr J Tudor Walters. The meeting was reported in *India* of 13 October 1905.

Gopal Krishna Gokhale (1866–1915) Member of Deccan Education Society, Poona; builder of the Fergusson College and editor of *Sarvajanik Sabha Quarterly* (1890); Founder of Servants of India Society, 1905, to train people to render services to the country; President, Indian National Congress 1905; went to South Africa at Gandhi's request. To Gandhi 'Gokhale was the image of truth, full of humanity, one who called nothing his own'. Gokhale used to say, 'Love of one's country must so fill the heart that all else shall appear as of little moment by its side'.

MEETING AT SHEFFIELD

MR GOKHALE said he had come as a representative of the Indian National Congress to arouse the interest of the British electors in the affairs of India. They had a great responsibility of 300,000,000 people, their fellow-subjects. All these millions together had not got a single vote, and they were entirely governed by officials who went out from England, and the morale of administration was anything but English. In the whole system of administration there was no control. The officials carried on the work of administration under a Viceroy from England, who had to work under the orders of the Secretary of State in England. The Secretary of State was assisted by a Council composed of retired Anglo-Indian officials, he was a member of the Cabinet, and he therefore had the majority of the House of Commons always with him, and he might, therefore, practically defy public opinion in India. The only class of men who controlled the Secretary of State effectively was the House of Commons. These men would take an interest in India if only the electors would make that necessary. (*Hear, hear*) The electors of England were not interested in keeping up a bad form of administration in India, and he was quite sure if the question was brought home to their minds they would at once say that nothing would be more agreeable to them than that the people of India should be contented, happy, and prosperous...

The discontent of the people had increased, and was steadily increasing. During the last few years a system of repressing the expression of discontent had been steadily pursued by the Indian Government. Criticism by the people was like a safety valve of a steam engine. The Government, unfortunately, did not see this. Like all other bureaucracies, they thought that if they could put down criticism everything else would take care of itself...

The English had become famed as the friends of constitutional liberty all over the world. They had stretched a helping hand to many struggling nationalities. Was it to be said that when it came to be their turn to take practical action in regard to people whom providence had entrusted to their care they chose the sordid and ignoble path of crushing and oppressing? ('*No*') Herein was the crux of the whole question.

SELF-GOVERNMENT REAL CURE

After all, the decisive power was in the hands of the British people; the electors must tell their representatives in the House of Commons that they wanted India to be governed according to English methods. Dealing with another phase of the question, the speaker emphasised the fact that it was impossible to exercise any fair and effective control over India at a distance of 6,000 miles. That form of government was alone in the best interests of the people, he urged, which was based on self-government. Whether there was to be Parliamentary institution in India depended on practical considerations, but the general proposition that self-government was the only cure for mal-administration would be accepted by Englishmen everywhere. England was pledged to the development of self-government amongst the people of India...

On the motion of MR R HOLMSHAW, seconded by MR CECIL WILSON, the following resolution was unanimously adopted:

That this meeting desires to express its cordial sympathy with the aspirations of the people of India, as represented by the Indian National Congress, for a steadily increasing measure of self-government. It recognises in such a policy the only effective way to obtain an improved condition of the people, without which the ravages of famine and plague cannot be checked, and the contentment and the happiness of the people ensured; the meeting is further of the opinion that for enabling Parliament to discharge more satisfactorily its responsibility in regard to the government of India, periodical Parliamentary enquiries into the condition of India should be revived, and the salary of the Secretary of State for India should be placed on the British estimates; and this meeting urges the Liberal leaders when in power to select for the offices of Viceroy of India and Secretary of State for India men prepared fearlessly to apply sound Liberal principles in the administration of India.

*   *   *

While Mr Gokhale spoke in Sheffield Mr Lajpat Rai addressed a meeting at the Union Church in Putney in London. The meeting was chaired by Mr Garratt who had lived in India for five years. He pressed for a generous consideration of India's claims. *India* of 13 October 1905 reported:

MR LAJPAT RAI AT PUTNEY

MR LAJPAT RAI, who was most cordially received, addressed himself to the disadvantages under which the Indian people laboured under the present system of government, and to the necessity of measures being taken to render them happy, prosperous and contented. Broadly and briefly put, their demand was: 'India for the Indians, under the guidance and control of Britain'. When he said that, he did not say it on his own authority, but on the highest authority within these realms. He based the claim on the Proclamation of the Queen-Empress when she took over the government of India from the East India Company in 1858 and upon the declarations of British statesmen. That Proclamation pledged the British Government to throw open the offices of the Government of India to all Her Majesty's subjects, irrespective of nationality, caste or creed in India. It was 46 years, or more, since the Magna Carta of India was promulgated. It was renewed in that great assemblage of Indian princes, nobles, gentry and people, when the Queen was proclaimed Empress of India. But the obligations which Her Majesty had declared should be faithfully and conscientiously observed had not been carried out, excepting in a very limited degree and in grudging measure, by those who had been entrusted with the administration of British rule in India. And Indians wanted to know why the government of India was not conducted on the principles thus proclaimed. The reason was not far to seek. Vested interests had grown up in connection with the official classes, who resented the measures which interfered with their predominance by giving increased opportunities to the Indian people to share in the government of their own country. Englishmen knew well the doctrine, and insisted on it in their own government, that there should be no taxation without representation. They recognised that in countries where the people were taxed without having a voice in the expenditure of the money taken from them, the system of government was unsound. There might be countries where the state of civilisation was such, where there was no education, where these principles could not always be applied. But in India, where there had been in the past a high state of civilisation, the people had proved in almost every sphere of life, in the universities, on political platforms, in the administration of justice, that they were capable of taking a part in the government of the country, to the advantage of the people and of the State. (*Applause*) He contended that the taxes should be raised with the consent of the people, and that they should be expended according to their wishes. (*Hear, hear*) The prosperity and the good of England, as well as of India, depended largely on the prosperity and contentment of the people of India. If the people of India were poor, unhappy, starving, discontented, it could rebound neither to the credit nor the good of England. (*Hear, hear*) The strength of British rule lay in the prosperity, loyalty, and contentment of India. They had to consider whether the condition of the peoples of India was better and more prosperous than since they had been under the British government.

*   *   *

While in Britain, the Hon. Mr Gopal Krishna Gokhale and Mr Lajpat Rai gave interviews to two national newspapers: The first to the *Manchester Guardian*, the second to the *Daily News*. They were in-depth interviews on the state of India and its legitimate rights. Both interviews were quoted by *India* on 13 October 1905.

INTERVIEW WITH MR GOKHALE
THE 'MANCHESTER GUARDIAN'

Mr Gokhale told me (writes a representative of the *Manchester Guardian* who interviewed him yesterday) that the Indians believe they have clearly outgrown the system of government which exists in India, and that a larger measure of self-government must now be conceded to them. 'This is necessary,' he says, 'both in fulfilment of the declared policy of British rule in India – that is to raise the people gradually to a position of equality with their fellow-subjects elsewhere in the Empire – and also because it is the only cure for the numerous evils, administrative and economic, from which the country suffers. Under the existing system there is no sort of control anywhere on the doings of the bureaucracy. We ourselves have no real voice in the government of the country; the Secretary of State, who controls the Government of India, being personally ignorant of Indian affairs, is in the hands of Council, composed of Anglo-Indian officials, whose bias is in favour of continuance of purely official rule; while the control of Parliament is merely nominal: 1, because the Secretary of State is a member of the Cabinet, and therefore has a standing majority behind him in the House; 2, because there is an understanding between the front benches that India is to be kept out of party politics; 3, and most of all, because most members of the House are absolutely ignorant about the state of things in India and are so much occupied with affairs near home that they simply do not trouble themselves about Indian matters. The result is that we are left to the mercies of a civilian and military bureaucracy, entirely uncontrolled in practice and enjoying a monopoly of power which makes it resist all attempts on the part of the people at any real association with them in the government of the country.'

Englishmen, Mr Gokhale continued, should have no difficulty in understanding that an administration is bound to give rise to many avoidable evils unless it is constantly subject to efficient control. 'And no control can be efficient unless it is largely "on the spot," and exerted by those who are directly affected by the administration. This is why the Indian National Congress urges that, in the interests of good government in India, a larger measure of self-government should now be conceded to the people.'

I asked whether the tendency during recent years had been in that direction.

'Unfortunately,' he replied, 'it has been all the other way, and the repression of popular aspirations has been at its worst during the last two years. A series of reactionary measures has been forced on the people in defiance of public opinion and in the face of fierce opposition, with the result that the faith of a large section in the desire of England to govern India in the interests of the Indians themselves has been well-nigh destroyed. These measures have had one great aim, namely, to increase the power of Englishmen in the land, and to make it more and more difficult for Indians to claim a position of equality with them. The popular element in the Calcutta Municipality has been reduced; the

Official Secrets Act has fettered the discretion of the Press; the Universities Act has officialised the universities; the abolition of the competitive test for many of the higher posts that are open to us has made employment in the public service a matter of official patronage; and the Viceroy has even tried to explain away the proclamation of the Queen Victoria – our Magna Carta. On the other hand, the salaries of English officials have been increased in all directions. And the bitterness of public feeling that has been aroused has been due as much to the manner in which these measures were forced on the people as to their substance. Now, on the top of everything, has come this partition of Bengal, which has almost driven the people of the province mad.'

I interjected a question as to the other side of Lord Curzon's work, whereupon Mr Gokhale said: 'Nobody admits more readily than I do that Lord Curzon has done some good things. He has made large grants to irrigation; he has increased the expenditure on primary education; he has reduced the salt-tax; he has tried hard to put down assaults by Europeans on helpless Indians; he has shaken local governments into greater activity; and, on the whole, he has laboured incessantly to increase the efficiency of the administration. But it is administration by English officials that he has been anxious to strengthen, while the Indians are kept always in a subordinate position. The fact is that he does not seem to believe in liberty and in national aspirations, and he has not understood the Indian people.' Mr Gokhale added that Englishmen in England had no interest in strengthening bureaucracy for its own sake, and therefore the Indians made their appeal to the British constituencies. . .

The following is the interview with Mr Gokhale in the *Daily News* which described him as an 'Indian patriot'.

'Experience has shown that in regard to India there is very little to choose between the two parties. An understanding exists between both sides that India shall be treated as an outside party, and though our best friends have come from the Liberal side, and the disposition to help us will, no doubt, continue on their part, yet, as between the two front benches, the understanding is pretty strictly observed. In practice this agreement is an agreement for what? – for doing nothing. India is brushed away out of sight, and left to the sole control of the bureaucracy, whose mouthpiece, whether under a Liberal or a Conservative administration, is the Secretary of State. In one respect we may even be worse off under a Liberal Ministry than a Conservative one. Our Liberal friends may sometimes fight our battles when in opposition, but they are not so ready to do so when it involves the criticism of their leaders, and the Conservatives, which in power or in opposition, are too indifferent about India to trouble themselves.'

'We of the Indian reform party,' continued Mr Gokhale, 'are naturally allies of the Liberals, and our hope is that by appealing to the electors and candidates who are concerned about India, enough pressure may be exerted to break down this unhappy state of things, I might almost say it is our only hope. The situation is growing very dark with us – it is worse than I have known it during the twenty years of my political life, certainly worse than in Lord Lytton's time, when the belief existed that England would come to the rescue. Now, as a result of the acts and temper of Lord Curzon's administration, the faith of the people in British rule has been destroyed, for the time being, and those who have hitherto relied on constitutional agitation are beginning to despair. That, to my mind, is a great evil. Politically considered, the Indian people are treated as non-existent. While I continue to admire England, and to trust her sense of justice, I will admit to you that to the new generation who have learned from England and the West to love liberty, it is a bitter thing to be governed by a bureaucracy, which knows nothing of popular government, political freedom, or confidence in the people. The system which you administer in India is the negation of all that you value in your own political system.'. . .

'It is a cardinal principle of my belief that no administration can be adequate or satisfactory, in which those who are affected by it have not a substantial voice. I ask the Liberal party and the Liberal leaders to apply that principle, which I assume that they also hold, to Indian affairs. I ask them to embark on a policy which shall gradually liberalise the foundations of the administration. I ask for extended opportunities to influence and control the Government ourselves...'

'And how would you proceed to liberalise the Government of India?' I enquired.

'The immediate steps we suggest are four. Starting with the Viceroy's Legislative Council, to which only four Indians are elected – I would have half the members elected by the people...

'With regard to the Provincial Councils associated with the Government of Bombay, Bengal, and Madras, which are concerned with purely internal affairs, we ask for a much larger measure of control than the Viceroy's Council.

'We claim that India should also have at least three members, one for each leading province, on the Indian Council at home, which advises the Secretary of State for India.

'Our fourth point is that its members – two for each of the principal provinces – for India should sit in the House of Commons. This would help the English people to realise that we are fellow-subjects with them, and free us at the same time from appealing to English constituencies of their charity to adopt an Indian as their member.

'Finally, I would have a large measure of decentralisation providing effective popular control on the spot over the powers exercised by members of the Civil Service, who are at present the virtual masters of the people...'

*   *   *

At the invitation of Sir William Wedderburn, a group of members of Parliament and others interested in Indian affairs met at breakfast at the Westminster Palace Hotel in February 1906.

After breakfast, a conference was held, 'with a view to reconstitute the Indian Parliamentary Committee, and generally to consider what action may be usefully taken in the new Parliament to advance the interests of the Indian people'. The Rt Hon. Leonard Courtney presided. As reported by *India* of 2 March 1906, among those present were: Lord Weardale, Sir W Wedderburn, Mr CE Hobhouse, MP, Mr AO Hume, CB, Mr P Lall, and Mr Dadabhai Naoroji.

Sir W Wedderburn stated that letters expressing regret for inability to be present had been received from a large number of MPs and others.

Lord Brassey wrote that he took a great interest in the subject of the Indian Parliamentary Committee.

Mr Bilson wished 'Sir William Wedderburn success in the exertion on behalf of the Indian people'.

Mr Brigg was 'in full sympathy with the objects of the meeting. One thing ought to be asked for, viz, an earlier day in the Session for the discussion of Indian Estimates'.

Mr Cremer said his views were well known, and that he need not repeat how deeply he sympathised with the interests of the Indian people.

Sir Charles Dilke said he would 'gladly serve again on the Committee'.

Mr Ramsay MacDonald telephoned his regret that an important meeting of the Labour party prevented his attendance.

Mr J Kier Hardie, MP, who was to have seconded the first resolution, wrote:

'I much regret that owing to a meeting of the Labour party I cannot be present at the breakfast. The prospects of having something done for India are brighter in this Parliament than I have ever known them before, and you may rely upon a strenuous backing from the Labour party.' [Mr Keir Hardie's letter was unfortunately received too late to be read at the meeting.]

SIR WILLIAM WEDDERBURN said he proposed that they should now resolve themselves into a Committee on Indian affairs. Fortunately, they had with them that morning a gentleman who had very worthily filled the position in the House of Commons of Chairman of Committee, and he was sure they would all approve that Mr Courtney should be asked to take the chair and guide their proceedings. (*Cheers*)

MR COURTNEY said Sir William must have his little joke and, especially from a Scotch point of view, it was distinctly a joke to put him in the chair of that occasion, for the whole burden, responsibility and credit of their gathering that day belonged to Sir William. Those of them who knew him in the House of Commons needed no word to recall what he had done and how he had striven to serve the cause of India. (*Hear, hear*)...

Sir William upheld the consideration of Indian affairs in the House of Commons during the years he had a seat in that assembly, and in so doing he was undoubtedly aided by a Committee which he himself called together, and which responded in the most admirable way to his invitation...

SIR WILLIAM WEDDERBURN trusted they would excuse the liberty he had taken in inviting them to that conference. His excuse was that he was chairman of the Indian Parliamentary Committee formed in 1893, so that he was very much interested in the revival of that Committee. He proposed to tell them in a few words how it originated, and how it carried on its work. Perhaps they would allow him to state that the basis upon which the Indian Parliamentary Committee was formed was that any member who joined it was not in any way committed to the support of any particular measure, but by joining only expressed his willingness to co-operate in supporting a just and sympathetic policy towards India. (*Hear, hear*)

As regarded the ordinary members of the Committee, it was understood that, most of them having specially onerous duties of their own to perform, thus should not be subjected to any unreasonable demand upon their time or attention, but that they should only be asked in important cases to give their support to Indian affairs, when the House of Commons was engaged in debating such questions. They were, in fact, expected to help make a House and to cast their votes for justice and right in that particular cause. (*Hear*) Next he would like to say a word as to the origin of the Indian Parliamentary Committee. It went back a good many years, because in 1883 Mr John Bright, who took a great, and, indeed, most powerful, interest in Indian affairs, approved of the formation in Parliament of an informal Committee to deal with Indian affairs, and he himself expressed willingness to become chairman of that Committee. It was accordingly formed and in 1885 Mr Slagg, who was then senior member for Manchester, obtained a place for a motion in the House of Commons having for its object an amendment of the Government of India Act, 1858, with a view to reviewing the condition of things and to saying whether reasonable steps might not be taken to bring the people more into the management of their own affairs.

MR DADABHAI NAOROJI

MR NAOROJI supported the resolution with the greatest earnestness, because the Parliamentary Committee, in his opinion, would have to deal with some very important questions.

*   *   *

Among the most enthusiastic voices of support for India was that of Dr V M Rutherford MP. A large audience at the Palace Theatre in Glasgow heard him speak on 'The Unrest of India and its Remedy,' on 8 September 1907.

THE TOUCHSTONE OF INDIAN POLICY
DR RUTHERFORD MP AT GLASGOW

In the country at large the general ignorance regarding India could only be described as colossal. And yet what subject of more vital or more pressing importance could be named for the consideration of Englishmen? No one, he imagined, had any longer any doubt as to the existence of a real growing state

John Bright (1811–1889)
Liberal politician and a friend of India; Member of Parliament. Suggested that government of India be made a department of the British Government 1853; proposed decentralisation in India 1858 and 1879.

of unrest in India, and it was idle to suppose that a policy of suppression could cure that unrest for it was due to a variety of causes, social, economic, and political, which no wise or conscientious man could afford to ignore. India should be bound to England by love and not by fear, than which no more contemptible means could be sought for the association with a great Imperial race of any set people in the world. But as a matter of fact they were always being told that the teeming millions of India were held by sword not by the heart. Was there not herein a wrong premise at the very start? Much was made of the racial and religious antipathies which divided India against herself. But he did not think there was really any antagonism between the various peoples who inhabited India. The antagonism lay between rulers and ruled, and it seemed to be part of our policy to imagine that this antagonism could be lessened by pitting class against class and creed against creed in India. This was, he feared, the fundamental defect which underlay the schemes of so-called reform to which Mr Morley had been committed by the Government of India; and it was much to be regretted, in his view, that a Liberal statesman should have sanctioned such proposals. He was sometimes asked: Would the English lose India and how? He could only suggest that we should not lose it to Russia. Russia had her own business cut out for her. The answer was that we should lose India to India and the Indians. It was only a question of time, and it was for Englishmen to decide whether the change was to be brought about by the sword or by the magnanimity or intelligence of this country. He hoped it would be the latter and that we would never drive the Indians to this struggle, where the sacrifice of life on both sides would be tremendous. We should make the country a self-governing part of the Empire, and then we should hold it in the best and truest way...

The enduring foundation of the unrest, however, was the very spirit of nationality which we ourselves believed in, and which our forefathers sacrificed their lives for. We admired and loved patriotism, and we must admire and love it in the Indians, and not seek to crush it and brand it as 'seditious'. It should never be forgotten that God made the nations and men made the Empires. The permanent root of the unrest was a great patriotic movement. Britain had been the very instrument to put this spirit into them, and we should rejoice in it rather than be afraid of it. The only remedy for India and other countries similarly situated was self-government. As Mr Gladstone had well and nobly said, 'Liberty alone fits for liberty'. (*Applause*)

*   *   *

In the 1892 British General Election Keir Hardie was elected the first Labour Member of Parliament, and Dadabhai Naoroji, the first Indian Member of Parliament. They were friends and Naoroji often helped out Hardie financially during the election campaign. In May 1908, Keir Hardie returned from India after a fact-finding tour of the country to see things first hand. On his return a great public meeting was held on 5 April at the Albert Hall in London for his welcome. The *Daily News* hailed the meeting as a historic gathering, and said that: 'Never, perhaps in the history of the Albert Hall has there been such a gathering. From the first to last the enthusiasm was spontaneous, tremendous and infectious.' The report continued:

MR KEIR HARDIE'S WELCOME HOME
GREAT MEETING AT THE ALBERT HALL

The history of the Labour movement has been marked by many remarkable incidents: but by common consent the meeting of Sunday was the largest and most successful demonstration that has ever yet taken place in London. Mr J Ramsay MacDonald, MP, presided and among the large number of friends and well-wishers who supported him on the platform were Sir William Wedderburn, Sir Henry Cotton MP, Mr O'Grady MP, Mr Grayson MP, Mr Llewelyn Williams MP, Mr Frank

Smith, LCC, Mr and Mrs S K Ratcliffe, Mr H E A Cotton and many Indian gentlemen. Conspicuous in a corner of the platform also was a group of Indian ladies in national costume, among whom Mrs P I Roy, Mrs P K Roy and Mrs J C Bose were specially noticeable.

MR J RAMSAY MACDONALD MP, was loudly cheered as he outlined the path which Mr Hardie had followed in his tour. He had 'rested' in India – India that was groaning and appealing for help to the British Democracy; India neglected; India that ought to be the jewel in the Crown of the Empire, but which was dimmed and tarnished by despotic rule within its borders.

MR KEIR HARDIE met with a unique reception. The British Empire could not be held together for twenty-four hours, he asserted, if we endeavoured to treat any part of Canada, Australia, or New Zealand as Ireland was treated. In another part of the Empire also there was no commitment, and that was India – India, the land of broken faith and unredeemed pledges. He had been accused of saying certain things concerning India and its reforms, of preaching sedition and the rest. It might be news to many that every suggestion he had made had been the subject of representations, speeches, or promises made in days gone past by responsible people. They were to be found in the promises contained in proclamations made by the late Queen, by Viceroys, Governors, rulers and other wise persons of that ilk...

MR J M PARIKH expressed his gratitude on behalf of the London Indian Society to the Independent Labour Party (ILP) for the opportunity of speaking at that large and magnificent meeting... The Government of India was essentially capitalistic; it was established on the principles of the old East India Company and had never been altered. The present Government was putting forward a sham scheme of reform for the support of ruling Princes, the territorial magnates, the merchants, and the wealthy people in India, which was simply a bid for the support of the capitalist class and merited complete condemnation. What India required was Home Rule. On the one hand people were determined to have Home Rule; and on the other the Executive authority were apparently equally determined not to give the people any share in the administration of their own government...

The Native Press was persecuted and those who were sent to prison for political offences were treated like felons, condemned to hard labour and insufficient food. Again, there was a campaign against Indian schoolboys and students, upon whom the very future of India most depended, in the course of which they were flogged in the public places. The British people at home were called upon by both the Liberal and Conservative Parties to give their assent by their votes to the permanence of this shameful system. They were told that the Indian people were unfitted for self-government. This last contention was a most remarkable condemnation of the continued British rule in India. They had been there for 150 years, and if in that time they had not educated the Indian people and made them fit for government of their own affairs then he failed to conceive any period which would prove adequate...

In concluding, he expressed the gratitude of many Indians to the Labour Party, its individual members, and particularly to Mr Hardie, in giving a helping hand to the struggling millions in that country.

'Fifty years of the Empire' was the subject of Sir Henry Cotton's address at Nottingham, and was reported by *India* on 2 October 1908.

'FIFTY YEARS OF EMPIRE'
ADDRESS BY SIR HENRY COTTON AT NOTTINGHAM

'Fifty years of the Empire' was the subject of an address by Sir Henry Cotton, KCSI, MP for East Nottingham, in the Addison Street Schoolroom, Nottingham, on Tuesday evening last (September 29). Mr W B Baggaley JP, presided.

Referring to the present situation of 'unrest' in India, SIR HENRY COTTON dwelt upon the character of the system under which Indian administration was carried on. 'It was,' he said, 'a system of pure absolutism – as autocratic as that of the Czar, from the Viceroy downwards. Indeed, it was no exaggeration to say that our Indian Government was the most perfectly organised bureaucracy in the world. That system had continued up to the present time, but the people, actuated by their new ideas culled from Western sources, now desired admission to a greater share in the government of their own country. When the Indians were reading Milton, Mill and Herbert Spencer, who could wonder that such a desire had arisen among them? The dissatisfaction came to a head after Lord Curzon's departure from India: and the question that had now to be considered was in what manner and to what extent could a change with advantage be effected. The great body of the Indian Civil Service had certainly, on the whole, rendered splendid service to the country, but people vested with great power were never willing to hand any portion of it over to others, and the friction which had recently come to a head was due to the desire of the people to possess more power, which the ruling class was more and more averse to surrendering.'

'No one knows the feeling of the educated classes of India more than I do,' continued Sir Henry. 'I have the confidence of all their leaders, and know the trend of thought there, and I can say with confidence that the feeling amongst the educated classes is not one of desiring separation from Great Britain. They realise the many advantages which they enjoy from British domination, including the maintenance of peace, and they are not ungrateful for the spread of Western ideas. Their desires, however, have been ruthlessly set aside, and no respect has been paid to their feelings. This policy has caused strong indignation.'

The complaint was general that the promises made to them had not been fulfilled, and, more serious still, that the country was not being governed in its own interest, but in accordance with British ideas. Of late years a more advanced party had arisen – a party which said that constitutional agitation had been futile in the past. The position today was a dangerous one, because the views of the moderates, who were in the majority, might likely become merged in the views of their advanced compatriots. Repression was not helping the cause of constitutional agitation. In every province of India there were educated men – men who had travelled in Europe – who were undergoing imprisonment with hard labour for identifying themselves with the Nationalist movement.

Having described the malady, Sir Henry proceeded to prescribe the cure. Lord Morley, he said, had to deal with a problem of terrible complexity; but he had thoroughly grasped the situation, and had in hand the adoption of reforms and concession which (he sincerely hoped) would go far to remove the acuteness and painfulness of the situation. (*Applause*) Those reforms, however, must not be illusory, or consist of mere pledges or promises. There would have to be an alteration in the autocratic character of the government and in the constitution of the Civil Service; reconstruction of the Legislative Councils on a representative basis; local boards must be to a very large extent released, and in many cases removed entirely, from official control; municipalities would require greater freedom and liberty; and a wider association of Indians with the administration of the 'districts' would require to be considered. (*Applause*). . .

*　　　*　　　*

Surendra Nath Banerjea on a return visit to England was honoured at dinner by the Indian residents of London at the Westminster Palace Hotel on 25 June 1909. It was chaired by Mr JM Parikh, and as reported by *India* of 2 July 1909, among the guests present were: Mr B Dube, Major NP Sinha, IMS (retired), Mr GS Khaparde, Mr Bipin Chandra Pal, Sir Henry Cotton MP, Mr FC Mackarness MP, Mr J Keir Hardie MP, Mr J Ramsay MacDonald MP, Mr JG Swift MacNeil KC MP, Mr J O'Grady MP, Mr Philip Snowden MP, Mr Arnold Lupton MP, Dr VH Rutherford MP, Mr WP Byles MP, Mr HW Nevinson, Professor AF Murison, Mr SH Swinny, Mr IW Ritch, Mr SK Ratcliff, Mr HEA Cotton, Mr AL Cotton and Mr WD Hall.

THE CHAIRMAN, MR JM PARIKH, proposed the health of the guest of the evening. This was, he said, a unique gathering. In reply to the criticism that India could never unite, Mr Parikh said that all the provinces of India were represented there that night, and that fact alone proved that if they were determined to promote a common object they were capable of being united. And if they were so capable were they not equally capable of uniting for the promotion of the welfare of their own country? (*Cheers*) What should he say as to the situation in India today! On the one hand they were told that the reforms which were about to be introduced would solve the situation. He admitted and he did so frankly – that the reforms, so far as they had gone, were good – (*Hear, hear*) – they were a step in a direction which they hoped would lead them to something better still. (*Hear, hear*) But when they were told those reforms would solve the difficulties of India he began to be very sceptical, because, after all, what was the greatest problem in connection with India? It was the poverty of the people. Lord Morley, in one of his budget speeches, said that though India was poor she was going to be prosperous. They who belonged to India thought otherwise. They thought that, owing to the enormous drain going on from India that country was getting poorer and poorer every day. How were they going to solve the financial question unless they gave the people of the country the power to manage their own finances? Until that was conceded there would be no solution of the Indian problem. (*Cheers*) They were all determined to have self-government in India. (*Renewed cheers*) A great deal of blame had been put on the shoulders of those who had been working on behalf of India – their Motherland. It was alleged that the present difficulties were the work of agitators. But if they looked calmly at the situation they would find that the Government measures – or some of them – were the great agitating factors in the country. (*Hear, hear*) Let them look at the recently issued Parliamentary Paper in connection with the Sedition in India. What did they find? That in a year – or even in nine months – there had been from 50 to 60 journalists sentenced to an aggregate of 150 years' imprisonment!...

MR SURENDRA NATH BANERJEA at once replied. He said there are moments in the lifetime of an individual when he may truly call himself happy. One of those moments has sounded for me now, when I find gathered together in this hall representatives of the culture, the civilisation, the wealth and the intellect of India, associated with you, Sir, to welcome me on my coming to this country. (*Cheers*) It is an index of the growing feeling of solidarity between the different races and peoples of India upon which the best prospects of Indian regeneration so largely depend. (*Cheers*) May this feeling grow and deepen to the lasting glory of the Motherland and the credit of the English rule in India. (*Cheers*). Today I find myself away from home, but yet in a second home surrounded by the loving kindness of friends who, like yourselves, have adopted me into the bosom of your little community...

You have asked me to discuss the problems of India – complicated and multiform problems, such as they present themselves to us today. I confess myself in a position of some little difficulty and embarrassment. A spectator sees more of the game than the actual players. I am not a spectator: I am in the thick of the fight. (*Cheers*) I may claim to be in the front rank of the battle surrounded by gifted self-sacrificing comrades in arms, some of whom, alas, have been deported without trial, and some of whom I would have liked to bring over to this country as samples of the race among whom a policy of repression has been introduced, and who in some quarters are considered unfit for self-government. It has often struck me that would be a most useful thing – beneficial to England and India alike – if we had in this country a session of the Indian National Congress (*hear, hear*) – and this impression has been accentuated by my experience in connection with the Imperial Press Conference. A Session of the Indian National Congress in London would be an object lesson the significance of which it would be difficult to exaggerate. We have been declared to be unfit for self-government. Let us come to face to face with the British public and let them see and decide whether the people of our great and ancient land is unfit for the inestimable boon. (*Cheers*)

*   *   *

MK Gandhi left England after being called to the Bar on 10 June 1891. He made his second visit to England in 1909 from South Africa where he had made his home. *India* of 22 October 1909, reported a lecture given by Mr Gandhi at the Friend's Meeting House in London on 22 October 1909.

Mohandas Karamchand Gandhi of the Transvaal British Indian Deputation spoke on the 'East and West', dealing with the sensitive question of a union between the nations of the East and the West. The meeting was organised by the Hampstead Peace and Arbitration Society, and presided over by Mr CF Maurice.

'EAST AND WEST' · MR M K GANDHI AT HAMPSTEAD

Mr GANDHI said that the question of East and West presented a vast and complex problem. He had had eighteen years' experience of contact between East and West and had endeavoured to study the question, and he felt that he might give an audience such as the present one the results of his observations. As he thought of the subject, his heart sank within him. He would have to say many things which would seem repugnant to his audience and use hard words. He would also have to speak against a system under which he had been brought up. He hoped they would bear with him if he hurt their feelings. He would have to break many idols which he and his countrymen had worshipped, and which his audience may have worshipped. He then referred to the lines in Kipling's poem that 'East is East and West is West, and never the twain shall meet,' and said he considered that doctrine to be a doctrine of despair and inconsistent with the evolution of humanity. He felt it utterly impossible to accept a doctrine of that nature. Another English poet, Tennyson, had in his 'Vision' clearly foretold the union between East and West, and it was because he (the lecturer) believed in that vision that he had cast in his lot with the people of South Africa, who were living there in very great difficulties. It was because he thought it possible for the two peoples to live together in perfect equality that he found himself in South Africa. If he had believed Kipling's doctrine he would never have lived there. There had been individual instances of English and Indian people living together under the same rule without a jarring note and what was true of individuals could be true of nations...

When he cast his eyes upon India what was represented there today under British rule? Modern civilisation ruled India. What had it done? He hoped he would not shock his hearers when he said that civilisation had done no good to India. There was there a network of railways, and telegraphs, and telephones; we had given them a Calcutta, a Madras, a Bombay, a Lahore, and a Benares – these were symbols of slavery rather than of freedom. He noticed that these modern travelling facilities had reduced their holy places to unholy places. He could picture to himself Benares of old, before there was a mad rush of civilisation and he had seen the Benares of today with his own eyes, an unholy city. He saw the same thing here as in India. The mad activity had unhinged us, and, although he was living under the system, it seemed to him desirable that he should speak to them in that strain. He knew it was impossible for the two peoples in India to live together until the British change their ways...

*   *   *

At a meeting of the East Indian Association at Caxton Hall, London on 31 January 1912, a paper on Home Rule for India was read by a veteran campaigner, JB Pennington. *India* of 9 February 1912 reported the discussion of both sides of the arguments.

'INDIA AND HOME RULE'
DISCUSSION AT THE EAST INDIA ASSOCIATION

SIR J D RESS strongly demurred to Mr Keen's suggestion, or rather statement, that the different races of India had shown themselves incapable of managing their own affairs. None the less, it was true that until we went to India not one of them was strong enough to impose on the country that peace which alone could give them the opportunity of managing their own affairs. The real question at issue was: if Home Rule was brought about, how was India to pay her way? The independence of India depended not upon the Army, but upon the British Navy, for which she paid next to nothing. . .

MR S S THORBURN expressed the conviction that Home Rule would come, but not for many generations yet. The country must first be living together in amity, and her peoples must be educated. . . No Englishman would admit that England would ever give up India until she was forced to. So long as we were a nation, we should never give up India, nor would the races of India desire it so long as they were justly ruled and had a fair share in the administration of their country. . .

*   *   *

The subject of Home Rule for India was approached from a different point of view in an address given by Dr V H Rutherford at a meeting of the Indian Association on 7 June 1916. He set out a scheme of reform and self government. *India* reported the meeting at the height of the First World War when large numbers of Indian soldiers fought under the Imperial colours in Europe and the Middle East.

INDIA AND SELF-GOVERNMENT
A SCHEME OF REFORM BY DR RUTHERFORD

Mr Syed Hossain, who was the chair, introduced Dr Rutherford as an old and staunch friend, who, both in and out of Parliament, had consistently served the cause of India. Dr Rutherford's was no new-found infatuation of the rights and liberties of India. He had long been associated with those with whom the principle of self-government for India was a living faith.

Insisting that the time was appropriate for the discussion of the question of India's future, when Indians were sacrificing both their lives and their money in a war for national freedom, Dr Rutherford advocated the setting up of provincial parliaments, with central imperial legislature in which the so-called 'native States' would be represented. All the members of those bodies should be elected on a franchise to be settled by Indians. At the same time the old village councils should be restored and municipal councils and district boards re-organised upon an elective basis. He would apply the principle of Home Rule strictly to the Civil Service. Indians should administer their own country. The present form of Government in India was pure despotism: and it was the worst in the world, however qualified it might be by benevolence. Arguments might, of course, be advanced against his proposals. It would be said that Hindus and Mahomedans were mutually antagonistic; but the signs of the times were all in favour of co-operation between the two great communities. The All-India Moslem League and the National Congress were about to meet in conference, and were united in a common desire to achieve the national aspiration. Next, it was urged by critics of the type of Mr Balfour, that parliamentary government was not adaptable to India, because of the many races which inhabited the country. The suggestion was worthy of those who had denounced the grant of a constitution to South Africa as 'a dangerous experiment'. Again, it was pleaded that India was not fit for self-government. What a melancholy reflection this was upon the British rule! It had been said so often that the English were in India to teach Indians to rule themselves, and yet after a century and a half it was to be acknowledged that they had failed. As a matter of fact, he (Dr Rutherford) had visited Baroda, which was administered entirely by Indians, and had found it better governed than any portion of India governed by Britons. He need only remind them of the one matter of free and compulsory education, in which Baroda was far ahead. Liberty, as Mr Gladstone had said, alone fitted men for liberty. Surely Indians were as fit to govern themselves as Serbs, Bulgars and Greeks.

*   *   *

The First World War ended in 1918, and in 1919 Indian troops were cheered at the Peace March in London. The invaluable support of the Indian soldiers in Britain's victory in Europe was recognised. But India's other fight for self-rule continued. Public meetings were held to put India's case and to criticise Britain for failing to fulfil reform promises. *India* reported one such gathering on 8 August 1919:

'BRITAIN AND INDIA' MEETING

A meeting was convened by BRITAIN AND INDIA on the 29th ult., in the Caxton Hall, to welcome all the delegations at present in Great Britain. After enjoyable social intercourse,

THE HON. MR SRINIVASA SASTRI, of the Indian Moderate Deputation, gave a brief explanation of Diarchy. It was considered that full responsible government was too much to introduce at once. Part of the functions of government, such as law, justice and police, were to be reserved to the executive. Other subjects such as education and sanitation, were to be carried out by Ministers subject to the control of the legislature. This devious method of introducing responsible government was such a novelty that much Indian opinion was alarmed by it, but many opponents fell into agreement after the visit of the Secretary of State. In his scheme the evils of diarchy were minimised and the process of subjects from reserved to transferred was to be genuine and real. The Government of India have recommended the fullest development of this scheme, the two halves of government to be kept as much apart as possible. This was dangerous. This had caused a withdrawal of moderate support from diarchy. The Government of India's scheme of diarchy was comparable to the divorce of a married couple before they had ever lived together.

MR RAMASWAMI IYER, of the All-India Home Rule League, dealt with the question of the Central Government of India. The average annual income for the United Kingdom is £42, but of Indians £2. Two hundred years ago India was exporting cotton and silk goods, but tremendous import duties were levied upon such goods and that flourishing trade decayed and India was now the poorest country in the world. To take a proper economic place India asked for economic freedom. Whether their economic dogmas were sound or unsound they demanded liberty to make their own experiments. Gratitude was of the essence of the Indian. Troubles would disappear if the Indian had some control over central government. The collocation of events leading up to the resignation of Sir Sankaran Nair was known – place without power was useless. . .

THE HON. MR VP PATEL, of the Indian National Congress, did not accept provincial diarchy. The Indian National Congress had accepted the August 20, 1917, declaration involving self-government by stages, but did not accept the principle that the Governments of England and India should be the judges of the stages. (*Applause*) They asked that a period should be fixed within the Statute within which responsible government should be achieved. It was in the interests both of India and Britain that India should remain within the British Empire.

Mrs Besant, for the National Home Rule League assured the audience that the deputations differed only on detail – all were willing to take stages, all willing to work in amity with Britain, but all were working towards Home Rule for India on the ground of human dignity. It was not right to monopolise foremost positions or to control the education of another race. The price of India's loyalty was India's freedom. (*Loud applause*)

*   *   *

Indian delegates of the Indian National Congress visited England to put India's case before the British people. *India* of 19 September 1919 covered the tour of Mr B G Tilak in Scotland that included the Trades Union Congress at Glasgow, an At Home party by the Glasgow Indian Union, a meeting of Women Workers and Edinburgh Indian Association. The theme of his talks was 'The Indian Problem':

Balganagadhar Tilak (1856–1920)
A nationalist leader. Editor, *The Maratta* and *Kesari* 1890; Professor of mathematics at Poona; wanted nothing short of total independence for India. Imprisoned several times to prevent him from taking active part in the freedom movement. Visited England and spoke at various public meetings as delegate of the Indian National Congress. Never became its President but inspired others, by words and deeds, for support for freedom movement. Disliked the weak policy of the Indian National Congress; believed that 'political rights will have to be fought, not by persuasion but by strong pressure'.

THE CONGRESS PROPAGANDA
MR TILAK'S TOUR

MR B G TILAK, spent a useful week in Scotland between the 6th and 12th inst. On Saturday he attended a social reception at Glasgow, held under the auspices of the Union of Democratic Control on the eve of the Trades Union Congress, under the chairmanship of Mr Wishart. The chairman in his speech extended a welcome to Mr Tilak and his Indian colleagues, and assured them of the support of the Union in their cause. On Sunday Mr Tilak delivered a lecture at the Avenue Theatre on the subject of the 'The Indian Problem'. The gathering was a pretty large one. Mr Velkar also addressed the meeting briefly. At the Trades Union Congress demonstration, held the same evening at St Andrew's Hall, which was attended by over 5,000 people, Mr Tilak was the first among the speakers. Called upon to address the gathering, Mr Ramsay MacDonald, who was the principal speaker, referred in his speech to Mr Tilak as an eloquent embodiment of the grievances of India, who was there to appeal to the British democracy to stand by Indians in their struggle for freedom, and he assured India, through Mr Tilak, that the Labour Party were prepared to do so. Whoever, he said, kept himself in touch with Socialism kept himself in touch with everything that stood for freedom, equality, and justice. Mr Tilak was given a tremendous ovation by the great gathering.

On Monday evening Mr Tilak attended an At Home party given by the Glasgow Indian Union, where there was a mixed gathering of English, Scottish, and Indian ladies and gentlemen. Mr Tilak, on being invited to address the gathering, spoke for about an hour on the present position in India. Mr Velkar also spoke a few words. The next day Mr Tilak attended a meeting of Women Workers, where Messrs. Henderson and Thomas were the speakers.

At Edinburgh the principal function was a lecture given by Mr Tilak under the auspices of the Indian Association on the subject of 'The Meaning of Indian Nationalism.' The meeting was attended both by Indians and Scotsmen. Mr Robertson, of the Independent Labour Party, in thanking Mr Tilak, said that, whereas he had heard of Mr Tilak as only an agitator, he now found in him only the right sort of a leader a nation should have. The problems for the people in India were nearly the same as those for the British people, and he assured Mr Tilak of the full sympathy of all right-minded Britishers. An Indian dinner by the Indian students completed the programme. Mr Tilak returned to London on Friday last.

Among other delegates was Mrs Sarojini Naidu, campaigning in the south-west of England.

THE CAMPAIGN IN THE SOUTH-WEST

Another batch of delegates from the Indian National Congress opened their campaign to enlighten the British public by holding a meeting at Bournemouth while the British Association was in session there. The speakers were Mrs Sarojini Naidu, Dewan Madhava Rao CIE, Hon. VJ Patel, and Hon. GS Khaparde, and they were fortunate in having as chairman Mrs Councillor Laney, who gave them a hearty welcome to Bournemouth.

Indian National Congress delegates to England toured Britain. *India* reported one of the most significant and momentous of such meetings at the Albert Hall on 7 November 1919.

INDIAN HOME RULE DEMONSTRATION
GREAT ALBERT HALL MEETING

The great Indian Home rule demonstration held in the Albert Hall on the evening of the 25th inst. was a triumph for the cause of India. Contrary to the expectation of some people, the magnificent hall was pretty full except in the upper stalls. The early stream of men and women seeking admission to the

Sarojini Naidu (1879–1949)
Poet and politician; sailed for England 1895; studied in King's College, London, and later at Girton College, Cambridge. Returned to India after three years; published *The Golden Threshold* 1912; *The Bird of Time* and, in 1917, *The Broken Wing*. Involved in politics from 1921. Went to Kenya and South Africa on behalf of Indian National Congress 1924–25, stating that 'let Congress be the voice of the people and not the voice of the politicians'. Gifted orator; went to America in 1928. Naidu met Gandhi in London for the first time in 1914 and joined him in his Dandi Salt March and for the Round Table Conference in London, 1931. Repeated imprisonments damaged her health. Wrote to Gandhi in 1920 from abroad, 'the specialists think that my heart disease is in an advanced and dangerous state, but I cannot rest till I stir the heart of the world to repentance over the tragedy of Martyred India'. Her speech at the Albert Hall, London, on 7 November 1919, is one of the best made by any Indian in Britain.

seats was an unmistakable proof of the eagerness with which the London democracy looked forward to be enlightened upon, and to support by their presence, India's demand for political self-determination. It was evident, of course, that they took more interest in the temporary Russian blockade than the permanent bondage of India. But there are also cogent reasons why this should be so. An Indian onlooker, however, could not but regard the interest shown by the London people in Indian affairs on the present occasion as a hopeful augury for the future.

After the usual orchestra music and the spirited songs sung by the choir, Mr George Lansbury opened the proceedings with a short but very pithy and convincing speech. He said a meeting like that for the cause of dependency was unthinkable in former times. But now the people of England, it was quite evident, did not want to have any subject people, but only fellow-citizens, with equal rights in the Commonwealth. After referring to the drain upon India's wealth and the fact that food was exported from India even while Indian people were dying of hunger in their own land, Mr Lansbury said that it all proved that the affairs of India were being mismanaged and that time had come for the Indian people themselves being allowed to organise them, as they assuredly could not do worse. If aliens were to be prevented from entering into this country, why should not India be entitled to do the same? The awakening in India was taking place even faster in India than it did in England. Indians might now demand and not supplicate. They might even demand that they should not be allowed to elect the Viceroy. Insults like the threatened appointment of the Duke of Northumberland as the Viceroy of India should only sting the demand for self-determination into action. The Viceroys were mere ornaments, and represented in India a thing which was of not much importance in England. After severely criticising the outrages in the Punjab [The Jallianwala Baag massacre], Mr Lansbury said Englishmen knew only as much of governing other nations as governing themselves well. They were there in India, not because they had any virtue in them, but only because they were perhaps superior masters of the art and craft of war. He ridiculed the idea that the English were a peace-loving nation. The blessings of gin and whisky were perhaps the only blessings of civilisation they had to give to India. In conclusion he rousingly appealed to the British democracy to stand by India and help her advanced political reformer.

Mr Jamnadas Dwarkadas, of Bombay, then moved the following resolution: 'That this mass meeting of British citizens, holding that the existence of the British Commonwealth is dependent upon the right of self-government being conferred upon each of the nations within its boundaries, hereby declares that the Indian people are entitled to receive at the earliest opportunity the full right of self-determination.'

The speaker reminded the audience of the assurances given from time to time by British statesmen, and said that the very fact that Indians demanded self-government proved their fitness for it. The fetters put upon expression of opinion in India perpetuated the shackles upon her people, and it behoved England to free India as well as herself from any political shackles in future

Mr Ben Spoor, who, Mr Lansbury said, was the man chosen by the Labour Party to watch over Indian affairs, was received with cheers and made an excellent, forceful speech. He testified to the vastness of the Indian problem, but expressed the conviction that interest in the cause of India was sure to be awakened in England now more than ever before. A false step now taken in Indian affairs would surely lead to irretrievable ruin. The East and the West had a common purpose in the world, and a better understanding must be established between them. The British took India before; the Indians wanted India back now. England so far exploited India; now India wanted to be exploited by herself and for her own interest. India had a great civilisation behind her, great poets and philosophers, but perhaps no business Government (*Laughter*), no commercial magnates. If a Viceroy is still necessary for India, he should rather be Robert Williams than the Duke of Northumberland! The speaker then dwelt upon the condition of labour in India, and contrasted the misery of wages with the wealth of dividends earned by British capitalists in India. The Indian people were horribly poor and were coerced in the bargain in any natural opposition they offered to maladministration. India restless and eternally chafing under alien rule was a menace to the peace of the world. She has been spurred into a natural interpretation of her fundamental rights, and she must be satisfied by giving her self-determination, the right of choosing her own rule and her own form of government. Mr Spoor then illustrated how India and England had much to give to and receive back from each other; but asserted that India could not be expected to give her best unless she was free and happy in her mind.

Mrs Sarojini Naidu, who was warmly welcomed by the audience, made a stirring speech. She began by saying that the British democracy should feel more ashamed for a woman like herself to have to stand before them and remind them of their duty and responsibility than that she should feel proud to make a speech before them. In scathing terms she analysed and exposed the boastfulness and the hypocrisy of the English people – rather English statesmen, who, while granting self-determination to Assyrians and Kurdish Christians – a mere handful of mountaineers – denied it to the three hundred millions of civilised India who had done so much for the Empire. Are you prepared, she put it point-blank to the audience, to say to India 'Stand up and be free'? And the appeal was answered by a ringing cheer and an enthusiastic 'Aye.' She then mercilessly ridiculed the idea of the foot-rule-and-thumb measure of English beliefs and English benefit; being used to determine the self-determination of India. She warned England that the so-called peace in India was a peril, and that Englishmen had better free their mind betimes from vain illusions and vanities concerning the government of India. She asked them to remember that it would be better for the English people to be dead and forgotten than that they should be hypocrites and their deeds should not tally with their word. India would go with England only as a comrade and not as a slave.

Mr Yakub Hasan supported the resolution as a Mahomedan and dwelt upon the importance of the united demand now made by Mahomedans as well as Hindus in India for self-government, for if the demand was not granted now a wide gulf would be opened by the rulers and the ruled, which might never be bridged over.

Mrs Besant was the next to support the resolution. As she rose she was greeted with opposition in some quarters, one Indian gentleman putting the question straight to her whether she had changed her policy of supporting repression and saying that brickbats must be answered with bullets. The Chairman having intervened, Mrs Besant went on with her speech. She said India was tired of asking for one bone of reform after another. She now wanted full equality of status within the Commonwealth. She wanted fragments no more, but Home Rule. She claimed self-determination ought to be given to the helpful people of India before anyone else. The British people who made and unmade the Parliament held the destinies of India in their hand, and they must give if the Parliament denies what Indian people wanted. India was willing to take the Bill which gives but imperfectly what she wants; and would not be enthusiastically received unless it gave power in the Central Government and fiscal autonomy. With this brief reference to the Bill, Mrs Besant went on to deal as eloquently as usual with other details, mainly about the poverty in India and her misgovernment by England. She referred to the Punjab, but she did not answer the question put to her about brickbats being answered by bullets, though the Chairman had said at the time she would answer it. She concluded her speech with a solemn warning to England, saying England and India were nearly at the parting of the ways. There was as yet not enough real hatred of England in India, and the time was now to give India her freedom. If there was a quarrel it was between the Indian people and the Anglo-Indian bureaucracy, not between them and the English people, and the latter should therefore befriend the former.

Colonel Wedgwood, who followed, said the time was for India now as it was on the eve of the Reform Bill of 1832 for England. The evidence before the

Select Committee proved that there was absolute unanimity of Indian opinion on one point – viz, that the Bill was illiberal, over-cautious and timid. The question was whether Indian people should refuse the Bill? His personal opinion was that not having any reasons to hope for a better Bill from the present Government, they should accept it for the present, as opening to them just the fundamentals of liberty, and wait till the Labour Party came to power. No nation, he said, was good enough to govern another nation. The millions of India asked for a voice in their own affairs, and he appealed to the audience to send a message of hope to India. The Indian deputations had opened the eyes of the British public by going up and down the country and giving lectures. He concluded with the expression of hope that England and India would stand shoulder to shoulder, and India would not only get but give the lead to other nations in liberty.

Mr B G Tilak, who was received with loud applause, could not commence his speech at once as some Indian gentleman had sent to the Chairman an addendum to the resolution and insisted upon being allowed to move it at that stage. The Chairman, however, ruled that he could not allow that at that or any other stage. There were consequently cries of dissatisfaction from certain quarters.

Taking up the point of the controversy as a convenient beginning for his speech, Mr Tilak said he had watched the controversy with some anxiety and would therefore deal with both the resolution and the proposed addendum. There was, however, no controversy about one thing – the demand by India for self-determination as put forward in the resolution. It was a new word ushering in a new era, and all welcomed it equally. He asked the question point-blank: 'Is there anyone in this assembly who does not want self-determination to be given to India?' There was of course, no dissentient voice, as there could not very well be, on this point. And Mr Tilak himself broke the silence which his tactful question had created for a moment by declaring, amid loud laughter and applause, that the proposition before the meeting was therefore carried unanimously. As regards the proposed addendum, he said he saw the point of it but, it could not be an amendment to that general proposition about self-determination only. He did not want to condone the Bill, he never did. But it was impossible to discuss the full details of the Bill in an assembly like that. There were differences of opinion about the Bill, but not about India's right to self-determination, which even the Government admitted. The Government, however, seemed to think that India's self-determination was to be determined not by the Indian people, but by the Government themselves. But that was a ridiculous interpretation of the term. The Government had convened a Convention to enable Ireland to choose for herself. But it failed. There out in India the Indian people had saved the Government that trouble, and the National Congress and the Moslem League, which were together the great Convention for India had already decided upon what they wanted by way of political self-determination. The door to Liberty was, as remarked by Colonel Wedgwood, indeed opened, but India was asked to walk, nay, run, if she liked, through that door with heavy fetters upon her feet. The Government would give Indian people mastery over their house – the word for which was responsibility-without giving them the possession of the house. They would make the masters occupy and wait in a sorry outhouse.

The Bill related to the Government of India, and the Government of India meant the Central Government of course – nothing else, nothing less. What would self-government be like or worth if the power of the purse, fiscal autonomy, and control of the administration in the Central Government were not included in it? The Government gave a promise to India in times of difficulty, and now when danger was over the lawyer was put forward to whittle down the promise. The word gradually was interpreted as if it admitted of centuries instead of, say, ten or twenty years. Colonel Wedgwood advised them to accept the Bill as a thin end of the wedge. But they would do so if they had power to drive the wedge deeper. In one sense what could a people do but accept any Bill which the Government might choose to pass? In that passive sense anything might be accepted. But unless the Parliament modified the Bill as they wanted it to be, they would go on agitating. The Bill [India Bill of 1919] might or might not pass, but the agitation would not cease. Militarism and Czarism were dead in countries like Germany and Russia, but not in India, and they might revisit the West now from the East. The Government had no excuse to wait for self-government being given to India, as in India there was not even an Ulster question.

But if they denied self-government to Ireland because Ireland was disunited, they denied it to India because she was united. That sort of juggling would, he said, no more do. Indians were far too serious a people for that. He did not support the Bill, and had faith in a future Liberal Government.

The last speaker was Mr John Scurr, who in a short but spirited speech asserted that the minimum that should be now given to India was the measure given to Canada. The Labour Party stood for full and complete self-government for India. The Trade Unions were determined to agitate for this and help the Indian cause. India and England shall be free together and stand four-square to the wind.

The resolution was then put to the vote and carried unanimously. At the request of certain gentlemen, however, the Chairman read out the proposed addendum, which advised the meeting to ask the Parliament to reject the present Bill as it was unsatisfactory. The Chairman said he quite understood the point and held that the movers were entitled to their opinion about the Bill; but that he could not allow the meting called for one purpose to be so used for another purpose. He then declared the meeting dissolved.

Hind of 2 June 1922, reported a notable gathering that took place at the Caxton Hall, London on 29 April 1922. A large audience filled the hall, attending the Second Session of the London Bharat (India) Conference, presided over by Mr B G Horniman. The notable feature of the meeting was the attendance of fraternal delegates from various organisations such as the Labour Party, The British Communist Party, and the Irish Self-Determination League and...

the passing of resolutions dealing with the deletrious effects of the imperialistic ambitions of the governments of Western countries on the people of those countries themselves...

This is the first Indian conference at which the discussion has travelled outside the immediate scope of India's own demand for the achievement of her rightful claim to control her own destiny. It is almost impossible in the space at our disposal to publish a detailed report of the speeches, and for the present we must content ourselves with the reproduction of the text of the resolutions and a very brief account of the proceedings. The following resolution were passed:

> This Conference expresses unabated confidence in Mahatma Gandhi and other leaders and workers in India who are engaged in the struggle for Swaraj and renews the expression of its determination to support them by every means possible.

> This Conference urges the Committee of the Indian National Congress to consider the necessity of maintaining political and national activities of the Indian community in Great Britain, while the self-imposed control of Britain over India lasts...

The first resolution, which was very ably moved and seconded by Mr H F Fruqui and Mr S A Hamid, respectively, was carried, at the request of the Chairman, by upstanding as a mark of request to Mahatma Gandhi and other imprisoned leaders.

The next resolution was moved and supported by Mr R Palme Dutt, Editor, *Labour Monthly*, representing the Communist Party of Great Britain, in a very educative and interesting speech, and Mr Shapurji Saklatvala, whose command of the language and mastery of the subject roused the Conference to a high pitch of excitement.

All the speakers dwelt on the great need for some organisation, purely Indian in character, to control and organise activities of this country, and the desirability of purging the life of the community of the evil influence of pseudo-philanthropic institutions, like the YMCA Hostel in Keppel Street and the institution in Cromwell Road, which, it was pointed out, by subtle and insidious methods, tended to obstruct the very growth of national spirit in the Indian youth. The Chairman's plea that it was inconsistent with the dignity and self-respect of Indian students that they should look to alien 'religious' organisations for the social and other amenities, was loudly cheered. Indian students, he said, should see to it that they were independent of foreign patronage in this respect, and it was the duty of the national institutions in India to assist them in maintaining their independence.

*　　*　　*

The Times of 27 October 1922 covered a news item on India's Claim and MR SRINIVASA SASTRI on Peaceful Revolution. He was the guest of honour at a luncheon given by the Royal Colonial Institute:

INDIA'S CLAIM · MR SASTRI ON PEACEFUL REVOLUTION

The Right Hon. Srinivasa Sastri was entertained at luncheon yesterday by the Royal Colonial Institute, Sir Godfrey Lagden presiding.

Replying to the toast 'Our Guest,' proposed by the Chairman, Mr Sastri said that he had arrived at a most interesting time in English public affairs. He found the country engaged upon one of its periodical pastimes of pulling down a Government and setting up another.

He wished that other nations knew the secret of accomplishing a revolution in so unsanguinary and peaceful manner. They in India had taken very good care not to be linked with any political party, and expected from any Government the entire fulfilment of pledges and promises that had been made. He had been surprised during the last few days to hear many people of influence ask what was the best thing to do with regard to India. It was not always possible to take the ideal course, and it was sometimes better to take the second best course in good time rather than to wait to take the best course at some distant time.

Great Britain was committed in 1919 irrevocably to the grant of responsible Government to India, and it was a matter of grave concern to read speeches delivered by statesmen of Cabinet rank who treated the subject as though it had not been settled, as if Parliament had not over and over again pledged its solemn word to the accomplishment of that high aim. Nothing remained now but to go forward.

*　　*　　*

On 29 June 1929, the Commonwealth of India Conference took place at the Caxton Hall, London, with Mrs Annie Besant in the chair. A resolution was passed at the end of the session, to be delivered to the Prime Minister and the Secretary of State for India.

This conference is in agreement with the object of the Commonwealth of India League (namely) 'to work for Dominion Home Rule for India' and invites organisations in sympathy with the object of the League to collaborate with it in order to realise the hope, expressed by Mr Ramsay MacDonald in July of last year, to become a self-governing Dominion.

Mrs Annie Besant delivered the presidential address:

The problem of the British in India and the East is a world problem, for there is a proposal to form not a League of Nations which meets at Geneva, but a League of Asiatic Nations which shall link together the nations of Asia in a common self-defence. . .

INDIA AWAKE

A nation has the right to throw over a monarch if he tyrannises that nation. You cannot deny this right, for you sent Charles I to execution, you drove another King into exile and you laid down principles of Government in Magna

Mrs Annie Besant (1847–1933)
Active Fabian in early life, a theosophist, and Indian politician. President of the Indian National Congress, 1917. Founder of Central Hindu College, Benaras, (1899); started the Home Rule for India League, 1916; imprisoned for her political activities, 1917; organised the Home Rule movement for India, 1917; changed the name to Commonwealth of India League (which later was to be the India League), 1922. Her whole life was dedicated to the cause of India. Also collaborated with another scholar for the translation of the *Bhagavat Gita* from Sanskrit into English.

Carta and the Bill of Rights . . . Long ago when I went over to India, I was told, when I spoke to them of their lack of liberty, 'India is dead', and I used to retort, 'India is not dead; she is only sleeping'. And now she is awake. . .

England has won her freedom, and this freedom is becoming wider and wider. Ramsay MacDonald refers to India as a country he hopes to see as a self-governing Dominion – and that is the dream of India at the present time.

INDIA'S DEMAND

We are asking for Dominion status. Why should not India also make that claim and have it willingly conceded by the British Government? Why should not India be put on a level in the Empire?

INDIA AND WORLD PEACE

She pointed out that there would never be peace in the world until the subject nations were free. . . A free India, friendly to Britain, interpreting the East to the West and the West to the East, was the only safeguard against a cleavage of the world into two camps. India had a right to be free – no power in the world could keep her in bondage, but more than all this, the peace of the world rendered it essential that the day of her liberation should be hastened.

Indian leaders, absent from the Conference made their views heard by sending messages from India:

MESSAGES FROM INDIAN LEADERS

Sent to the Commonwealth of India Conference, held at Caxton Hall, London, on June 29th:

From SIR TEJ BAHADUR SAPRU:

I sincerely hope and trust that those who will attend the Conference will make it abundantly plain to the Government in England, whatever may be its political complexion, that nothing short of the recognition of India's right to Dominion status will satisfy Nationalist India. The way in which several prominent English statesmen and nearly every English newspaper have approached and discussed during the last two years the question of India's future makes one feel that a great change for the worse has overtaken the attitude of English public men towards India. If political faith has to be revived and resuscitated as it must be then absolutely the first thing to be done is that the claim of India to Dominion status must be admitted without equivocation. Once this is done there can be a basis for discussion and exchange of ideas. But if the claim of India, which rests upon most solemn declarations and pledges, is repudiated or whittled down I am afraid I cannot look upon the future with any degree of hopefulness. Further it must be remembered that Dominion status with us is no longer a far-off dream, but a real live issue, and we should like an approach to be made to it in a manner which would command the maximum amount of consent and agreement. Nationalist India has expressed its views definitely in the Nehru Committee report, and notwithstanding some dissent that has been raised in certain quarters I feel that it is going to stand by it. I sincerely hope and trust that the efforts of the Conference may be crowned with success and that it may be the rallying centre of all those who sincerely believe that India is entitled to be placed on the footing of a Dominion within the British Commonwealth of Nations.

From CHINTAMANI, Chief Editor, *The Leader*, Allahabad; Member Legislative Council, and formerly Minister of Education, United Provinces:

India must be deeply beholden to Mrs Annie Besant for organising a Conference in London in support of Dominion Status for this country. Every Indian patriot is behind her in this plea. The present position of dependence is ruinous to India materially and degrading to her morally and politically. India's national consciousness is thoroughly aroused and Indians will not tolerate much longer the unsatisfactory position to which they have been con-signed. The only condition on which she can willingly remain associated with Britain is that she should be accorded the same status as Canada, Australia, South Africa, the Irish Free State, and New Zealand. She should have the same full rights of national self-government as the Dominions enjoy and exercise; the Indian States and the British Indian Provinces forming one Federal Union – the Commonwealth of India, which will be an equal member of the Commonwealth of Nations at whose head will be the King of England, to whom all the members of the Commonwealth will owe allegiance.

To this there will be but one alternative: a violent effort by India to win Sovereign Independence after the manner of the present United States of America. The people of India do not wish to be forced to such drastic action. They bear no ill-will to the people of England, whose great qualities they admire. For His Majesty the King they feel the most sincere devotion.

Will England, who has been called 'the Mother of free nations,' do the right in time, retain India's friendship, and win gratitude? Or, will she act like any of the discredited Continental despotisms?

*   *   *

The Commonwealth of India League, started by Mrs Annie Besant, organised meetings all over the country. *The Indian News* of 13 June 1929 covered them at Hull, Bristol, Birmingham, Wolverhampton, Liverpool, and Sutton Coldfield with an impressive list of speakers:

Mr T H Redfern (National Organising Secretary of the Commonwealth of India Group) delivered an address on India. He reminded his hearers that the respon-sibility for the government of India still rested with the voters of England. . .

The question which they had to consider was: is India to be offered Dominion status within the Empire and so kept as a friend? Or would we drive her to range herself against Europe with the other nations of the East?. . .

WOMEN'S GUILD LECTURE ON INDIA

At a meeting of the Women's Co-operative Guild at Cotham recently, Miss Merrie (Organising Secretary of the Bristol Branch of the Commonwealth of India League) gave a lecture on India, expressing the hope that more and more people would take an interest in the affairs of that country, for she felt that in a peaceful union between India and England lay the security of peace between East and West.

THE WOMAN OF INDIA
MRS SAROJINI NAIDU

The greatest achievement of the Women's Movement, said Mrs Sarojini Naidu, speaking at a meeting of the British Commonwealth League, should be that there should be no sex consciousness but perfect comradeship. Indian tradition and legend was always about 'proud women, brave women, who never folded their hands and appealed to others, but whose sword was their own spirit.' 'I am Indian enough to believe,' said Mrs Naidu, 'that there is no difference between man and woman in psychology and destiny. Man and woman are complemen-tary. In the words of the Quoran, they had to be a garment one to another.'

*   *   *

Meetings organised by the Commonwealth of India League were increasing in numbers and in audiences all over the country, such as the Bristol Women's Conference, presided over by Mrs William Graham, the wife of the then President of the Board of Trade, on 25 September 1929, and reported by *The Indian News* of 3 October 1929.

The Conference was attended by representatives of no less than 70 organisa-tions, who accorded to Mrs Graham an enthusiastic reception. In her opening address the President drew attention to the serious state of affairs in India, and appealed to the women of this country to realise their responsibilities and take an active interest in the cause of Indian emancipation. Mrs Graham made very pointed references to the ignorance prevailing in this country on Indian affairs, and also to the gross misrepresentation of facts concerning India by interested writers and the British Press. 'India', the speaker declared, 'should have fair play; she does not get it now'.

England continues to ignore India's demands, the result of which can only be the complete alienation of the Indian people. Some English people today, unfortunately a majority, think that British rule in India is an unmixed blessing to that country and that India has no cause to grumble. This view is continually put forward by the enemies of India who trade on the ignorance of the British people.

We as a people are pledged to mete out justice to India since the times of Queen Victoria. The Indians say that our pledges are unredeemed and few Indians trust our promises any longer. India is tired of pledges and England will soon have a rude awakening if she is not careful.

Now that the women of England have the vote, continued Mrs Graham, it was up to them to do their utmost for India's cause. India had culture and learning thousand of years older than that of England, and yet within a few decades of British rule that country has been reduced to a state of comparative illiteracy. The condition was becoming intolerable.

We must wake up to facts and give no peace to the Government or Members of Parliament. In the days of the Women's Suffrage Movement the women of this country made sacrifices and asserted themselves. It is worth while to remember that in the suffrage days British women were fighting for the removal of disabilities and evils which, when compared with India's grievances, are very small. Can we, with the memories of our struggles for freedom and our own national traditions of Liberty, ignore India's demands? It is shocking to think that the British representatives in India have been responsible for hindering social reform. The Child Marriage legislation recently passed is the result of India's fight against official obstruction. In concluding, Mrs Graham once again appealed for strong and persistent action, and said, 'Give no peace to your Government, agitate for all your worth for India'.

*   *   *

As the Indian population in Britain grew, so too did the numbers of Indian organisations. The Indian Freedom League was one such body organising social events for the purpose of conveying and creating the spirit of nationalism to its members. *Indian and Colonial Journal* of 31 January 1931 was present with a photographer:

The Indian Freedom League: members and friends in London on the occasion of the Indian National Flag Salutation Ceremony on 9 January 1931

LOCAL NEWS

The Indian Freedom League, London, held a social and a dance at 12 Archer Street, on Friday, 9th January. The greatest event of the evening was the performance of the Indian National Flag salutation ceremony. Under the soft twinkling lights there assembled young India to pay their respect to their National Flag – the Indian Tricolour. When India's banner was being unfurled with dignity and sanctity the dearest song of Indian hearts – their own Nationalist Anthem *Vande-Mataram*, was sung to the accompaniment of music. On this occasion young India stood upright and respectfully saluted their country's flag. They all, like soldiers true to their country's call, sang their national anthem. Their faces beamed with joy. Their hearts jumped and danced and kept beating in tune with the music. This was the greatest moment in their lives. It was a dream that came true in the very heart of the Metropolis of the British Empire. When the flag salutation ceremony was over one was able to see vividly the radiant joy that lingered in the minds of all Indians and their friends. After a little pause, Bengali youths charmed the guests of the evening by their enchanting Bengali melodies. Their harmonious voices, their songs with Indian philosophical depth of meaning, their sweet expression was peculiarly their own. It was like India's voice that came across thousands of miles away. There is magic in Indian music. There is love in Indian songs. There is sweetness in Indian voices. And that is why Bengali tunes melted all hearts away into a stream of a heavenly dream. Never before the history of England was there such a ceremony to honour and salute the Indian National Flag. – *Vande-Mataram*

In 1932 *India Bulletin*, organ of the Friends of India was published. The monthly paper, edited by Horace Alexander, with Will Hayes, Reginald A Reynolds and Atma S Kamlani on the Editorial Board, presented the British support for India, as it did in its July-August issue.

Horace Grundy Alexander (1889–1989)
Quaker, born in Croydon and educated at York and Cambridge; secretary of the Friends Peace Committee 1915; lecturer in international studies at Quaker College, Birmingham 1919–1943; friend of CF Andrew who persuaded him to visit Gandhi at his ashram in India; became good friends with Gandhi, based on their shared commitment to the principles of non-violence; became involved with establishing civilised communication between the British government and the congress party, scarcely on talking terms, first through the India Conciliation Group and later as a member of Gandhi's entourage; spent much time in India between 1946 and 1951; received the Padma Bhushan medal in 1984, in recognition of his services to the freedom movement, the highest civilian honour the Indian government can give to a non-Indian.

India Bulletin, February 1932
Annual Subscription 2/-
Published by Friends of India, 46 Lancaster Gate, W2.

Vol 1 No 6–7
July-August, 1932

BRITISH SUPPORT FOR INDIA

The Friends of India held a meeting in Trafalgar Square on Saturday, June 25. Mr Peter Freeman was Chairman and the speakers were Reginald Reynolds, Rev FA Wentyon, Rev William Riley, Syed Abdul Huck, Mrs Haidri Buttacharji, R E Kumana, Dr V Thalmankar and Atma Kamlani. Some 400 people were present and the various speakers were followed with the closest attention. The following resolution was carried unanimously.

'That this meeting strongly protests against the policy of repression which is being pursued by the British Authorities in India and calls upon the Government to withdraw the Ordinance regime. The meeting further protests against the attempted suppression of the National Congress which represents the Indian masses and demands release of all political prisoners in order that the leaders of the Congress may be in a position to draw up a Constitution for Independent India.'

CHAPTER 2

Organisations and their activities

INDIA REFORM SOCIETY

The first ever joint British-Indian organisation, the India Reform Society, was formed by the Friends of India, in London on 12 March 1853. It was established mainly through the efforts of John Dickinson, a writer on Indian and British bureaucracy. He saw the necessity and importance of promoting well-directed action among the friends of India and providing them with true and accurate information regarding Indian affairs. There was also a need for 'bringing public opinion to bear on the Imperial Parliament in the case of India, so as to obtain the attention to the complaints and claims of the inhabitants of that vast Empire'. The immediate objective of the society was that the customary enquiry by Parliament into the renewal of the Charter of the East India Company, due in 1854, should be full and impartial.

BRITISH INDIA ASSOCIATION

This association was first formed in Calcutta for the purpose of sending representatives to the British Government. Impressed by its strength and purpose, at a meeting in Bombay on 26 August 1852, the Bombay India Association was formed. In 1859 it drew up a petition to the House of Commons asking for reforms in India. In the aftermath of the 1857 rebellion, it acknowledged the new governing body, the British Crown and began:

Sheweth that:
   Your petitioners hailed with delight the Proclamation of our gracious Sovereign, whereby she assumed the direct administration of her Asian Empire.
   Your Honourable House will deem the interest of your loyal Indian fellow-subjects (who are politically unrepresented) as intimately of national, if not domestic concern.

   With this sentiment, your petitioners take the earliest occasion to crave your Honourable House a hearing to defects of administrative, legislative, judicial and executive, demand the deliberations of your hearing.
   That your Honourable House regard India as an integral portion of the British Empire, and as therefore, entitled to the active sympathy of Britain's representatives.

In all there were 43 points detailed in the petition demanding attention and reforms to Legislative, Council, Courts, Civil Service, Education and Land Tenures regulations in the country.
   The petition was signed by the Committee with a final plea: 'the petitioners earnestly pray that these entreaties and suggestions may be deliberated upon and that thereby renewed confidence may be conveyed not merely to your humble petitioners but to the millions of Indians'.

LONDON INDIAN SOCIETY

The origins of the London Indian Society lie in an organisation founded in Calcutta, by a group of intellectuals, in order to present a united voice in dealing with the British authority. Soon afterwards the news of its formation reached Bombay, and a meeting was held in 1852 at which it was decided to follow Calcutta's success and establish its own Bombay Association. One of those present at the meeting was Dadabhai Naoroji. Three years later he came to Britain and eventually gave the Association its London voice.

Dadabhai Naoroji founded the London Indian Society in England in 1865 with W C Bonnerjee. The idea was to hold public meetings and dinners in order to project the affairs of India before the British public. The other objective was to bring together students from India, offer them a warm welcome and help them adjust to a new life in Britain. There appear to be no records of any other all-Indian organisation in Britain before 1865.

One of the major and well received functions of the Society was the annual conference of all Indian residents in the United Kingdom. On 28 December 1898, the conference at the Westminster Town Hall was convened and presided over by Dadabhai Naoroji. 'A large force of Indians, various in race, religion and profession, together with a considerable sprinkling of English ladies and gentlemen, received with acclamation the venerable and revered President, Mr Dadabhai Naoroji', is how the conference was described.

Naoroji attacked the unjust aspects of British rule in India and the failure of the authorities to fulfil their declared pledges, enshrined in Acts of Parliament and Proclamations of the Queen, to treat Indians exactly as British subjects were treated in England. He reminded the audience that the British should never forget the 'loyalty, heroism and soldierly qualities' of Indian soldiers in the war, the North-West Frontier Campaign of 1897. He deplored all legislation restricting self-government in India and condemned the Sedition Law of India.

Others who spoke at the conference were: Mr Romesh Chunder Dutt; Mr S Ziauddin; Mr Mehtab Singh; Mr A A Khan; Mr W S Caine; Mr A K Donald; Mr R C Sen; Mr Bipin Chandra Pal; Mr P N Chakrabutty; Mr J Baptista; Mr Martin Wood; Dr Sarat K Mullik, MB, CM, Vice-President; RV Paranjpe Esq. and Raghubar Dayal Esq., Secretaries.

Between the years 1875 and 1885 Naoroji lived in India, toured the country and managed to get donations for the upkeep of the Society from the Indian Princes. He also published a journal *Asiatic Quarterly* and the *Voice of India*.

The London Indian Society started with membership for Indians only. Later on the membership was opened to the British. Its name was then changed to East Indian Association, and it received much needed support and sympathy from Naoroji's British friends. He and his friends devoted much time to the reading of papers on Indian affairs – and in no time became a popular London Indian organisation.

Some years later, after much useful and successful service to the cause of India, the Association was taken over by a few very sharp and shrewd enterprising Anglo-Indians belonging to the Civil Service. Naoroji was powerless and deeply hurt by the takeover. The 'new' East India Association started publishing pamphlets in 1909 from its offices at 3 Victoria Street, London. These were favourably prejudiced views of

British rule in India. The British were doing a wonderful job in India and administering it for the benefit of the natives. They attributed India's financial drain on the 'wreckless expenditure on marriage festivities'. It also had a grudge that India never paid tribute to England; it became an anti-Indian organisation. It was ironical that the East India Association should ask Naoroji if he would be good enough to send his reminiscences of the Association, or at least his blessings and good wishes for its Golden Jubilee in 1916. Naoroji refused. He replied that the Association had departed widely from its original aims and had caused him much anguish.

INDIAN PARLIAMENTARY COMMITTEE

In 1883, a decision was taken to have an informal Indian Committee with a view to secure combined Parliamentary action in matters affecting Indian interests. Ten years later, in 1893, the subject was taken up again by Sir W Wedderburn. The scheme was a revival of an older organisation founded in 1853, named the India Reform Society, initiated by John Dickinson.

INDIAN NATIONAL CONGRESS

The idea of establishing the Indian National Congress in 1885 has generally been accepted as the brainchild of Allan Octavian Hume. However, there was an element of irony behind its creation. Lala Lajpat Rai, in his book, *Young India*, quotes Hume's biographer, Sir William Wedderburn:

In initiating the National movement, Mr Hume took counsel with the Viceroy, Lord Dufferin and whereas he was himself disposed to begin his reform propaganda on the social side, it was apparently Lord Dufferin's advice that he took up the work of political organisation as the first matter to be dealt with.

Lord Dufferin apparently told Hume that:

As head of the Government, he had found the greatest difficulty in ascertaining the real wishes of the people and that for the purposes of administration, it would be a public benefit if there existed some reasonable organisation through which the government might be kept informed regarding the best Indian public opinion.

History has shown that the idea actually backfired: Lord Dufferin, quite innocently and in good faith helped create a genie that would come to haunt the Raj and eventually supplant it. What Dufferin had hoped for and expected was a tame political organisation run by tame spirits. He did not for a moment suspect that the Congress would represent institutions for the Indian people: the seedbed for full democracy.

Hume wrote a manifesto in the form of a letter, dated 1 March 1883, which he sent to the graduates of the Calcutta University. In it he made a candid and moving appeal, pointing out to them that they were: 'the most important source of all mental, moral and political progress in India.' He told them they were the favoured sons, that India looked upon for initiative. He proposed the formation of an association, to be named Indian National Union. Hume even came to England with the proposal to put before his friends and sympathisers inside and outside of Parliament.

The formation of the Indian National Congress as an institution was unique and without equal in India's national life. It dominated Indian

Marquess of Dufferin and Ava (1826–1902)
Initiated establishment of the Indian National Congress. First Marquess of Dufferin and Ava. Under-Secretary of State for India 1864–86; Governor-General of India 1884; dealt with India's land questions; annexed upper Burma 1886; Retired from India 1888.

politics for over a century and produced the country's greatest men and women. It was both national and secular in composition. As it grew, in membership as well as in influence, the Indian National Congress went through different phases in its outlook, tactics and goals.

From 1885 to 1905 it was an organisation driven by moderate nationalism and loyalty to the British Crown. Between 1906 and 1918 there were parallel currents of militancy and moderation, of direct action and constitutional propriety. However, there was broad nationalist support for the British war effort in the First World War. It was during this period the Congress came to its own with Gandhi's leadership, with his unique and effective policy of non-violent civil disobedience or non-cooperation. Thus began an era of passive resistance in India. Under Gandhi Congress became a mass movement; he combined constitutional activity with direct action.

The Indian National Congress in India needed a voice in England, and Dadabhai Naoroji was invited to be its representative, and in 1889 the British Committee of the Indian National Congress was formed. Sir William Wedderburn became its first chairman, a post he held for life. The Congress in India had the utmost confidence in his ability to gain the sympathy of the British people for India's cause. To promote news of India and views of Indians in Britain, the British Committee launched a periodical called *India* in 1890, first as a monthly, later as a weekly; it was edited by William Digby.

The financial responsibility for running the Committee and its journal *India* was taken up mostly by Sir William Wedderburn and, to a lesser degree, by Dadabhai Naoroji. Help also came from AO Hume. Only when reports from India reached London, complaining that *India* was a financial burden to the Congress, did Wedderburn disclose that it was he who had been footing the bill in the main, both for running the journal and for the British Committee.

Congress in India and its organ in Britain became a visible symbol of enlightenment and nationhood; the more successful it became in uniting the people of India in a common struggle, the more it became determined to release India from colonial bondage to Britain.

The Congress of 1929 at Lahore introduced the word *Swaraj* (total independence) in its resolution and declared 26 January 1930 the day of independence, with a pledge that this anniversary would be celebrated annually.

The 1942 Congress passed a 'Quit India' resolution. It was at the time of the height of the Second World War in which more than 36 thousand Indian soldiers gave their lives for the defence of Britain and India against Hitler and fascist Japan. The Congress made an appeal to Britain and the United Nations to respond to the 'call of reason and justice' by granting India its independence and enabling it to join the Allies as a sovereign nation in the war against the Axis. Historically, these have been the most significant resolutions passed by the Congress.

At the end of the war in 1945, the General Election in England put the Labour Party in power with a landslide victory. With a huge majority in Parliament, Prime Minster Clement Attlee and his Government was acutely aware of a rising swell of anti-British feeling in India. India was clearly determined on achieving full independence. No longer could the British take for granted the loyalty of the Indian soldiers. The Bombay naval mutiny was a sign of growing unrest in the Indian armed forces. Attlee had no wish to lose the goodwill of the Indian people. For him, Indian independence was the fulfilment of British rule in

Indian troops being inspected by Mr Leo Amery, Secretary of State for India

the subcontinent. It was time to leave. India became a sovereign nation on 15 August 1947. Britain transferred power to an Indian government comprising the leaders of the Congress Party. Sixty-two years after its formation in 1885, the Indian National Congress took India to full nationhood.

The tragedy was that it was a partitioned India. Hindu-Muslim bloodshed cast a dark shadow on the subsequent history of the subcontinent.

CONGRESS IN BRITAIN

After the founding of the Indian National Congress in 1885, a deputation came to Britain every year to meet the British people and members of Parliament. This was a propaganda mission to familiarise the British public with various resolutions passed by the Congress. They aimed to awaken the British public in the cause of India. The delegates offered friendship to all non-official circles in Britain but stood firm in their attitude to the Government, putting their views before the Select Committee with candour. They carried a message of hope back to India, not hope of immediate radical reforms in India but of the increasingly favourable climate for the future agitational work in Britain. The Congress delegates visited important provincial cities in Britain to put before the public India's demands for self-determination. For example, at a representative conference in India at the Steinway Hall in London on 4 October 1919, presided over by Mrs Annie Besant, the Hon. Mr Srinivasa Sastri spoke on 'What India wants'; Col. JC Wedgwood, MP, spoke on 'The House of Commons and India' and Mr MA Jinnah on 'Indian Reform and Hindu-Mohammedan Relations'. There were other fine speakers on a variety of other India-related subjects.

The Indian National Congress had become the official voice of India in the struggle against British imperialism. On 30 April 1888, Mr AO Hume delivered a speech at a public meeting in Allahabad on the origins and aims of the Congress. He explained that no other movement had acquired in so short a period, such an appreciable hold on the minds of people of India. No other organisation had provided such wide-reaching and beneficial results,

the labour of a body of cultured men, mostly born natives of India, who, some years ago banded themselves together to labour silently for the good of India. To understand Congress thoroughly, it is necessary to understand, first, what were the basic principles laid down by that body. It was primarily and directly as a political institution that the Congress was founded. The objectives are:

(1) The fusion into one National whole of all the different and till recently discordant elements that constitute the population of India.
(2) The gradual regeneration, mental, moral, social and political, of the nation.
(3) The consolidation of the unions between England and India, by securing the modification of such of its conditions as may be unjust or injurious to the latter country.

The 50th anniversary of the Indian National Congress was celebrated throughout India in 1935 as a significant milestone in India's struggle for independence. The Congress President forbade any form of illumination as part of the celebrations since 'when repression is still rife, and thousands of men and women are in internment without trial'.

HOME RULE LEAGUE

Mrs Annie Besant was one of the early Indophiles totally immersed in Indian politics and culture. As early as 1910 she was active in India's freedom campaign and in 1915 decided to launch her own Home Rule League, after she found the Indian National Congress difficult to deal with. She considered her League concept to be an auxiliary to the Congress and not its rival. Her project was criticised and opposed. Undaunted, she even approached Dadabhai Naoroji and Sir William Wedderburn to accept the presidentship of the League, with the principal branch in India and another in England. The aim was to promote and publicise her Home Rule for India League. Besant even founded a newspaper, *New India*, but success did not come until 1917.

The function of the Home Rule League was to act as a pressure group for India and eventual Indian independence.

In 1922 the Home Rule League changed its name to the Commonwealth of India League, to promote and publicise its work throughout the British Empire, making it a subject for debate for students everywhere. A young student, Krishna Menon was Mrs Besant's protégé as well as being a pupil of Professor Harold Laski at the London School of Economics. He became a Joint-Secretary of the Commonwealth of India League in 1928 and its General Secretary in 1930. The driving force of the League was Henry Polak, who was inspired by Mrs Besant. They promoted the message of the Indian National Congress in England but never became its official representatives.

The League and the Congress kept their separate identities, but in time they worked with increased co-operation just before the years leading to Indian independence in 1947.

Krishna Menon personified the League. He was a man of action. Not content with the League's soft approach to politics, he quit, taking with him some of its more militant members to form a newer India League. This desertion was seen as an act of ruthlessness and betrayal and he was never forgiven by Polak.

India League today is the surviving half of the Commonwealth of India League, which was originally called the Home Rule League, established

Mrs Annie Besant

For the first time in Congress history, you have chosen as your President one, who when your choice was made, was under the heavy ban of Government displeasure, and who lay interned as a person dangerous to public safety. While I was humiliated, you crowned me with honour, while I was slandered, you believed in my integrity and good faith; while I was crushed under the heel of bureaucratic power, you acclaimed me as your leader; while I was silenced and unable to defend myself, you defended me, and won for me release. I was proud to serve in lowliest fashion, but you lifted me up and placed me before the world as your chosen representative. I have no words with which to thank you, no eloquence with which to repay my debt...

ANNIE BESANT, Presidential speech, Indian National Congress, Calcutta, 1917.

This speech was brought out almost in its entirety by India for the British public. It was also published by the Home Rule for India League under the title The Case for India.

in India in 1917 by Mrs Annie Besant. She made it quite clear that home rule was the birth-right of the people of India, and not a reward for their services or their loyalty to the British Empire.

Krishna Menon attracted the sympathies of many Britishers who were in the Committee of the League. They included Bertrand Russell as Chairman; Harold Laski, President; J Horrabin, MP, Vice-Chairman; Reginald Sorensen, MP; Fenner Brockway and Michael Foot. They all helped carry India's cause to the people, Parliament and Government of Britain. The testing time for both the British Government and the demands of India were the periods of the First World War and the Second World War. India wanted the same liberty and democratic rights that Britain was fighting for with the support and loyalty of the Indian soldiers. India had to wait till the end of the Second World War and a Labour Party victory in Britain in 1945, for her freedom. The India League gave Krishna Menon a perfect opportunity to mix with the British and to build up contacts with various authorities that was to prove a valuable experience when taking up the post as India's first High Commissioner in Britain.

INDO-BRITISH ASSOCIATION

At the start of the First World War in 1914 it was generally accepted that questions of India's internal politics, reforms and reconstruction would have to be put on hold in order to concentrate on the war effort. Soon after the war ended in 1918, the Indian issue was taken up in 1920 by the newly formed Indo-British Association, presided over by Lord Sydenham GCSI, GCMG, GCIE, GBE. Other members were: Lord Ampthill GCSI, GCIE; Sir Charles Armstrong; J Duncan Esq; Sir William Garth; Sir Herbert Holmwood; A Hopkins Esq., MP; A D Jackson Esq.; Sir Charles McLoed; Sir West Ridgeway GCB, GCMG, KCSI; J C Shorrock Esq; Sir Harry Stephen; Sir Harold Stuart KCSI, KCVO; and Sir David Yule.

The Association strongly believed that those who were aware of the conditions in India would have no hesitation in supporting their programme of proposals for a 'substantial step' in the direction of granting self-government to India. Their proposals, detailed in a special booklet, were:

(1) Re-adjustment of responsibilities of the Secretary of State in Council in order to put an end to the interference in financial matters which are injurious to the interest of India.

(2) Reconstruction of the India Office in London.

(3) Decentralisation of the excessive powers wielded by the Government of India, with a Federal State.

(4) Establishment of Government by Council in all Provinces.

(5) The reconstruction of the electorates of the Provincial Legislative Councils, on the basis of communal representation as well as of a special or property qualification, by electing communal representatives to safeguard their own interests which are in danger of being neglected.

(6) The transfer of all municipal and local government to elected bodies, to give Indians large powers and develop a sense of responsibility.

(7) The immediate reservation of 25 per cent of the higher appointments in the Indian Civil Service.

INDIA CONCILIATION GROUP 1931–1950

India Conciliation Group was the creation of Gandhi when he came to Britain for the Second Round Table Conference in 1931. It was his wish to establish a conciliation body to represent him in order to resolve deadlock through conciliation and negotiations with the authorities in London. Horace Alexander was invited to organise it with Carl Heath as its Chairman and Agatha Harrison as Secretary. The role played by the Group was that of a mediator between the Congress and the British Government. It continued to put pressure in Britain for India's cause and for the release of an increasing number of political prisoners in India. The group aimed at getting the support of liberal-minded Britishers and had the support of Lord Halifax, Lord Lothian, Lord Allen, Sir George Schuster, Henry Braisford and Sir Stanley Reed.

After accomplishing the main objective of the Group when India became independent, there was a possibility of working with the India League or merging with it, but the idea was rejected. It ceased as an organisation when Carl Heath died in 1950. Only Agatha Harrison kept up her interest in the post-independent India through the India League, often contributing to its short-lived monthly *India Today*.

Before returning to India, Gandhi was invited to speak from the India League platform to explain the situation in India and, in particular, the role played by the Indian National Congress.

Carl Heath (1869–1950)
Member of National Peace Council 1909; Chairman of Council for International Service 1919; met Gandhi in London in 1931; became good friends; Chairman of the India Conciliation Group, liaised with Viceroys and the Secretaries of State for India; worked to win friends in Britain and to influence them regarding responsibility of policy on India.

INDIAN EMPIRE SOCIETY
An anti-Indian organisation

The Indian Empire Society was a British organisation devoted to British Imperialism. Demands for Indian independence were seen by the Society as a threat and a danger to the Empire in India. It criticised the Indian political leaders as well as British politicians sympathetic to India's cause. The Society viewed the Round Table Conferences in 1930–32 with disfavour.

INDIAN PROGRESSIVE WRITERS' ASSOCIATION

A group of Indian writers and journalists, resident in London, formed the left wing IPWA with the sole purpose of bringing together writers with progressive ideas, in order to hasten a literary revival in India.

*   *   *

Indian organisations in Britain were originally established for the study of the history of India. As the population of Indians living or visiting Britain increased so did the number of different societies, which were devoted to a variety of causes. These organisations or associations covered religious, cultural and regional issues. Gradually these different societies formed into pressure groups and political organisations. In 1922 they were listed by a journal called *Hind*.

The Woking Mosque, The London Dharamsala, The London Indian Association, The Indian Conference, The Bharat Conference, The Central Islamic Society, The Indian Majlis, Various university centres, The Workers' Welfare League, Indian Muslim Association, Indian Social Club, Parsi Association, Indian Information Bureau, Bengal Literary Association, Urdu societies at Cambridge and Oxford.

According to the journal, there were roughly 3000 Indians in Britain, including residents, doctors, and lascars. London Indian Society held annual conferences, which brought together all Indian residents in the United Kingdom, convened by Dadabhai Naoroji. The December 1898 Conference was held at Westminster Town Hall, London.

*   *   *

The November 1946 issue of *United India* produced a diary of activities of different organisations, just a few months before India's independence. Some had a celebratory atmosphere.

The Indian Workers Association celebrated the formation of an Indian national government; The Gandhi Society, London, and Indian Social Club celebrated Gandhi's birthday; The Hindu Association celebrated the Dusserah festival; The India League and Swaraj House celebrated Gandhi's birthday; Sikh Gurpurb celebrated Baba Nanak's birthday. The journal also reported the activities of the Indian Institute, London, and the Universal Human Society.

INDIA

A Journal for the Discussion of Indian Affairs.

REGISTERED FOR] [TRANSMISSION ABROAD.

No 1. VOL. I.] FEBRUARY, 1890. [PRICE TWOPENCE.

While the English mind in India has been tempted to stand still, arrested by the contemplation of the fruits of its efforts in former times, and by the symmetry of the shrine, the pride of its own creation, in which it lingers to offer incense to its past successful labours, the Indian mind has been marching on, eager and anxious to expand its own sphere of action, and to do what it, for its own part, has to do. Rapidly maturing under the influence of great facilities for communication; stimulated by more frequent contact with England; and encouraged by the opportunities afforded during successive years of profound peace, it has succeeded at length in awaking to the consciousness of its own powers, and the assurance of its own success. The breath has come into the bones, and they are about to live and stand up upon their feet, an exceeding great army.—*Anonymous, but trustworthily credited to* SIR AUCKLAND COLVIN, *Governor of the North-West Provinces and Oudh, who is, however, opposed to the Congress.*

THE INDIAN NATIONAL CONGRESS.

ENGLISH COMMITTEE.

Sir WM. WEDDERBURN, Bart., *Chairman*, Gloucester.
W. S. CAINE, M.P. | W. S. B. MCLAREN, M.P.
J. E. ELLIS, M.P. | DADABHAI NAOROJI.
GEORGE YULE.
WM. DIGBY, C.I.E., *Secretary.*
OFFICES : 25, *Craven Street, Charing Cross, London.*

OFFICERS IN INDIA.

President for 1889-90 : Sir WM. WEDDERBURN, Bart.
General Secretary : A. O. HUME, C.B., Simla.
Joint Secretary : The Hon. AJUDHIA NATH PANDIT, Allahabad.
Standing Council : Bengal—W. C. BONNERJEE.
Bombay—Hon. PHEROZSHAH MEHTA, M.L.C.
Madras—ANUNDU CHARLU, M.A.

STANDING COMMITTEES.

1. Presidency, Burdwan and Chittagong Divisions, Assam and Orissa.
2. Dacca Division.
3. Rajshahye Division.
4. Bhagalpur Division.
5. Chota Nagpur Division.
6. Patna Division.
7. Benares Division.
8. Meerut, Agra, Allahabad, Jhansi Divisions, Bundelkhund and Ajmere.
9. Oudh.
10. Rohilkund and Kumaon Divisions.
11. Delhi Division.
12. Punjab, excluding Delhi Division.
13. Sindh.
14. Guzerat, Kuch, Kathiawar, Panch, Mehals.
15. Bombay Island, Colaba, Thana, and Rutnagiri Districts.
16. The Dekhan, Khandeish, and North Canara.
17. Sholapur.
18. Berar.
19. Central Provinces.
21. Madras Presidency.

CONGRESS SESSIONS.

PLACE.	Year.	PRESIDENT.	No. of Delegates.
Bombay	1885	W. C. BONNERJI, Hindu, Brahmin.	72
Calcutta	1886	DADABHAI NAOROJI, Parsee.	484
Madras	1887	BUDRUDIN TYABJI, Mahomedan.	604
Allahabad	1888	GEORGE YULE, Non-Official, Englishman.	1,248
Bombay	1889	Sir W. WEDDERBURN, Bart., Ex-Official, Englishman.	1,913

NUMERICAL PROPORTION OF DELEGATES IN 1888.

(*Latest analysis available.*)

Race, Religion, etc.	Number Present.	Population in 1881.	Representation to which entitled.	Actual Representation.
Hindoos	964	154,222,303	937	964
Mahomedan	222	47,098,603	286	222
Parsee	7	75,588	1	7
Jani	11	738,146	4	11
Sikh	5	1,848,257	13	6
Christian	38	1,091,511	7	38
TOTAL	1,248	205,074,407	1,248	1,248

INDIA TO BRITAIN.

Britons ! to your professions now be true !
If selflessly ye seek my lasting good,
Stand fast to me ! For, rightly understood,
My cause and yours in sooth are same, though few
Seem willing yet to realize this view
In deeds, bespeaking that calm mental mood,
Which sees in mine and England's Sister-hood
My right to claim from her a Sister's due.
Blest heirs of Freedom ! act as freemen should !
Some of her blessings on my sons bestow,
And thus secure my endless gratitude,
And one more wreath of glory for your brow !
O spread those blessings through this Empire wide,
And let my sons march onward by your side !
RAM SHARMA.

NOTES.

THE sonnet published above is from the pen of a Hindu gentleman whose cultured taste and whose power of versification are freely acknowledged by men of all shades of opinion in Eastern India. "Ram Sharma" is a *nom de plume.* The writer of the patriotic and friendly lines we publish is the author of a book of poems in which Indian latter-day topics are handled with much breadth of thought and with considerable literary faculty combined with high intellectual acumen. In December, 1888, the Congress about to meet at Allahabad was greeted with a burst of song which, under like circumstances in Britain, would have been set to music and portions sung by reformers at many public meetings and on all suitable occasions. The sentiment of the sonnet we publish to-day is unexceptionable, and should call forth a corresponding feeling in the hearts of all who wish well to India and to the United Kingdom.

Mr. Bradlaugh's constituents have lost no time in expressing their delight at the handsome manner in which their Member was treated by the people of India during his recent visit to Bombay. At a meeting held on the 7th instant, attended by an enormous throng of Northampton citizens, an address of congratulation on his recovery from his serious sickness was presented to Mr. Bradlaugh. In the address the following passage occurred :—" We especially rejoice at the magnificent reception given to you by the people of India, and indeed we feel honoured that the interests of that vast Empire have been entrusted to your care at the wish of the people themselves. We are satisfied that the best interests of India are safe in your hands, and that you will ever be the friend of her people, ready at all times to correct all abuses, to remove all inequalities, and to secure the realisation of their just demands and aspirations."

Those words have an excellent ring about them.

CHAPTER 3

Journals and other publications

THE BRITISH EMPIRE OF INDIA was perhaps the most unique in modern history, yet as Macaulay noted in his essay on Clive, it was remarkable how few Britons possessed an appropriate knowledge of Indian events. A free Press and Press freedom have been one of the enduring legacies of British rule in India. It was a battleground of ideas, a source of information and an instrument of national struggle. One of the first of these special journals was *The Asiatic*, established in November 1869. It was published in London every Tuesday and Friday evening, with the annual subscription of one pound and six shillings and sold throughout the United Kingdom, in India and the Empire. It tackled the issues of taxation, irrigation, the grain market, etc. But the issue that most disturbed the Liberals was the salt tax. The British treated the Indian consumption of salt as a 'luxury' and not a necessity. The tax was therefore a terrible burden upon the poor. At the time, in 1871, salt in Britain cost half a farthing per pound; in India its official market value was thirty times as much. This anomaly was well illustrated in *The Asiatic* of 14 February 1871 in its Editorial – 'The groans or curses of a suffering nation are but a sad accompaniment to a prosperous rule; and it is a poor satisfaction to a righteous Government to have removed the grievances of the higher classes, and left the wrongs of the poor without redress.' The journal returned to the iniquitous nature of the tax in its issue of 26 August 1892. Tax on salt became a recurring theme of other later journals. *India*, established in February 1890, published from London, showed on 16 January 1891, how salt tax in India was administered and cited the harsh persecution of the women affected by it.

THE SALT TAX ACT IN INDIA: HOW IT IS ADMINISTERED
ALMOST INCREDIBLE PROSECUTION OF TWO WOMEN

Two prosecutions of Indian women under the Bombay Salt Act of 1890 have just been disposed of by the Bombay High Court. It will be remembered that the Congress in its recent session, as indeed it has done in all its sessions, protested against the crushing tax on salt. That is an evil; and it is not the only evil. The salt laws of India are of the most Draconian character. Here are the facts of the two cases: 'The child of the first accused threw some water on some salt, weighing three tolas (about two ounces!) that lay in a pot, and the mother, with that thrift which characterises native housewives of the poorest classes, in these days of burdensome taxation and dear salt, dearer than gold in the native eye – boiled it down to save the salt from being completely melted away. The second bought some dirty salt, and refined it. Both were perfectly innocent of the existence of the law which holds this process, miracles of miracles, to be offensive, and punishable by fine and imprisonment!' Comment on such a decision is superfluous. Fortunately the case was taken before the High Court of Bombay. Still more fortunately it came under the review of the most humane of Indian judges, Mr Justice Birdwood.

Journals, sympathetic to India's cause, and organisations representing the voice of India in Britain complemented each other in India's struggle. Opposition to these objectives often took the form of being ridiculed, as

The first issue of *India* – A Journal for the Discussion of Indian Affairs – price twopence.

was the case of the East India Association in *The Asiatic* of 11 April 1871, following an inaccurate statement regarding the (East India) Association in the *Hindoo Patriot* of 6 March, which published a statement from an anonymous correspondent:

'The East India Association is only a non-cohesive gathering of gentlemen professing an interest in Indian questions, but disagreeing among themselves at almost every point. It is a dilettante institution, having the slightest possible power or influence. Indeed, it is scarcely known in political circles; and, so far as the general public cares, its meetings might be held at the North Pole on the top of an iceberg.' And, again, 'Mr Dadabhai Naoroji is, in fact, the Association so far as its working power is concerned. Without his strenuous exertions it would collapse altogether, and even he thinks more of Bombay than he does of India in general.'

To counteract, then, the possible effect of the writer's misrepresentations, we think it advisable to indicate the three points on which the censor is at fault. His first statement is that the East India Association is a 'non-cohesive gathering of gentlemen professing an interest in India, but disagreeing among themselves at almost every point!' Whether the gentlemen who form this Society are 'non-cohesive', or whether their interest in India is merely a 'profession', we will not enquire; but that they disagree among 'themselves at all points', we are able, from a perusal of the reported discussions, to pronounce an absurd and unfounded statement.

The second misstatement is that the Association possesses only 'the slightest possible power or influence'. That the Association does not possess all the influence that its friends might desire may be the case; but it is impossible to have watched the proceedings of the Society during the last two or three years without clearly perceiving that its influence has lately increased in a remarkable degree, and its discussions have been followed by the most satisfactory results. We may, we apprehend, safely assert that it is principally to the influence exercised by this body that we owe the appointment of the present Parliamentary Committee – a result which ought to give satisfaction to all the friends of India, and is in itself sufficient to stultify the assertions of the anonymous correspondent of the *Hindoo Patriot*.

The third and the last misrepresentation is, that the 'Association and its most energetic hon. secretary (Dadabhai Naoroji), thinks more of Bombay than of India in general'. Perhaps of all these misstatements this is the most unwarrantable. A perusal of the subjects selected for discussion during the last two years, and a reference to the speeches of Mr Dadabhai himself, as well as the other members, will be quite sufficient to prove the groundlessness of this disparaging statement. To corroborate our assertions, we give below a list of the subjects which have come under the discussion of the Society during the last two years, and recommend the *Patriot*'s anonymous critic to profit by the perusal. They are:

The Material Improvement of India; by F Login, Esq., CE.
Agricultural Condition and Prospects of the Godavery District (Madras Presidency, East India), with especial reference to *Irrigation and Navigation Works*, by W Bowden, Jun. Esq.
The Establishment of a 'Mussafir-Khaneh' or 'Guest-house' for Asiatics in London, by Lord Stanley of Alderley.
A Retrospect of the Afghan War, with reference to Passing Events in Central Asia, by Sir Vincent Eyre.
Lecture at Bombay on the Work of the East India Association, by Dadabhai Naoroji, Esq.
Indian Civil Service Clause in the Governor-General of India Bill, by Dadabhai Naoroji, Esq.
On the Population and Mortality of Bombay, by P M Tait, Esq.
On the Admission of Educated Natives into the Indian Civil Service, by Dadabhai Naoroji, Esq.

On Transport in India in reference to the interest of England and India, by Hyde Clarke, Esq.

The Advantages of Encouraging the English Language to become the Colloquial Tongue of India, with a Practical System for its Development, by George Simmons, Esq. CE.

On the Beneficial Effects of Caste Institutions, by R H Elliot, Esq.

The Bombay Cotton Act of 1869, by Dadabhai Naoroji, Esq.

On the Industrial Settlement of Europeans in the Hilly Climates of India, by Dr A Graham.

On the Relations between the Native States and the British Government, by I T Prichard, Esq.

On the Grant-in-Aid System in the Presidency of Bombay, by P M Mehta, Esq. (Paper read before the Bombay Branch)

The Bonus System in the Indian Army, by Lieut.-Col. J C Phillip.

The Delay of Justice to Indian Appellants in England: its Causes, Consequences, and Possible Remedy, by W Tayler, Esq.

On the Work done by Miss Carpenter for Female Education in India, by Miss Carpenter.

On the Present and Future Product of Cotton in India compared with that of America and other Cotton-producing Countries; by W S Fitzwilliam, Esq.

Is India a Conquered Country? and if so, What then?, by Major Evans Bell.

On Indian Finance, by I T Prichard, Esq.

On Public Works in India, by Sir Bartle Frere.

The Wants and Means of India, by Dadabhai Naoroji, Esq.

On the Finances of India, by Sir Charles Trevelyan.

The Shortcomings of the present Administration of Hindoo Law, by Dr L Goldstucker.

On the Proposed Plans to cut a Ship's Channel between India and Ceylon, by Sir James Elphinstone, Bart. MP.

On the Commerce of India, by Dadabhai Naoroji, Esq.

We have thought this subject worthy of remark, because statements, even of the most superficial character, when repeated, without refutation, in the leading column of an influential journal, are apt to be accepted by the careless reader as correct; and the description, which we have quoted, of a body of gentlemen who are earnestly labouring for the good of India, without recompense or reward, may, unless its inaccuracy is exposed, be prejudicial to its future development. We are glad to see, from a paragraph in another portion of the same journal, that the British Indian Association has a better appreciation of the services of the East India Association than the superficial critic whose effusions we have noticed. In the last report of the Committee of that body, submitted at their late annual meeting on the 2nd February, the following observation is recorded:

'The East India Association promises to be a powerful ally to the Indian associations in furtherance of their objects. During the last year the Committee were in correspondence with the Secretary of that Association on several important subjects.'

Despite Press attacks on the workings of the East India Company's government, it continued with its labours in India. Emphasis was placed on the importance of ascertaining and recognising the feeling of its Indian subjects on matters pertaining to Indian administration. It also made proposals for the gradual introduction of advisory councils and village level participatory *panchayats*. The plea was that Indians were entitled to a voice in the management of their own affairs. *The Asiatic* also advocated the right of Indians to hold positions in the executive service of their country as 'most important' and suggested practical steps towards comprehensive administrative reforms.

The Statesman was launched on 29 November 1879 in London as a weekly journal of home and foreign policies and published in parallel with *The Statesman and Friend of India*, Calcutta. The editorial in the first issue declared that:

'Western ideas are a solvent of tremendous power; and under their influence India is changing with a rapidity that must be watched to be understood. It results from this, that an English journal desiring to disseminate the truth regarding India, must obtain its information fresh, from writers in immediate contact with the facts, convictions, wishes, and aspirations which they delineate. By the establishment of a London *Statesman*, in direct connection with the *Statesman* in Calcutta, this will, it is hoped, be accomplished. Englishmen entrusted with despotic power have too often succumbed to its corrupting influences. They have learned to believe that in their case might was right, and that because they were entrusted with a mission to elevate and improve the people of India, they might, in their dealings with that people, dispense with those moral laws without which no elevation of character is possible. Everything was to be done *for* the people; nothing was to be done *by* the people. And the consequence has been, that the people of India have been treated by us as a *corpus vile*, on which administrative theorists and crotchet-mongers had full power to experiment as they pleased. There has been neither continuity of principle, nor consistent purpose, in our administration, but a series of vast experiments, precipitate in their inception, and disastrous in their consequences. Thus it is that at the close of a century of British rule, carried on to a ceaseless chorus of self-congratulation, we find these singular effects: A profound gulf existing between rulers and ruled; a peasantry sunk in poverty and indebtedness, and swept away in millions by periodical famines; an army, the most costly in the world, and yet so deficient in organisation, that we cannot, in three months, collect 30,000 men on our own frontier; a heavy public debt, an increasing expenditure, and the Empire on the very verge of bankruptcy. We do not say that this comprises the whole of the picture, or that there are not brighter scenes to be found in it. But this we do say, that the above facts are strictly true, and demand that we should cease from contemplating, Narcissus-like, our own perfections, and try to ascertain how and why we have so grievously failed.'

The weekly *Statesman* was devoted to political, social and literary topics, especially to those related to administrative and economic reforms in India. However, it declared on 3 January 1880, that although it hoped to make the journal an authority on Indian affairs, it was not an Indian paper because 'there is not sufficient interest taken in Indian affairs in this country, to allow of any reasonable hope that such a paper would succeed', and added:

And now as to India, the affairs of which great Empire will be a *spécialité* of the journal we propose to establish. When the Government of India was transferred from the Court of Directors to the Crown, it was inevitable that, sooner or later, the initiative in policy and legislation should also be changed from Calcutta to London. The effects of this transfer are, that the authorities in India are relieved from responsibility to even such feeble public opinion as exists there; while from the ignorance and indifference at Home, the Indian Government in London becomes more despotic than ever. A government which rules India from Calcutta, cannot entirely close its eyes and ears to the effect of its measures upon the people; but an irresponsible bureaucracy attempting to govern India from Downing Street legislates in the dark.

But though India will be our speciality, the paper we establish will not, as we have said, be Indian, but will deal with the whole range of English politics, domestic as well as foreign, insular as well as Imperial. Social questions and current literature will also receive their due share of regard therein.

While journals like the weekly *Statesman* were at pains to tell the truth about the British administration of India, *The Times* was frequently accused of 'misinformation' on India. The former on 14 February 1880 put *The Times* in its place, and explained the Real State of India, by criticising both *The Times* and its cronies among the officials at home.

While a chorus of Indian officials at home have been assuring us that everything is well under our rule in India, and *The Times* has been endorsing their assurances, and telling the world that they who say otherwise are mere 'slanderers' of their countrymen. One of the oldest and most experienced members of the Civil Service in India, has been quietly passing through the Press of this city an essay on *Agricultural Reform in India*, which should settle the controversy, we think, in the mind of every one who seeks to know the truth upon the subject. The author of this invaluable essay is Mr Allan O Hume, a son or nephew – we have forgotten which – of the late Mr Joseph Hume. Mr Hume has occupied a prominent place in Indian administration for many years. He greatly distinguished himself in the Mutiny, and was made a CB for the singular gallantry and administrative energy displayed by him, during that terrible crisis. It is to Mr Hume's exertions mainly, that we owe the abolition of the Salt and Customs line in Northern and Central India.

The *Statesman* introduced Mr Allan O Hume, who in subsequent years was to play a crucial role in the formation of the Indian National Congress. He was also to make a major contribution to the activities of the Congress in Britain.

In February 1890 *India* was launched in London. It was the voice of the Indian National Congress, which was established in December 1885, in India.

It was launched with the help of Sir William Wedderburn, who spent a lifetime keeping India's cause at the top of the British imperial agenda, as its first fierce editorial in February 1890, showed only too clearly.

INDIA'S REASON FOR EXISTENCE

'Well, if you really wish to have my opinion I must say I look upon the movement with great mistrust. I am afraid there is more in it than appears on the surface, that there is sedition in it, and I know not what else.' Thus remarked a Member of Parliament in reply to a friend of Indian Reform who had mentioned the Indian National Congress efforts to him, and expressed the hope that he would give them his support. After a while, when the subject had been further discussed and light thrown upon it, the Member said, 'You have put a different complexion upon the matter. I shall be glad to look into it'.

The Member in question is typical. There are many thousands such as he, – hundreds in Parliament, hundreds of thousands outside Parliament. India is lacking many friends at this moment simply because her object is misunderstood, because ignorance is the prevailing characteristic regarding our Eastern Empire. Owing to this ignorance, and also because when the ignorance is dispelled the demands of the Congress are easily understood and are found to be eminently moderate, this journal has been established.

No space will be found in the pages of *India* for acrimonious or rancourous discussion. Their own aims being wholly sincere, pure, and upright, no railing will be indulged in by its conductors or permitted by its correspondents. Imputation of motives to opponents will be unknown in these colums. The sole dependence of the people of India in their desire to secure justice at the hands of their fellow-subjects is in the reasonableness of what they seek, in the advantage which they are convinced will accrue to the United Kingdom as well as to India if their desire be gratified, and in the constitutional manner in which they have urged and will continue to urge the programme which, through the National Congress, they have put forward. Sooner or later they will, if they continue firm in their efforts, command success. When success is obtained it will be found to have been well deserved. There will be no bar sinister across the Indian record of agitation and instruction. Unshaken determination and unsparing effort will be the only weapons in this warfare so far as we are concerned.

There was of course, the inevitable response to the Indian National Congress as seen in the letters pages of *India* which reflected most shades of British opinion.

The main object of *India* was to educate 'The British people on the Indian question'. It carried the torch for the Congress in Britain, often organising, but always reporting, its meetings throughout the country.

For *India*, unfinished or ignored business in the House of Commons on matters relating to India, was justification enough for coverage in its columns. For example, Lord Cross's Indian Councils Bill was given an airing in its issue of 21 June 1890, since the Bill was being so casually delayed.

LORD CROSS'S INDIAN COUNCILS BILL

This measure has now, thanks to the muddling of public business in Parliament, been more than three months in the House of Commons awaiting its second reading. On the date these lines are written (June 16), the measure stands thirteenth on the Order of the Day; there is little chance of its being considered or, if ever brought forward, no chance at all of its being adequately debated. It is nevertheless probable the Government will force the Bill through this session. Should this course be taken, little regard must, necessarily, be shown to the grave and most urgent necessities of that portion of the British Empire which contains five-sixths of the Empire's population. The present temper of the Government indicates that such a course is not merely possible but highly probable. Whatever may now happen it is impossible for the bill to receive, during the present session, adequate consideration.

By December 1890, *India* had been in circulation for almost a year. It became a journal of the record and comment on India's struggle. In its issue of 5 December 1890 it traced the history of the English political organisations and Indian reforms, a chronicle of all that had been attempted so far, starting with the Viceroy, Lord Ripon's resolution on the local self-government in 1881.

ENGLISH POLITICAL ORGANIZATIONS AND INDIAN REFORM
A RECORD OF WHAT HAS BEEN ATTEMPTED

Elsewhere we comment upon the future of the Indian Reform Agitation in regard to a possible alliance with the great party organisations in Britain. Whether Indian Reform should be worked into the warp and woof of British politics, or should be conducted wholly on an independent and non-party basis, deserves the most careful consideration. That consideration we endeavour elsewhere to give. Here we are content to tell the story, in detail, of what has been done in one or the other direction during the past ten years.

1881

During this year, Mr William Digby, CIE, who returned to England from India in 1870, and was a year later – after having for nine months edited the *Liverpool and Southport Daily News* – editing the *Western Daily Mercury*, published at Plymouth, exerted himself to bring Indian Reform under English consideration. The course he proposed to himself was to work through the Liberal organisations. He did not consider any good would come of an attempt to get the Conservatives to interest themselves in such a matter. Under the title of *Indian Problems for English Consideration*, Mr Digby wrote a pamphlet-letter addressed to the Council of the National Liberal Federation. This letter, consisting of sixty-eight pages, after a few pages of introductory matter, treated Indian problems under three headings: (1) The people of India as they are; (2) The country as it is; and (3) What Englishmen can do for India. To this was added a postscript having reference to Lord Ripon's projected reforms. Through the generous help of a Birmingham Liberal friend, Mr Richard Tangye JP, ten thousand copies of this pamphlet were printed and circulated. Many newspapers, both in England and in India, commented upon the suggestions made, and the Federation itself, at the annual meeting held in Liverpool, on October 25th referred, in its report, to the matter in the following terms:

'The officers have also had under consideration matters of importance concerning India, and in this direction they specially direct the attention of the Liberal Associations throughout the country to a letter on Indian problems for English consideration, addressed to the Council by Mr Wm Digby CIE; the letter is in general circualtion. Mr Digby, who is now resident in England, has lived in India. In his letter he gives his own experiences of the people, and describes their political and other needs. More than that, however, he brings under review the most recent official literature of the Empire, and from that literature shows our rule in India to be far other than it should be, or what the people of England desire it to be. The need for such reform as it is in the power of Liberal Associations through their representatives in the House of Commons to effect is urgent. It will be seen that Mr Digby makes a number of practical suggestions, both in respect to organisation on the part of the Federation and in regard to the particular reforms in India which call for immediate attention.'

India also published a letter prepared for circulation to the various Associations connected with the Federation and approved by the Council, and signed by four office-bearers of the Federation.

THE NATIONAL LIBERAL FEDERATION
INDIAN REFORM

Atlas Chambers, Paradise Street,
Birmingham, November 1881.

Dear Sir,
We venture to ask the early and best attention of your Association to the subject of Indian Reform as detailed in Mr Digby's letter to the Council, copies of which have already been sent to you. We shall be happy to send you such further numbers as you may need for distribution among the members of your Association.

There can be no doubt, we think that Mr Digby has shown there is most urgent need for immediate reform in India, and we feel sanguine that the Federated associations will be glad to share in the work of endeavouring to procure that reform. We would invite special attention to the statements on pp. 12–14, 31–42, and 49–62, of Mr Digby's letter, wherein we feel sufficient evidence is produced to render energetic action imperative, if we, as Englishmen, are to show ourselves alive to our responsibilities. Appended to the present communication will be found the digest of a Decentralisation Minute issued by the Viceroy of India, which not merely affords a justification for effort, but renders effort a sacred duty. Reading this digest in the light of Mr Digby's letter, and with the illustrative remarks which will be found following the Viceroy's Minute, we trust it will be in your power to arrange for a meeting of your Association to consider the whole question, to invite discussion thereupon, and to pass resolutions somewhat of the kind we have drafted. If you could procure the attendance of your parliamentary representative or representatives, and enlist his or their interest, a great step would have been gained. Should it seem well to you to do so please arrange for your meeting being open to the representatives of the Press, and send us two copies of such reports as may appear. The Council of the Federation would like, before the end of the year, to be in a position to approach the Secretary of State for India upon this important subject: we should, therefore, be additionally obliged if the matter could receive your attention before the end of this month, or in the early part of December. Copies of resolutions agreed to should be sent to us, and if you think well, forwarded simultaneously to the Marquis of Hartington.

Confidently counting upon your earliest and prompt co-operation in this movement, on behalf of greater freedom for our fellow-subjects in India.

India reported that in 1882 Mr William Digby was appointed a member of the General Committee of the Federation and added that during 1883–1884, an organisation called the British India Committee was formed and worked assiduously during the two years. Agitation in support of Lord Ripon's measures was carried on.

INDIA, 5 DECEMBER 1890

The organisation did really good service. But it was crippled for want of funds, and especially suffered from the lack of a really representative organisation in India.

During this period also, Sir William Wedderburn, though not in connection with the Party organisations, made strenuous efforts to create an Indian Party in Parliament. This record would be incomplete if it did not set forth Sir William's earnest endeavours. What he did is best described in his own words in a circular which, a year or two ago, he prepared for semi-private circulation, but which has found its way into print in India and portions of which may be reproduced here. We quote as follows:

(1) In 1883, Mr John Bright approved the organisation of an informal Indian committee, having for its object to secure combined Parliamentary action in matters affecting Indian public interests.
(2) This scheme commended itself to Mr Bright as being a revival of a valuable organisation, which, under the name of the India Reform Society was founded in 1853, mainly through the exertions of Mr John Dickinson, for the purpose of promoting combined and well directed action among the friends of India, and furnishing them with trustworthy information regarding Indian affairs. From the records of this Society it appears that the movement was initiated on the 12th of March 1853, when a meeting of the Friends of India was held in Charles Street, St James's Square.
(3) Unfortunately, however, in one most important particular the position of Indian reformers was very seriously damaged by the legislation of 1858, under which the Crown assumed the direct administration of India. As long as the administration of India was with the East India Company the proceedings of this privileged Corporation were watched in Parliament with great jealousy, and each renewal of the special charter furnished a natural opportunity for a Parliamentary enquiry into complaints and grievances.

But since 1858, when the Crown took over the direct administration, this self-acting provision for a periodical enquiry into grievances has been lost. There is now no day of reckoning. And Indian reformers find all their efforts exhausted and wasted in the vain attempt to obtain a Parliamentary hearing.

The report also introduced the leading figure of the Indian National Congress, Sir William Wedderburn, the force behind the establishment of an Indian Party in Parliament.

1885

This year is memorable in connection with the present narrative. Sir William Wedderburn, in the memorandum from which a quotation has been made, tells what was done in Parliament. He says:

The statutory arrangements, sanctioned in 1858, for the control in England of Indian affairs, were confessedly transitional and imperfect. Since 1858, a period of nearly thirty years had elapsed, and the needs of India were more pressing than ever.

1885 was the year when the Indian National Congress was set up. There was a general election in Britain and Dadabhai Naoroji emerged as the leading voice in Britain.

India lost no opportunity in reporting events or meetings, however small, wherever in the country, when these related to India, drumming the message of Indian reforms. On 11 March 1892 it reported a lecture at the Cambridge Liberal Club:

INDIAN REFORMS

At the Cambridge Liberal Club, on Sunday evening, February 28th, Mr HS Gour delivered an interesting address on 'Indian Reforms'. He remarked that before he could possibly deal with the subject it would be necessary to give a few elementary points relating to India. About 150 years ago it came, owing to an inscrutable Providence, into the hands of the British, and up to 1858, it was the property of the British [East] India Company. In that year it was formally transferred to the hands of the Queen. Since then the country has been ruled by a Viceroy, who every four or five years was sent from England. He was assisted by six paid members, who formed the sole executive. These men were appointed in England and, consequently, knew little about India. For legislative purposes it was true that certain natives were admitted, but they were always outnumbered by European non-official members. The result of this system was grinding taxation, which reduced the people of India to the greatest poverty and destitution. Their income in fact was only £1 10s, as against £13 of the English, per head and still they had to pay no less than double the taxes of the British people. This was the real cause of the frequent famines which destroyed millions of people, and not want of rain as naively urged by the Indian authorities during the periods of scarcity. The reforms he suggested were the substitution of the native for foreign and civil military services. Englishmen who went out to India were honest and just, but India could not afford to maintain them. What India wanted was a government of its own people, maintained at a minimum of cost. He finally contended for representation, which he considered to be the only effective means for the better government in India. It was never denied that India did not require reforms, but the Government failed to enact them. In conclusion the lecturer claimed sympathy on behalf of the Indian National Congress, which, he maintained, demanded only what was an elementary right of civilised humanity – representation. He hoped that the British people who adored liberty and freedom would not deny that boon to India. A vote of thanks to the lecturer terminated the proceedings.

These were the early days of demands for Indian reforms. Demands for full independence were to come in the next century.

India was keen to enlist the sympathy of the British public so that its views could eventually penetrate Parliament. It was, therefore, essential that all matters dealing with India were regularly and accurately reported in its pages. Furthermore it dealt with the unsympathetic views of the national Press.

India did not have it all its own way, in spite of the efforts it made to reach a large section of the British population.

Parliamentary and political history was made in Britain in 1892. At the general election Dadabhai Naoroji was elected as a Liberal to represent the Finsbury Central constituency, London. He was the first Indian to take his seat in the House of Commons. *India* gave his canditature worthy coverage in its issue of 10 June 1892:

INDIA AND THE GENERAL ELECTION

Will India occupy a prominent position among the great matters placed before the people of the United Kingdom on which, in a few days, their judgement will be asked? There is but one answer and that is, 'No', India will not attract the attention which the importance of its many grave problems deserve.

As compared with the General Election of 1885, for example, the present contest displays a sorry state of things. Seven years ago India and Indian topics occupied a very large place among the matters referred to the decision of the British people. Delegates from India spoke in nearly every great town. Crowded meetings presided over or addressed by some of the greatest statesmen of the day – John Bright, Joseph Chamberlain, Sir Charles Dilke, Dr Spence Watson – were held. Although the candidates most favoured by the Indian people were then beaten, the situation was full of promise and potency for future good, if only the progress made had been followed up. A good foundation had been laid; it only needed that the structure should be proceeded with, 'with both hands earnestly,' to have procured, ere this present year of grace, great boons for the Indian people. But, alas! 'the eyes of the people were holden and they could not see'. The National Congress was in course of formation. All attention in India was devoted to the upbringing of so valuable an infant of progress. England, and the need for work, unceasing, hopeful labour, in this country, was forgotten. This was a misfortune almost incalculable in its consequences. Later, an attempt has been made to repair the mischief which was done by the neglect of previous years. Many circumstances, however, have conspired to prevent this late effort bearing its expected fruit and, as a consequence, Indian reform is a lost cause so far as adequate attention in the hurly-burly of the supreme contest is concerned.

Nevertheless the situation is not wholly without its compensations. A Bill has just passed through Parliament which, honestly and heartily worked, will do great good. The Congress Party in India possess power enough to ensure that the objects which its supporters in Parliament had in mind shall be carried out. It is a matter for great gratification that this is being recognised by the Congress leaders generally, and that steps will shortly be taken which are calculated to leave no peace to Viceroy, Governor, and Lieutenant-Governor, until all Mr Gladstone affirmed, and Mr Curzon acquiesced in, are carried out. In the prosecution of this enterprise, those working in India will find most efficient coadjutors in England.

No definitely-arranged campaign or propaganda on behalf of Indian questions has been undertaken in the present crisis. Such a state of things has not arisen through a policy of drifting. The situation was carefully considered by the members of the British Committee of the Congress, and active abstention in the electoral struggle was, for sufficient reasons, deliberately adopted. In the present tumult, with Irish Home Rulers, Labour Eight Hours' men, London Government Reformers, Ground Landlords' Taxers, Temperance Enthusiasts, all pressing for the first place, Indian Reformers could not have obtained a foremost position. Not to be in the front rank at such a time, is equivalent to being out of the contest altogether. In a quiet way, however, much is being done which will bear fruit. More than that, however, India is likely to be well served by many devoted friends who, with prospects more or less excellent, are endeavouring to return to, or to enter, the House of Commons. Of the present Parliamentary friends of India there is not one whose seat is in serious peril. Mr Schwann, Mr S Smith, Mr J E Ellis, Mr W S B Maclaren, Mr Conybeare, Mr Seymour Keay, Mr Swift MacNeil, Mr Burt and others, are all reasonably certain of being returned. Mr Ellis may be selected for office, and the ranks thinned to this extent, but that, perhaps is all. Then, among newcomers, are Mr W S Caine, Sir W Wedderburn, Bart, Mr Dadabhai Naoroji, Mr William Digby, CIE, none of whom are fighting hopeless seats, but all of whom have a very fair prospect of success, – Mr Dadabhai not least of all if only his rival Liberal candidate retires before the nomination day, and leaves the veteran statesman-economist a fair field. Should the gentlemen named enter the

House, an Indian Party will, in all probability, be formed, whose object will be, not to embarrass Mr Gladstone and his colleagues and, of course, not to desert their Party on any critical occasion, but to ensure that proper attention is paid to the important interests of India. On the whole, though there is no excited movement of a public kind going on in the constituencies on behalf of our Great Eastern Empire, most excellent work is being done, and good results may be expected. Always supposing, however, that Indian reformers recognise *their* duty and see to it that the British organisation is properly maintained. There is no way of salvation for India save by the way of the British Parliament, and by adequate agitation and effort in England.

Four months later, in December 1893, *India* reported the progress of the Indian Parliamentary Committee. It was seen as a year of great importance in the history of India. Under the title of 'India In Parliament' it pointed with satisfaction that:

INDIA IN PARLIAMENT

The year which is now drawing to a close has been a year of special importance in the history of India. Looking over the records of the protracted Session of Parliament one fixes naturally upon the formation of an Indian Parliamentary Committee as a central starting point. For this work of organisation – which has already resulted in solid advantage – we are largely indebted to the initiative of Sir W Wedderburn. It was on July 27th that he and Mr Caine invited to dinner at the House of Commons a few leading members of Parliament with the view of forming them into a recognised Committee to watch the interests of India at Westminster. The idea was not novel. Others had realised before the need of associating India's Parliamentary friends in a compact band. 'You and I are,' says Thackeray, 'but a pair of infinite isolations, with some fellow islands a little more or less near to us'. What is true in this respect of the human race is still more true of individuals working separately though for a common cause in the House of Commons.

Twenty years earlier, thanks chiefly to the efforts of Mr John Dickinson, the India Reform Society was founded. Both of these organisations aimed specially at securing full Parliamentary inquiry into the government of India. In 1853 the charter of the East India Company was on the point of expiry, and the periodic stock-taking was at hand. In 1885, again, Mr John Slagg's motion to inquire into the Government of India Act of 1858 was only prevented by a change of Government. The present year saw no diminution, but rather increase of the need of special effort to obtain a full inquiry. For forty years there has been no stock-taking, and the present Viceroy is of opinion that 'to leave matters as they are means for the Government of India hopeless financial confusion; for the taxpayers of India the prospect of heavy and unpopular burdens, and for the country as a whole a fatal and stunting arrest of its development'. In these circumstances the time appeared to be opportune for the revival of an Indian Committee in Parliament which would not only insist upon the imperative need of stock-taking, but would continually watch and, if need were, direct the course of Indian affairs in the House of Commons. The scheme met with immediate success. A committee, of which Sir W Wedderburn MP was appointed chairman, and Mr T H Roberts MP, secretary, was formed. It seems safe to assert that July 27th, the date of this event, will remain a red-letter day in the annals of Indian reform.

But the formation of an Indian Committee is far from being the only fact upon which those who favour a just and sympathetic policy towards India can regard with satisfaction in the year's Parliamentary history. The return of Mr Dadabhai Naoroji for Central Finsbury has shown what Indian pluck and determination could achieve in a political contest in England. It remained for Mr Naoroji to turn his victory to account, and nobody who knows anything at all of the House of Commons will deny that he has discharged his duty with conspicuous ability and success. Mr Herbert Paul, who is not in the habit of using superlatives, paid in a recent speech, reported in another column, a remarkable tribute to the capacity displayed by Mr Naoroji in his great speech for the appointment of a Royal Commission. He was speaking in a language that was not his own He was addressing a comparatively strange and exceedingly critical assembly. Yet the speech struck Mr Paul and many others members as being one of the finest speeches to which they had ever listened. Nor is it as a speaker alone that Mr Naoroji has already won for himself a high place in the esteem of the House of Commons. On all sides he is recognised as second to none in devotion and disinterestedness and loyal effort for a great and worthy cause. It is to be hoped that India will, within a measurable period, return many native representatives.

By the turn of the century, there was an increase in the number of Indians coming to Britain as delegates to a variety of conferences. What they said was quoted in *India*, as were the remarks of Lala Lajpat Rai on 4 August 1905 on the tricky subject of Home Rule for India and its possible compatibility with loyalty to Britain.

That Home Rule for India is perfectly compatible with loyalty to Britain is a proposition that needs no insistence; it might, indeed, be argued that loyalty in any worthy sense compels Indians to desire it. The germ lies implied in the statute of 1833, in the Proclamation of 1858, and the other solemn declarations of authority to which appeal is so often made. The bureaucrats themselves do not openly repudiate it in essence; they see it plainly enough, and carefully avoid or thwart tendencies in the direction of it. Eventually, unless things be badly mismanaged on the part of the Indian people, Home Rule 'is inevitable,' as Mr Lajpat Rai said. There need be no dispute about that. The thing that we are specially concerned for is the practical proceeding for the accomplishment of the change. Evidently it cannot be done in a day. The contentions of the bureaucrats, too, are not to be waved aside: they are to be looked at squarely, calmly, and, as far as possible, judicially. The forces and the means, the men and the methods, are also to be scrutinised and tested. The bureaucrats may, and often do, govern badly; but, in any case, their task is a fairly big, complicated, and hard task, and it behoves those that aspire to take an oar to make sure that they have the strength and the skill to row. By the way, we must suggest that Mr Shyamaji's calculation 'that every man, woman, and child in this country takes £1 from the Natives of India, and that the Natives of India give them forty millions of pounds, for nothing' needs revision and restatement, or else justification.

Apropos the possible danger of India being invaded through Afghanistan, a speech was made by Lord Roberts and reported in the *Investors' Review*: *The Times* commented upon the speech which was quoted by *India* on 18 August 1905:

THE NORTH-WEST FRONTIER
LORD ROBERTS AS ALARMIST

The *Investors' Review* scarifies most properly the recent speech of Lord Roberts. It says:

Lord Roberts does not appear to be of the same opinion now as he was when he wrote that memorandum quoted by Colonel Hanna in his recent letter to *The Times*. In sounding that deliriously alarmist note at the meeting of the London Chambers of Commerce on Tuesday last he begged the people not to listen to anything that may be told them as to the impossibility of India ever being invaded through Afghanistan. India has been invaded no fewer than twenty-one times from that direction; he proceeded, 'and though I do not propose to enter into my reason today for the conclusion I have arrived at, I have no hesitation in giving it as my opinion that a twenty-second invasion would be a far less difficult undertaking than any of those that have gone before, unless we make up our minds to take the necessary precautions to safely guard 'the brightest jewel in England's crown'. He ought to state his reasons, seeing that the opinion he now expresses is entirely contrary to that formerly held and most ably defended by him. Does his lordship seriously mean to maintain that without our assistance in the shape of roads and railways driven through the mountain passes, it would be easier for Russia, crippled, bleeding, exhausted Russia, to bring an army of the size necessary to conquer India, with all the modern furniture of war required to maintain a successful assault through the Afghan passes, more barren of supplies now than ever they were? Did any of the former twenty-one invasions involve the dragging of heavy guns, of enormously heavy ammunition, and all the other appliances now required by a modern killing force, across mountains, through defiles, roadless and often waterless? If not, where does the analogy between the past and the present come in? It is to be hoped that the public is not going to lose its head over any such nonsense as this raving by the late Commander-in-Chief.

India on 24 November 1905 reproduced an article entitled 'Revived Suggestion of Reform for the United States of India', from a contributor to the *Investors' Review*.

THE UNITED STATES OF INDIA
A REVIVED SUGGESTION OF REFORM

An Anglo-Indian of large experience and of tried sympathy with the Indian natives (says the *Investors' Review*) sends us the following suggestions for reform in the method by which the Indian dependency is now governed – or, it would be more accurate to say, held down. The idea, he says, adumbrated in this memorandum 'seems Utopian today, but with extending education in India of the yearly growing number of her sons who are qualifying for the public service in all branches, this scheme or some scheme on similar lines will become inevitable, and at no distant day'. In that opinion we quite agree, and think that there is much more hope for India in development along the lines like these than in any such suggestion as that put forward by Mr Gokhale. He, we gather, would like to see at least six men elected by the natives of India, and sent here to represent them in the British Parliament. He does not know what that would mean. Under existing conditions, such men would have no weight whatever. They would be voted a nuisance, and relegated to the same position as the far more numerous Nationalist representatives of Ireland. India must work out her own salvation, and by passive resistance and continual educative effort strive to win domestic self-government.

UNITED STATES OF INDIA

A federation of autonomous, self-governing States, each with its own Governor and State capital.

A Federal Council, to which each self-governing State shall send two (or more) representatives.

The Federal Council to be presided over by a statesman nominated by the Crown. Race to be neither qualification nor bar to appointment either to this office or to Governorship of each State.

The State capital to be the chief city of each State. The Federal capital to be Delhi.

Each State to have sole legislative power as regards local laws; subject, however, to confirmation by the Federal Council in cases where such laws have more than local operation.

Posts, telegraphs, railways, Customs and diplomatic relations, either with Great Britain or with foreign States, to be reserved to the domain of the Federal Council.

Each State to have its own military force, and to be a separate army corps unit, both as to financial control and command – but to be liable to be mobilised as a Federal Army, under a specially appointed Commander-in-Chief, in case of a defensive war against attack by a common enemy.

The following might be the separate States contemplated in the above memorandum: Mysore, Hyderabad, Central Provinces, Punjab (with Scind), Madras, Bengal (proper), Burma (with Assam), Bombay, Rajputana (subject to regrouping, or contraction, or extension, as might be found advisable).

The franchise in the several States to be (for the present) limited to educational qualification. Election by ballot.

[The election of a half-dozen Indian representatives to the British Parliament is only one of Mr Gokhale's suggestions. His main plea has been for extended self-government, and he is keenly alive to the necessity of 'continual educative effort'. – Ed. *India*]

The Times for once showed understanding when it quoted Sir Henry Campbell-Bannerman on 23 November 1905, that, 'To secure a good administration was one thing, but good government could never be a substitute for government by the people themselves.' HS Swinny, quoting Sir Henry Campbell-Bannerman, wrote an article on 'Home Rule for India', published by *India* on 30 March 1906.

For a long time all proposals to introduce reforms into India, to associate the people more closely with the government of the country, and to give them more power in the administration of their own public affairs, have been met by the cry that such measures would impair that efficiency in administration for which our rule was famous. Now it may be at once admitted that efficiency and self-government are sometimes at variance, that modern democratic constitutions are not always favourable to the choice of the best rulers, and that in the past the Indian Civil Service has been fruitful in skilful administrators. Yet these considerations are very far from deciding the question at issue. One necessary condition of efficiency is a certain harmony between rulers and ruled. Without that the ability of administrators, instead of being exerted for the advancement of the community, will be expended in attempts at obstinate repression or ungracious conciliation. In such a position the party spirit which is held up to our abhorrence by the opponents of popular government appears in its most dangerous shape, and rulers and people enter the lists as contending factions. The Government is under the temptation to use the public resources as a means of silencing the public voice, and the people are prone to oppose the most ordinary acts of administration as designs of the enemy. In the end, even the administration of justice becomes tainted in the public estimation. The authorities are suspected of using the law to accomplish ends which are none the less factious because the party involved consists of officials and their hanger-ons; and their opponents in return cease to lend any active support, even if they do not show an open hostility, to the proceedings of the officers of justice.

Home rule in that country means a Government observant of, and guided by, Indian public opinion, and administered by men in whom Indians have confidence, whether formally elected or not. It means a government all the positions in which are freely open to Indians, and in which, therefore, Indians must gradually obtain a preponderance – for strangers are not likely permanently to remain in possession of authority, unless they are given some artificial advantage. It means, as Mr Gokhale so eloquently set forth in his Presidential Address at the recent National Congress, a Government which has as its goal an India as much the mistress in her own house as are the Colonies of Canada, Australia, and New Zealand.

If *India* was for Home Rule for India, then the *Pall Mall Gazette* was for the British Rule for India. *India* reproduced the *Pall Mall Gazette* article from an 'occasional correspondent' on 4 January 1907:

THE FUTURE OF INDIA
AN EASTERN'S CRITICISM

An 'Occasional Correspondent' contributes the following suggestive article to the *Pall Mall Gazette* of December 28:

The very remarkable address of Dr Rashbehari Ghose and others at Calcutta cannot, it is to be hoped, fail to arouse the interest and engage the attention of all Englishmen who really care for the British Empire in its real sense. The writer had the good fortune today to enjoy a prolonged conversation with a distinguished Indian scholar and statesman – for India produces statesmen, though she finds as yet little for them to do. The views he expressed are not only of supreme interest in themselves, but, since they amplify, and, in some cases, explain, the remarks and observations of the more eminent speakers at the Indian National Congress, they are well worth reading in connection with that event.

'I am a little afraid,' he began by saying, 'that the dominant tone of the Congress may sound in English ears as a warning note of what the political agitator will not scruple to call 'insurrection' – a desire to throw off what silly people describe as 'the British yoke'. I judge by the headlines in some of the morning papers. Now, intelligent Indians do not regard British rule in India as a yoke, in the sense, that is, of an intolerable burden. The conquest of India has been a blessing to the Indian people in more ways than one. It has been a civilising agency to some extent, though it should not be forgotten that we have, in parts of India, a vast civilisation still subsisting which is Eastern, which is, in many respects, our own, and which, though different philosophically from that which has spread over the West, is capable of producing a greater reverence for art, letters, and for true morality than we are able to perceive in England or America today.'

At this point I should state that my friend is, philosophically speaking, a Rationalist, and may, on the whole, be regarded as looking as impartially as a man can on the religious systems of the world, and with the tenets of most of these I know him to be familiar. I should also say that I have rather anticipated his remarks.

'Intelligent English people,' I said, 'fully realise the measure of appreciation which British rule has received at the hands of the more enlightened Indian people; but we are not blind to the fact that the proposals embodied in the speeches at Calcutta will be taken advantage of by many collocations of Indians, who, differing from you in sympathy and in race more widely perhaps, than he, will cheerfully range themselves on your side for purely religious and racial reasons. These are the people whose internecine fanaticism we have long held in the check, from whose semi-barbarity India has been spared by pure efforts alone, and over whom, as yourselves as interested parties you could never wield an effective sway. Talk of the kind recently indulged in can only serve to fire them with that sort of zeal for independence which in such a country as yours only makes for civil war. Is it not so?'

'The policy we propose to pursue precludes, I think, the possibility of that.' My friend smiled. 'You did not quite let me finish my preliminary exposition,' he continued good-temperedly. 'I spoke of the civilisation which British rule has introduced. I spoke of it as a blessing; it is not an unmixed blessing, because civilisation is but a relative term, and the Eastern mind, more speculative (more logical; you will forgive me for saying), is quick to see the faults of a new system while not the less ready to adopt whatever seems useful in it. You will admit that we have, some of us, been apt learners. We have taken readily to your language and your literature; we have become learned in your law, in your military system, in your sciences, particularly in those involving applied mathematics, and in medicine; but so far as your civilisation is based on Christianity and on a mediaeval European system of morals, you have failed with us – failed not only to convince us, but you have strengthened our primitive opposition.'

'Has not Christianity made great progress in India?' I asked.

'Progress?' I got the answer. 'Such progress as it has made in Africa – among the ignorant and the time-serving! Among those who desire 'respectability' among the Westerns and such occupations as the reputation for this quality may bring them. The brains of India have been either strengthened in their Eastern faith – Mahomedan, Buddhist, or Hindu – or they have adopted the agnostic standpoint. And can you expect it to be otherwise? The Western missionaries are rarely learned in their own theology, still more rarely than in any of ours. How can they make way, for instance, against a learned Mahomedan Imaam? The Mahomedan clergy (if I may use the word) are in reality scholars. You send preachers to cope with dialectician! The contest, my friend, is unequal! One more point before I pass from this aspect of the question – your system of morals. We see it at work in your own country. We do not see anything to astonish the pious in our system. We permit many things which you dub dishonourable, and which you render illegal, but to which one cannot trace the long list of illegitimacy, suicide, disease and insanity, which disfigures your social system and undermines your race. Most of these very special curses (as they seem to me) you have done much to spread in India.

'Now I have one final complaint to make before I speak of the immediate future. It concerns the men you send to administrate the affairs of our land. I am not speaking of such as hold the one or more high military and civil offices; such a name as that of Lord Curzon will be remembered with honour among us as long, perhaps, as there are those who care for our history; but I do speak of the sending in shiploads of young men, born, bred, and educated in 'Westernism', unschooled for the most part in the language or the culture of the people over whom they are to hold a petty sway, and, too often, wholly without any bent towards Orientalism or any aptitude for the excision from their minds of that intellectual tumour, the fixed idea.'

'What have you,' said I at this point, 'to congratulate us upon? What have you to be especially grateful for?'

'For the opportunities you have hitherto given us for the study of your methods, the educational facilities we have enjoyed – the equable system of justice, the freedom of the Press – in a word, for the chance you have given us to beat you at your own work!'

'So,' my friend added, with a touch of Eastern cynicism, 'you see you have, in this liberal rule of yours, rather tended to forge the axe and sow the hemp for your own ultimate extinction!'

'Has it come to that?' said I.

'Perhaps not yet,' he laughed. 'We only ask a trial. Perhaps you will send us better men, perhaps you will show us that you can still manage everything better than we can; but, we say, since we pay the piper, let us at least have a share in calling the tune!'

'Do you seriously,' I enquired, 'mean to suggest a Parliament, a Home Rule system in many-peopled, creed-divided India?'

'Oh no; not for ages! But we want a reasonable chance of competing with you for every administration position, and we want a proper representation at the India Office. We want these offices and the emoluments attached to them, if we can win them in fair competition. We pay for them, my friend! Let us see first, as between English and Indians, who will win; and then, as between India and India, what races, what creeds, will predominate. This, we ask, not as a favour, but as a right accorded in principle to every British subject. Do you fear the contest? Need you fear it? For, whatever the primary issue, the result can only be a contented and well-governed land, and such would prove to you a more valuable and more loyal possession than any or all of your much-boasted colonies. Is not the relation of friendship between pupil and master better, more delectable, and more reliable than the sentiments usually entertained amongst near relatives?'

'And do you expect to obtain any or all of these concessions from the present Liberal administration?'

'I hardly know what to expect. India is certainly not afraid of the party represented by the *Pall Mall Gazette* – India is an aristocratic country. The caste system which obtains over a wide area is the embodiment of a real aristocratic ideal; and where this system does not absolutely obtain, the feeling in recognition of which it exists – reverence for long lineage, pure blood, culture, and refinement, courage – is the dominant social factor in the lives of our people.'

The activities of the Indian National Congress was never off the front page of *India*, nor was criticism of the organisation published in other British journals. The *Spectator*, in the same mould as the *Pall Mall Gazette*, often received letters from friends of India correcting or criticising misleading comments. These letters were also published by *India*. *India* of 18 January 1907 reproduced a letter from Sir William Markby to the *Spectator*; it was seen as a corrective to the bias of the *Spectator* and other contemporary journals who were strongly critical of the Congress. It said :

SELF GOVERNMENT FOR INDIA
SIR WILLIAM MARKBY AND THE 'SPECTATOR'

The following interesting letter from Sir William Markby appears in the last number of the *Spectator*. It supplies a much-needed corrective to the mass of undigested reflections in which the *Spectator* and other journals have been indulging on the subject of the Congress movement. Sir William writes:

'Whatever the *Spectator* says on Indian subjects must always command the greatest respect, yet I cannot refrain from expressing a doubt whether in your last issue you deal quite adequately with the present situation. So far as you contend that it would not be possible in any circumstances to introduce into India any form of representative government no one need complain. This must be a matter of opinion. I would only observe that, after what has happened in Japan, it is difficult to be sure of what changes may not come about in other Asiatic countries. But what surprises me is the reasons you give in support of your contention, particularly where it is said that 'if we are to continue to give to India good government, we must give it her in the absolutist and autocratic form'. You apparently have no fault to find with the present government of India, but where is the absolute autocrat? I do not wish to quibble about words, and I know that all monarchs, even Oriental ones, are rarely, if ever, able to do exactly as they please. There is generally some class of persons – nobles, priests, or soldiers – whom they must be careful about offending. This is a check upon absolute authority; but the checks on authority in India are altogether different. They are checks imposed by the law. Not only is 'sloth and corruption' restrained, but everyone, from the Governor-General down to the lowest officer of Government, is bound to act within the limits of the law. If he exceeds these limits the Courts of Law can interfere. This is a power which is wholly inconsistent with 'absolute and autocratic' government. It is a power which the Courts of Law do not possess even in Republican France. Of course, from the point of view of the people of India, the Government may be called despotic, because, though the checks upon arbitrary power which I have noted above are a very substantial protection to the people of India against oppression, yet, whatever be the forms of government, the ultimate powers of sovereignty are absolute and unrestrained. The King and Parliament are a despotic power in England, and in exactly the same sense they are a despotic power in India. The true grievance of India, however, does not lie here, but in the practical exclusion of Indians from all share in this power, which in England is diffused very widely. In short, it is exactly the same grievance as is now felt by many women in England. To them, as to the people of India, the government is a despotism. And it would be a great mistake to suppose that this grievance is only felt by a minute fraction of Indians. Does the native Press, not only of Bengal, but of Madras, of Bombay, of the Punjab, of Lucknow represent nobody? Are we to imagine (as Mr Meredith Townsend once asked) that the Indian Press alone in the world represents precisely the ideas which its constituency disapproves? And are we for ever to go on saying that to share the government with Indians is an absolute impossibility? Surely it is not on moral grounds that this can be said, for we have already handed over to them the larger share in the administration of justice. Do we not pride ourselves on the efficiency and purity of our administration of justice, and do the moral qualities of the judges contribute nothing to them? Again, have we not established in a large part of India a system of co-operation between British and Native authority which, whilst it places the ultimate responsibility for good government on British shoulders, leaves to the Native Princes a large freedom of action? If co-operation in this form between ourselves and Indians (not as our nominees) is possible, why should a like co-operation in any other form be so absolutely inadmissible?'

To which the *Spectator* rejoins:
We pointed out that the antiseptic of despotism in India is its dependence on the free democratic Government of Britain, and we realised that this also involved the supremacy of the law. We were careful, therefore, not to describe the Indian Government as arbitrary, for that it most certainly is not. We admit, however, that despotic, non-representative, or non-democratic would be a better description of the government that we hold to be suitable to India than autocratic. If the ultimate power is not to be with the representative body, it is better not to establish such a body.

On the same page as the letter to the *Spectator* above, *India* reproduced another letter, this time published by *The Speaker* on 12 January 1907, by Mr S H Swinny whose 'Home Rule for India' appeared in *India* in March 1906. This apparently was his second letter to the journal. The editorial note appended to his letter asked whether it is 'seriously maintained that either the Mahomedans or the people of Madras are joining in the demand for a self-governing India'. The surprise is not about what Mr Swinny said, but that this should be printed by *The Speaker*.

'THE SPEAKER' AND THE CONGRESS
A FURTHER LETTER FROM MR SWINNY

Mr S H Swinny has the following further letter in *The Speaker* of last Saturday (January 12):
You ask, in the editorial note appended to my letter in your last issue, whether it is 'seriously maintained that either the Mahomedans or the people of Madras are joining in the demand for self-governing India'. As your previous statement was that the 'whole' of the Mahomedans regarded the movement with antipathy, and that Madras was 'practically untouched' by it, this question of yours is at least a retreat from the extreme and untenable position you had previously assumed. The Mahomedans are certainly divided in opinion, though there are some indications that their attitude does not so much imply hostility to self-government as a belief that more can be gained for their community by posing as the special friends of the British – an attitude warmly condemned by many of the most eminent Indian Moslems. As to the Madrassis, they are not behind the other provinces in zealous support of the Congress, but they have had no question so nearly touching them as the partition of Bengal has touched the Bengalees. The Indians are, indeed, a hard case, if their desire to have a voice in the government of their country is only to be recognised when they have been forced into a state of unrest by some intolerable wrong. In all countries until lately, in most countries even now, politics in quiet times interest only the more intelligent classes and individuals – a fine reason for excluding a people from almost all share in the management of their own affairs. But the last sentence in your note raises a still more serious question. You appear to agree with a reactionary newspaper in England (the *Spectator*) and a few revolutionists in India that the destruction and replacement of the present Government of India is the proper object to be aimed at by

all who desire a greater measure of self-government for that country. The Congress, on the contrary, avoiding discussions on the ultimate form of government suitable to their country, desire a 'gradual' enlargement of their liberties, a 'gradual' increase in the number of Indians holding high office, and a 'gradual' reform of their institutions, so as to give greater weight to the wishes of the Indians in the policy of the Indian Government. And they think that now, when there is once again a powerful Liberal Government, it is time to make up for the long period of stagnation and even retrogression, and by a decisive step show the Indian people that there is some meaning in Liberal principles, and as keen a desire among Liberals to extend the liberties of their Indian fellow-citizens as to preserve and augment their own. Finally, to those Liberals who are so struck by the goodness of the Indian Government I would recall the words of the present Prime Minster: 'To secure good administration was one thing, but good government could never be a substitute for government by the people themselves.'

To which the Editor replies: 'Mr Swinny misinterprets us, and if his statement of the views of the leaders of the Congress be correct our difference with him is not very serious'.

The success of *India* was complimented by the appearance of *The Indian Age*. It was first published in London in January 1908 with an editorial justifying its voice in Britain in the wider context of science, philosophy, art, literature and commerce. Its mission was to draw attention to the educational aspects of Indian life.

OUR MISSION

We all have our own ideas as to what is best for India in its present circumstances. Politicians are busy affirming that India must politically assert itself as a nation, either under the suzerainty of, or independently of, Great Britain. Others affirm that, before all things, commercial regeneration is the one thing needful. Others again, think that neither political nor commercial reform is possible until education has spread itself, and exercised its potent influence upon the mind and imagination of the people. For ourselves, we think that all are right and all are wrong. You cannot have political regeneration without education; you cannot have commercial life without political liberty. Nations cannot become great on a lop-sided basis – all-round development is a condition precedent to healthy national growth. Therefore *The Indian Age* will endeavour adequately to discuss all questions, whether political, commercial, educational or social. Our problem and our difficulty is to maintain a right sense of proportion.

Sketch writers on Lord Curzon were for ever denting his ego. It was said that 'Lord Curzon would have been a great man if he could occasionally have forgotten Lord Curzon. He has dwelt in a house of mirrors. Whenever he has turned he has met the dazzling vision of himself. Oxford was but a setting for one magical figure.'

'Parliament the stage for one inimitable actor; India the background for one radiant form in purple and gold. Lord Curzon has never laughed at himself. He has only admired.'

The *North American Review*, in its issue of July 1910 published the thoughts of Lord Curzon on the British Rule in India. *India* was quick in reprinting an extract of his contribution in its issue of 22 July 1910.

LORD CURZON ON INDIA'S VALUE TO THE EMPIRE

To the current number of the *North American Review* Lord Curzon contributes the first of two articles on 'British Rule in India', from which we take the following extract:

First, let me endeavour to state what India gives to Great Britain and the

Empire; for that she is a source of great material and political advantage to them has always been one of my favourite propositions. From her abounding population she has supplied England with labour for the exploitation of Empire lands in all parts of the globe. Few persons probably have any clear idea of the extent or variety of this service. After the abolition of slavery in the West Indies, had it not been for the supply of Indian labour, many of the islands must have fallen out of cultivation, and would probably long before now have been transferred by cession or secession to another flag.

The benefit is reciprocal, both in relief to the congestion of India and in occupation and wages to large numbers of poor men.

Not a war can take place in any part of the British Empire in which the Indian princes do not come forward with voluntary offers of armed assistance; and the fact that the native army was not allowed to stand by the side of the British in repelling the Boer invasion of Natal in 1899 was actually made the subject of attacks upon the Government in India – so keenly was the popular sentiment in favour of Indian participation aroused.

Only Lord Curzon could talk about Indian labour as if it was some kind of commodity of trade.

In the following issue of *India* quite the opposite views expressed in *The Times* were reproduced on 26 August 1910.

Letters or articles in *The Times* were written for two distinct reasons. One was to put right any forward arguments for or against India's right to nationhood. *India* very often reprinted arguments from both sides from *The Times*. First was the article on 'India and Self-Government' and the view of British administrators – and then the comments of Sir Francis Younghusband, as if obliging India for what it did there! This was a vain bit of 'sacrifice' of Britain!

INDIA AND SELF-GOVERNMENT
THE VIEWS OF BRITISH ADMINISTRATORS

In a leading article on August 17 *The Times* made reference to the general belief, lately repeated by Sir Henry Cotton, that the older British administrators looked forward to an India, which should be self-governed, and worked towards that end. 'But ideals change,' said *The Times* and there were a good many impossible ideals in the early Victorian era. Cobden dreamed of universal peace under the inspiring supremacy of the commercial traveller, and others wanted to 'cut the Colonies adrift'. We doubt, however, whether the majority of the rulers of India of those days ever cherished the views ascribed to them by Sir Henry Cotton. He takes more than one unwarrantable liberty with great names. Elphinstone, for instance, whom he quotes, declared that the time when Indians could stand alone was at 'an immeasurable distance'. Herbert Edwardes made his declaration avowedly contingent upon the wholesale conversion of India to Christianity. Failing that, he said, Englishmen could not 'get like cravens into their ships,' and leave India 'to become again a very hell of anarchy and war'. Malcolm held the ideal described, but his political judgment was not infallible, for he actually tried to demonstrate that meanwhile Company rule was the best. Macaulay's eloquent mistakes about India are now known to be legion. Sir George Campbell stood in the seventies very much where Sir Henry Cotton stands today – a solitary and not very convincing figure. The fact is that all developments in India in the direction indicated are bound, owing to the character and traditions of its people, to be exceedingly slow. A very great and powerful Indian once fixed the period within which India might be able to govern herself at two hundred years, and that was a very sanguine estimate. Meanwhile, it is an imperative duty for English administrators in India to abstain from encouraging false hopes and premature aspirations.

SIR FRANCIS YOUNGHUSBAND'S COMMENT

Sir Francis Younghusband writes to *The Times* as follows: 'To abstain from encouraging false hopes as to India being able to govern itself within any measurable distance of time is, as you, Sir, have so opportunely pointed out, an imperative duty. Not that it would be to our disadvantage if she were thus able to stand alone. If India were so strong and developed that we could, without administering the country, trade and reside there, invest our capital and set up business there as freely as we can in a European country, we should be freed from an immense burden, and the military, naval, administrative, and political energy and expenditure which we now put into India and the communications between it and England we could then direct to the development of our own country, our own Colonies, and our own race.

...We know that if we were not there Mahrattas would be fighting Mahommedans for supremacy, Gurkas would be raiding Bengal, and the Afghans adding yet another fiery ingredient to the strife, and that, even if all their differences were composed and the united Indians were strong enough to resist invasion by land, there is no possibility of their being able to raise either the money or the men to defend themselves by sea as well; because we recognise that an India with such a weakness would soon have to appeal for protection to one or other of the strong Powers of the world and so become, like Morocco and Egypt, an apple of discord among the nations, that practical men have come to realise that for many a long year, yet we must remain to preserve order in India.

Indians are developing rapidly under British rule. They might not flourish so well under their own.

If India gains self-government will Britain lose India? This was a constant 'fear' in the minds of those for whom the greatness of Britain rested on its control and possession of India. For others it was a matter of indifference or blessing in disguise as it was not worth the great expense and sacrifices Britain had to endure. An article along these lines appeared in the *Weekly Despatch* which *India* reprinted on 16 December 1910, written by Robert Blatchford. It was an unusual expression of 'good riddance' if India went.

WILL ENGLAND LOSE INDIA?
BY ROBERT BLATCHFORD
From the *Weekly Despatch*

We have spent immense sums in securing the safety of the route to India, we have fought several wars with the idea of strengthening and protecting our Indian frontier.

THE ENGLISHMAN'S INDIFFERENCE TO INDIA

Now the more I think about India and about Britain, the more convinced am I that we shall lose India. In the first place, it seems to me that the bulk of our people do not care a rush whether we keep India or lose it. Important as India has always appeared in the eyes of our merchants and statesmen, it has never gripped the public attention. Our people know very little about India, and care perhaps less. India has never interested them. Frankly, it does not interest me. I think I shall express the feeling of the average British citizen when I say that 'anybody is welcome to share my India'. I cannot feel about India as I do about Australia, or Canada, or New Zealand. If India is really worth the trouble and expense we have spent upon it, I feel quite sure that it is not worth the great sacrifices we shall have to make in the future if we are to keep it.

CAPTURE – NOT EVACUATION – THE DANGER

I write this article in the hope of turning the attention of a few of my country-men to a question which seems to me important: shall we keep India? Before we can answer that question we have to decide whether it is right to keep India, and whether India is worth the price we shall have to pay if we do keep it. Whether we keep India or not it is important that the British people should make up their minds. When I say that anyone is welcome to my share of India I do not mean that I am indifferent as to whether or not India may be taken from us. There is a difference between the idea of relinquishing India voluntar-ily and the idea of being driven out of India by some foreign Power. It may not be worth our while to fight for India; but it can never be worth our while to be defeated and deprived of India. Our evacuation of India would not trouble me; but the seizure of India would. I hope that is quite clear.

THE NEED OF AN 'UNDERSTANDING'

I think the British people ought to come to an understanding among them-selves about India while there is time. I have said that I believe we shall be unable to hold India. I will now give my reasons. I believe that India is disaf-fected. I do not think the mass of the Indian people are very loyal to our rule. I am sure that the British people are divided as to the wisdom of holding India. I mean that there is not that national unanimity as to the value of India which would be needful if it became necessary to make great sacrifices for the defence of India. There are two reasons why I think we shall lose India: because our own people do not seem really to want India, and because India does not seem to want us.

We are weak, indifferent, selfish, divided. There can only be one end of such a state of things.

It is incumbent upon the Democracy to make up its mind, and that quickly. But I believe that, do what we may, we are going to lose India in the near future.

On 20 September 1912 *India* reprinted 'An Imperialist View of India and Self-government' that appeared in the Imperialist quarterly, the *Round Table*. It was a long article headed 'India and the Empire' which is noteworthy for its honesty in recognising the Indian claim for self-government within the British Empire. The unsigned article took a sweeping view of Indian history from the Aryan times to the British period. In a somewhat remarkable thesis it stated that :

INDIA AND SELF GOVERNMENT
AN IMPERIALIST VIEW

British rule in India 'represents in fact, if not in democratic theory, the people of India'. The writer goes on to contend that it is 'the astounding moral ascen-dancy of the English' that has given them their position in India, not their achievements in making roads or railways or developing industry. These things can be paralleled elsewhere. Moreover, the British have been 'vigorous to a degree unknown in India before'. They have 'knowledge, public spirit and an impartial enthusiasm for the practical business of government'; and 'as a result the British are indispensable to India'. But the East is moving, the pace at which change is proceeding has been enormously increased by education, and Indians claim with ever greater insistence a larger share in shaping the policy of the Government. The writer proceeds:

'Their entry into the arena in which the British have held unchallenged sway is bound to have momentous consequences. Their claim is not like that of an uneducated mass of barbarians, as some people appear to think. Previous pages may have given the impression that Indians were all of one level, and that the problem of the British in India might be compared to the problem of ruling the negro tribes in Africa. Nothing could be more fallacious. India is full of highly-educated, thoughtful, and competent people. It has great ruling families comparable to those represented in the House of Lords. It has numberless country gentlemen exactly like the country gentleman of England. It has professional men of the highest qualifications and standing, lawyers, judges, doctors, many of them trained in England. It has a huge hierarchy of public officials holding all but a few hundreds of the topmost positions. It has a growing financial and commercial class. The potential influence of these men is prodigious. It has not been exercised in the past, because they have been traditionally indifferent to politics. They are rapidly ceasing to be indifferent, and their demand to be allowed to share in the control of public policy is one that cannot possibly be ignored.'

'If Indians are to free themselves from the reproach that they are wanting in public spirit, that they are unable to shoulder responsibility, that they are incapable of dealing fairly with their fellows in politics, they can vindicate themselves only by being allowed to prove in practice that the reproach is no longer true.' Ever since 1882 the experiment of limited self-government has been in progress. 'There is, therefore, in India today a system of representation influencing the action of Government at every stage. No one can attend the debates at the Imperial Legislative Council without being impressed with the high level of knowledge and debating power, and the sense of public responsibility, displayed by the Indian representatives.'

'India also demands progress in the political sphere, and progress means a change in the character of British rule. Here is the supreme problem. Nobody doubts that India ought to progress towards self-government; but nobody knows how the process is to be carried out, or what the ultimate end will be. The ideal goal is clear. It is that some day or other India should acquire the status of a self-governing Dominion, independent of the control of her own internal affairs, a loyal and willing partner with the other units of the Empire in their common concerns. Whether she will ever be able to attain complete self-government will depend entirely upon the capacity of her people to progress in knowledge and self-control.'

The process must, of course, be slow: it will be long before India can govern herself on democratic lines. Yet 'progress, if slow, will be steady'; and the problem is the same in essentials as that of the British Dominions, for they 'remain within the Empire solely because they wish to do so'. 'If in the future India also remains within the Empire, it will not be because we are strong or because we govern justly and well, but because we retain her respect and goodwill.' It is a profound mistake to imagine that India today is hostile to British rule: 'Only one thing can make a rupture inevitable – if the British in India or elsewhere should allow their policy to be swayed from the paths of equity and justice by pride of colour or race. The belief that we treat them as inferior or inherently incapable of development, not on their true merits, but because of their blood or the pigment of their skins, will unite all Indians, Mahommedans with Hindu, high caste and low caste, north and south, in revolt against our rule, as nothing else will do. If such danger exists it is to be feared rather from the Englishmen living in the other parts of the world than from those who know India.'

Finally, while we talk about Colonial self-government for India is to look far ahead, 'it is well that those outside India, who are ultimately responsible for its government, yet who only occasionally have time to glance at its affairs, should see where things are moving.' For 'to dam the tide would raise a flood which would overwhelm not only our rule, but India herself, in a torrent of desolation.'

The *Indiaman*, a weekly journal devoted to the affairs of India was first published on 15 May 1914, from London. It incorporated *The Overland Mail* and the *Homeward Mail*. Its first editorial summed up its reasons for being published:

NOTES OF THE WEEK

People rarely want to read about India. The subject is associated in their minds with dreary essays on India's problems or tiresome expositions of long administrative reports. *The Indiaman* has perforce to carry a heavy cargo, but in unloading it we shall endeavour to display it in as interesting and attractive a form as possible.

Our task, we grant, will not be easy. Only on Monday Lord Curzon initiated a debate in the House of Lords on a subject which gave full scope to his knowledge and eloquence. Yet even he failed to stir the public out of its attitude of habitual neglect. A visitor to the House expressed surprise at the emptiness of the Strangers' Gallery, and inquired of an usher as to its cause. The usher glanced at his order paper. 'Oh, it's only India,' he replied.

The launch of the *Indiaman* had the blessings and best wishes of Lord Landsdowne and Lord Ampthill and was whole-heartedly welcomed as a necessary journal to add to the voice of India in Britain.

To the Editor of *The Indiaman*
Sir, – I am glad to hear that you are bringing out an Indian newspaper in London, and I feel sure that it will be wisely and honourably conducted.

The public here is, as a rule, badly informed about Indian questions, and is apt to arrive at very erroneous conclusions with regard to them. *The Indiaman* will supply a real want, and I cordially wish it success.

Yours truly,
LANSDOWNE
Lansdowne House, Berkeley Square, W.

To the Editor of *The Indiaman*
Sir, – I have just received a printed notice setting forth the aims and objects of *The Indiaman*, and I hasten to assure you that I shall welcome the appearance of this new paper. I have constantly felt the need of some periodical of an unrestricted and entirely impartial scope which would enable those who have lived in India and who love India to keep in touch with Indian affairs. I am sure that if you adhere to the lines of the prospectus your paper will find many keenly interested readers, and I do not doubt that it will go far to promote that better understanding which you have in view, and which is above all things, desirable. I wish all possible success to your enterprise.

I am, yours very faithfully,
AMPTHILL
65, Ennismore Gardens, SW, May 14.

1914 was the year the First World War began. Britain was given loyal support by India – both civil and military. Questions of self-rule were put on hold. Testimony to India's loyalty came when the Indian National Congress deputation visiting England issued a letter endorsing full support for Britain. Mr Mohandas Karamchand Gandhi and Mrs Sarojini Naidu and several other distinguished Indians 'unconditionally' offered their services to Britain in its hour of need. The view of the Imperialists was that the war was not a British question but an Imperial one – and that the employment of Indian troops simply meant fighting for the life of the Empire.

There were others who took an objective view of the war and the part played by India. There was a passionate debate on the issue of India's loyalty and Indian aspiration. One who had the wisdom and benefit of being able to see both sides of the argument to weigh up the situation was Sir William Wedderburn. *India* on 15 January 1915 reproduced Sir William's thesis on the subject he wrote on the Common Cause, six months into the war.

Sir William Wedderburn emphasised that the issue of India's right to self-government was not forgotten; it was simply put on hold. Nevertheless, there was no wavering or weakening of the Indian demand. He explained:

INDIA'S LOYALTY AND INDIAN ASPIRATION
BY SIR WILLIAM WEDDERBURN, BART.
(FROM THE 'COMMON CAUSE')

No one can doubt that if India had turned against us in the world crisis through which we are passing, the great fabric of the British Empire would have been strained, even to the breaking point. Indeed, the position would have been serious if the response from India had been doubtful, or half-hearted; if there had been hesitation on the part of the Indian princes, who command the hereditary allegiance of the masses, or of the educated class, who control advanced public opinion. Happily there has been no hesitation either among the thinkers or the fighters; and India has shown 'a serious and unswerving loyalty,' placing personal service and her vast resources at the disposal of the King-Emperor.

If we ask why the princes and people of India are eager to stand by England in this time of storm and stress, we find that it is because they believe that – whatever its shortcomings may be – the British Empire stands, on the whole, for freedom, toleration, and progress. But it would be fatal to assume that India is satisfied with her political condition, and that, as regards reform, the time has come to rest and be thankful. The blighting influences of official distrust must be put away for ever; we must boldly carry to its logical conclusion the doctrine of trust in the people; and India must be welcomed to an equal partnership in a free Empire.

A CONTINUING POLICY

This is the only right – and the only safe – course to pursue; the only way to strengthen and perpetuate the existing good feeling. And the true note was struck by Mr Charles Roberts when, speaking in the House of Commons on behalf of the Secretary of State, he said that 'in the atmosphere of friendship and goodwill which unite England and India today there is surely a bright hope for the future: the common endeavour of these days will enable India to realise that she is occupying, and is destined to occupy, a place in our free Empire worthy alike of her ancient civilisation and thought, of the valour of her fighting races, and of the patriotism of her sons.'

'TRUST IN THE PEOPLE'

As regards the comfort of the people in their daily life, the remedy must be sought in decentralisation, with the development of local self-government, and the employment of voluntary unpaid agency in the districts and villages.

In the India Council at Whitehall the Secretary of State is dependent for advice and information on retired members of the permanent service, and in order that he may be master of the situation, he should have on his Council a due proportion of Indians representing independent Indian public opinion.

As regards the European crisis, we shall now learn the considered view held by India's unofficial Parliament. What that view will be, no one in India doubts. It will be voiced by the President, Mr Bhupendranath Basu, a trusted member for many years of the Viceroy's Legislative Council, whose pamphlet, recently published in London under the auspices of the Victoria League, explains, in the words of the title, *Why India is Heart and Soul with Great Britain*.

What we ask is, that the British people, being now convinced of India's loyalty, will give a fair and kindly hearing to India's aspirations.

In August 1921 another Indian weekly, *Hind*, was published in London with a banner 'Swarajya Is My Birthright'. It was to fill the gap left by

India. *Hind* was launched in order to continue supplying information on London affairs to Indians resident in Britain – and to the British public interested in India. The first editorial explained the situation:

'HIND'
FOREWORD

We feel that the state of affairs in India, both political and otherwise should be placed before our compatriots here through Indian eyes first. Once they have grasped that fully, they can see, with some advantage, too, the other side of the picture available here. But the latter will not make a substitute for the former. And thus there is all the more reason that *Hind* should come in the field to make up for the deficiency. There will be, of course, several other equally important local items of programme which we are sure the readers of *Hind* will find no less interesting. We have also reason to believe that this organ will go a long way to serve as a reliable agency for the supply of all shades of Indian views and news.

There is also a great majority of our countrymen, who visit this country for joining the educational, technical, and various other like institutions. It is a matter of common knowledge, that they are working under great disabilities. We want to assure them – one and all – that they can always count on *Hind* for the ventilation of their grievances, the redress of their wrongs, and the expression of their sane views. With us, it is but sound politics, that we must try to assist our young friends – our budding leaders and our hopes of tomorrow – not with an air of leadership, but with a real earnest spirit of service. And we can only hope that they will find *Hind* truly serviceable to them.

The measure of the success of *Hind* will chiefly depend upon the measure of the support we are able to secure at the hands of our compatriots in the British Isles. If every Indian resident in this country makes it a point to place an order for a copy of *Hind*, *Hind* will undoubtedly be a success.

GURDIT SINGH DARA

Dated, London, August 1st, 1921

There had to be some satire, some attempt to prick the bubble of British imperial conceit. The first issue of *Hind* did just that with a scene: An Anglo-Indian House in England.

From *Marhatta* (India)

Q Father what is India?
A A distressful country.
Q Why is it distressful, father?
A Because the Indians are fools.
Q Why are they fools, father?
A Because they do not know when they are well off.
Q When are they well off, father?
A Now.
Q Then why is there so much firing and shooting?
A That is due to the Non-cooperationalists.
Q What do they want to do?
A They want to manage their own affairs.
Q Is that very wicked, father?
A Very wicked indeed.
Q What ought we to do then, father?
A We must be firm.
Q Is that the right policy, father.
A Of course.
Q Then I suppose India is nearly settled now?
A Not quite. But we must be firm.
Q Why, father?
A Well, think how our prestige would suffer otherwise.

Q   What is our prestige, father?
A   Our honour.
Q   Why would it suffer, father?
A   Because people would think we could not keep the Indians down.
Q   Are we keeping them down, father?
A   Of course we are.
Q   Then is our prestige all right?
A   Quite all right.
Q   Father, what is repression?
A   It is another name for justice.
Q   Justice for whom, father?
A   For the Non-cooperators, of course.
Q   What is the meaning of repression?
A   It means violence for violence, etc.
Q   Do the Non-cooperators commit violence?
A   Invariably.
Q   Then do we have to commit violence too?
A   This is not violence.
Q   Why not?
A   Because it is done by the Government.
Q   What is the difference, father?
A   The difference is that the English Government has a united people
    at its back.
Q   Has the Government got that, father?
A   Certainly.
Q   Father, have the Indians ever managed their own affairs?
A   Certainly not.
Q   Why not?
A   Because they could not do it.
Q   Can we do it for them, father?
A   We must. It is our duty.
Q   What is our duty?
A   I mean we must set them an example.
Q   Is that what repression is for, father?
A   No. That is to show that this great Empire –
Q   Yes, father?
A   Which has just emerged from this devastating catastrophe –
Q   Yes, father?
A   Do not interrupt! – is not going to be intimidated by a numerically
    insignificant gang of moonlighters and footpads.
Q   (Admirably) You know that bit off by heart, father! Is that all the Non-
    cooperators are?
A   What?
Q   A gang of what you said?
A   Certainly.
Q   How clever a few men like that must be to subdue the whole country.
A   Oh, they are supported by outside influence.
Q   Who are supporting them, father?
A   The Bolsheviks, of course.
Q   What a lot of things the Bolsheviks seem to be doing, father?
A   That is true.
Q   What is Home Rule, father?
A   Complete madness.
Q   Why, father?
A   Because Mr Tilak invented it.
Q   Was everything that Tilak did mad, father?
A   Quite.
Q   What does Indian Swarajya mean?
A   It would mean the ruin of England.
Q   Why, father?

A Because the Indians would drive the British out of India.

Q But, father, surely this great Empire –

A You don't understand.

Q Which has just emerged from this devastating catastrophe is not going to be intimidated by –

A Cyril, your hair is a disgrace, go and wash.

    (Exit.)
  (With apologies to him to whom they are due.)

BG Horniman, the *enfant terrible* of the Press, had a lot to say about 'India's Way to Victory' in *Hind* on 10 February 1922. It was one of the fiercest attacks on the British rule of India.

Indians as soldiers in the war were valued differently to ordinary Indians as British-ruled subjects.

INDIA'S WAY TO VICTORY

BG HORNIMAN

India is on the eve of the greatest crisis which has yet occurred in her national history under British rule. For the past three years the British Government has gone from one blunder to another in its mad career of repression of popular aspirations, defiance of the national will and open violation of its own solemn pledges. Beginning with the Montagu-Chelmsford reform scheme, which constituted a glaring betrayal of the promise of self-determination so freely shouted from the house-tops by British statesmen during the war, it passed to the Rowlatt Act, a direct and insolent attempt to rob the Indian people of the very elements of liberty; then to the Treaty of Sevres, a flagrant breach of Britain's most solemn pledges to the Indian Moslems and the grossest outrage on their religious sentiments and principles, and finally to the orgy of massacre and atrocity perpetuated by Sir Michael O'Dwyer and his satellites in the Punjab, under the benign encouragement of Lord Chelmsford and his advisers. All this, let it not be forgotten, was the prelude to, and cause of, the situation as it exists in India today. No people with a vestige of self-respect, with the smallest concern of their own safety and progress – even their very existence – as a nation could or would have acquiesced on their national liberty and their dignity as a people.

The Government might have had peace two years ago, as they might have it today, had they been prepared to recognise the error of their ways, to redeem their pledges to the Mahomedans, to punish the wrongdoers in the Punjab, and requite the sufferers and to give the Indian people the control of their own destinies, to which they are entitled. They have preferred, in the alternative, a dishonest and criminal policy of make-believe and repression, and now that they are faced with such a stirring of popular revolt, that even the complacent organs of Imperialism have been shaken out of their sublime belief in the unshakeable stability of British rule, they are able to see no better way of escape from the fruits of their own folly than a further plunge into the stormy waters of repression, which already threaten to overwhelm the Empire of Great Britain in the East in a final flood of disaster.

Well let it be so!

India is prepared. If the British Government have steeled their hearts in a final resolve to go to the uttermost lengths in an endeavour to crush the manhood of India by brute force, the Indian people are equally resolved to make the last sacrifice in a passive resistance to this attempt to destroy them as a nation. But let the issues be clearly stated. Let there be no doubt as to the terms on which peace and friendship, even at the eleventh hour, could be obtained. Even at the last Lord Reading has been offered, once more, the alternative of a frank conference with the object of bringing about a peaceful settlement of the dispute. But he cannot have it on his own terms. Mahatma Gandhi and his fellow-leaders are not prepared to go into a conference in an atmosphere which would preclude the possibility of a solution. The Government must meet them on the terms of equality in an atmosphere free from the polluting influence of the measures of repression and provocation now in operation all over the country. And the leaders, now in gaol, whose freedom is essential to a discussion which shall be fully fruitful in its results, must be released; and the Government, on its part, must come prepared to right the wrong and to give the people, on such terms as their leaders may see fit to accept, the freedom they demand. The Viceroy and the British Cabinet have only to decide whether they are prepared to make this concession to what justice and reason demand, or whether they are prepared to face, on the other hand, the paralysis of administration and general anarchy into which the country will inevitably be plunged if they decide to go further with their policy of repression.

In the end the result will be the same – India must and will be free. Her people may have to pass through a greater agony than that which afflicted the Punjab three years ago. But the victory will be theirs in the end. That the sinister forces which have held the reins of power in India for so long are preparing an intensified orgy of tyranny has been apparent by the events of the past year. Nothing would please those who believe in the policy of holding India by force more greatly than the outburst of popular violence, which Mahatma Gandhi and his followers are pledged to resist and avert. From every province of India, stories come of intensive provocation, which can have no other object than the creation of a situation in which popular violence would provide the excuse for another experiment in the forcible repression of which Sir Michael O'Dwyer and General Dyer were such super experts; and there is no doubt that those who are urging the Viceroy and the British Government to an obstinate resistance against the Indian people are doing so in the belief and expectation that, should they succeed in provoking an outbreak of violence on a large scale, an immense expenditure of force will be necessary for the conflict that would ensue. Fifty thousand British troops have been released from service in Ireland, and that some of these are already under orders for India, while others are to be held in reserve, there is little doubt. Deliberate preparations are being made for the eventuality of a conflict in India on the largest scale.

But those who are looking forward to so gruesome an outcome of the challenge which has been given to the Government may, as we hope and believe they will, prove to have been gravely mistaken in their calculations. That the arrest and deportation or imprisonment of Mahatma Gandhi, should it take place, and a wholesale onslaught on the leaders of Non-Cooperation may be followed by sporadic outbreaks of disorder here and there is possible – the police will, no doubt, see to that. But the spirit and intentions of the people, as a whole, is very different. And very different, too, will be the problem which the Government will have to face. Peaceful, non-violent resistance is a form of opposition which bayonets and machine-guns cannot break down and hold in check. Lord Reading and his provincial satraps will have to face the development of a movement all over the country, already begun, backed by a supreme spiritual resolve and spirit of sacrifice which no physical force can hope to conquer. It will bring their government to naught and reduce to a paralysis their whole system of administration. In Ireland it was the spiritual resolve of the people and their refusal of co-operation with British administration and institutions, more than forcible resistance, which brought the final surrender of the British Government in its effort to force upon them foreign rule. In India there will be no force but spiritual force, and the will to suffer and sacrifice. And through them the victory will inevitably be won.

BGH

From his experience of being a second-class citizen in South Africa, Mohandas Karamchand Gandhi was now experiencing the same humiliation in India. Having returned to India in 1914 from South Africa, he found himself at odds with his rulers. If there was one lesson that he learnt in racist South Africa, it was to defy unjust laws with his unique brand of passive resistance. His non-cooperation in India grew out of his South African experience. His argument was quoted by *Hind* of 17 February 1922:

NEWS AND NOTES

I stated clearly that I am open to conviction, and that I would preserve neutrality concerning civil disobedience until the Government refused to yield to the clearly expressed opinion of the vast majority.

The alternatives before the country are mass civil disobedience on the one hand, and the lawless repression of lawful activities on the other. It is impossible to remain silent while assaults on innocent people and the looting of property are going on all over India – even though it is done in the name of law and order!

Gandhi encouraged Indians to volunteer for service in the British Indian Army, and raised an ambulance unit on his return to India in 1914 during the First World War. His sudden change of heart took place after the introduction of the Rowlatt Acts and the Amritsar Massacre in 1919. Thereafter British rule in India became his prime foe.

Hind, on 21 July 1922, published a poem by an anonymous Indian attacking the Rowlatt Acts.

INDIA TO BRITAIN

She shall escape – she shall aspire,
Bind her with your Rowlatt Acts,
Spurn her with your teuton arrogance,
Sweep her with your machine-guns,
Make her grovel like a worm,
Flog her like a wild bull,
Brand her as a nation of savages,
Paint her as a lunatic and fanatic,
Cast her ashes into the gutter;
She *shall* escape, she shall aspire,
Lighting, and shall light evermore,
The lives that are yet unborn.
Soul supreme, soul eternal – India!

The Indiaman, 15 May 1914, No 1, Vol 1

The 25 August 1922 issue of *Hind* enlisted all the Indian organisations in Britain. These had kept pace with the growth of the Indian population in the United Kingdom.

INDIAN COLONY IN THE BRITISH ISLES

21 Cromwell Road, the Indian YMCA Hostel, the Woking Mosque, the Putney Mosque, the London Dharmsala, the London Indian Association, the Indian Conference, the Bharat Conference, the Central Islamic Society, the Indian Majliss, at various University centres, the Workers' Welfare League, Indian Muslim Association, Indian Social Club, Parsi Association, Indian Information Bureau, Bengal Literary Association in London and some Urdu Literary Societies in Cambridge and Oxford. The list may not be considered exhaustive in any sense, for we have had to leave alone some institutions, with whose right titles and designations we are unfortunately not aquainted. Apart from these, there are also the resident Indian community, a number of practising doctors, and a host of starving Lascars. One and all are to be dealt with if we are to arrive at a relative and then collective idea of something like three thousand prominent Indians staying in this country. For each one of them to assume shortly the position of a leader, when we shall be looking upon him as an Indian leader first and an English servant afterwards.

Not all associations and societies were established and run by Indians. The British Indian Union was formed and organised by Lady Lutyens and inspired by Mrs Annie Besant. Not all Indians welcomed this. *Hind* published a critical view of *The Searchlight* on 22 June 1923:

It is an undeniable fact that all this talk of cultivating social relations and better understanding and mutual co-operation between two races – however grand the idea may be in the abstract sense of the term – must be wholly futile so long as this country is exploited and ruled with an iron hand by Britishers, that is as long as Indians continue to smart under the domination of British rule and as long as all the aspirations and rights of Indians are mercilessly trampled under foot by the bureaucracy. How can there be a better understanding so long as Indians continue to be alien in their own land? The only way to introduce healthy relations between the two countries is to make India free.

The Searchlight

Hind of 20 March 1924 takes to task Lord Oliver for his 'mistaken, ill-informed, ill-inferred and unjustified', utterances in the Lords:

WHY INDIA IS UNFIT FOR SWARAJ!
LORD OLIVER IN THE LORDS
Hinoz Dehli door ast

Another milestone is raised on the road to Indian Reactionary-Freedom. His Majesty's Government 'having themselves the same ultimate aim for India as the Swaraj Party,' would, none the less, refuse to translate it into action by discussing the position on a Round-table Conference with the Swarajists, although the position is causing 'a very great anxiety' to Lord Oliver. His lordship would rather discuss the terms of the 'Resignation' of the Government of India with themselves, than taking the Swarajists into confidence, who claim to force such 'Resignation' by virtue of the Resolution they have carried in the Assembly. The Council Resolution for the Round-table is already thrown to the winds by the Secretary of State. Nevertheless, he appeals to the Councillors for 'patience, circumspection, and co-operation in using the councils'. Among the 'causes of distrust' towards the Britisher in India, his lordship, however, has found some 'unfortunate things,' and discovered some 'injudicious language' too. The 'unfortunate thing', however, is a reference to the Resolution passed in the Lords, appreciating the services of General Dyer, who massacred at Amritsar about 2,000 unarmed Indian men, women and children. While the 'injudicious language' is an allusion to the steel-frame speech of Mr Lloyd George on the Anglo-Indian services in India, to increase whose pay and prospects (twice increased already during the last six years) the Lee Commission has already finished its tour of India. We are, however, glad to note that some discovery has, after all, been made into these causes by the Secretary of State! But he ought to have also discovered that a denunciation of crime is not the vindication of justice. Unless he were trying to explore the history of crime for his own political ends, we should expect him to go forward. Get the Resolution rescinded in the Lords. Bring the Punjab criminals before a court of law for trial. Remove the name of Dyer, as also of the Lt.-Governor Dwyer (who 'approved' the massacre) from the Indian Pension List. Failing which, to resign himself and establish his *bona fides* thereby.

His lordship, we are assured, has taken great pains to make some other discoveries too. And one of them is the 'mistaken, ill-informed, ill-inferred and unjustified' belief, on which the manifesto of the Swaraj Party is based. That in spite of this belief, described in characteristically Imperial fashion, the Imperial Government should still remain 'unequivocally friendly' towards the Swaraj Party, does indeed provide us with a still further discovery. The rest of the theme in the Secretary of State's sermon, however, is too well-known already. It refers to the 'disastrous religious and other differences,' 'mutual intolerance and antagonism,' Gandhi's philosophy and the 'excesses' of his followers, which we propose to discuss on another occasion. Then we are also reminded that a Capitalist Government, three years ago, were 'convinced that the establishment of full responsible government would be worse than perilous to the people of India'. And to this now is added the verdict of the Labour Ministry that it 'would be big with disaster,' if India were to have a Home Rule or Swaraj. It is 'impossible for the Indian people or Indian politicians to leap at once into the saddle,' says the Secretary for India. This amounts to saying that *Hinoz Delhi door ast*: That India is far farther from Indians yet. How farther or nearer are our homelands from us, we will deal at length, when we have had an announcement on the subject from the ex-convict of the Jerwada Jail. For it is with Mahatmaji that the final word rests.

In September 1928 *India* published a 'Song for Slaves' explaining that, owing to the inexplicable silence of Mr Kipling, a poet-correspondent has brought up to date *Rule Britannia!*, which he suggests might be used for community singing in India:

A SONG FOR SLAVES

When India first at *our* command
Arose from out of the azure main (*bis*)
This was the charter, the charter of the land
And guardian angels can approve this strain:
Rule, Britannia, and take out £sd
India never, never, never shall be free.

Hind was a short-lived venture. In January 1929 *United India* replaced *India* and *Hind*. It was edited and published by GS Dara, barrister-at-law from 31 High Holborn, London. The Goodwill Message for its launch came from CF Andrews who in his message said he hoped the paper 'will at all times represent faithfully the ideals of Mahatma Gandhi, which are non-violence and truth. I firmly believe that India's independence and unity are to be won by these weapons alone'.

United India in its first issue called Gandhi the Soul of India – as Naoroji had been the spirit and culture of India of the nineteenth century.

The Indian News, another publication, appeared on 30 May 1929. Yet another Indian organisation, as well as giving it the publicity, also set out its objectives and appealed for membership.

India's demand for self-government had now turned into a cry for freedom! The first editorial stated quite clearly:

EDITORIAL

Events in India have reached a stage when the greater knowledge and understanding of Indian affairs by the British people has become imperative. India is restless and discontented. She will no longer tolerate autocracy. The starvation and illiteracy of the majority of her people, their outraged self-respect, from time to time, have combined to be one of the hardest problems of our century.

Britain is ignorant of India. She has taken it for granted that her rule is for the benefit of the Indian people. She has hardly ever recognised an Indian point of view. She has made pledges to India which have, unfortunately, been frequently broken. Under her rule the soul of the Indian people has been crushed. India with her glorious civilisation and great knowledge is, today, an enslaved nation. The civilisation which she came into contact with in the British conquest has some vigorous elements in it. India, unlike Britain, has assimilated these foreign elements. But she refused to be absorbed.

While all this is true, we do not believe that the mistakes of Britain in India are acts of deliberate vandalism. But ignorance, where that ignorance affects the happiness of millions of people and tends to stifle the best in a people, is a

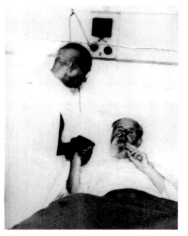

Mahatma Gandhi visiting Charles Andrews, a great friend of India, in hospital.

crime. If the British public knew the facts about India they would refuse to be party to the mal-administration and exploitation of India. The British Press has served India very badly. India has not received fair play. She has been almost invariably the victim of misrepresentation or a conspiracy of silence.

The Indian people will no longer tolerate the present state of affairs. They demand the right to self-government, for which India fought side by side with Britain, and made far greater sacrifices than any of the Self-Governing Dominions. Britain promised India self-determination. She has not implemented her promise. The majority of Indians are willing to be friendly with Britain, and to remain as equal and free partners in a future Indo-British Commonwealth. British policy has already driven a minority into desperation, who declare that the self-respect of India is incompatible with the 'British connection'. Britain has only herself and her purblind administrators to thank for the birth of this school.

Mistakes, admittedly, have been made. Let not their number be increased. It is to us a wonder that in spite of all that has happened in India, leaders of Indian opinion are still willing to treat with Britain and to meet her half way. This is more than South Africa or Australia was willing to do. India's moderation, the courtesy of her people, and her willingness to look at things from more than a mere national point of view is misinterpreted by British politicians and the Anglo-Indian officials as weakness on the side of the Indians. Britain will, of course, give way when she can no longer resist. This may be sound policy in business, but not in dealing with nations whose self-respect and liberty are at stake.

India's freedom is vital to the peace of the world. It is essential for the amelioration of her economic and social condition. It is essential for the prosperity of British business and British labour. The denial of freedom in India is reacting adversely on British freedom. India in revolt, or India suppressed, is, at any rate, a greater danger than India free.

India has made her demand. She has kept the door open. *The Indian News* supports that demand, and will draw the attention of the British public, to the best of its ability, to the real facts about India. There are millions of men and women of goodwill in this country to whom the Indian question means nothing. We think that such ignorance is a danger. We ask them to listen to India's case, and to insist that justice be done, in their own interests as well as those of civilisation. *The Indian News* looks forward to their support in its campaign for enlightening the British public on India, and in demanding that India's moderate claim to freedom as a self-governing country, like Canada or Australia, be immediately accepted.

A commission to India was led by Sir John Simon, to 'investigate in India the possibility of constitutional changes only', without consultation with India. The Simon Commission was boycotted by political parties in India in 1928, that is the Indian National Congress and the Muslim League. Clement Attlee, a backbencher, later to become the Prime Minister who put through the Indian Independence Bill in 1947, was one of the members of the Simon Commission.

When the Commission returned to England from India, a procession formed by the Indian Nationalists and the League Against Imperialists (British section) went to Victoria station in London to 'greet' them with black flags. The police intervened at Hyde Park Corner and broke up the demonstration. *United India* of May 1929 described the 'disturbance' between London Indians and Sir John Simon.

LONDON INDIANS AND SIR JOHN SIMON

Indian demonstrators and spectators numbered about 150. The police, foot and mounted, together with the plain-clothes, armed detectives, appeared about twice as many. They took up positions at 'strategic' points. Streets were patrolled, and even roofs of some of the shops and offices were held by groups of police. Not only the arrival platform was heavily guarded and barricaded, but the police were posted all over the station and outside, at the exit and entrance of the Underground Tube. Even access to the telephone boxes was stopped. The police came into frequent clash with groups and individuals. A thorough comb-out from the waiting throng of Indians was made, and several young men who resisted strenuously were carried bodily down the street. The black flags and banners, bills and boards were promptly seized by the police, torn up, or wrested from their bearers. On some of them was written: 'To hell with the Simon Commission,' 'Release our Prisoners,' and 'Complete Independence for India'. A number of young English ladies, who were supporting their Indian friends, were ordered to quit the place at once. They were all lining up along one of the streets adjoining Victoria station, behind the police squads. Notwithstanding this state of siege and battle array, the Simon Commissioners were spirited away by a side entrance, under heavy guard, thus leaving the demonstrators alone. Indeed, Sir John, the hero of a hundred Black-flag battles, has truly exhibited to his countrymen, the wonderfully courageous way in which he had all along faced similar Indian crowds that followed him from town to town and village to village.

As a sequel to the Indian demonstration at Victoria station against the Simon Commission, four persons were charged at the Westminster Police Court. Three of them were Indian students: Mr Nalin A Saynal, Mr Yousuf Md Dadoo, and Mr A Chandra Bannerjee, were charged with 'using insulting words and behaviour,' and Mr Bob Lovell, Secretary of the ICWPA, with obstructing a police officer. Mr Dawson, barrister defending, stated that all four would plead 'Not guilty,' and put in defence. They were released on their own recognisances.

Both as a reminder as well as a notice to act fast and faithfully, *The Indian News* of June 1929, boldly printed the resolutions at the Annual Conference of the Labour Party at Blackpool in 1929. They were:

Resolution passed at the Annual Conference of the Labour Party at Blackpool in 1927: The conference reaffirms the right of the Indian peoples to full self-government and self-determination and therefore is of opinion that the policy of the British Government should be one of continuous co-operation with the Indian people, with the object of establishing India, at the earliest possible moment, and by her own consent, as an equal partner with the other members of the British Commonwealth of Nations.

From Labour and the Nation: It (the Labour Party) believes in the right of the Indian people to self-government and self-determination, and the policy of a Labour Government would be one of continuous co-operation with them, with the object of establishing India at the earliest possible moment, and her consent, as an equal partner with the other members of the British Commonwealth of Nations.

The Rt Hon J Ramsey MacDonald MP, presiding at the British Labour Conference at London, 2 July 1928. 'I hope that, within a period of months rather than years, there will be a new Dominion added to the Commonwealth of our nations, a Dominion of another race, a Dominion that will find self-respect as an equal within this Commonwealth. I refer to India.'

In the same issue, *The Indian News* published an article by Annie Besant, originally written for *New India*, which she agreed could be used by *The Indian News* as a main feature. It was written after the General Election in Britain when the Labour Party came to power. Coming as it did soon after the fiasco of the Simon Commission, it made a number of interesting points regarding India's future:

BLACKPOOL TORY

INDIA ANSWERS

The subject of India was raised by **EARL WINTERTON, M.P.**, in the following motion :—

"That this conference, while faithfully pursuing the achievement by the Indian peoples of self-government within the British Commonwealth of Nations, with all the rights and freedoms enjoyed by other British Dominions, affirms that it is the duty of Parliament whatever happens to make sure that in any settlement which may be proposed the rights of minorities and of the Indian States shall be effectively safeguarded and the mission of Britain in India be honourably discharged.

"There is a hard, concrete, inescapable duty," he said, "laid on Parliament to see that in the Act setting up the new constitution there are proper safeguards for the safety, honour and welfare of the minorities.

"It is utter nonsense to say that in passing this resolution we should be pursuing the old British plan of divide and rule. The only time in her long history that India has been united is under the period of British rule. She can retain the unity in spirit and fact under self-rule only if the rights of the religious and racial minorities are safeguarded. There must be no dominance through Congress rule.

"There is a tremendous danger to be avoided—the use of British troops in a self-governing India as mercenaries to prevent armed conflict between Hindu and Moslem or between caste and other Hindus. Why is Premier Nehru, who has shown himself in two wars to be so bitter an opponent of the British connection, been so strangely silent about the date of withdrawal of British troops from India? Because he wants to use them for his own purpose."

MR. L. D. GAMMANS, M.P. (Hornsey), seconding, said that the recent settlement plan for India was not a settlement by agreement but a settlement by scuttling from our responsibilities.

"We are handing over India," he said, "to a minority party that stands for the worst form of class privilege the world has ever known. We are handing it over to men who were prepared to stab India, the Empire and the cause of freedom in the back at the time of their greatest danger and ours."

MR. DOUGLAS READ (North Norfolk), speaking as one who had spent 23 years in India, six of them as an elected representative in a legislature, said that as a pious hope this resolution would not do much harm, but it had a taint of patronage and superiority which took away its effectiveness and offended a great people.

The party must not go on with its old die-hard attitude, but realise that this new Dominion was worthy of us and worthy of good and kind treatment. He was an optimist and believed that these people were going to work out their salvation, but they wanted our help, trust and good will.

MR. R. A. BUTLER, replying for the executive, said that he had worked and fought for the granting of self-government to India and proposed to go on doing it whatever Mr. Read or anyone else might say.

As a party they had a moral position which was set up by the late Government from which he saw no reason to depart. This was that India should have the right to frame her own future destiny on the understanding that the ultimate form of government arrived at included the main elements in India's life.

MR. WINSTON CHURCHILL: I am glad the conference has passed the resolution about India. "The way in which the Socialist Government have handled this problem," he continued, "has been such as to give the vast masses of the people of India hardly any other choice but to become separated from the British Crown, which has so long shielded them from internal convulsions or foreign invasion.

"I fear that calamity impends upon this sub-continent, which is almost as big as Europe, more populous, and more harshly divided. It seems that in quite a short time India will become a separate, a foreign, and none-too-friendly country to the British Commonwealth of Nations. Indian unity created by British rule will swiftly perish, and no one can measure the misery and bloodshed which will overtake these enormous masses of humble, helpless millions, or under what new power their future and destiny will lie.

"At this moment, and in the presence of this unparalleled act of voluntary abdication in India, we are still ceaselessly abused by the Soviet wireless and by certain unfriendly elements in the United States for being a land-grabbing imperialist Power seeking expansion and aggrandisement.

"While Soviet Russia is expanding or seeking to expand in every direction, and has already brought many extra scores of millions of people directly or indirectly under the despotic control of the Kremlin and the rigours of Communist discipline, we, who sought nothing from this war but to do our duty and are, in fact, reducing ourselves to a fraction of our former size and population, are successfully held up to world censure.

PANDIT NEHRU: "Certain speeches delivered at Blackpool indicate a hostile attitude on the part of some leading members of the Conservative Party towards the interim Government of India. These speeches are irresponsible, full of malice, and calculated to stir up strife and prevent unity and settled government in India.

"A charge has been made that I am silent about the withdrawal of British troops from India, and that we seek to use them fo quelling communal disturbances. This charge, like much else in the speeches delivered at Blackpool, is completely false. We do not want to use them for quelling internal disturbances. It was our policy before we took office, and it is our policy now, to have the British troops withdrawn from India immediately, or at any rate with the greatest possible speed. We do not want them to stay on in India for a day. It is unfair to us and unfair to them to keep them here.

"I invite the leaders of the British Conservative Party to support us in these demands, and to help in giving effect to them in the immediate future. While we have expressed our willingness to co-operate with the United Kingdom, I want to make it perfectly clear on behalf of myself and my colleagues in the Government of India that there will be no co-operation with those who adopt an unfriendly attitude towards us or trifle with the independence of India."

MR. M. A. JINNAH: His paper *The Dawn* says the resolution on India advocates "in traditional Tory way, the Dominion Status for this country. It seems that all the changes in socio-political values, that the world has undergone, have failed to impress on them (the Conservatives) the need to revalue their ideas and conceptions."

The Indian Moslems "do not lag behind anybody in demanding complete Independence for India, and will not be satisfied with anything else. Die-hard Tory jingoism in relation to India has robbed them considerably of the goodwill of this country. Their sympathy for the Minorities, genuine though it may be, lacks convincing force against the background of their undying Imperialism."

SHEIKH ABDULLAH: The Muslim Nationalist leader and the Vice-President of All-India States Subjects' Conference (Pandit Nehru is the President), was sentenced to three years' imprisonment by a judge in the Kashmir State on charges of "sedition." S. Mohamad Abdullah and his three colleagues went on hunger strike in jail. At the intervention of the Director of Medical Service and Prisons, the strike is now given up.

CALCUTTA INQUIRY: Sir Patrick Spens, Chief Justice of India, in opening the inquiry into Calcutta riots, stated that he had requested and obtained "very special powers" to inquire into conduct of members and officials of Bengal Muslim League Ministry. More than 6,000 people are awaiting trial on charges arising from the riots.

The report of the Conservative Party conference in Blackpool – with comments by Pandit Nehru and Mr Jinnah – from *United India*, November 1946.

'THE INDIAN NEWS'
13 JUNE 1929
WHERE DOES INDIA STAND?
BY ANNIE BESANT, DL

The Report of the Parliamentary Commission, headed by Sir John Simon, cannot be ignored by the Parliament to which the Report is to be presented, and that it may even be probable that a Labour Government may be willing to submit that Report, *together with the Nehru Report, and any others that may have been made*, to a Joint Committee of Lords and Commons, associating with it a Committee of leading Indian representative politicians, for examination and report to Parliament.

Many of us are prepared to negotiate with the Labour Government, in which are many good friends of India, seeing that the Labour Party has had Indian Self-Government as part of its programme for many years, and that its Head, the Rt Hon. Mr Ramsey MacDonald, is an ancient supporter of India's claims. Moreover, a few months ago he expressed a hope that the addition of a new Dominion within the Empire was a matter of months rather than of years, and the Congress demand of Dominion Status before the end of this year exactly chimes in with that gallant and generous hope.

Ramsey MacDonald

India and Britain in 1929 were at cross purposes. Britain wanted to keep India as long as possible. India wanted to be free of the British yoke as soon as possible. On 31 December a resolution was passed by the Indian National Congress declaring complete independence for India with the hoisting of the tricolour. The President of the Indian National Congress read the resolution: 'We believe that it is the inalienable right of the Indian people, as of any other peoples to have freedom'. In December 1929, *United India* stated:

INDIA AND ENGLAND ON CROSS ROADS

The feverish activity of 1921 is indeed wanting still. But the desire for freedom is more widespread. Mass awakening is much greater, and the hatred against alien rule has gone still deeper.

Indian nerves have been rendered over-sensitive by a prolonged history of broken pledges and dishonoured promises at the hands of English Imperialists. As if this were not enough, untold harm to the cause of reconciliation has been done by letting loose the flood gates of immeasurable hostility against India, both in Press and on platform.

The discussions in English columns have ranged over familiar grounds: Our 'Sacred Mission' in India, 'Our position as Trustees of the countless natives,' the 'anarchy in India when we left her shores,' and other made-to-order phrases, that we are all so very familiar with. It is seldom that a day has passed without some one or other organ uttering some sort of fresh libel seeking to justify the prolongation of the political servitude in that unhappy land known as India. The millionaire Press in this country has never been louder in insults directed against India as now. In fact, everything Indian has been held up to contempt and ridicule. The issue of Indian freedom came in for an open attack at almost every point where it was found assailable. The *sati* and the *untouchability* have been specially selected for a frontal attack in the belief that these two systems are specially vulnerable.

3 January 1931 saw the launch of yet another pro-Indian journal from London, the *Indian and Colonial Journal*. The title was different but the message was the same, as conveyed by the previous publication: *Freedom*. The editorial summed up the purpose and policies of its publications:

EDITORIAL

With the first issue we send our greetings to all the people in India, the Colonies and their sympathisers in this country and all over the world. We desire to make this journal an organ that shall express the demand for independence of India and the Colonies. The need for a publication of this nature is very great at this moment. It is becoming more and more manifest that the political and economic freedom of India and the Colonies is very closely linked. It is our earnest desire that individuals and organisations carrying on a struggle for freedom in all parts of the world will make this paper their own organ. Our columns will always be open to express the needs and aspirations of all subject peoples. Authentic local news and short articles from all parts will always be welcomed. By publishing this paper in the heart of the Empire we desire and hope to bring together and unite the people in their common struggle for independence and freedom. This journal is not subsidised or controlled by any organisation or any party and is, therefore, free to express the views of its readers without reservation. We have started in the present small size, but we confidently hope to increase the size and scope of this publication. We urge and request our friends and supporters in England, India, the Colonies and all other parts to help us by writing in our journal, themselves subscribing to it, sending us a list of prospective subscribers and obtaining new readers.

At the time of the Round Table Conference, a new journal, *India Bulletin* was published from London on 2 February 1931. The cry now was 'India has had enough of British Misrule – get out'.

This new tone was in contrast to the relatively soft approach of the Naoroji days. Be that as it may, *India Bulletin*, proclaimed an all-out attack on the British Raj with a message: 'Hands off India'.

'INDIAN BULLETIN' · 1 FEBRUARY 1932
OUR OBJECT

Our object is to awaken England and to attack the century-old prejudices and ignorance which prevail among Englishmen in regard to India. The time has come when Britain must understand India. Otherwise she will be led to endorse a repressive policy which will not only be a denial of British tradition, but will end all trade connections between the two countries. India's destiny is of vital importance to people in this country. By unwise action in India, not only may the present connection end in one of the greatest failures of history, but also all chances of the revival of British prestige in the world will be shattered.

India wants her freedom. She wants to be rid of the exploitation which has continually impoverished her during the past 150 years, and which is leading to a revolt of the starving masses.

India wants to govern her own destiny. She has a civilisation which dates back thousands of years. She wants self-expression and self-control. Can any Briton deny these legitimate rights?

What then are the obstacles to self-government for India? The general British public is sympathetic to India's aspirations, but it doubts the ability of Indians to govern themselves. In English schools boys and girls are taught to consider themselves superior in intelligence. False press propaganda further strengthens these prejudices and magnifies the difficulties in the way.

It is our intention to show that the various objections raised to self-government in India are based on ignorance and on wrong information. We would convince the best minds in this country that the only way of avoiding a disaster in India is to let India choose her own path. We shall prove from official documents how the country has been misgoverned under British rule, in order to benefit the few Britishers who have stakes there. We shall indicate how close study reveals that self-government for India will in the long run be to the advantage of this country.

We shall, further, point to the significance of the non-violent movement in India: how under Gandhi's saintly leadership India is reviving some of her best traditions and fighting with clean weapons. The West has replied to this moral idealism of the East by employing methods of savage terrorism to crush it. With machine guns, bombing aeroplanes and bamboo sticks, Britain is proclaiming in India that 'Might is Right'. This force is being employed under the name of 'Law and Order'; but no amount of terrorism can suppress the awakened spirit of a people.

People in this country are kept in ignorance of what is being done in their name. We believe that if Englishmen knew and understood what is happening, for very shame they would force their government to put an end to those barbarities. Against us is the Censor and the British Press. We, however, believe that the truth will make itself known, in spite of all the engines of perversion. In these columns the strictest attention will be paid to the truth, and the authenticity of the statements made.

We urge all friends of India to help us to make the truth about India known. Circulate this *Bulletin* amongst your friends and help us to get subscriptions. Remember that in the present struggle in India, the whole moral tradition of England is at stake. Do not let your friends justify an immoral policy in India. Let public opinion rouse itself to save Britain from the blind folly of her statesmen.

Winston Churchill, a staunch imperialist and opponent of Indian nationalism, spoke from the platform of the Indian Empire Society. In a special Jail Number, *India Bulletin* of June 1932 was quick to point out that Mr Churchill's success would be short-lived; his hope that 'sooner or later you will have to crush Gandhi and the Indian Congress and all they stand for' was not going to happen. In fact, it said, 'sooner or later an Indian agreement will have to be reached with Mahatma Gandhi and the Indian National Congress'.

'INDIA BULLETIN' · THE JAIL NUMBER
MR CHURCHILL HAS TRIUMPHED – BUT FOR HOW LONG?

As time goes on, the truth of this statement will become apparent even to the hard-baked bureaucrats. They ought never to have closed their eyes to this inevitable end. But those who govern India remain in such isolation from the people, they hold so much irresponsible power in their hands and the machinery of the Government is so well organised, that an arrogant administration can easily over-estimate its capacity of imposing its will. It forgets that the sanction of the most autocratic and powerful government in the world rests, in the end, on the consent of the governed. Mahatma Gandhi claimed in London that 85 per cent of the masses were behind the Congress.

The brutality inflicted on the Congressmen is making martyrs of them and is bringing more and more people into the active line of resistance. Every week's reports from India confirm this impression. Before long, the Government will realise that though it had driven the Indian movement underground, the people are more than ever attached to Congress.

Mr Churchill likes using phrases which smack well. He was naively unaware that he was talking utter nonsense when he advocated the crushing of 'Gandhi and the Indian Congress and *all they stand for*'. It is not sufficiently known here that Congress is the most progressive force in India today. It is not merely a political body, but it has made strenuous efforts at social reform and economic uplift of the masses.

To try to crush the Congress is to crush the renascent forces which are bringing a new nation into being.

During the coming troublous months, while politicians may be making compromises, which will not work, we shall steadily advocate a settlement that will be acceptable to the Congress. Indians feel that they must be really masters within their own house; nothing else will satisfy them.

Gandhi visited London for the last time when he came for the Round Table Conference in the winter of 1931. The Press and news film-crew followed him around in London. Naturally his activities were reported and relayed in India. Whatever the motive, a ban was put on showing the films of his stay in Europe. In February 1933, *India Bulletin* gave the news under the heading of:

BAN ON FILMS ON MR GANDHI – BOMBAY ORDER

The following films dealing with some incident of Gandhi's stay in England and his activities in India have been banned in Bombay Presidency by the Board of Film Censors, according to a notification published in the *Bombay Government Gazette* of December 1932.

1. 'Gandhi in England' produced by the British Screen News Company.
2. 'Gandhi sees the King', produced by the British Screen News Company.
3. Gandhi's activities in England.
4. Epoch-making voyage of Mahatma Gandhi to England.
5. Mahatma Gandhi in London.
6. Gandhi's visit to Lancashire.
7. Arrival of Mahatma Gandhi in London.

Monica Whatley, British sympathiser, joined one of the Indian organisations, the India League. She was a member of its delegation to India and gave her first hand report to *India Bulletin* for its issue of February 1933. She began by asking: 'Must England Lose India?'

'MUST ENGLAND LOSE INDIA? BY MONICA WHATELY (MEMBER OF THE INDIA LEAGUE DELEGATION)

Must England Lose India? is the title of a book, in which the writer, Lt-Colonel Osburn, shows in a very striking way that this country and India are at the parting of ways. Those of us who have just returned from an investigation in that country cannot fail to realise that morally England has already lost India. Rule by Ordinance has destroyed any feeling of respect for British justice – and police excesses, any belief in Britain's love of fair play. Since 1917 this country has promised to do justice to India – today official figures give the number of political prisoners as twenty thousand, while the great Nationalist organisation of Congress tells us there are more than double that number in the Indian jails. Wherever I went, on my 12,000 mile journey through that vast country, I was told the story of jails crowded – not with convicts, but with men and women, boys and girls paying the price that Britain demands for freedom. The morning that our delegation arrived in Bombay we were told that Miss Slade, an English woman and disciple of Mahatma Gandhi, had been arrested on her way to meet us. We at once got into touch with Sir Patrick Kelly, the head of the police, and asked of him permission to see Miss Slade, who was at that time an untried prisoner. Permission was categorically refused, in spite of the fact that I pointed out to Sir Patrick that such a refusal would be bound to create a bad impression in England, where a prisoner is innocent in the eyes of the law until tried and proved guilty.

The fact that a whole nation is suffering as India is doing under British rule by Ordinance – that in spite of the most savage provocation, the people in the main remain non-violent, and are carrying on their fight for freedom without arms, and without hatred – speaks volumes for Mahatma Gandhi's teaching.

The India League Delegation, of which I was a member, wanted to see the inside of the Indian prisons, about which we heard such terrible stories, but in the majority of cases we were refused permission.

These fighters for India's freedom are not criminals, but doctors, professors, judges, barristers, teachers, merchants, landowners, students. I should say the greater number are drawn from the professional classes, though the simple villagers have also gone in their thousands. It is a marvellous thing, that though the Indian patriot knows what he, or she, will have to face, once locked away behind those prison walls – they face it over and over again. But their willingness to suffer does not take away from us our responsibility for what is done by the Prison Authorities, who must account for their actions – not to an Indian Administration, but to a British.

If we do not want to lose India, our policy must be changed – before it is too late – we must hold out the hand of friendship, and ask India to forgive and forget.

India Bulletin was published as the 'Organ of the Friends of India'; its motto was 'Seek Truth'. When others spoke truth, the *Bulletin* was quick to quote and comment on it, as it did on H G Wells' opinion of England's work in India, in its issue of March 1934, titled 'The Great Failure'.

THE GREAT FAILURE

'The English rule in India is surely one of the most extraordinary accidents that has ever happened in history. We are there like a man who has fallen off a ladder on to the neck of an elephant, and doesn't know what to do or how to get down... In some manner we shall have to come out of India. We have had our chance, and we have demonstrated nothing but an appalling dullness of our nation's imagination. We are not good enough to do anything with India.'

India Bulletin did not agree and argued that:

The going of the East India Company to India might have been an accident – (though adventurers of several European nations were busy over a number of years trying to find a suitable sea route to India) but the British conquest cannot be regarded as such. It took the East India Company hundred years of hard fighting and piece-meal consolidation to create an Empire in India, and it was done with great deliberation. Nor can we agree with H G Wells that, having got onto the elephant's neck the Britisher does not know how to come down. The trouble is that he does not want to get down.

Mr Wells, however, puts his finger on the weak spot of the British rule. The British as a race lack in imagination, and this has been all the more palpable when dealing with a highly sensitive people. The Britisher has failed to understand an Indian; that is the great failure. With the best intentions in the world, let us suppose, he is ignorant of India's culture, and he prefers to remain so. He has cared little about India's previous history and has tried to create England in India on a larger scale disregarding the genius of the people.

But can a Britisher claim to have acted in India with the best intentions? The chief object in holding India is profit. Human beings act from mixed motives, but without this factor of economic gain Britishers would not hang on to India for a single day.

And what have they not done to retain their control? They have disarmed the people, demoralised the nation, created factions and often crushed a new urge to life and constructive efforts.

The Government has deliberately chosen to join hands with the reactionaries instead of the reformers in order to keep its political hold on India. By the very nature of its alliance it must discountenance all progressive forces in the country. That is the great failure of England's political mission in India. Instead of relying on the consent of the governed, the Government is relying on force. Instead of speeding India's progress, it is holding back the natural forces of evolution. Can there be a worse commentary on British rule?

After the necessity of having the symbol of nationalist movement in the form of a flag, there were now in 1935 discussions about the national anthem. The discussions had to be held in 'secret' lest the Government found it out. In fact the provincial governments had asked its servants not to pay respect to India's national anthem, the *Vande Mataram*. The governments sent a circular asking its servants not to participate in the singing of the song or to stand up as a mark of respect.

The *India Bulletin* of April 1935 went on to explain and expose the absurd instructions of the Government, tantamount to being ludicrous:

THE INDIAN NATIONAL SONG AND THE GOVERNMENT

The Home Secretary argued that India's national anthem could not be different from that of England! If at all, however, people want to sing it, let them do so after *God Save the King* had been sung.

Then again, Mr Bell [Home Member of Bombay] would have the *Vande Mataram* song sung sitting. He thinks it absurd of Indians to glorify it as their *National Song*! Indeed, Indians are a race of incorrigibles. Bell, and all well-wishers of his ilk, have repeatedly asked Indians not to be foolish and love their own national flag and national anthem! What an idea! India to have a national song and a national flag! It is not in their interests to indulge in such luxuries! It is not good for them! So the Government of Bombay has issued the fiat!

Is it not ridiculous and childish to issue a circular like that? *Vande Mataram* is a song which was originally composed by Bankim Chandra Chatterji, himself a Government servant. Since 1906 the song has received extraordinary currency and is accepted as the national song by all sections of Indians. Hindus and Mahomedans sing it with equal fervour and devotion. In 1908 the Government banned it, proclaimed it seditious and sent young men to jail for singing it. The song survived all persecution. In 1930–31 at the height of the Civil Disobedience Movement the *Vande Mataram* had become at once the solace and the inspiration of millions. Men, women and children gladly went through unspeakable repression singing the song.

Whether the Government like it or not, *Vande Mataram* has come to stay. The circular in question only shows the pettiness of British rulers in India. It also serves to show the peculiar methods the Government are using to placate public opinion in India.

Vande Mataram, by Bankim Chandra Chatterji was translated from Bengali to English by Sri Aurobindo. *India Bulletin* of April 1935 reproduced the whole version of the 'controversial' song that the Government in India was so irrational and irritated about. Their sensitivity to such a harmless song showed how terrified they were with the slightest show of unity – lest India runs away from its iron fist.

VANDE MATARAM
By Bankim Chandra Chatterji

Mother I bow to thee!
Rich with thy hurrying streams,
Bright with thy orchard gleams,
Cool with thy winds of delight,
Dark fields waving, Mother of Might,
Mother free.
Glory of moon-light dreams,
Over thy branches and lordly streams,
Clad in thy blossoming trees,
Mother, giver of ease,
Laughing low and sweet!
Mother, I kiss thy feet,
Speaker sweet and low!
Mother, to thee I bow.
With many strengths who art mighty and stored
To thee I call, Mother and Lord!
Thou who savest, arise and save!
To her I cry who ever her foemen drove
Back from plain and sea

And shook herself free.
Thou art wisdom, thou art law,
Thou art heart, our soul, our breath.
Thou the love divine, the awe
In our hearts that conquers death.
Thine the strength that nerves the arm,
Thine the beauty, thine the charm.
Every image made divine
In our temples is but thine.
Thou art Durga, Lady and Queen,
With her hands that strike and her swords of sheen.
Thou are Lakshmi lotus-throned
And the Muse a hundred-toned.
Pure and perfect without peer
Mother, lend thine ear.
Rich with thy hurrying streams,
Bright with thy orchard gleams,
Dark of hue, O candid fair
In thy soul, with jewelled hair
And thy glorious smile divine,
Loveliest of all earthly lands,
Showering wealth from well-stored hands,
Mother, Mother, mine!
Mother sweet, I bow to thee,
Mother great and free!

1936 was not a good year for Britain. It had to cope with the abdication crisis – as well as to put up with the barrage of home-grown criticism of its management of India. And if that was not enough, Gandhi was becoming a real irritation. His vast following in India was as unwelcome as it was effective. Then there were those like Laurence Housman, President, Friends of India, who took the theme of 'India and Peace' in his *India Bulletin*. To be on the side of India was to be against the Government. Housman had previous experience of aiding another freedom movement, that of women's suffrage. This provoked the hostility of some of his friends.

'INDIA BULLETIN' · OCTOBER – NOVEMBER 1936

INDIA AND PEACE

By Laurence Houseman

When I presided at the meeting of welcome given to Mahatma Gandhi when he came to London for the Round Table Conference; and in my remarks as chairman said that our attitude toward India should be that of 'unconditional good-will' not dependent on good behaviour, or on meek submission, officially described as 'loyalty', to a form of Government which had not the free consent of the people.

It happened rather amusingly that just when two friends had given me a patriotic scolding for keeping such bad company, the Mahatma had gone by invitation to Buckingham Palace to meet the King; and I suggested that it was rather absurd to tell me that company which was good enough for the King was not good enough for me. It was a short way of shutting two foolish mouths, but I knew as a matter of fact that Gandhi had only gone reluctantly, and as an act of courtesy, and that his acceptance of the invitation did not mean either loyalty or allegiance.

That representative statement of facts which leaves the average Englishman quite unashamed, and which even has his general approval, quite decided me on which side I must align myself. To the fundamental claim of India for self-government and independence, sporadic or even organised terrorism makes no difference. It did not in the case of Ireland: it cannot in the case of India. The doctrine of racial superiority as a justification for racial dominance and the imposing of our ideas of Government on races which would far rather govern themselves, becomes more and more a superstition in proportion to the standard of civilization to which we try to apply it. Toward India, with its ancient civilisation, it becomes fantastic.

As regards the Peace Movement, of which Mahatma Gandhi is the greatest living exemplar, I have come to see that it is no use saying you believe in Peace, unless you cease to believe in War. Any belief in War as an ultimate remedy vitiates the whole process of peace-preparation – reduces it indeed to foolishness.

More and more I have come to recognise that the problem of World-peace is closely bound up with the problem of India; and that until we have the heart to admit India's right to full freedom we shall not have the heart for a full Peace-policy. And it is because Mahatma Gandhi stands for each of those policies in its fullness with uncompromising honesty, that I continue to regard him as the best politician of our day; and even if years of failure to achieve those two great ends still lie before us, I shall continue so to regard him.

His statement that what the Nations most need is a change of heart, remains the truest of all political utterances of our day; and it is a truth which our politicians continue persistently to wriggle away from: they are very ready to tell other nations that they have sinned; but it is the last thing they will admit about their own.

During the 1930s, Fascism and Nazism appeared in Europe. The system believed in the supremacy of one national group over other races. Could there be an Indian Fascism? The prospects of such a situation becoming a reality concerned Vernon C C Saunders of Oriel College, Oxford. He put his arguments in *United India* of March 1937. He also put forward his plans for India's future.

COULD THERE BE AN INDIAN FASCISM?

In many speeches and writings on the question of India's freedom there is a tendency which must inevitably be dangerous if India ever gains autonomy, and that is to divorce Indian nationalism from socialism and industrialization, and to regard the termination of British rule as an end in itself. It is for this reason that I regard Gandhi and Gandhism with a very qualified admiration. India's future, whether before or after liberation, must depend on the scientific mobilization of her natural resources in the Russian style, mechanization both of industry and agriculture, a vast campaign for hygiene and health, and above all the education of the masses, political, technical and intellectual, to enable this programme to be carried out, and for India to become a twentieth-century nation with modern ideas and a modern standard of living. Nationalism divorced from this and linked instead to mysticism, back-to-nature and home-spinning movements is worse than useless. I would go further – I would say that until the country is soaked in Socialist doctrine, freed from the poison of reactionary mysticism, and prepared to bury its religious and tribal fanaticisms, independence for India is definitely undesirable. The examples of China and Ireland should be enough; in both of these countries before they had thrown off the yoke they talked glibly of Socialism. Now there is Fascism in one and every prospect of it in the other. Suppose India gained autonomy tomorrow with the Socialist Nehru as leader. China did the same with the Socialist Sun Yat Sen. Sun Yat Sen died. So may Nehru. What is to prevent the rise of an Indian Chiang Kai Shek?

For it must not be overlooked that there is a large class in India to whom Socialism would be as unwelcome as to its counterpart in Europe, and it might very well be that their reaction would take a similar form. Nationalism, too, to which Indian Socialism has become linked, can easily be diverted to other uses, and those to whom in India the capitalist and caste systems are worth maintaining would have little difficulty in raising a cry of 'saving India's traditions' and might well play on the theme of the 'materialism' of Socialism to bring round mass religious feeling to their own ends. Add to this the mystic and other opposition to 'Western' ideas of science, education, women's emancipation, and industrialization, and it will be seen that there are potentialities for a successful counter-revolution. What is more, Fascist Germany and Italy, if still surviving, would be fully prepared to foment this movement for their own ends to bring about a domination of their own over an India lost by Britain.

Rather than turn India over to an unholy Fascist alliance of native capitalists, princes and mystics, let us have a steady preparation of the country by native Socialists, with a maintenance of the British rule as the lesser evil for some time to come.

VERNON CC SAUNDERS,
Oriel, Oxford.

CHAPTER 4

Student activities

THE INDIAN STUDENT POPULATION in nineteenth and early twentieth-century Britain, mostly male, were driven by the need for British academic qualifications. They were to be found in various disciplines and in universities throughout the country. These students were open to the diverse intellectual, moral and social currents and the British imprint on their formative years was often deep and lasting. One of the most popular courses of their study in Britain was the Bar.

Debates were organised according to the contemporary issues of the day, which was usually India. Their debating societies in the universities provided an ideal opportunity to put forward, to defend or defy India's claim for self-rule.

Two of the earliest debates on India took place in the splendid debating hall of the Oxford Union Society in May 1890. The following reports appeared in *India* of 6 June 1890:

MR SURENDRA NATH BANERJEE AND MR EARDLEY NORTON AT THE OXFORD UNION

'That this House views with regret the non-recognition of the elective principle in the Indian Councils Bill now before Parliament.' Moved by Mr Eardley Norton, BA, Merton; opposed by Mr J F W Galbraith, Oriel, Secretary.

The splendid debating hall of the Oxford Union Society was well filled on Thursday, May 22nd, to hear Mr Eardley Norton and Mr Surendra Nath Banerjee, the delegate from the Indian National Congress, upon the subject of Indian Reform. There was a large and appreciative House, which greeted the delegates with much enthusiasm; while the visitors' gallery was crowded to overflowing, the audience including Mrs Norton, Mr A O Hume CB, HRH Prince Kitiyakara of Siam, and Miss Cornelia Sorabji BA, who is now studying at Oxford.

The Chair was taken at eight o'clock by Mr F H Coller, Christ Church, President of the Society, who, after some formal business had been transacted, called upon Mr Norton to move his resolution.

MR EARDLEY NORTON BA, Merton, who was received with cheers, said, that after an absence of sixteen years from his University, he could not have wished to renew his connection with it upon a more honourable occasion than the present. What they had to do with that evening was an appeal from all the best of the people of British India to the people of England, asking them to recognise, in some modified fashion, perhaps, but still asking them to recognise that they were sentient human beings, not mere serfs, and to remove if only partially the ban which was keeping the peoples of India from all voice in the administration of their home affairs. . .

MR J F W GALBRAITH, Oriel, opposed, and said it seemed to him that the real reform which India needed was in social questions. The phrase 'Empire of India' struck the key-note of the position he wished to take up. Did the Hon. mover think, with his great knowledge of Indian affairs, that any system of Empire in India could be consistent with a representative system? We were in such few numbers in India that it made it absolutely necessary that we should keep in our hand the highest executive and legislative powers, and if we attempted equality with the natives in that respect we might as well pack up our baggage and leave India tomorrow. . .

MR SURENDRA NATH BANERJEE, Principal of the Ripon College, Calcutta, who met with an enthusiastic reception, said he was greatly indebted to the House for the cordial reception which had been accorded to him, and he could assure the House that that reception would be to him a source of encouragement and

Cornelia Sorabji (1866–1954)
First Indian woman to study law in Britain at Sommerville Hall, Oxford 1889; social reformer; campaigned for women's education; helped women in purdah; second Indian woman to be called to the Bar (Lincoln's Inn) 1923; against complete independence for India, favoured Dominion Status.

inspiration in the somewhat difficult task which he had undertaken that night. He craved the indulgence of the House for a few moments – he was afraid he would take some little time of the House – in discussing the numerous points which had been raised. He thought he would best discharge his duty by stating in the first place, in a few plain words, the situation in India, and the demand that they made in conformity with the requirements of that situation. What they said was this. The English Government had given them high English education, it had conferred upon them the inestimable boon of a free Press, and last but not least, it had conceded to them the gift of local self-government based partially on the representative system. (*Cheers*) They had now for a period of more than fifty years lived under these influences. For more than fifty years they had enjoyed these blessings, and he thought the House would think they must be something less than human if, after living under these influences and imbibing these impressions, they were not inspired with a lofty enthusiasm to transplant into their country something of the spirit of the constitution which they had learnt to admire in the noble literature and noble history that England had taught them. (*Cheers*) They asked England and the English people to gratify those aspirations which they had kindled in their breasts, and they made that demand not only upon pure sentimental grounds – grounds of emotion, grounds of sensibility, grounds of vague, undefined feeling – but because they were distinctly of the opinion that the result of such a concession would be to add sensibly and visibly to the efficiency, and he was going to say the stability, of British rule in India. (*Cheers*) Such was the case, such were the grounds upon which their appeal was made to this House. (*Cheers*) He was somewhat surprised at some of the statements that had been made (*Laughter*) – by the gentleman (Lord Hugh Cecil) who had opposed the motion. He was somewhat in sympathy with him in his ignorance (*hear, hear*); ...

He thought as far as the educational aspect of the question was concerned it might be taken for granted that they were not the barbarians they were represented to be. (*Cheers*) The statement was made in the course of this debate that the Indians before the advent of the English were a pack of barbarians or semi-barbarians; he believed that was the language that was used. Let him remind this House that they came – the Hindoos of India, the race to which he had the honour to belong (*Loud cheers*) – they came from a great and ancient stock, that at the time the ancestors of the most enlightened European nations were roaming in their native woods and forests, their fathers had founded great empires, established noble cities and cultivated a system of ethics, a system of religion, and a noble language which at the present moment excited the admiration of the civilised world. (*Loud cheers*) They had only to walk across the way, and place themselves in the Bodleian library to witness the ancient records of Indian industry, Indian culture, and Indian ethics; therefore it seemed to him the remark was somewhat out of place. (*Cheers*) If the remark was made to prejudice the claim which they had now the honour to put forward, to prejudice their claim for representative institutions, never was it more misplaced, for the simple reason that self-governing institutions formed an essential feature of the civilization of the Aryan race, and they came from the Aryan stock. (*Cheers*) The Hon. opposer of the motion was pleased to refer to the authority of Sir Henry Maine in reference to certain quotations he made. He (the speaker) was prepared to bow to that authority, and accept him as an authority on Indian matters. What did he say in reference to India? The first practical illustrations of self-governing institutions were to be found in the early records of India. Their village communities were as old as the hills. (*Cheers*) When they asked for representative institutions, or a partial concession of representative institutions, they asked for something which was in entire accord with the genius and the temper of the people of India, in entire accord with the traditions of their history, and in entire accord with the tenor of British rule in India...

Was there in this demand any approach to democratic Government, to Home Rule, or to Parliamentary institutions? (*Cheers*) And was it not desirable to consider the great advances that had taken place in the circumstances of

Surendra Nath Banerjee (1848–1925)
Distinguished Indian politician and enlightened educationalist. Appeared successfully for the Indian Civil Service Open Competitive Examination in London in 1869. His career in the ICS was shortlived on account of a conflict with the authorities, in which it was subsequently felt that he was unjustly treated. He later threw himself into public life and became a passionate and eloquent advocate of Indian rights and aspirations. He was a staunch member of the moderate camp in the Indian National Congress. He was the founder of the Indian Association in Calcutta (1876), one of the precursors to the Indian National Congress, of which he became President in 1894 and 1902. He was one of the earliest Indian National Congress delegates to Britain. He was knighted in 1921.

the Government and of the country, and was it not necessary that some reform of this kind should be made! (*Hear, hear*)

He just wished to point out to that House, before he sat down, that this was really not a party question at all. (*Cheers*) It was a question of national and Imperial justice. England was the home of representative institutions; from England as the centre, representative institutions had spread far and wide until this country had justly been called the august mother of free nations. The people of India were children of that mother, and they claimed their birthright; they claimed to be admitted into the rights of British citizens and British fellow-subjects. He was perfectly certain that such an appeal made to the English people could meet with but one response – a response of sympathy, and a readiness to grant it. (*Cheers*) He pleaded before that House for justice; he pleaded for liberty not inconsistent with British supremacy but tending to consolidate its foundations and he was perfectly convinced that so long as these words, these sacred words, had any weight, any meaning, any signification amongst Englishmen and in that House they would record, by an unanimous vote, an emphatic vote, their sympathy with their aspirations, their desire that India should be governed according to those eternal principles of justice and liberty, which were engraved deep in the hearts, the convictions, and feeling of Englishmen to whatever party, to whatever creed, to whatever sect they might belong. (*Loud and prolonged cheering*)...

MR EARDLEY NORTON. If the House that night decided in favour of the motion he would carry to the peoples of India a new message of confidence and consolation. (*Cheers*) But, if the House decided against him, he and his friend would still labour hopefully and courageously, because no temporary defeat would divert them from the advocacy of a cause which sought to cautiously and tentatively apply to the peoples of India principles which had built up on so sure a foundation the moral and political grandeur of this country. (*Cheers*) He did not think the people of England would turn a deaf ear to demands urged on behalf of the people of India in a manner at once loyal, constitutional, and temperate. (*Loud cheers*)

The result of the division was announced as under amidst much cheering:

For the motion	73
Against	13
Majority for the motion	60

*   *   *

The question of Representative Institutions for India was under the consideration of the Cambridge University Union on 6 February 1892. The subject of the debate was: 'That India can never be well or justly governed, nor can her people be prosperous or contented until they are allowed through their elected representatives to have an effective voice in the Legislative Councils of their own country':

THE INDIAN QUESTION AT CAMBRIDGE
SUCCESS OF THE INDIANS AT THE UNIVERSITY UNION
From our correspondent

The question of Representative Institutions for India was under the consideration of the University Union at this week's meeting and attracted a good attendance, conspicuous amongst whom were a number of Indian members of the University, who were all on one side of the House, and there were many sympathizers in the Strangers' Gallery, some of whom were so carried away by the eloquence of an English sympathiser with the aspirations of the Indian people as to applaud, which nearly led to their expulsion. The subject was introduced by:

MR MAHOMED AHMED, of St John's College. The honourable opener lodged a very severe impeachment against the English administration of the affairs of India urging that all the most lucrative posts were monopolized by Europeans in contravention of the statutes which form the Charter of Indian Liberty. He complained of the high rate of pay of the English civil servants and of the executive and judicial function of government being in the same hands. The Salt Tax and the system of periodical assessment of the land came in for strong condemnation, as did also the Opium Policy, the Frontier Policy of small wars, and the irresponsibility of Indian civil servants. He urged that if the laws were to be obeyed, they should be made by a popular authority, and he asked if it was not a much prized principle of the English nation that there should be no taxation without representation. He expressed his gratification that many English statesmen who knew India well had given their support to the scheme of elected representatives in India, and he hoped the Union would take its place in the van of progress by supporting the motion.

MR O MADDEN, of Clare, who led the opposition, contended that India was not a nation, but a geographical expression, was composed of many races naturally hostile, so that self-government was an impossibility, and the Indian people would regard Representative Institutions as a burden rather than a blessing. He contended that the so-called Indian National Congress had no more right to that title than that House, and added that India was unfit for those western ideas which it was proposed to apply to it.

MR YUSUF ALI, of St John's, supported the motion by an eloquent speech, and urged that the objection, that because there were many races self-government was impossible, was wrong, as where a common interest existed it was quite possible. The English Reform Bill agitation of 1832 was met by precisely the same arguments or objections as were now urged against the proposal. The name of the Marquis of Ripon elicited tremendous applause from the Indian members of the House. He reminded them that the noble Marquis, whilst Viceroy of India, had introduced some attempts at an elective system in municipalities which had been attended with success. Some of the Indian universities elected their own Fellows. He urged that the Indian Civil Service added another caste, and was quite out of touch with the people, and in impassioned terms he predicted more strained relations between the people of India and the Government if their just demands were not granted.

MR EA KENDALL, of St John's, defended the Civil Service, and contended that India was well and justly governed, and charged the Indian National Congress with scattering untruths abroad, and so creating discontent.

MR SC AGNEW, of Trinity, pointed out the difficulty of ascertaining the real wishes of the Indian people. The Hindus and Muhammadans were mutually hostile, and only anarchy could result from the introduction of the elective principle.

MR FATEH CHAND MEHTA, of Christ's College, in moderate and well considered language, explained the demands of the Indian National Congress and the Indian people behind it, and urged with great force that British influence ought to have educated the people up to representative government, if it had not done so.

MR JB MASTERMAN, of St John's, charged the supporters of the motion with exaggerating their grievances and ignoring the benefits received from England, but he was very severely taken to task by:

MR FA BERTRAM, of Caius (Vice-President of the Union), who spoke well and urged the necessity of some agency to keep the Government informed of the real wants of the people. It was simply nonsense to talk of British sacrifices for India's good. We had regarded India simply as one of our possessions, and more unselfishness would be shown in giving Representative Institutions to India than guarding it by the sword.

MR HS GOUR, Non-College, spoke eloquently of the poverty and misery rife in India, and argued that the elective system would, as it always had done, prove a blessing to the people to whom it was given.

MR AC DEANE, of Clare, reminded the House that England, with all its representative advantages, had its poverty and misery as well, as in India.

MR TG THOMAS, Sidney, desired to call the attention of the House to what he could not help considering an anomalous condition of affairs, that an Indian should be compelled to seek the suffrages of the English electors of Finsbury, in order to bring India's demands into public notice. He held that the concession of popular representation to India, would do much to consummate that Imperial unity which was so much desired.

MR MAHOMED AHMED having briefly replied, the House divided at 11.15, when there were:

For the Motion	49
Against	44
Majority	05

a result which was greeted with much enthusiasm.   (*India*, 11 March 1892)

* * *

At Cambridge 13 years later there was great attention both for the subject and the participation of one of the leading Congressmen visiting England from India. On 31 October 1905, a spirited debate took place at the Cambridge Union Society on the motion of the Hon. Mr GK Gokhale CIE that 'This House would welcome the introduction in India of government on more popular lines'. He had the full attention of the House, both in number and enthusiasm. It was rated as a triumph for India.

MR GOKHALE AT CAMBRIDGE
IMPORTANT DEBATE AT THE UNION
TRIUMPH FOR INDIA

...The House was crowded, and many Indians were present.

MR GOKHALE remarked that it was now a hundred years since the destinies of India and England came to be linked together. The men who were at the head of affairs in England one hundred years ago had a double task before them when India was brought under their rule. The first task that confronted them was that of consolidation, and the second, conciliation. The first task had been on the whole well done, and he thought the men who went out to govern India undertook the work of consolidation in a spirit of devotedness, and they produced results which might be regarded with satisfaction and pride. (*Applause*) The task of conciliating his fellow countrymen to the new rule was carried out, aided by the introduction of Western education, also satisfactorily. Consolidation and conciliation having been accomplished, it became necessary to reconstruct the foundations of the English rule. That had, however, been put off from time to time. India had now been under the rule of England for one hundred years, and in what state did they find India today?

PRESENT CONDITIONS IN INDIA

He applied two tests: the material and political condition of the people. The whole country was kept disarmed, and recruiting generally took place amongst frontier tribes. England had entered into an alliance with Japan, and statesmen of both parties had been proclaiming the alliance with a sense of satisfaction. Had they ever considered how that Anglo-Japanese alliance affected the people of India and their feelings? They entered into an alliance with Japan in order to repel foreign invasion and to keep the people of India in a state of bondage. (*Applause*) Was that worthy of England? In the government and the administration of the affairs of the country all the 300 millions of people had not as much voice as a single working man in England. Was that satisfactory? Alluding to the material condition of the people of India – which he regarded as the supreme test – Mr Gokhale said first of all they would find plenty of evidence of the absolute poverty of the people. The annual average income of the people of this country was £45, and the annual average income of the people of India was at the most £2. The impoverishment of the people had been growing worse and worse, and things could not possibly go on much longer at the same rate...

AN OUTGROWN AND DEMORALISING SYSTEM

Proceeding to deal with the government of the country, Mr Gokhale said India was divided into 250 districts, at the head of which were English gentlemen who had the entire administration of the district in their hands. He did not want to blame the men, but the system. They in India had surely outgrown that system. There were one million men in India who had had an English education, and surely a certain number of those should be drawn upon for the government of their country. The system was a demoralising one. Although India was a great loser, materially and morally, England was a greater loser morally than India. It appeared that the position of England as the friend of liberty was being seriously affected by the British administration of India. The Secretary of State for India had never been to that land (*Laughter*) – and it was impossible to study India properly from a distance of 6,000 miles. (*Applause*)

Already, he proceeded, a feeling of great bitterness was growing up in India, so much retrogression having taken place and unnecessary offence having been given to the people...

MR FG SELWYN (King's College) opposed the motion which, he said, rested on two fundamental misconceptions: first, that England was bound to do everything for India, and at last give her the right to govern herself; and, secondly, on a sort of malady of the Liberal mind, which was that popular government was a panacea of all woes – a sort of political Beecham's pill. (*Loud laughter*) God knew they had done everything they could for India. They had spent their life blood on India, and were now asked to go on educating her for ever and ever, and give the people arms – for peaceful purposes? No they wanted arms for fighting, evidently. (*Laughter*) They were told that the material condition of India was unworthy of England. The cause of the distress, was it England's fault? Hard Cheddar if it was. (*Laughter*) Could they say that popular government was a success for the Romans? Some persons, well competent to judge, had said there was little doubt that England gave popular government to Cape Colony too soon. In China did they see any signs of popular government? (*Laughter*) Yet, the Chinese seemed to get on very well. (*Renewed laughter*) He did not think they had any right to say that because popular government was good for England it was also good for any other country. He thought they should be very chary about taking it for granted that popular government was the right thing for India. (*Applause*) If they looked at the general circumstances of the nation they must admit that the people of India were not yet fit to govern themselves, by reason of their lack of independence and unpracticalness. There were still racial differences and the religious difficulties. If they gave India popular government it would only be driving in the thin edge of the wedge. They could not have any experimenting over that business. The only way of governing India was by autocracy, benevolent, but still perfectly strong. (*Applause*) The result, in his opinion, of allowing India to govern herself would be the desolation of homes and the ravaging of the country, with blood flowing like water. They were asked to hand India back to bloodshed and struggle, and cover England and India with ruin and shame. (*Applause*)

MR RM PATTISON MUIR (Caius College) supported the motion, and asked the House to consider the question imperially. There were alternatives to the courses that had been suggested, viz., (1) that they should colonise India, and (2) help India to become a nation. The first alternative was entirely out of the question, because the climate of India prevented English children living there. With regard to the second, he said India would become a nation, but it must not become a nation in spite of England, but by her help. (*Applause*)

SIR ET CANDY, CSI, opposed. He said he had been unable to see the connection between the lamentable picture drawn by Mr Gokhale – a friend of his own – and the resolution he moved. The proposer did not show how the material condition of the people was to be improved by popular government. As regarded the point that the people of India were disarmed, he did not know for what purpose they wanted arms, and he was quite surprised at Mr Gokhale's interpretation of the Anglo-Japanese alliance. (*Applause*) The lack of status of

Indians in our Colonies was the fault, not of our Government, but of men that had got that self-government which India so much desired...

Of course, all well-wishers of India hoped that in time the people might become more and more associated with the government of the land. But the progress must be slow. (*Laughter*)

He could not see any reason why India should not be represented in the English Parliament as suggested. The idea was in operation in regard to the French possession in India, but he had never heard of the deputy having any effect upon the French Government.

There also spoke: For the motion: Messrs JM Keynes (King's), RHEH Somerset (Queen's), GSW Epps (Emmanuel), SA Bilgrami (Christ's), A Pickles (Trinity), HAI Laidlaw (St John's), WG Elmslie (Pembroke), GS Shaw, (Trinity), and B Nath (Trinity). Against the motion: Messrs May Oung (Downing), HFF William (Clare), AC Caport (Trinity), EA Gubboy (Trinity), and AS Hedderwick (Clare).

The voting resulted as fellows: Ayes, 161; Noes, 62; majority for the motion, 99. (*India*, 10 November 1905)

MEETING AT LEAMINGTON

The Hon. Mr Gokhale, on Friday last, addressed a meeting at the Liberal Club, Leamington. Councillor Norris presided, and Mr THD Berridge, prospective Liberal candidate for the constituency, was also present.

THE CHAIRMAN said they were there to hear an address from a gentleman who came from the other side of the Empire, and would give them a very interesting account of affairs in India. When the late Mr Charles Bradlaugh was alive he was one of the greatest friends India ever had, and was looked upon in the House of Commons as the 'Member for India'. At that time he (Councillor Norris) was a political follower of Mr Bradlaugh, and he was glad to know that Mr Bradlaugh did so much for the people of our great dependency. They would probably hear from Mr Gokhale why the Government was dividing Bengal, and he might also tell them something of the great trade between India and the rest of the Empire. They sympathised with the poor of India, and also with those educated natives of that country who had not the opportunity of taking that part in the government of their own country which they ought to have. (*Applause*)

MR GOKHALE, who was received with great applause, explained the object of his mission to this country, and laid stress on the responsibility that lies upon the British electors, who 'alone could in any way influence the Government'. He sketched the relations of rulers and ruled in India, setting forth the great promises made authoritatively to his countrymen, and showing how inadequately they had been fulfilled, and how necessary it was for the Government now to make a generous response to the developed spirit and instructed intelligence of India. He dealt very fully with the financial, industrial, commercial, and educational aspects of the administration, and handled with severity the repressive policy of Lord Curzon. He recognised the enormous difficulties in the way of giving self-government to India, but urged that the people must be more and more associated in the work of government till the final goal was attained and India found a place among the other Colonies, inside the Empire, and working for the common glory and the common prosperity of the Empire. (*Loud applause*). (*India*, 10 November 1905)

LORD MORELY AND MR GOKHALE

We are glad (writes the *Daily News*) that Lord Morley took the opportunity on the Third Reading of his Indian Councils Bill to reply to certain attacks upon his measure and his methods. There is always a kind of treacherous critic who professes great admiration for a scheme in general and then proceeds to water it all away bit by bit. In the case of Lord Morley's scheme of Indian reform, they have been saying that nothing could be more excellent, only the whole thing had better be postponed for the present. Finding that device no good, they worked up a so-called Mahomedan grievance. When Lord Morley gave way on that, they discovered that the proposed Executive Councils were the point of danger, and persuaded the Lords to cut them out of the Bill. When Lord Morley maintained that the Government of India favoured the Executive Councils, they asked who was meant by the Government of India. Lord Morley replied that the Viceroy was meant, and that ought to silence them on that point. But already they had gone off upon another objection. They had been writing to *The Times* to say that the reforms were not designed by the India Council nor suggested by the Government of India, but were 'wrung' from Lord Morley by the representations of an Indian leader. They named Mr Gokhale, who is known to have had interviews with Lord Morley during last summer. Lord Morley's answer to the charge was strong and complete. He had consulted Mr Gokhale as he had consulted other Indians, Mahomedan as well as Hindu. He only regretted that he had not consulted more. It was an answer worthy of Lord Morley's best Liberal traditions. Mr Gokhale is known as a highly educated, incorruptible, and moderate leader of Indian opinion. He has won the admiration even of Lord Curzon for his wisdom, and of large numbers of friends in England as well as in India for his entire and sincere devotion to the best interests of his country. If such a man is not to be consulted on the future of his own people, who is to be consulted? That Lord Morley's reforms agree in the main with Mr Gokhale's own proposal for the immediate progress of India is, in fact, their highest commendation. (*India*, 19 March 1909)

NATIONALISM IN INDIA
DEBATE AT THE OXFORD UNION SOCIETY

The question for debate at the Oxford Union Society on Thursday evening, March 11, was 'That this House views with alarm the present national movement in India'.

MR R A KNOX, of Balliol College, the President of the Society, was in the Chair.

MR C S T WATKINS (Lincoln), in proposing the motion, maintained that those who opposed the revolutionary tactics of the nationalist movement in India had, nevertheless, got the interests of India at heart. There was a tendency in Eastern countries that had become inoculated with Western ideas to imitate them in their political institutions. But it had to be remembered that national movements on the part of conquered nations had frequently in the past been a source of self-destruction. Moreover, India was not a nation – it was a continent, comprising races of different sorts, different religions, different conditions of living, different climate, and it was also under the rule of a Western nation. The unity of such a continent was not within the range of practical politics, and the strength to be gained by such a union was somewhat doubtful. The Indian people, as a whole, had certainly raised themselves to a higher condition in the presence of a strong central power, and it was their contention that the English rule had induced that intellectual activity which has produced the national movement. But this could hardly be called national, since it was influenced by men who might have been sufficiently educated to imbibe democratic ideals under the Liberal rule of England, but who had not realised the incapacity of their fellow-countrymen to appreciate such ideas. Again, this movement was encouraged by commercial and political rivals amongst other Powers. English public opinion was alarmed, not because of the existence of the movement, the sign that India was gradually awakening, but because it feared the present conditions in India tended to revolution, and were only likely to militate against India's own interests. It threatened to arrest the development of educational reforms, and, ultimately, the independence of the Indian States.

MR G E DODDS (New College) opposed the motion. He agreed that it was necessary to bear in mind Lord Morley's warning against regarding India as if it were a State like Ireland or England. The national movement which they heard of in the Press was engineered by a number of fanatics. But it was not merely a political movement. There was a large amount of discontent, which made the movement broader and deeper. It was associated with bomb throw-ing and murder in the minds of the average Englishman. All would, however, approve of repressing Anarchism, and the only real method of getting rid of it was to get the Indians into co-operation with the Government. The movement aimed only at a larger share for Indians in the government of their country, and ultimately for perfect autonomy. The reception that had been accorded Lord Morley's reforms showed that they were content with constitutional reform. It was not an argument to say that India was incapable of governing herself, since she, in common with Ireland, had not the opportunity of trying.

MR S HERBERT (Balliol) commented on the manner in which the result of the Russo-Japanese War had operated as a distinct challenge to Great Britain's supremacy in India. It was popular some years ago to suppose that the Russians were our main danger in Asia, but now the belief was that the Japanese, in spite of the alliance, were our greatest enemies. The few years that had elapsed since that conflict had seen the rise of much harm in India. He quoted the discussions in the Indian National Congress as an example of what government by a society of educated Indians would mean. Taking all things into consideration, however, what were we going to do with India? Were jus-tice and education to be the only functions of the Central Government? Were we going to stand by and help her to digest the political food we had given her? There were sixty nations in India, and more than seventy languages. It was all very well to talk of educated Indians, but what about the half-castes?

MR LEP SMITH-GORDON (Trinity) thought that hon. members opposite were labouring under a misconception. They had probably relied for their facts on the tender mercies of those papers that lived on sensation. They took present manifestations as evidence of a national movement. Not that he approved of bombs in the least, in fact, if he met a man with such an engine he would be the first to run away. But there were two kinds of patriotism – the individual patriotism, and the world patriotism. The former was that of a rising nation, and such a nation was India. It could not be said that the country had been well governed during British occupation. It was the duty of an empire-power to further the intellectual development of the whole world, and when this was accomplished it was time for it to retire gracefully. If they looked back to his-tory, they would see that not one of the Empires of the past had retired in this manner, on the contrary, they were absorbed in eating up everything gradu-ally. What had happened? Nothing but pieces of clay and stone remained for the interest of the archaeologists. They should be taught to realise what an infinitely glorious thing it was to make such a sacrifice. People, though Indians, did not throw bombs for pure amusement. We had destroyed in part their religions and customs. We must reconcile ourselves to the result.

The debate was continued by MR KC MACARTNEY (New College), MR AD COOPER (New College) and MR AI JOHNSTONE (Exeter), who spoke in favour of the motion.

The opposite view was put by two Indian speakers, MR N CHAND (Worcester) and MR SM HUSAIN (Jesus), and also by MR EP SWAIN (St John's), ex-Junior Treasurer, MR ET WILLIAMS (Balliol), MR EH WALL (Lincoln), and MR JHG GIBBS (Merton).

On a division being taken, there voted for the motion 51; against 49. The motion was therefore carried by a majority of two.   (*India*, 19 March 1909)

YOUNG INDIA AND THE FUTURE
MR. HORNIMAN AT THE CAMBRIDGE MAJLIS DINNER

The annual dinner of the Indian Majlis, Cambridge, took place at the Lion Hotel, Cambridge, on February 27. Mr MC Bhat, President of the Majlis, presided over a large gathering, which included Mr BG Horniman, the guest of the evening, representing the British Committee of the Indian National Congress; Mr Bernard Manning, adviser to the Indian students in Cambridge; Mr RM Joshi, repre-senting the London Indian Association; Mr JIC Rodrigo, representing the Oxford Majlis; Mr MA Azim (Hon. Secretary); Mr RS Inamdar, ex-President; Mr Pariya, ex-President, Mrs Lolita Roy, Mrs and Miss Tata, and Miss Ram.

Mr B G Horniman, proposing the toast of 'India' was accorded a very enthusiastic reception. He dwelt on the present condition of the Indian people, their grinding poverty, their political subjection, the tyranny of the repressive laws, and their recent sufferings. They could not think of the recent 'Reform' Act as a measure of emancipation in the light of all these circumstances. There was a great deal of discussion about 'acceptance' and 'rejection'. But the terms were meaningless and the discussion was wasteful. If a man who had been kept for years in solitary confinement was then allowed to emerge from his cell and gaze for a few hours daily on 'that little tent of blue which prisoners call the sky', it was not a question whether he accepted or regretted this slight leavening of his sufferings; and, if he took advantage of the few hours' relief, it did not mean that he accepted it as his freedom, or even the beginning of it. He was still a prisoner. And there was no question of acceptance or rejection when they came out to gaze on the little patch of freedom which Mr Montagu called Dyarchy. They wanted their full freedom, and they must go on struggling for it strenuously, whole-heartedly, and without compromise. (*Cheers*) He did not know how any patriotic Indian could accept half-measures which left an autocracy, still with full powers to enchain the people, when he remembered what his people had suffered and were now suffering. The hope of the future was with the young men of India. Let them not forget their honour, let them not barter the freedom of their fellow-countrymen, let them not compromise with their national self-respect or abate one jot of their claim for their independence. (*Loud cheers*) If they were to be part of a great Empire, they wanted to be a partner on their own terms, and as free and independent as Australia, Canada, or South Africa, taking as much as they were asked to give. (*Renewed cheering*) When they returned to India, let them go with the full determination honestly and loyally to strive for her emancipation and to rescue her people, who lay chained and bleeding, from the rule of the civil and military bureaucracy that had inflicted on them the Rowlatt Act and the Punjab Terror. (*Prolonged cheers*)

The President, in replying to the toast, said the eloquent and inspiring appeal to which they had listened would strike a responsive chord in all their hearts. In an able and well-delivered speech, he dealt with the features of the Indian problem as they presented themselves today.

Other toasts followed. Mr Pariya proposed 'Cambridge University', to which Mr B L Manning, who was very cordially received, responded. 'The Guests' was proposed by Mr N M Shah and replied to by Mr Horniman. Mr M A Azim gave 'Sister Societies', and Mr R M Joshi replied. Mr Rodrigo, in a witty speech, proposed 'The Majlis', and Mr C Sittamplam was also delightfully witty in his response. 'Homegoing Members' was proposed by Mr M I Rahim and replied to by Mr R S Inamdar.

During the evening it was announced that Mr Mahomed Ali, Mr Syed Hossain, and Syed Sulleman, Maulana, of the Khilafate Deputation, who had been invited, had sent an expression of their regret that the time was too short, after their arrival the previous day, to enable them to accept the invitation. Their message of greeting, delivered by Mr Horniman, was received with cheers. Cheers also greeted a warm message of cordial good wishes from Miss Helena Normanton. (*India*, 12 March 1920)

* * *

In February 1921, Mrs Sarojini Naidu was at the Indian Students Union and Hostel at Keppel Street, London. The occasion was an address by Dr A F Garvie of New College, London, on 'Political Idealism'. The Chief Guest was Lord Reading, Lord Chief Justice of England.

Principal Garvie's lecture had been characterized by vigorous radicalism, and Mrs Sarojini Naidu, who wore Indian costume, had taken the opportunity to speak before Lord Reading of India's aspirations. Liberty, justice, and love, she said, using a substitution of these words by Dr Garvie for the French principles of 'liberty, equality, and fraternity', were the three things which summed up

the whole of India's idea of politics. If he who was to be for five years custodian of the Imperial honour in her country would remember what the lecturer had said, 'Be the other fellow', she thought there might be peace for India. India was setting out on the path to freedom. It was for the custodian of England's honour to see that freedom was born of mutual understanding and respect for their liberty...
(*The Times*, 28 February 1921)

THE ANNUAL CAMBRIDGE MAJLIS DINNER
From a correspondent

The annual dinner of the Cambridge Indian Majlis was held at the Lion Hotel, Cambridge, on February 12th.

The President, Mr Purshottam Merchant, was in the Chair, and was supported, among others, by Mr George Lansbury, Mr B G Horniman, and Dr Bond, Master of Trinity Hall. Several ladies were present, as well as representatives of the sister Association at Oxford and the London Indian Association. Mr Lansbury, in proposing the toast of 'India', delivered an eloquent address, expressing sympathy with India's struggle for freedom and admiration of Mahatma Gandhi. India, he said, was teaching the world new lessons, and would show a new way, he hoped, to the Western Hemisphere, in which the ugliness and cruelty of highly developed commercial industrialism, as we saw it in this country, would be absent.

Mr B G Horniman, replying for 'Our Guests', said he had been asked many times since his arrival at Cambridge, whether he thought Mahatma Gandhi's movement could succeed. He was glad to have that opportunity to declare that he had the utmost faith that Mahatma Gandhi had found the true and only way to India's salvation.

Referring to Mr Montagu's speech in the Commons, Mr Horniman described as indecent his threat to the Indian people that they would suffer the fate of the Germans if they challenged 'the most determined people in the world'. Mr Montagu might have remembered that Indian blood and money enabled Britain to face the German challenge. But, while he believed English people could show determination, above all others, in a cause in which they believed, he did not believe that there would be any determination in this country for a campaign of 'blood and iron' against the Indian people. (Mr Lansbury: '*Hear, hear!*') The Secretary of State for India would have to reckon on the determination on the other side. When all the machine-guns, bombs, aeroplanes, and other material resources that Britain could provide had been exhausted, India's vast resources of spiritual determination would not have been exhausted. (*Cheers*)

DEBATE – On Sunday, February 19th, there was an interesting debate at the Indian Majlis on the motion that 'This House has lost faith in Labour policy towards the East'. The motion was proposed by Mr Zaidi. Mr Horniman and the Hon E S S Montagu (nephew of Mr E S Montagu) were among the opposers. The motion was defeated by 42 votes to 17.
(*Hind*, 10 March 1922)

The debate was hailed as a great success for having the rare privilege of providing two eminent authorities on the subject on the same night. The hour-long debate was considered one of the finest ever heard at the university. There were other such occasions down the years. These events are self-explanatory and reports about them are reproduced.

THE INDIAN ASSOCIATION, LONDON
MR JINNAH ON 'WHAT INDIA NEEDS'

A very successful meeting was held at the Caxton Hall, on Saturday, June 9th, under the auspices of the Indian Association, London, which has recently been started by the Indian Student Community in the Metropolis. The occasion was marked by a very interesting address on 'What India Needs' by Mr M A Jinnah, whose interest in and activities on behalf of the students in London have

Mohamed Ali Jinnah (1876–1948)
Studied Law in England. Barrister,
Bombay High Court; Secretary to
Dadabhai Naoroji when he was President
of the Indian National Congress. Joined
Muslim League 1913; opposed Gandhi's
support of the Khilafat movement and
the non-cooperation policy of the Indian
National Congress, resigning from it in
1920. Came to England for the Round
Table Conference 1930–31 and stayed
on till 1934; returned to India to devote
time to the Muslim League. Prime
mover behind the League's Pakistan
resolution 1940, which demanded a
separate homeland for the subcontinent's Muslims. Governor-General of
Pakistan (1947–48).

always been a feature of his visits to this country. 'What India Needs', in Mr
Jinnah's view, is a United Front.

There are divisions and schisms everywhere, he emphasised. Divisions
among Non-Cooperators, division among Moderates, divisions between Hindus
and Moslems. Until they could close up their ranks and present a United Front,
they would achieve nothing. He spoke with the utmost reverence of Mahatma
Gandhi, but he said he was not a believer in the Non-Violent Non-Cooperation.
The only thing that impressed Englishmen was just the opposite of that. Mr
Jinnah went on to say that he was losing all hope of India gaining anything by
continual association with Britain. It was no wonder, the Indian people should
despair and give up hope in Britain, when a man, who had been so loyal as
Mahatma Gandhi, was forced at last to refuse cooperation with the British
Government. He admitted that Non-Cooperation had achieved great things
and given a tremendous impetus to Nationalism but he was not a sentimental-
ist and he did not believe the ultimate goal could be achieved by such means.
England had yielded to violence in Egypt and Ireland. Let us hope the English
would not drive them to such extremes in India.

There was a large attendance and among those present were Mrs Jinnah,
Dr S S Mohamadi, Sjt. ML Bhargava, (LLB) Vakil, Madame and Dr Leon and
Mr G S Dara, Editor, *Hind*. Letters of apology were received from Mr Horniman
and Mr Arthur Field, both of whom were not in town.   (*Hind*, 22 June 1923)

Lala Lajpat Rai (1856–1928)
Took leading part in organising relief of community distress of all kinds. Joined Indian National Congress in 1888. Member of the Congress deputation to England (1905). Deported to Burma for Sedition (1907); to escape political harassment he spent eight years in America where he ran a paper called *The Young India*, 1915. President of the special Congress Session in 1920 that adopted the programme of non-cooperation. Author of *Unhappy India, Arya Samaj*, etc. While leading a demonstration in Lahore in 1928 he was hit by a police baton and died from his injuries. Wrote foreword for Josiah C Wedgwood's book: *The Man and His Word*.

The following are excerpts from an interview with Lala Lajpat Rai, published in *Hind* on 15 June 1924:

INDIAN STUDENTS IN ENGLAND

Question: Could you favour me with your view on the Indian students coming to this country, particularly in view of their future prospects, both in Government service and other lines?

Answer: I am not very favourably disposed towards the idea of a large number of young Indian students coming to Europe for the purpose of education. I am afraid it results in their de-Indianisation, and a majority of them do not derive proportional profit from their stay in Europe. By proportion, I mean in proportion to the expenses their parents incur on their stay over here. I am of the opinion that only selected students of mature age should be sent to different Western countries to acquire special proficiency in subjects for the teaching of which adequate provision does not exist in India.

Q.: Perhaps you would kindly explain a little further the import of this term 'selection'.

A.: By selection I do not mean selection by Government. Though, if the Government gives scholarships, the selection of scholarship holders will necessarily be made by official or semi-official bodies. By selection, what I really mean is the selection by parents themselves.

Q.: And you know, Lalaji, how many come to England every year – without even knowing what they are coming for?

A.: To me it seems absurd that young men should come to the Western countries without deciding what they were going to study here. That shows that study with them is a secondary matter; the primary being their visit to Europe. I am disposed to strongly disapprove of the young Indians coming to this country in such numbers to study law, or for merely a degree. I do, however, wish that they should come down to Europe and America for higher studies in sciences and technical subjects, especially in marine and aerial navigation.

THE MEERUT TRIAL

Published Monthly.

INDIA BULLETIN

ORGAN OF THE FRIENDS OF INDIA.
President: Laurence Housman.

Vol. 2. No. 1.   FEBRUARY, 1933.   One Penny

INDEX.

"MUST ENGLAND LOSE INDIA ?"
By MONICA WHATELY.
(Member of the India League Delegation.)

" Must England Lose India ? " is the title of a book, in which the writer, Lt.-Col. Osburn, shows in a very striking way that this country and India are at the parting of the ways. Those of us who have just returned from an investigation in that country cannot fail to realise that morally England has already lost India. Rule by Ordinance has destroyed any feeling of respect for British justice—and police excesses, any belief in Britain's love of fair play. Since 1917 this country has promised to do justice to India—to-day official figures give the number of political prisoners as twenty thousand, while the great Nationalist organisation of Congress tells us there are more than double that number in the Indian jails. Wherever I went, on my 12,000-mile journey through that vast country, I was told the story of jails crowded—not with convicts, but with men and women, boys and girls paying the price that Britain demands for freedom. The morning that our delegation arrived in Bombay we were told that Miss Slade, an English-woman and disciple of Mahatma Gandhi, had been arrested on her way to meet us. We at once got into touch with Sir Patrick Kelly, the head of the Police, and asked of him permission to see Miss Slade, who was at that time an untried prisoner. Permission was categorically refused, in spite of the fact that I pointed out to Sir Patrick that such a refusal would be bound to create a bad impression in England, where a prisoner is innocent in the eyes of the law until tried and proved guilty. Later the Delegation had an opportunity of witnessing what Sir Samuel Hoare in the House of Commons has been pleased to call " The staging for the party's benefit of Congress demonstrations which would involve clashes with the police." Following their usual custom, the local Congress organisation announced by the distribution of handbills that a raid on the Secretariate would take place on a certain day—at a certain hour—and it did. As a raid it compared badly with the great demonstrations that some of us remember in the days when the women of England and America were fighting for their emancipation. In India the day for such big spectacular demonstrations is over. With so many of their finest men and women in jail—they rightly conserve the strength of those who are outside, and the manifestations which take place now,

though frequent, are on a much smaller scale. The Secretariate or Government Offices stand in their own grounds, and face a large open space, used before the day of the " Ordinances " for public meetings, sports, etc. On the day announced, the whole of that open space was crowded with onlookers, a quiet and orderly crowd, demonstrating by their presence—their moral support of those who were prepared to pay the price in the protest they were about to make. A comparatively small number of Congress volunteers mingled with the crowd. An enormous number of police patrolled the streets, while the officers stood in groups clutching their heavy sticks. Cars filled with more police passed back and forth—while the whole staff of the Secretariate gazed from the windows and balconies—work for them was out of the question that day. There was a feeling of suspense in the air, attention was riveted on what might happen, rather than what did—that was so quickly over. One or two white-clad figures would detach themselves from the crowd, make a dash across the road, waving their Congress flag and attempt to enter one of the closely-guarded gates leading into the Secretariate. Immediately there was a rush of police in that direction, a surging forward on the part of the crowd, and the Congress volunteer would surrender to arrest quietly, and without protest. That was all. There could be no justification for the beating which many received at the hands of the police—the indiscriminate lashing out with those heavy sticks, the sickening thud of the blows on those slight, sparely-clad bodies—the hauling and mauling as they are thrown into the waiting police vans. It was a spectacle that could not fail to shock and humiliate any fair-minded British man or woman—but that is India to-day.

The fact that a whole nation is suffering as India is doing under British rule by Ordinance—that in spite of the most savage provocation, the people in the main remain non-violent, and are carrying on their fight for freedom without arms, and without hatred—speaks volumes for Mahatma Gandhi's teaching.

"Mahatma Gandhi is the best policeman that the British have in India," was a remark made to me by one of the permanent officials at Poona. " Nevertheless, we do not like this non-violence," he said. " It is so difficult to attack—if the Indian people became violent we could crush their movement in a month, for we should know what to do."

Violence, it is true, exists—but it is to be found less among the Indians fighting for their freedom than amongst those seeking to suppress these national aspirations. It was with a sense of horror that many of us, on opening our papers a few days ago, saw the heading " Prisoners Assaulted." We went on to read of a European jailer named Roach who with a deputy jailer named Jackson had thrashed a political prisoner under their charge in Nasik Jail—thrashed him with a stick with an iron knob until he became unconscious.[*] If the reading of such incidents causes a shudder to pass through the ordinary citizen—what can be the feelings of those of us who have just returned from India, where we have been in personal touch with prisons and prisoners? We who know, that for every jailer who is prosecuted for his ill-treatment of prisoners there are hundreds who behave just as brutally as Roach, and get off scot free.

The India League Delegation, of which I was a member, wanted to see the inside of the Indian prisons, about which we heard such terrible stories, but

[*]See reports on "Trial of Nasik Jailers," page 8.

CHAPTER 5

Correspondence in the Press

B RITISH ACTIVITIES, PRIVATE, PUBLIC AND DIPLOMATIC, were believed by the Raj to be above critical scrutiny by Indians. In fact a gagging vernacular Press Act of 1878 had to be introduced, following the hostile tone of the Indian language newspapers towards the British rulers. The often declared and pledged policy of the British people through acts and resolutions in Parliament and Queen Victoria's Proclamation of 1858 had not been redeemed. A trio of famous Indian historians described it thus:

The Queen's Proclamation, described as the Magna Carta of the Indian people, confirmed the treaties and engagements of the East India Company with the Indian princes and to pay due regard to the ancient rights, usages and customs of India; disclaimed all desire for the extension of British territorial possessions in India through 'encroachment on those of others'; granted a general amnesty to 'all offenders, save and except those who have been, and shall be convicted of having directly taken part in the murder of British subjects'; proclaimed a policy of justice, benevolence and religious toleration, enjoining the Government to 'abstain from all interference with the religious belief or worship' of the subjects; and declared that all 'of whatever race or creed, may be freely and impartially admitted to offices in our service, the duties of which they may be qualified, by their education, ability and integrity, duly to discharge'.

— MAJUMDAR, ROY CHOUDHURI AND DATTA: *An Advanced History of India*

However, injustices remained and were a regular subject of debate in the British press. Arguments were put forward by sympathisers of India, and defenders of the Raj; they were published as letters to the Editor. Judging by their size, it would appear that they were published without any editorial censorship. One such letter was published on 17 January 1880 in the *Statesman*; it was a reaction to a comment in *The Times*, on the subject of 'The Growth of Native Loyalty in India', and written by HM Blair on 8 January 1880 from 11 Stanhope Place, Hyde Park. The writer dismisses the assumption and goes on to say:

I venture to say that a greater delusion, as regards the loyalty and patriotism of the people of India towards our rule, was never attempted to be palmed off on the people of England by any journal professing to be acquainted with the true direction of native public opinion.

There cannot, indeed, be a greater mistake (as must be well known to all who have had practical acquaintance with the native character) than to suppose there is any real attachment among the people of India to their European rulers. The reason of this it is not difficult to account for. Differing in language, in habits and feelings – in everything, in short, that conduces to social intercourse, there exists a great gulf between the rulers and the ruled which cannot be bridged over; and anything like *loyalty and patriotism*, in our sense of the terms, is utterly unknown to the native mind. This may seem strange to those who are unacquainted with the peculiarities of the native character, and the effects produced by long habits of subjection. But the fact is, that so long as they are not oppressed or overtaxed (as there is much reason to believe they are at present), and are left to the enjoyment of certain civil rights and religious practices, and the kind of self-rule they have for ages been accustomed to in each village community, it is a matter of perfect indifference to the mass of the people what may be the supreme power under which they live. In short, as we won India by the sword, so by the sword we must keep it, and no one who has any practical knowledge of the country can entertain a doubt that, were our 65,000 British troops withdrawn from it, our hold on India would not be worth a month's purchase; and the mass of the people would witness the advent of Russia or any other power to rule over them, with stoical submission, hoping, no doubt, they would be less heavily taxed than they are under our Government.

A great deal has been made of the Imperial proclamation, in 1877, before the largest assemblage of native princes ever seen in India, as creating an increased feeling of loyalty to the British Government. On the native chiefs themselves – as related by Sir William Wedderburn in an article in the *Nineteenth Century*, who was himself present on the occasion – it created a feeling of keen disappointment, when they found that they had come so far to hear so little, and to receive no boon more valuable than medals and ribbons. That the proclamation had any moral effect on the mass of people, where it happened to reach them, is the merest delusion.

As an independent witness, making a long tour in India, with peculiar opportunities of observing the country, and mixing with the natives, well acquainted with the native language and literature, Mr Monier Williams, Boden Professor of Sanskrit at Oxford, gives the following testimony.

Speaking of our connection with the native States and our manner of dealing with them, he observes, 'I fear that the people everywhere prefer maladministration, and a limited amount of oppression under their own rulers, to good Government under ours'. Again he says, 'And in the last place, what is the attitude of the natives of India towards our Government? The most intelligent are quite ready to admit that they enjoy greater benefits under our rule than they would under any other, but the mass of unthinking people would rather be badly governed by their own chiefs than well governed by us. In the Native States they will acquiesce in exactions which, in our own territory, would be regarded as intolerable.' Mr Monier Williams concludes his interesting impressions with the following remark: 'In my opinion the great problem that, before all others, presses for solution in relation to the Queen's Eastern Empire is, how can the rulers and the ruled be drawn closer together? How can more sympathy and cordial feeling be promoted between them?' This certainly does not look like 'sympathetic *rapprochement*' which *The Times* would have us believe exists between the rulers and the ruled. 'But,' says *The Times*, 'the utmost enthusiasm, and outburst of patriotic and quasi-national feeling of Indian people under British administration, was called forth when it was known that the Government was actually dispatching Indian troops to the Mediterranean.' 'I doubt,' says the writer of the article, 'whether, in the history of the world, there has ever been a more remarkable revulsion of national feeling than that which now occurred throughout all India.' For this he quotes specimens of the most extravagant nonsense, culled from certain Mahommedan newspapers, of what the troops were to effect when marshalled against any European forces, "who would hardly dare stay to meet them". All this sounds more like burlesque than a real representation of public opinion, and it must have required more than the usual assurance of *The Times*, in trusting to the ignorance or credulity of people in England, to believe in the sudden conversion of the people of India from disloyalty to loyalty, by the expedition of the native troops to Malta. We all know now the beginning and the end of bringing these 7,000 sepoys to Europe, though we shall probably never know the policy which dictated the measure. As to the effect which the measure must have produced in the minds of the intelligent population in India there can be little doubt. The news must have travelled in every bazaar, and to every native court, that England required the help of her sepoy army to fight her battle with Russia – an evidence of her inability to contend with that power singlehanded. What other conclusions, indeed, could be drawn from such an unprecedented event?

Our dominion in India, as is well known, rests in a great measure on opinion – on the belief of our military superiority – and anything that tends to lower that opinion must weaken our influence and authority in the country. The fact of our having called upon our native Indian troops, bribed by high pay, to support our military power in Europe, must have had the effect of lowering the prestige of our name in Asia.

We have had of late more than enough of the language of extravagant boast and confidence in our national resources, and it must appear somewhat strange to our neighbours that we should, nevertheless, have to resort to Indian mercenary troops to raise England to the rank of a numerically great military power.

It has hitherto been considered that Indian, and not British interests, have been our chief concern in the administration of the affairs of our Eastern possessions; but there seems reason to fear that in certain quarters it is now considered that India should be made to contribute to the support and welfare of England. Let the injustice of such a measure become generally felt among the people of India, and especially among the educated classes, numbers of whom now visit England, and it will not be long before disaffection to our rule may become a serious danger. Indications of such a feeling are not wanting at the present time, as, with reference to the Licence and other taxes, enthusiastic meetings have been held at Bombay and other large cities, to petition against the arbitrary acts of the Calcutta bureaucracy, and to ask for the grant of representative institutions, in order to prevent such neglect of popular opinions in future.

The lesson which we have yet, as a nation, to learn about India, and which must be preached in season and out of season, till it is learned, is that India is *not a rich, but a very poor country*; and that to increase the already overburdened military expenditure there for the sake of our home interests, would, as Mr Gladstone has said, be 'injustice – gross and monstrous injustice'.

In what I have expressed on this subject I have not spoken without some authority, but having held positions of some importance in the Civil Service, and been in charge of a province in Southern India, which had just been in a state of insurrection, I am not unacquainted with the character and feelings of the people; and, from what I hear, there exists more discontent at present, especially among the educated classes, with our rule. Again, the social estrangement between the European and the native is greater than of old, arising from special circumstances which I cannot enter upon here. I would refer those who may wish for further information upon the subject, to a valuable article on 'The Stability of our Indian Empire', by Sidney James Owen in the *Contemporary Review* for February last.

The Indian National Congress, established in 1885, set up a British Committee in 1890. Its main objective was to 'Campaign for Educating the British People on the Indian Question'. This it did by holding public meetings all over Britain, as well as by establishing a weekly journal called *India*, for the 'Discussion of Indian Affairs'. There was a mixed reaction to both the British Committee and its journal *India* from established British newspapers. The columns headed 'Wise' and 'Otherwise' gave their verdict and views, for and against the presence of this Congress body, which was a joint British and Indian organisation. British opinion was divided and local papers helped them put their views to the test.

Comments on the Congress appeared in February 1890. The 'divide and rule' stigma attached to the administrators of the Empire is easy to see in the 'Otherwise' column. It clearly illustrates that if they, the British, run out of policy of ruling other nations, then the final weapon left in the imperial armouries was to create a division among the subjects. The Hindu-Muslim division was thus created to divert attention from Britain's own misrule.

When it is seen that the objects of the Congress are sought by great numbers of people, and are pursued constitutionally, rationally, and steadily, sober people will at least not straightway condemn them, without learning for themselves what it is that is asked, and why change or reform is demanded.

Manchester Guardian, 3 January

In their demands, now patiently and respectfully urged for years, there is surely nothing but what is just and fair. One only wonders that they do not ask for more.

Darwen News, 25 January

The native of India wants above all things a hearing from Parliament. He cherishes the memory of noble speeches made in that assembly when the Government of India was the all-absorbing question there. He never forgets the Charter Act of 1833, opening up offices to the natives, irrespective of caste, creed, or race. He clings to the Queen's Proclamation of 1858, renewing the promises of equal treatment and renouncing any policy of further conquest. He believes that all the demands made in the Indian National Congress are strictly within the rights accorded to him in these Charters; and he has every reliance on Parliament if he can only get his case placed fairly before the Legislature, cleared of all the prejudice and misrepresentation which are apt to cloud it when it can only be transmitted through an official class, who are, at the best, not disinterested in this matter of the native claims to further influence in the legislative and administrative functions of Indian government.

Daily News, 26 December

The great curse of our Indian administration, however, is that our best and most enterprising administrators have no effective public opinion to fall back upon for sympathy or support whilst they are in office. The Indian National Congress will not only create that opinion, but it will give it more or less authoritative expression.

Daily Chronicle, 28 December

It is sad to think that responsible Englishmen should in their philanthropic wrong-headedness side with such a disloyal and unhealthy crew. The spouting Hindus no more represent the Indian nation than the unwashed Socialists of Trafalgar Square represent the British nation. It is high time these dusky-skinned gentry and their white-skinned sympathisers were taught a salutary lesson.

Mirror (London), 27 January

Whatever may be conceded to native wishes in the distant future, it is the unanimous opinion of the most competent authorities upon Indian affairs that the time has not come yet, and that to encourage attempts at Hindu predominance at the present time would be not only intensely distasteful to the other peoples of India, but also be fraught with peril to the very existence of our Indian Empire.

Morning Post, 28 December

As for the alleged representative character of the Congress, it would just as much represent the inhabitants of Saturn or Jupiter as those of Hindostan.

Globe, 28 December

We would like to know by what right the native members of the Congress take upon themselves to speak for the people of India. These Congressmen are simply our friend the educated *baboo* – an artificial creature produced in the forcing-houses called schools and colleges set up by ourselves. He has acquired a dreadfully fluent command of English formulas, and can pour them out at will. We have seen, and daily see, the *baboo* here; we are familiar with his faculty for gaining prizes, his memory, his docility, his imitative faculty, and his absolute incapacity to think or act for himself when deprived of leading-strings. Of such is the Indian National Congress.

St James's Gazette, 28 December

That elaborate and ridiculous farce known as the National Congress is again being played in India – this time in Bombay. 'We call him Jim because his name is William' is a sharp saying in a modern play; and on the same principle the collection of *baboos* in Bombay is called National because it is not in any sense representative.

Bristol Times, 30 December

CORRESPONDENCE IN THE PRESS

A section of natives (Indians) aided by a number of discontented and malcontent Europeans are simply seeking to upset the existing order of things, in order to realise their own ambitious and sordid ends.

Cheltenham Chronicle, 4 January

The public also had a chance to voice its opinions on the rights and wrongs of the activities of the British Committee of the Indian National Congress, whose meetings were followed all over the country – and often became subject of sharp comments. Following one such public meeting at Northampton on 14 June 1890, the following letter appeared in *India* from the Secretary of the British Committee of Indian National Congress, Mr W M Digby, to a Member of Parliament, the Right Hon. George J Goschen, on 21 June 1890.

MR GOSCHEN AND INDIAN AGITATORS

The following correspondence explains itself:

George J. Goschen (1831–1907) Liberal MP; declined Viceroyalty of India.

British Committee of the Indian National Congress
25 Craven Street, Charing Cross, London,
May 21st, 1890

The Right Hon. George J Goschen MP,
House Commons, SW.

Sir, – In your speech at Northampton on the 14th instant, when referring to Indian Reform, you are reported to have said: 'Some agitators in India put themselves into communication with officers of the Irish-American League'. It is evident from the context that you refer to the National Congress and its efforts on behalf of Legislative Councils reform. So far as my Committee are aware there is, at least as regards the Members of the Indian National Congress, not a single word of truth in the statement. I am desired to ask you to be so good as to give me the names of the agitators you referred to. If any members of the Congress have been so misguided as to take the course which you describe the organization to which they belong will know how to deal effectually with them. The Congress movement for reform, I may add, is thoroughly loyal and constitutional. The Congress has never countenanced, it does not intend to countenance, any action but that which is an accord with law and order.

Again, you are reported to have said: 'Agitators in India find the columns of Irish newspapers particularly open to receive their complaints'. We do not know of a single Congress agitator in India who has written a single line to any Irish newspaper. Will you, please, state in what papers and on what dates the complaints you refer to appeared?

You speak strongly against the Congress reform movement and declare it is the work of a political party. At the present time meetings, on a non-party basis, are being held in various parts of the United Kingdom to instruct the English people on Indian matters, and to create a sentiment in favour of Indian reform. Liberals – Home Rule and Unionist – attend and take part in such meetings. One such, held in Birmingham last night, was presided over by a prominent Unionist. Should the Indian reform question become a Party question, the fault will not lie with the Indian reformers themselves or with their English allies.

I am, Sir,
Yours faithfully,
WM. DIGBY, *Secretary.*

Mr Digby wrote again on 6 June after receiving a reply from Mr Goschen.

You spoke at Northampton. The junior Member of that constituency is popularly (and most deservedly) spoken of as 'the Member for India'. Last year he attended the Session of the National Congress at Bombay. To the English people no Indian agitators are known other than those connected with the Congress. As a matter of fact there are no agitators in India who, in however remote a degree, wish for an extension of Parliamentary institutions in India. You made special reference to Parliamentary institutions. By ninety-nine people out of every hundred your observation would be taken to apply to the Congress agitation, and would be understood to imply that Mr Bradlaugh was associated with the agitators you condemned.

Your remarks, it appears, were based upon events which happened more than five years ago. The political situation has not more changed in England during the past five years than it has in India. Your present official position is a proof of the greatness of the change here. In India, at the time you mention, the Indian National Congress did not exist, nor were the Provincial Congresses, which fulfil so useful a function in the respective Presidencies and Provinces, then in existence. It may well be that some Indians, for reasons best known to themselves, did communicate with members of the Irish-American League. Indeed, it is clear that one at least did so.

Public meetings organised by the British Committee of the Indian National Congress in Britain were often organised jointly, the platform being shared with the Westminster Liberal Association. Their support was often constructive and specific, as expressed by C H Norman on 18 September 1904 in a letter to the editor of *India*.

THE NEXT SECRETARY FOR INDIA

Sir, – I have read your article on Sir Henry Cotton's acceptance of the Presidency of the Indian National Congress with great interest.

As one who takes a great interest in Indian problems, may I suggest that the next Liberal Government should show whether its desire to grapple with Indian grievances is genuine or not by appointing Sir H Cotton Secretary of State for India in the next Liberal Government.

Why should a man be allowed to occupy a position where he has to deal with questions which he probably knows nothing about, and which, generally, he has had no practical experience of? I think that is a fair summary of the qualifications of the recent Indian Secretaries that 'poor India' has been blessed with. However, perhaps this is too big a cake to take away from our hungry professional politicians, and therefore the alternative might be the creation of an Advisory Committee of three experts to assist the Secretary of State – let us say, Sir H Cotton, Sir W Wedderburn, and one native-born Indian. 'Too many cooks spoil the broth', but you equally 'spoil the broth' if you have an inexperienced cook. It seems to me that such a Committee would be of great assistance to the Secretary of State for India, and, what is more important, to the Indian people. By this means the conspiracy of silence that has been adopted towards India by both parties would not then be so harmful as now, as the people of India would know that their interests were in safe hands.

Yours, etc.,
C H NORMAN
4N Hyde Park Mansions, London W.   *18 September 1904.*

Updating the activities of the British Committee of the Indian National Congress through the Press was viewed as a means to appeal to and influence public opinion. The fact that a senior member of the Committee felt it necessary to publish a thank-you letter in *India* adds a human touch to the story of a political organisation.

ANOTHER FRIEND IN NEED
TO THE EDITOR OF 'INDIA'

Sir, – Some little time ago the Rev. Philip Wicksteed very kindly sent certain contributions to our fund, and I (without previously obtaining his permission) ventured to address you on the subject, saying that I had been unable to resist the temptation of letting cheering light shine before men. The letter has not been without its uses, for now Captain Arthur St John writes that he desires to follow Mr Wicksteed's lead. 'I now send you a cheque' (he writes) 'for £6 from my wife and myself: £5 for well-digging or other material relief, and £1 for extending information in this country as to the facts of India's condition and our relations thereto.' I need hardly say how gladly we welcome such instances of spontaneous help from friends known only by name as fellow-workers. The amounts have been at once allocated to the purpose indicated, that for well-digging being sent to our trusty Bombay Committee, and the balance credited to the fund to meet the expenses of the delegates expected from the Indian National Congress.

Yours, etc.
W WEDDERBURN
Meredith, Gloucester, 16 November 1904.

On the same page was another letter from J B Pennington, expressing views on the subject of 'Prospects of Indians in India'. There was also a human touch in the exchange of letters between Dadabhai Naoroji and Viscount Baring on the death of the latter's father, Lord Northbrook, who had been Viceroy of India in 1872.

'PROSPECTS FOR INDIANS IN INDIA'
TO THE EDITOR OF 'INDIA'

Sir, – I hope I may be allowed to congratulate the writer of the paper entitled 'Prospects for Indians in India,' on the excellent tone of his remarks and the reasonableness of his criticism. As the writer of the paper on Lord Northbrook says, 'O! Si sic omnes'!

There are only one or two remarks I should like to make with reference to the last table in the second column, and that is that (although some of us may not agree with them), the Government of India may perhaps think it has arrived for the present at the irreducible minimum of Europeans still necessary for the successful government of the country.

I think it should be admitted also that Eurasians have a right to be considered rather as Indians than as 'foreigners', and it seems that the proportional increase in the numbers of Hindus and Mahomedans between 1897 and 1903 is nearly double that amongst the Eurasians.

I see Mr Dadabhai still quotes the promises of 1833 and 1858 as if they were absolute, and does not inform his audiences that they were always specifically conditional on the maintenance of British supremacy, the need for which he himself admits. Where he always seems to me to fail is in not specifying, at least approximately, the smallest proportion of Europeans he thinks necessary.

Yours, etc.
JB PENNINGTON
18 November 1904

THE LATE EARL OF NORTHBROOK

The following correspondence has been sent to us for publication:

Viscount Baring, 10 Belgrave Square, SW

My Lord, – I read in the *Daily News* with much regret about the death of Lord Northbrook. As Viceroy of India he was fair and sympathetic with the people, and I personally, as Dewan of Baroda, owe him a signal act of justice. After his retirement from India he had always kept up his sympathy and good feeling towards the people of India. I express my sincere condolence with your Lordship in your bereavement.

I remain, yours truly,
DADABHAI NAOROJI
22, Kennington Road, London, SE.
16 November 1904.

Dadabhai Naoroji, Esq.

Dear Sir, – I beg to thank you for your kind letter, and for your expression of sympathy with me.

My father kept to the last the great interest in the welfare and happiness of the people of India which he had felt since he went to India as Viceroy – now more than thirty years ago.

Yours faithfully,
BARING
Stratton, Micheldever Station, 19 November 1904.

The year 1905 was the year when Lord Curzon, the Viceroy of India, angered Indians with his undiplomatic utterances which cast aspersions upon the integrity of Indian people and their sacred writings. A meeting was held by the Indians resident in the United Kingdom at the Caxton Hall, Westminster, in May, to protest against him. Mr Dadabhai Naoroji presided, and among those present were Mr WC Bonnerjee, Miss Alison Garland, Mr Muhummud Anwar Ali, Mr BC Chatterji, Mr E Dalgado, Mr Dwarka Dass, Mr JV Desai, Dr Dikshit. Mr W Douglas Hall, Mr JA Hobson, Mr MB Kolascar, Mr Parmeshwar Lall, Mr Moola, Mr JC Mukerji, Shams-ul-Ulma, Munshi, Mr CJ O'Donnell, Dr Pereira, Mr K Prakasam, Mr Hans Raj, Mr RN Ray, Mr S Shapoorji, and Mr Martin Wood. Support and sympathy came by way of letters from the meetings in Edinburgh and Manchester, which were read by the President.

University Union, Edinburgh.
12 May 1905.

Dear Sir, – I have much pleasure in informing you that a special meeting of the members of the Edinburgh Indian Association was held at 6, Nicolson Street, on May 10, 1905, when a resolution was passed cordially sympathising with the proceedings of the public meeting to be held in London on the 13th inst., under the chairmanship of Mr Dadabhai Naoroji, one of the honorary presidents of the Association.

I remain, dear Sir,
Yours faithfully,
KR TAMFIR,
Secretary, Edinburgh Indian Association.

The Manchester Indian Association,
155, Acomb Street, Manchester,
11 May 1905.

Dear Sir, – I have the honour to communicate to you the following resolution passed unanimously at our meeting on the 7th inst.: 'That the members of this Association approve of the objects, etc., of the protest meeting to be held on Saturday next at Caxton Hall, Westminster, by the Indian residents of the United Kingdom.'

I have, etc.,
SJ MOODGAL,
Vice-President.

Members and officials of both the Indian National Congress and the British Committee of the Indian National Congress, were in constant touch with each other. Communication between the two Conferences were continuous and kept up to date. Representatives of the Indian National Congress came to Britain and their detailed activities were chronicled. News of their arrival and departure made news in the United Kingdom, India, Europe and other parts of the world. Those who could not meet the Congress delegates expressed their support for Congress and India's rights, in the letters to *India*. In an important letter to Mr Gopal Krishna Gokhale CIE, Hodgson Pratt, on 30 October 1905 (published in *India* on 10 November 1905), conveyed the following message of loyalty and understanding for India's cause. It is a detailed observation of the situation in India within a historic context – almost a thesis on morality and rights of the individual.

MR HODGSON PRATT ON INDIA'S RIGHTS
IMPORTANT LETTER TO MR GOKHALE

Hon. Gopal K Gokhale, CIE,
National Liberal Club,
Whitehall Place, SW.

Sir, – As a former member of the Bengal Civil Service, and as a personal friend of many of your countrymen, I beg to address you for the purpose of expressing my great satisfaction that you have come to England in order to inform the British public regarding important matters affecting the welfare of India.

In common with many, I am grieved that there is so much ignorance as to the condition of the Indian people and their requirements, because this ignorance must often preclude useful intervention on their behalf in the British Parliament.

If, however, it should become possible through such action as you are now taking to awaken a widespread interest in Indian affairs, our representatives in the House of Commons would feel constrained to inform themselves as to pressing questions, and would be able to bring about a public discussion in the House – and out of it.

It must be recognised that no people having a civilisation such as that of India can be satisfactorily governed for any length of time by foreigners of a different race.

British officials who during the last century have exercised authority in India have been men of high character and excellent intentions, but their good qualities did not prevent them from committing serious errors, to the disadvantage of vast populations of people affected thereby.

Necessarily, the time arrived when your countrymen, Sir, becoming conscious of their fitness for a larger share in the management of their national affairs, began to ask for a recognition of the justice of their claims.

As regards the possible causes which have delayed the admission of Indians to a larger share in the management of their national affairs it surely cannot be said that there is any evidence of moral or intellectual unfitness.

I may be allowed to add perhaps that in the sphere of religion the Hindu race has produced a very remarkable number of men whose teachings have attracted the respect of the followers of other creeds, and when such men as Ram Mohun Roy and Keshab Chunder Sen have visited Europe, they have won the profound esteem and affection of great religious teachers.

In view of such facts as these, it is indeed difficult to understand on what ground justice has not been done to the legitimate aspirations of our fellow-subjects in the East. They are but asking for the right of participating in the noble duty of serving their country.

For generations past we have regarded the desire of a people for self-government as a test of their fitness for its enjoyment. It is, moreover, generally admitted that national independence is for all nations who have reached a certain stage of civilisation, absolutely essential for the highest development. It is indispensable as a means of giving adequate stimulus to the development of great virtues, and of calling forth increasing efforts for the welfare of the native land.

To restrain the young men of a nation from cherishing the highest and most legitimate ambitions would involve a cruel wrong because it makes the full manhood of the people impossible.

I trust, therefore, that you may, Sir, receive a hearty welcome from the English people, and thorough co-operation in the prosecution of your great task. I hope that other countrymen of yours may follow your example, and that by this means a large part of our people may be led to give a due response to your appeal. Englishmen generally have yet to understand how great a debt they owe to India; and I pray that a consciousness of this may be gradually developed.

The mission you have undertaken cannot be accomplished in a day, but our democracy loves justice and fair-play, and I trust that the best men of all classes will recognise the claims of the Indian people.

Hearty union in ideals, and a spirit of fraternity between our people and yours, is essential for the true welfare of both. God be with you.

Yours heartily,
HODGSON PRATT.
Douarnenez (Finistere), France,
30 October 1905

Support for India's cause came from abroad, and an effort was made by the British Committee of the Indian National Congress to see that their well-wishers were rewarded with information on the nature of their propaganda in Britain. The Chairman, William Wedderburn sent a letter for publication to the *Boston Transcript*, a leading paper in the United States of America, in October 1905. It was introduced 'as an extremely important and interesting communication' and as reported in *India*, 24 November 1905, it said:

INDIAN VIEW OF INDIAN AFFAIRS
LETTER FROM SIR WILLIAM WEDDERBURN
TO AN AMERICAN CORRESPONDENT

Under the heading 'Home Rule for India', the *Boston Transcript*, which is perhaps the foremost paper in the United States for light and leading, publishes the following (October 31):

An extremely important and interesting communication has just been received in this city from Sir William Wedderburn. It is dated at the office of the British Committee of the Indian National Congress, 84 and 85, Palace Chambers, Westminster, London, September 21, 1905, and is as follows:

Dear Sir, – We have to thank you for the sympathetic interest you have shown in the scheme under which Indian delegates are coming to England, in order to place before the British public the Indian view of Indian affairs. You have also been so good as to suggest that they might pay a visit to America. May I, therefore, be allowed briefly to indicate the nature of the propaganda which they propose to undertake on behalf of the people of India?

As you are aware, the delegates receive their credentials from the Indian National Congress, an assembly of elected representatives, numbering about 1,500, drawn from every province of India, which meets annually at Christmas time, and passes resolutions voicing the independent opinion of India on all the most important matters affecting the welfare of the people. Each year these resolutions are respectfully submitted for the favourable consideration of the Viceroy in Council and the Secretary of State for India. The position taken up is both constitutional and patriotic. The Congress frankly accepts British rule as the national rule, so far as effect is given to the just and progressive principles laid down in Acts of Parliament and in Queen Victoria's Proclamation of 1858; but it contends that those principles have not been sufficiently carried out in practice; and it claims that the time has come to give to the people of India a larger share in the management of their own affairs.

In times past the British nation granted to India certain far-reaching concessions, such as those relating to the freedom of the Press, trial by jury, municipal and local self-government, and university education. The concessions thus wisely granted have hitherto proved the sheet anchor of British rule: for the people of India have shown themselves worthy of the confidence placed in them, and under the sympathetic and progressive administration of Lord Ripon and Sir Evelyn Baring (now Lord Cromer), all classes were contented and hopeful. But twenty years have elapsed since that happy period; a new generation is coming to the front, and further developments are needed to meet altered circumstances. Looking to the law-abiding character of the population, and to the trained intelligence of the educated classes, the Congress claims that a further advance is now due, in the interest alike of India and of England. But, unhappily, of late years, a spirit of distrust and reaction has infected the administration, especially during the Viceroyalty of Lord Curzon. The concessions courageously granted in earlier and less settled times have one by one been withdrawn; blows have been struck at the independence of the Press, at municipal self-government, and at higher education; instead of bringing experienced and trustworthy Indians into the higher offices of the State, as enjoined by Queen Victoria's Proclamation, all authority is jealously kept in the hands of the foreign officials, acting through great centralised departments. Thus the administration year by year becomes more and more out of touch with the people; and the natural consequences follow: ruinous public expenditure, with crushing taxation; the educated classes disheartened and alienated; and chronic and increasing destitution among the masses of the people.

With a fertile soil, a fine climate, and labour cheap, skilful and abundant, India might, and ought to be, a garden of plenty. Instead of that, the vast rural population are constantly on the verge of starvation. So destitute are they of any reserve, whether of food, money, or credit, that the failure of one harvest causes countless deaths by famine, with the consequent fevers, cholera, and plague, among the exhausted survivors. The great majority of the peasantry not only possess nothing, but much less than nothing, being hopelessly in debt to the village money-lender. These facts are patent. But they are denied by the official authorities, who persist in saying that the peasantry are lightly taxed, that they are increasing in prosperity, and that (to use the phrase of Sir Henry Fowler, late Secretary of State for India) they are enjoying 'the unspeakable blessings of British rule'. Here, then, is a plain issue of fact as regards the condition of the people. Accordingly, the Congress has asked the Government to have this issue tried and determined; again and again it has petitioned the Government to hold a detailed economic enquiry into the condition of typical famine villages in the different provinces, in order to ascertain the real facts, with a view to measures of famine prevention. Without a diagnosis of the patient it is impossible to prescribe remedies. But this enquiry has been refused, although the prayer of the Congress was supported by the Indian Famine Union, which addressed to the Secretary of State for India a memorial signed by leading representatives of every important class in England.

Under the circumstances nothing remains for the people of India but to appeal to the British Parliament and the British electorate. In times past, when India was under the East India Company, a full Parliamentary enquiry into the affairs of India was held every twenty years, before the renewal of the Company's charter. It was from these enquiries that all the most beneficial reforms took their origin. But since the direct administration has been taken over by the Crown, these periodical enquiries have ceased; for the last 50 years there has been no account of the official stewardship, and the executive has been practically without control. One of the principal prayers of the delegates will be for a revival of such periodical enquiries. Before a Parliamentary committee the true facts will come out, and the British electors will be placed in a position to discharge their trust to the people of India.

In conclusion, I may state that the delegates will be headed by the Hon. G K Gokhale, CIE, a member of the Viceroy's Legislative Council. He is a thorough master of Indian questions, and an excellent speaker, and should he be favoured with an invitation to lecture in the United States, I feel sure that a great benefit would accrue to the cause of justice to India.

W WEDDERBURN,
Chairman.

The British constitutional adage is that the Sovereign reigns but does not govern. The truth about Queen Victoria, the Empress of India, was that in the welfare of the Indian people, she took a deep and abiding interest, going as far as to even learn the language of 'her people', but she never ever set foot in India. Instead, she communicated through letters. There were few questions of importance on which she did not express her firm opinions. One such subject was India. A number of bulky volumes of letters written by her were something of a revelation. One of the earliest letters expressing regret was written from Buckingham Palace on 23 April 1844 and addressed to Sir Robert Peel, following the recall of Lord Ellenborough as Governor-General of India, and the services he had rendered to the East India Company. She was not happy about his treatment. A letter eleven years later to the President of the Board of Control, on 20 June 1855, was quoted in *India*, 26 June 1908:

THE LETTERS OF QUEEN VICTORIA · SOME EXTRACTS OF INDIAN INTEREST · THE QUEEN TO THE PRESIDENT OF THE BOARD OF CONTROL

She takes a deep and natural interest in the welfare of her Indian Empire and must consider the selection of the fittest person for the post of Governor-General as of paramount importance. She has frequently discussed this point with Lord Palmerston, but the name of Lord Canning never occurred amongst candidates alluded to. The Queen is even now quite ignorant as to the reasons and motives which led to his selection in preference to those other names, and Mr V Smith will see at once that were the Queen inclined to object to it, she could not now do so without inflicting a deep personal injury on a public man for whose personal qualities and talents the Queen has a high regard. . .

Next in order may be quoted with advantage the text of the remarkable, if not altogether inspired, communication which was addressed to the Queen by the retiring Governor-General on the arrival in India of Lord Canning, barely a twelve months before the outbreak of the Mutiny. . .

Following the famous Proclamation of 1858, a year after the Mutiny, the Queen's letter, written on 15 August, made her objections to the draft of the Proclamation. History shows that these were just the words of a sovereign that reigned but could not govern...

The Queen would be glad if Lord Derby would write it himself in his excellent language, bearing in mind that it is a female sovereign who speaks to more than one hundred millions of Eastern people on assuming the direct government over them after a bloody civil war, giving them pledges which her future reign is to redeem, and explaining the principles of her Government. Such a document should breathe feelings of generosity, benevolence, and religious feeling, pointing out the privileges which the Indians will receive in being placed on an equality with the subjects of the British Crown, and the prosperity following in the train of civilisation.

*   *   *

One of the most unexpected examples of support came from Mr A E Pacefaite, a Spanish Correspondent, writing from Estancia La Libertad, Cordoba. It was published in *Public Opinion* on 'India and Self-government' which *India* reproduced on 2 October 1908. While he has the right idea of India's need and justification for self-government, his solutions to the problem must remain just an improbable dream. What is rather endearing and moving is the effort made to not only write, but to expand in ways and means for a 'peaceful' solution. The time taken to free India was 39 years away.

Public Opinion publishes the following letter on 'India and Self-Government' from Estancia La Libertad, Cordoba:
Is not the time ripe now for the British to do what the Americans have done in respect to Cuba – give India self-government and so retire magnanimously from continuing a work which has already produced good results, the rousing of 'a people's national consciousness?' Each province might have a governor, chosen by its own people in a federative sense; all the governors to recognise a head in the person of a chosen president, who should abide in a central province, this province to have a governor equally with the rest of the provinces. The form of government to be unitarian in the sense of responsibility of all the governors to the central government. In the central province only should there exist a congress, consisting of senators and representatives, all chosen by the votes of each province, and these two bodies to elect the president for a certain number of years, the only one eligible to be natives born in India. The administration of justice to be under British control for a specified number of years, a friendly agreement to be made between the British and India in the sense of a preferential commercial treaty, and complete freedom given to British enterprise in a social, industrial, religious, and commercial sense. Thus would a true and lasting and binding friendship result between the two peoples. If things are allowed to drift as at present there will be, increasingly, war, rebellion, and expenditure on a vast scale for the British; besides, the opportunity of anarchy would be taken advantage of by the enemy (always on the watch) to add to the trouble. Finally, let me add that it would be expedient, till the new Constitution were firmly established in working order, that the British troops should remain as the guarantee of a peaceful reconstruction. If this were all realised in the reign of our gracious King Edward VII, he would assuredly merit the well-earned name of 'The Peace-maker'.

In May 1914, a new magazine was launched which was published between the First World War years 1914 and 1917. To wish it success, Aga Khan sent the following cable:

LETTER TO THE EDITOR

BY CABLE. I wish *The Indiaman* every success. Would have written more fully, but have just returned from North Africa and starting for East Africa, so am very busy.

AGA KHAN

The Indiaman, 15 May 1914. No1 Vol I.

The Editor invited correspondence from its readers. It published a page of letters from other noble well-wishers.

At the height of the First World War when Indian soldiers were fighting alongside the British soldiers in Europe and both their death rate and awards of Victoria Crosses to them were rising, a rather ungracious editorial appeared in *The Times* on 19 June 1916, against the Home Rule for India League.

A MISCHIEVOUS MOVEMENT

We have received copies of a leaflet circulated by an obscure organisation calling itself 'Home Rule for India League', which appears to have opened offices in London, and proposes 'to inform the British people of the real condition of things in India'. If the statements in the leaflet are a fair example of the type of 'information' which the League intends to circulate, the sooner it receives official attention the better. Thus it is said that Indians are 'becoming alarmed at the frightful poverty of the agricultural population, the destruction of indigenous industries by foreign competition, and the decreasing vitality of both the educated and the uneducated classes, but especially of the latter'. Each of these statements is untrue. The condition of the peasantry is steadily improving; industrial development has become almost the main preoccupation of the Government of India; and the standard of comfort and vitality among all classes has shown a great advance during the last twenty years. The subsequent reference to 'our constant demands for her money while we refuse her men' is merely ridiculous, for the Indian revenues have not contributed a rupee to the cost of the war. The most poisonous feature of the new propaganda is a wicked attempt to set Indians at loggerheads with the British in India. The most ominous feature is concisely summarized in the declaration that 'the government of India must cease to be foreign and must become Indian'. A movement of this kind need not, perhaps, be taken too seriously. Nevertheless, we feel bound to point out to well-meaning people, who may be attracted by it, that the exaggeration and falsehood on which it is founded are the very surest means of checking the natural growth of the great Dependency which we hold in trust for civilization. Cranky people in this country do many mad things, but surely the maddest is to encourage a 'Home Rule' agitation in India at a moment when we are just entering upon the gravest crisis of the war. No Viceroy has ever shown more sympathy with Indian aspirations than Lord Hardinge, but the warning which he uttered in his last Budget speech at Delhi is plainly more applicable than ever. He spoke of self-government for India as an ideal, and went on to say: 'In the present position of India it is not idealism that is needed, but practical politics... Lightly to raise extravagant hopes and encourage unrealizable demands can only tend to delay and will not accelerate political progress.' We commend these wise words to any ingenuous person who may have been invited to countenance the activities of the 'Home Rule for India League'.

Within two days they printed a reply to the Editorial from an Indophile, Emily Lutyens, in support of Mrs Annie Beasant's All India Home Rule League. Emily Lutyens had inaugurated the English Home Rule League with the first meeting at Bedford Square in London.

Emily Lutyens (1875–1964)
Daughter of Lord Lytton, Viceroy of India (1876–80); Married Edwin Lutyens (1869–1944), the architect of New Delhi, including the Rashtrapati Bhavan, the former Viceregal Lodge.

'A MISCHIEVOUS MOVEMENT'
TO THE EDITOR OF 'THE TIMES'

Sir, – With reference to your leading article on the Home Rule for India League, may I correct an impression which might be misleading to the general public? The League has not, as you seem to suggest, been organised to carry on an agitation either in this country or in India to press for action on the part of the British Government during the war. Its aim is rather to educate the British people on the question of India's needs, so that when the war is over and the whole question of Imperial reconstruction is being considered India may not be forgotten. That there is a danger of this forgetfulness is proved by the fact that although even now, while the war is in progress, the question of Imperial federation is being discussed by leading statesmen and in the Press, India's place is never mentioned.

Yours truly,
EMILY LUTYENS.

Lady Emily Lutyens is mistaken in supposing that 'India's place is never mentioned' by those who discuss Imperial relations in the Press. We suggest that she should study any periodical which deals with these questions, such, for instance, as the *Round Table* and our own recent Empire Number.

Having her letter in *The Times* gave publicity to the League. In spite of her good intentions, the publicity and the letter were criticised as it was feared, it would harm her husband, Edwin Lutyens. 'I think you should keep out of this', was the advice given to her by Annie Besant.

Against the drama of the war in Europe, all talk of self-government for India became a secondary issue. Yet, there were those who could and would keep India in the forefront. The British had to be reminded, as the writer puts, of the 're-settlement of the Empire'. Britain's war was fought with the whole-hearted support of the Indians. In the end Britain won, but the Indians gained nothing. A letter in *India* by Sheikh Mushir Hosain Kidwai, from the National Liberal Club address, was published on 27 October 1916.

THE DEMAND FOR SELF-GOVERNMENT
TO THE EDITOR OF 'INDIA'

Sir, – The news that nineteen elected members of the Imperial Legislative Council have presented a memorial to the Viceroy, advocating constitutional changes after the war, is very welcome. The signatories are to be congratulated upon acting at exactly the right time. Hindus and Mahommedans are united in the demand for self-government; and the reforms suggested, if the cabled summary is correct, appear to be framed on sound lines.

Everyone who has studied the problems in India is aware that it is the Civil Service, with its vested interests, which constitutes the chief obstacle to reform. Under the present system, the bureaucracy frames the laws and regulates the finances exactly as it pleases. And, so long as the Viceroy remains under the domination of the Civil Service, it is useless to imagine that even a Ripon or a Hardinge can undertake any genuine step forward in the direction of progress. I hold that it is only from this country that real constitutional changes in the nature of self-government can be expected. It is, therefore, most desirable that a deputation of Indian publicists should come to England in order to prepare the public here for the time when the claims of India must be discussed in connexion with the re-settlement of the Empire. The memorandum which has been presented to the Viceroy should be circulated to every member of both Houses of Parliament.

It has been stated that the signatories to the memorandum do not include any representatives of the 'military caste' or of backward provinces. But India does not seek transition through violent methods, and the support of the 'military caste' is unnecessary. It is not revolution that is demanded, but reform – radical, indeed, but within sound constitutional limits. Nevertheless, the choice of the character of agitation is still, to a large extent, in the power of the educated Indians, and the British public. Even now, in one of the provinces of India, the life of the leader of the constitutional party is being threatened by the anarchists. Self-government is the only concession that can avert the danger and satisfy the awakened consciousness of India.

SHEIKH MUSHIR HOSAIN KIDWAI (of Gadia)
National Liberal Club

Hind was launched as the Indian organ in the United Kingdom in August 1921 following the closure of *India*. Under the slogan 'Swarajya Is My Birthright' it put forward the state of affairs in India, political and otherwise, for readers in Britain. It prided itself in being a reliable agency for all views and news of India.

A PERSONAL EXPLANATION

For the last sixteen months I have not asked for a holiday. My engagements with the Bharat Conference, the Sikh Conference, and the Bazim-i-Hind, independently of my work with the journal *Hind*, have been responsible for a heavy strain on my health, and I think I deserve a little rest. Instead of closing the office for a holiday, I propose issuing communiqués in a reduced size of *Hind* for a fortnight. I also trust that instead of sending me any sympathetic letters, my supporters will send me their Subscriptions in arrears which is the real cure for the disease I am suffering from.

Khadim-i-quam,
GS DARA

The editor G S Dara and Arthur Field, Hon. Secretaries of the Indian National Congress Association, London, published a letter in *Hind* on 18 August 1923, regarding the Indian Swaraj flag.

INDIAN NATIONAL CONGRESS ASSOCIATION, LONDON
INDIAN SWARAJ FLAG

There seems to exist some misunderstanding in some quarters on the subject of the Indian National Flag, as seen lately at the No-More-War Demonstration in London. The Association think it would be advisable to issue a manifesto on the subject: (1) the cloth of the national flag should be square. Its length should be one and a half times its breadth. (2) There would be three equal pieces of cloth one over the other in the National Flag. Above all there would be a white coloured piece, in the middle green and lowest red. (3) There would be a sign of spinning wheel in the centre, it may be printed or stitched, and equal portion of cloth should be left round the wheel. The measurement of this wheel would be one-fourth of its breadth. (4) The National Flag over the breast should always be on the left side. Ladies should use it on the left shoulder; the red of the hand flag should always be kept erect.

August 8th, 1923.   GS DARA, *Editor Hind,*
31-33 High Holborn,   ARTHUR FIELD,
London   *Hon. Secretaries*

Having established various organisations it became necessary to give a simple symbol of authority to their activity and identification.

British support for India's cause was wholehearted and open. Some, as A Fenner Brockway did on 6 January 1923, even wrote a letter to *Hind* of his willingness to do all he could to fight for self-rule for India. It came as a New Year's Message to *Hind* but it was also a message for India's future

END THE BRITISH RULE OF FORCE
RIGHT OF INDIAN PEOPLE
A NEW YEAR'S MESSAGE TO 'HIND'

Dear Mr Dara,

I hope that the Indian Nationalist Movement may during the coming year advance steadily towards its goal of the absolute right of the Indian people to decide their own form of Government and their own allegiances. Your movement has given the world an example of applied idealism. I hope that it may continue to understand that liberty is a thing of the spirit and that it can only be won by spiritual and non-violent means. We in this country must endeavour to end the British rule of force in India from outside, whilst you seek to end it from inside; and then hand-in-hand we must go forward as partners in the cause of world betterment.

Yours sincerely
A FENNER BROCKWAY
(*National Organising Secretary of the Independent Labour Party*)

1924 was the year M K Gandhi became President of the Indian National Congress. The war had been over six years and King George V was the King Emperor. Self-rule for India was nowhere in sight. The non-cooperation movement was making effective inroads into the business of British administration. Gandhi, who had been arrested a year before for sedition was *persona nongrata* to the Raj. A veteran of South African political struggle, he was not easily defeated. His imprisonment and state of health gave rise to anxiety everywhere. As Editor of *Hind* and the Secretary of the Indian National Congress Association, G S Dara published two letters, on 2 and 4 February 1924.

INDIAN CONGRESS ASSOCIATION, LONDON
HIS ILLNESS

The manner in which the British press has treated the illness of Mahatmaji is only equalled by the methods adopted by the Anglo-Indians in India in keeping close secrecy of the whole episode till the last moment. The present, however, is not the occasion to utter anything that would disturb its serenity. What really is wanted at the moment when our hearts are throbbing with grief, is to raise our hands for prayer, and kneel down before Him, with all humbleness that the gravity of the occasion warrants, and pray for his speedy recovery to health. For a prayer to be of any value, it should be offered in all sincerity, unaccompanied with any resentment towards his persecutors, who have thrown him in gaol for the crime of preaching what Jesus preached. Let us ask forgiveness from Providence, for both the persecuted as also his persecutors, for they 'know not what they do'. Not only in India and Asia alone, but indeed true Christians in the West, too, will have received the news from the Yerawada Jail with great concern. But still greater undoubtedly is the concern of his countrymen, in whose service 'the greatest living man on earth' lies but a condemned criminal today in a prison cell in India. Indians, in whichever corner of the world they happen to be, must all hasten to realise the deep debt of gratitude they owe him and the motherland. The Congress Association in London therefore expects every Indian in England and abroad irrespective of his political complexion, to turn his eyes to the Yerawada Jail, and offer prayers

Kabaa Roo, on February 18, the next Gandhi-day, invoking His mercy on the prisoner in the cell, and wishing heartily that Providence may spare him long to guide the destinies of the weak and the poor in India, England, and elsewhere. *Amen.*

	GS DARA
February 2, 1924	*(Editor, Hind),*
31-33 High Holborn, London.	*Secretary*

HIS ILLNESS

The Congress Association in London, in a previous communiqué, has enjoined on the Indian colony in this country, as also on their compatriots abroad, to observe February 18, the next Gandhi-Day, as the day of 'fasting and praying', to demonstrate their affection and esteem in which they all along held Mahatmaji. In order to effect a uniformity, however, it is further urged, that the meetings for the day should be held all over, if convenient otherwise, at 3pm. No unkind or ungenerous thought should be given expression to, lest it may mar the sanctity of the occasion in any respect. Also it is humbly expected from Indians who have not yet imbibed the idea of taking to intoxicating liquors and breaking the barriers of *Halal* and *Haram*, to abstain, if only for the day, from deliberate assaults on the tenets of their respective faiths, as known to their elders and understood to the rest of their countrymen. The Association further trusts that even those who frequent the hostels at the Cromwell House and the YMCA will try to see in it an appeal worthy of their response, too.

	GS DARA
February 4, 1924	*(Editor Hind),*
31-33 High Holborn, London	*Secretary*

By 1928, Indian aspirations for a self-government for India were growing rapidly. But the British were not moving as fast. They made a decision to send a fact-finding commission to India, headed by Sir John Simon, to see what constitutional changes could be made. It had three fundamental flaws: 1. No Indians were consulted; 2. It was answerable to the British Parliament; 3. Indians could be invited to give opinions, but their wishes could not become the basis of the Commission's recommendations. All Indian parties boycotted the Commission. Congress passed a resolution in 1929 demanding Indian independence. *The Times*, on 18 April 1928 published a remarkable letter from M F O'Dwyer.

INDIAN REFORMS
SWARAJISTS AND SIMON COMMISSION

Sir, – The return of the Simon Commission lends interest to the recent manoeuvres of the Swaraj party that is unsuccessfully attempting to boycott it. The Lahore cable in *The Times* of April 14 summarizes the views placed before the Congress meeting at Amritsar by Mr Jawaharlal, son of the extremist leader, Pandit Moti Lal. After rebuking the Punjab, the 'Indian Ulster' for its lack of 'great speakers or thinkers' and its consequent failure to join in the boycott, he outlined the Swaraj programme as follows: Dominion status would be useless to India, as she would still remain under British economic subjection. Hence complete independence, with the severance of the British connexion is the only sound political ideal. India could defend herself; if not, better foreign invasion than British protection. Then follows the bait that so often deluded our British Socialists into supporting a Brahman oligarchy striving under the catchwords of democracy to recapture its lost Dominion:

India should be made an independent democratic State, aiming at Swaraj for the masses, based on Socialism, and not on a transfer of power from a British oligarchy to an Indian oligarchy.

It was anti-British incitements of this nature that stirred up the revolutionary outbreaks of 1919; and, however futile they may be in Madras or Bengal, they may be a real danger in the 'virile province' of the Punjab. From this and other recent Swaraj declarations one may deduce the following conclusions:

(1) There is a section of the Swaraj party, including the discredited Caliphate 'rump,' which would be willing to invite foreign invasion and foment local rebellion, as it did in 1919, in the hope of pulling down British rule, and in the resulting chaos re-establishing the Brahman dominion which, having survived ten centuries of Buddhism and ten centuries of Moslem supremacy, may in their view, also supplant British rule.

(2) But the great mass of Swarajists and their 'Liberal' allies are not quite so foolish. Their ultimate aim may be the same, but their methods are subtler. They pose as the representatives of the 160 million caste Hindus – one-half of the Indian population, but divided into over 2,000 sub-castes – and therefore hope to reassert the domination of the Brahmans – roughly ten millions – not only over the inferior Hindu castes, whom they can keep in subjection by their religious and social supremacy, but also over 'the lesser hordes without the law' – seventy million Moslems, twelve million Buddhists, ten million aboriginals, four million Sikhs, five million Indian Christians, and the sixty million outcastes, created such by the Brahmans.

(3) The boycott movement is not a foolish gesture dictated merely by wounded vanity, or even that sense of inferiority to which Mr Ramsey MacDonald ascribes it. It has a deeper origin. Co-operation with the Commission would require the Swarajists to put all their cards on the table and prove their claim. Realizing the difficulty of this, they have adopted the more astute policy of challenging the statutory right of Parliament to decide the issue, and stand aloof demanding complete independence, with Dominion status as a possible transitional stage. The tactics are those of the Indian *bazar*. The seller begins by asking three time the value of the goods and at least double of what in the long run he will gladly take. Now and again the non-Indian purchaser is foolish enough to offer him at the start one-half or more, only to find that he has been duped; the goods are not what he was led to expect. This is the game the extremists are now playing. But they are becoming uneasy at the Commission's success in getting into touch with the saner elements of the Indian peoples – those who are not led by the Hindu lawyer-politician.

Mr Jawaharlal's rhetoric cannot conceal his misgivings; he urges that the boycott should continue 'in spite of the defections of the weak and the well-meant attempts to bridge a gulf which is not easily bridged'. He and his kind are looking out for that bridge.

The Commission is now master of the situation; it has realized that the Swarajists do not speak for the diverse Indian peoples, but only for a small minority, whose real aim is to restore a Brahman-controlled autocracy of the higher Hindu castes, under a camouflage of democratic form with which they hope to delude the British public.

I am, &c.,
M F O'DWYER
The Athenaeum, April 15

Jawaharlal Nehru (1889–1964) shown here with his father Pandit Moti Lal Nehru. Politician and statesman, he was India's first Prime Minster, 1947–64. Educated at Harrow and Trinity College, Cambridge; read for the Bar at London's Inner Temple 1910–12.

Between November 1930 and December 1932 three Round Table Conferences were held in London, which brought the Indian demands and discussion of constitutional issues to Britain's doors. Every move of the delegates was monitored and reported in the press. Equally, the press watched and followed the activities of the British delegation to India. The reporting was not always accurate as illustrated by a letter from the representative of the India League:

INDIA LEAGUE PARTY'S TOUR
TO THE EDITOR OF 'THE TIMES'

Sir, – May I be permitted to correct certain misstatements made by your Delhi Correspondent concerning the delegation recently sent to India by the India League?

Your Correspondent alleges that the delegation was financed by Congress. The fact is that subscriptions were received towards the delegation's expenses from all kinds of English and Indian sympathizers, including many Indians who are not only opposed to Congress methods but who are represented in the present Round-Table Conference. As a matter of fact, a considerable section of Congress was actually opposed to the delegation's visit, regarding English opinion on India as not worthy either of conciliation or information.

Your Correspondent's further suggestion that the delegation's tour was stage-managed by Congress is equally incorrect. The members of the delegation visited Indians of every class and every school of thought, and also received hospitality from many English officials, who advised both as to their procedure and the places which they should visit. The suggestion that Indians arranged for themselves to be beaten in order to provide the delegation with sensations is rather too ridiculous to deserve serious reply. It is perfectly true that demonstrations arranged in honour of the delegation's visit did, in certain cases, lead to counter police demonstrations, but it is equally clear that this result would have followed whether the delegation had been present or not.

I am, yours faithfully,
JF HORRABIN, Vice-Chairman,
The India League,
72, Gower Street, WC1

STATUS OF INDIA
THE WORK OF A CENTURY
TO THE EDITOR OF 'THE TIMES'

Sir, – In the matter of India's status we must look far and we must look deep. India is perfectly justified in wanting and working to be as free as she possibly can be. And it is surely in keeping with the deepest wishes of the British people that we should not block the way with unnecessary restrictions, but put our backs into helping Indians achieve their ambition. Constitution-making is a long and tedious process. And Indians must be patient while it is going forward. But in the crucial moments in this next week we can by our expressions in Parliament and in public leave upon India the impression that we are half-heartedly and niggardly in our Constitution-making and more intent upon safeguarding our own interests than upon helping Indians to govern themselves; or we can show them decisively and distinctively that we mean business, that we mean to do the big thing in the big way. We cannot possibly go against the whole trend of our national character, of the character upon which our whole Empire is built up, and of the character of the entire world-movement.

FRANCIS YOUNGHUSBAND
1 Vicarage-gate, W8, November 25

(*The Times*, 28 November 1931)

Reported Indian issues in the Press in Britain had the advantage of being read by all English-speaking nations of the world – and especially the North Americans. Frequently, there was a feedback by way of an informed comment in the form of a letter to the Editor as was the case from Michigan USA in January 1934.

Those who campaigned on India's behalf were treated as heroes, and appreciated for clarifying India's rights. India was honoured to have such loyal friends.

LETTER FROM ANN ARBOR, MICHIGAN, USA,
1 DECEMBER 1935

To the Editor of the India Bulletin.

As you know Mr Fenner Brockway is in this country on a lecture tour in the interest of Labour and the Freedom of India. He is speaking widely in the cities and universities and doing strong work on behalf of both causes. I have just had the pleasure of meeting him and listening to his address here in Michigan University and to the people of the town. They were very effective. He is doing much to help the cause of Labour and to give to America a true understanding of conditions in India.

JT SUTHERLAND

Support for India's cause came from all quarters and classes of society in England. Some had a great desire and ability to put across their views, both on their own behalf and on behalf of the organisation they represented. *United India* published a letter of moral support in June-July 1937, written by a AW Wood of Balliol College, Oxford, who was the editor of *Oxford Guardian* and ex-president of the Oxford Union Liberal Club.

INDIA

Like most people in England, I know nothing about India. I once, however, had the misfortune to travel from Bombay to Marseilles in company with a large number of Anglo-Indians returning on leave: and no knowledge of Indian affairs could engender a greater sympathy for the cause of Indian independence than personal contact with the actual lords and masters of India.

As a Liberal, I cannot but sympathize with hopes for the eventual achievement of Indian autonomy. In the first place, my party has a fine record as the champion of Subject nations: and in India we have a great nation of 350,000,000 people subject to a foreign Parliament which may devote one day per year to discussing their problems. Secondly, I oppose dictatorships: because it is better for a people to govern itself, even if it governs itself badly, than to be governed well by a despot at the price of liberty. India today is one vast Public School ruled over by the Old School Tie: and the fact that Indians want to emerge from their school-boy status and overthrow their schoolmaster merely proves their manhood.

AW WOOD
(*Editor Oxford Guardian, & Ex-President OU Liberal Club*)
Balliol, Oxford.

Mahatma Gandhi, The Aga Khan and Mrs Sarojini Naidu in London for the Second Round Table Conference.

The 1931 Second Round Table Conference showing the specially made oval table.

CHAPTER 6

Round Table Conferences

THE FIRST SESSION of the Indian Round Table Conference was held between 12 November 1930 and 31 January 1931. The Second Round Table Conference, attended by Mahatma Gandhi, took place between 7 September 1931 and 31 December 1931, chaired by the British Prime Minister, J Ramsay MacDonald. The Third Round Table Conference was held between 7 November 1932 and 24 December 1932.

Delegates from India for the Second Round Table Conference included Mr GD Birla, Mr MA Jinnah, Dr BR Ambedkar, HRH The Aga Khan, Mrs Sarojini Naidu, Begum Shah Nawaz, Pandit Madan Mohan Malaviya, The Rt Hon. VS Srinivasa Sastri and Sir Tej Bahadur Sapru.

Mahatma Gandhi, during his visit to Britain for the Second Round Table Conference, toured the country to meet people. He was well received wherever he went.

IN THE CLOUDS.

DAY OF SILENCE.

David Low produced a series of wonderful cartoons about the Second Round Table
Conference. The top cartoon appeared in the *Evening Standard* on 2 January 1930
and the bottom cartoon in the *Evening Standard* on 12 September 1931 in the
early days of the conference.

**Madan Mohan Malaviya
(1861–1946)**
Graduated from Calcutta University;
President of Indian National Congress
1909 and 1918; High Court Vakil 1893;
opposed the Press Act and the Seditious
Meetings Act. Delegate to Second Round
Table Conference, in London, 1931.
Always dressed in immaculate white
which earned him the nickname of 'the
spotless Pandit'.

The conference was organised to discuss a new constitution for a self-governing India. It was not a success and ended without any agreement. In his vote of thanks Gandhi told the Chairman that Britain and India had come to the parting of the ways. For Pandit Madan Mohan Malaviya, the conference had failed to address Indian problems, leaving very little hope for India's future. Gandhi had huge publicity but very little by way of success at the Conference.

Away from the Conference, Gandhi went round the country to meet British public figures and the ordinary people, notable amongst whom were Jan Smuts, George Bernard Shaw, Maria Montessori, Harold Laski, the Archbishop of Canterbury, Charlie Chaplin and Lancashire textile workers. He also made a radio broadcast to America. Gandhi also went to Oxford where he addressed Indian undergraduates, and spoke at the Raleigh Club, a university society devoted to Imperial subjects.

Gandhi's Dandi Salt March in April 1930 was already widely seen in the cinema newsreels of the West, making him an instantly recognisable celebrity during his travels in Europe. He was warmly received wherever he went.

When he returned to Bombay from London, Gandhi announced 'I have come back empty-handed'. To make up for the failure, he embarked on his campaign of civil disobedience to fight the British. Four years later, the Government of India Act of 1935 was introduced. It allowed basic reforms offering Indian Provinces some local autonomy. The Act was to become the constitutional structure of Independent India in April 1947.

Gandhi's visit to England was not, however, a total failure. When he went to Oxford, he stayed with the Master of Balliol, Dr A D Lindsey. A meeting was arranged to discuss the problems of India with Mr Henry Black, Dr S K Datta, Mr Malcolm MacDonald, Mr C F Andrews, Dr Lindsey, Lord Lothian, Professor Coupland, Mr Horace Alexander and Professor Gilbert Murray. No solution were found in such a short period, but a decision was made to keep open a channel of communication with the British Government. It was considered vital that this dialogue should continue. The India Conciliation Group was thus founded in 1931.

Carl Heath became its first chairman and Agatha Harrison its secretary, and regular meetings were held at Friend's House in London. As the name suggests, it was a low key organisation designed to quietly lobby ministers and politicians in Britain for India's cause.

At the time of the Round Table Conference, it was the wish expressed by Lord Irwin that Churchill should have a discussion with the visiting Indian delegates. Churchill's reply was, 'I am quite satisfied with my views on India. I don't want them to be disturbed by any bloody Indians'.

The Federal Structure Committee
of the Second Round Table
Conference. Pandit Madan
Mohan Malaviya, who helped to
present the Congress case is on
Gandhi's left hand side.

In Nairobi, Kenya, one of the most influential and active women's associations was the Bhagini Samaj.
The 1946 Working Committee included:

FRONT ROW SEATED (LEFT TO RIGHT)

Maniben Patel; Zaverben Patel; Lalita Ben Desai (President); Gangaben Patel; Damyantiben Adalja (Secretary);
Kalavatiben Topiwala (Joint-secretary); Champaben Vadgama (Author's mother)

STANDING

Jadavben Shah; Hansaben Sheth; Jayantibala Jani; Sarlaben Naugankar; Shantaben Sachania; Sushilaben Kolhatkar

STANDING BACK ROW

Dayaben Bakarania; Savitriben Kotecha; Durgaben Bhatt; Vimlaben Vora

CHAPTER 7

Support in other countries

SUPPORT FOR INDIAN HOME RULE was not limited to British shores. There was a growing interest in Indian affairs across the Atlantic. Understanding India's problems and allowing their public discussion was America's way of showing support. The American Press followed the activities of the Indian National Congress in India and in England and was quick to highlight its progress. It also welcomed warmly the views of leading activists in the campaign as it did to Lala Lajpat Rai in 1905. The New York *Evening Post* reported the man and his mission. He had come to England as a delegate to the Indian National Congress.

MR LAJPAT RAI IN NEW YORK

The object of the Indian National Congress is to present to the Government the defects of its administration. Our chief aim is to get, by gradual concessions, a system of representative government, by which the Natives of India may get a voice in the imposition of taxes, and in the administration of affairs. On my arrival in England our deputation will tour the country and address the people at public meetings, hoping so to excite their sympathy, and asking them to demand from their members at the next election, pledges to reform the condition of Indian government.

Unfortunately, England is now under an Imperial wave, and the attitude it maintains towards its subjects is not of trust, but of suspicion. The Indian National Congress thinks that there would be greater contentment throughout India if there were some local government, and that there would accordingly be no need of so large an army.

The object of my visit to the United States was to study your educational institutions. One lesson that India should learn of this country is the spirit of unity and nationality that obtains here among a mixed population composed of all nations of the earth...

Lord Curzon was a very unpopular Governor-General among the Indians, but Lord Kitchener is already still more unpopular. Lord Curzon's policy was one of interference and distrust. But while Lord Curzon was unpopular in regard to his civil administration, Lord Kitchener is still more unpopular on account of the military rule which he is establishing.

Politicians as well as other notable individuals visiting America were equally recognised for what they had to say about the affairs of India. Swami Abhedananda in 1906 attracted a great deal of attention for his series of six lectures, 'India and Her People' at the Brooklyn Institute. He was heard by a large and interested audience and received prominent coverage in the *Daily Standard Union* of Brooklyn. Tracing the history of the British domination of India since the days of the East India Company and life under the Crown, he began with an attack on the unpopular Lord Curzon.

A SWAMI IN THE UNITED STATES
LECTURES ON INDIA IN BROOKLYN
LORD CURZON'S ONE GOOD DEED

'Lord Curzon has done one good thing by his oppression. He has created a national feeling in India. Let us hope this will bring the English autocrats and despots to their senses. If the United States wishes to know what it would have become under British rule, let it look at India.'

'And this,' said the Swami, 'will give you a rough idea of how India has "progressed" under English rule. The East India Company has been gone since 1858, but its spirit is still there. The administration of the Crown doubled the debt in nineteen years. The expenses of the various expeditions are all added to the debt left by the old Company. Great good these expeditions do to India.

'As an example of what India has to pay, the expenses of the India House in London were cited, where even the charwoman is paid by India. England has not spent a penny for the good of India. The Government of England in India today is as despotic as that of Russia. The people's part is to pay the taxes and that is all.

'Lord Curzon was the most unpopular Viceroy India ever had. Liked at first, he became as much disliked because of his policy of oppression and distrust, and because he has taken away the freedom of the Press and the right to trial of a political suspect. In India a man can be arrested at any time and sentenced without trial. These things are happening in the twentieth century and there is not one nation in the world that takes cognisance of it today.'

The Swami spoke of Queen Victoria's Proclamation of fair treatment as something on which the Indians have built their hopes of better things, especially as its assurances were renewed by King Edward. But Lord Curzon said it could never be realised because the Indians are of another race, therefore cannot have equal rights with the English.

Criticism of the British rule in India came from Canada, a country once governed by Britain but moving on to become a self-governing Dominion. From an unusual platform and to an unsuspecting audience, Rev. TJ Sunderland preached in a sermon in the House of God in Toronto in 1906, on India's freedom movement.

THE WRONGS OF INDIA
SYMPATHY FROM CANADA

There are some wrongs which ought to press particularly upon our attention and weigh particularly upon our hearts, because of the fact that we are citizens of the British Empire.

In what with pride we call 'Our Indian Empire,' we have the spectacle of hundreds of millions of people ruled without their consent by a nation in a distant part of the world. The Indian people are the most intellectual in Asia; they had a high civilisation centuries before Great Britain had emerged from barbarism. Before the Christian era they had produced a great literature and great philosophical systems. We have the testimony of the highest English officials who have spent their lives in India, to the effect that hundreds of thousands and millions of the Indian people are equals of the English people themselves. Tens of thousands of them have been educated in colleges and universities in their own land, in England, and in the continent of Europe, and are trained not only in the learning of the Orient, but in the knowledge and science of the West, and yet they are given no part whatever in the direction of the affairs of their own nation, in shaping their own political history or future. They are ruled absolutely by foreigners. A single blacksmith or coal miner in England who can vote for a member of Parliament has more power in shaping the policy of the Indian Government than have all the people of India combined. This is tyranny. It is a wrong that should be righted. If they do not, then there should be protests from other lands. Especially should Canada take an interest in this matter. India is under the same government with ourselves. We have freedom. We have self-government. We have practical autonomy. We should have sympathy with those who are deprived of the rights which have been granted to us. We like to sing 'Britons, never, never will be slaves'. A more practical matter is, are we willing to keep others slaves? There ought to be a strong popular sentiment in Canada, reinforcing the sentiment which is growing in England, in favour of a gradual, steady, and real extension of privileges and rights to India.

In Europe, Germany took notice of the struggle for self-rule in India, in 1906. *India* took notice of what *Vossiche zeitung*, the most influential Liberal paper of Berlin had to say about *Bande Mataram*. 'As a novice', the paper said. 'the new Secretary of State for India thought at first that *Bande Mataram* was long ago 'legally prohibited'. This is not so yet, in point of fact, it is locally (in Bengal) under a ban'. The article was full of praise for the work and dedication of Sir William Wedderburn and Sir Henry Cotton for India's political struggle.

*   *   *

In America, the Indian cause was carried to sympathetic audiences all over the country by the Press, and coverage given to visiting Indian delegates and by founding various organisations. Simply understanding India's problem was not enough. Some Americans wanted to show an act of solidarity. The pressing need of an Indian voice in America gave rise to the Indo-American National Association at Green Acre, Maine, USA. A letter from the Association President, Mr Myron H Phelps was sent to Dadabhai Naoroji in London on 5 September 1907. It laid out the aims and objectives of the Association and informed him that he (Naoroji) on behalf of the Indo-American National Association had been chosen the Honorary President for India of that body.

AMERICAN SYMPATHY WITH INDIA
A NEW INDO-AMERICAN ASSOCIATION

We have pleasure in publishing the following correspondence which has passed between Mr Dadabhai Naoroji and Mr Myron H Phelps of the New York Bar:

Dear Sir, – I have the honour to inform you, on behalf of the Indo-American National Association, organised at Green Acre, Maine, USA, on the 5th instant, that you have been chosen Honorary President for India of that body.

The declared objects of this Association are as follows:

First: to assist in co-operation with individuals and associations the educational advancement of Indians, by the careful selection of young men and women of suitable character and promise by aiding them, as well as all Indian students now in this country, to find the most favourable locations in which to secure the best technical and industrial training, together with opportunities for self-support while engaged in study, and further to aid such students in the difficult task of adapting themselves to the conditions of American life and by all desirable means to render the sojourn of Indian students in America pleasant and profitable.

Second: To secure space in the American Press for the presentation and discussion of questions relating to India; to disseminate correct information about India through the Press and from the platform; to awaken an interest in India, and to create an intelligent public opinion on Indian questions in this and other countries.

Third: To arrange for entertaining in American homes, representative Hindus who may desire to visit the United States of America and to procure for them facilities for obtaining correct information about American institutions, and for becoming acquainted with the best side of American life; and so far as may be found practicable, to obtain for Americans travelling in India similar facilities for becoming acquainted with the real life of the people, and for learning the true character and the actual effects of British rule in the country.

Fourth: To convey through the Indian Press, and all other available channels, the sympathy which we feel for the Indian people in their present unhappy condition, and to encourage them to persist by all lawful means in their efforts to re-establish their industrial and economic independence, and to secure from the British Government that measure of self-rule which is essential to their well-being; to impress upon them the necessity of cultivating among themselves an all-embracing sentiment of unity, solidarity, and brotherliness, and of presenting an absolutely united front in all Indian affairs.

The membership of this Association is already considerable, and will, it is believed, rapidly increase; and it is composed of men and women who earnestly desire, and propose to work for, the welfare of the people of India. I shall hope to be authorised by you to convey to the Association your acceptance of this office.

I am, my dear Sir, with great respect, faithfully yours,
MYRON H PHELPS
42, Broadway, New York, USA. 9 September 1907

Reply from Dadabhai Naoroji:

My dear Sir, – I have received your letter of 9th inst., informing me on behalf of the Indo-American National Association organised at Green Acre, Maine, USA, on the 5th inst. that I have been chosen Honorary President for India of that body. I appreciate deeply and gratefully the honour done to me, and I accept it with great gratification. It is indeed, extremely gratifying to see this Association formed which has for its objects to promote the best interests of India, and I on my own behalf as well as that of India, offer our best thanks to the Association. I am glad to read that the membership of the Association is already considerable, and will rapidly increase. Composed as it is of men and women who earnestly desire and propose to work for the welfare of the people of India, the Association cannot fail to be of great benefit to India.

Yours Sincerely,
DADABHAI NAOROJI

India, 27 September 1907

British injustice was aimed at all Indians. It was irrelevant whether they resided in India or in one of the British colonies. Indians in British East Africa were just as nearly badly treated as were those in South Africa. There was a dual humiliation on the grounds of racism as well as oppression. Their pleas of equality and justice were always ignored. *India,* on 30 September 1910, reported the unfair treatment of the large Indian population in East Africa, expressed by Seth Alibhoy Mulla Jeevanjee. He was the first Indian to be appointed to the Legislative Council of the British East Africa Protectorate. On a visit to Manchester he aired his grievances regarding the British Indians in the Protectorate. Though his theme was trade, his complaints were about the misery of being badly treated. He was interviewed by the *Manchester Guardian.*

INDIANS IN BRITISH EAST AFRICA

'For about 300 years,' Mr Jeevanjee said, 'there has been a constant trade between India and East Africa, and it was indeed through the existence of that trade that East Africa became at last a part of the British Empire. There are at the present time about 25,000 British Indian residents in the country, mostly businessmen and their families. They are settled all along the coast and in the interior, and many of them have been born and brought up in the country. A few years ago the British Government in East Africa adopted a legislative and administrative policy adverse to the interests of the British Indians resident there...

'Members of European and American nations are allowed full trading and property rights in the Protectorate. The restrictions are directed only against Asiatics, and this arouses much resentment among Indian subjects of the Crown.

'British East Africa is being run by the British tax-payer who is, through this dog-in-the-manger policy, denied the proper return for his money. At the same time the British Indian, feels himself under an injustice. He holds that this policy is a deviation from that freedom of trade and intercourse which is characteristic of the British system; that it is an exceptional measure directed against himself alone. It cannot be to the interest of the British Government either in East Africa or in India that this sense of injustice should be allowed to exist.'   *India*, 30 September 1910.

Through the patriotic effort of Lala Lajpat Rai the case for self-determination for India was formally put before the Foreign Relations Committee of the United States Senate on 29 August 1919, through Mr Dudley Filed Malone, representing the people of India. The Indian National Congress at Delhi had appointed Mr Tilak, Mr Gandhi and Mr Hasan Imam to represent India at the Versailles Palace conference. Mr Tilak, who was in England at the time, was refused a passport to attend. He submitted a representation to the Conference President, Woodrow Wilson, which was not acted upon. Instead, the matter was taken up by the Foreign Relations Committee of the US Senate and the case for India was put on the official record, with the hope of making a report to the League of Nations. India was a founding member of the League of Nations and as such the question could not be treated as a domestic question.

Mr Tilak's arguments were that no civilised nation should be governed by any other nation without its consent. He demanded India's representation at the League of Nations along and on a footing of equality with the British Dominions. Mr Tilak also published a brochure on self-determination for India and circulated it among members of the British Parliament and the Ministry, the British press and the public generally. A copy was sent to President Wilson with a letter on 2 January 1919, stating:

MR TILAK AND PRESIDENT WILSON

The world's hope for peace and justice is centred in you as the author of the great principle of self-determination. I therefore feel impelled to bring the enclosed brochure to your notice for consideration and such action as the peace of the world and the principles of right and justice for all nations may demand in the case of India.

On 14 January, Mr Gilbert Close, writing for President Wilson, replied to Mr Tilak as follows:

I am instructed by President Wilson to acknowledge the receipt of your letter, and to express to you his high appreciation of your kind thought of him, and to assure you that the matter of self-determination for India is a question which will be taken up in due time by the proper authorities.

The next that Mr Tilak or any other body heard of in this connection was that India was made an original member of the League of Nations; but the words that:

'the matter of self-determination for India is a question which will be taken up in due time by the proper authorities' remained as enigmatic as ever.
                                        India, 26 September 1919.

Extracts of Mr Dudley Field Malone's speech to the Senate:

INDIA BEFORE THE SENATE
CITIZEN MALONE'S SPEECH

I come here, Sir, today not as counsel in any technical or legal sense to speak for the people of India. I come as an American citizen; I come, however, as their chosen representative, largely because it has been decreed, I understand, by this Committee that only American citizens are to come here as representatives. Otherwise, I should ask you to hear the most distinguished citizen of India in this country, Mr Lajpat Rai, who is here today.

However, I speak today for a people who represent one-fifth of the population of the world, who are 350,000,000 in population, and who have a territory about two-thirds the size of the United States.

The plea that I make is based upon the humanitarian purpose for which we are supposed to have gone into the war, and the humanitarian purpose which is alleged to be the purpose of the covenant of the League of Nations, and I do respectfully submit that if the covenant in its present form is passed it may break the hearts of the world.

The Government of India is only the agent of the Government of England. In the Montague-Chelmsford report, issued by the authority of the British Parliament in 1918, it is specifically admitted that the Government of India by England is an absolute despotism. The chief body which actually represents the people of India is the Indian National Congress, which of course, under the consequences, is unofficial. It met, however, very completely and very fully but unofficially last December after England had appointed two representatives, and passed the following resolution:

That this Congress urges that in justice to India it should be represented by an elected representative or representatives, to the same extent as the self-governing Dominions, at any conferences that may be held to deliberate or settle the terms of peace or reconstruction.

Now, gentlemen, it has been said publicly and privately that the question of India is a domestic question for England to decide. No question, gentlemen, to my mind, of any nationality, of any people, whether they be 1,000,000 or 350,000,000, can be a domestic question, if the whole world is called upon in more or less common council to decide upon it and it has the machinery which will make the liberty of mankind not a domestic but an international question.

I am not here in any anti-British spirit. I surely am not. Mr Chairman, I am not here making any argument against the English people. I am making arguments against the present Government of England over 350,000,000 people.

I should like to point out in conclusion what India did during the war. India gave 1,475,000 men to the war. She contributed $1,000,000,000 in money, more than any other Dominion of England. Besides untold quantities of stores and provisions, she suffered war losses of 100,000 men.

India, 26 September 1919.

An American view of the meaning of India's demand for Home Rule came from Mr J T Sunderland, President of the India Home Rule League of America and Editor of *Young India*, from New York on 31 July 1920. This letter was published by *India* on 10 September 1920.

THE MEANING OF INDIA'S DEMAND FOR HOME RULE
AN AMERICAN VIEW

What do the people of India mean when they agitate, as for many years they have been doing, for Home Rule like that of Canada and Australia?

Do they mean continued slavery to the British Empire, or slavery of any other kind? No, they mean freedom. Canada is free, Australia is free. Both make and administer their own laws. Their connection with the Empire is voluntary;

they could break it if they choose; but they prefer not to break it; they see advantages in preserving it. Thus they hold in their own hands the power of self-determination. Essentially this is what India means and wants.

The Editor of the London weekly, *India*, which is the British organ of the Indian National Congress, discusses this question well in a recent issue. Says that able English interpreter of India:

'As to the question of India's remaining or not remaining in the British Empire, the position may be clearly stated thus: The policy of the Indian National Congress (which can be said without question to represent the people of India), is, and has always been, self-government within the Empire. But it is and always must be a matter of their own choice. Theirs must be the final decision. The Congress has stood for self-government within the Empire, not as some seem to suppose, because loyalty to the British Empire, in any and all circumstances, is a sort of divine injunction imposed upon all peoples who have come, either with or without their consent, within its capacious fold, but because the Empire stands for certain ideals, and because Indian interests have become through political and economic associations inextricably bound up with the British Empire. For that reason there is ground for hope that the people of India will prefer to remain as part of the Empire (as Canada and Australia are doing) as soon as their aspirations have been met by the granting of adequate measures of autonomy.'

The essential thing is, India must have freedom; must have self-determination. If and when these are assured to her, then the closer her association and co-operation with England the better.

To be sure, England is not India's mother-country, as she is the mother-country of Canada and Australia; therefore, India cannot have just the same reasons for desiring to maintain permanent connection with England that Canada and Australia have. But there may be other reasons hardly less weighty, if the connection can be made one of equality, of co-operation and therefore of mutual advantage. Some have thought the distance of England from India an obstacle to their union. But why? That Canada and Australia are on different sides of the globe from England makes their union with her in some respects more desirable and more useful to both parties than if they were near one another.

India has had a long association with Great Britain as her subject and slave. May not a happier future have in store for both nations a better relation, a partnership in freedom, and thus a joint mission as leaders of the world to a higher and better civilisation? But if they cannot be associated as real partners, each respecting and treating the other as an equal, and co-operating in ways to be mutually advantageous, then they should part as two separate and friendly nations, each to pursue her own path and to fulfil her own distinctive mission in the world.

The question of vital importance to both nations, and of tremendous consequences to the world is, will Great Britain be wise enough and noble enough to choose either of these courses of action? Or will she persist in tempting to hold in subjection a nation of 350,000,000 civilised people – one-fifth of the entire human race – against their united wish and will? If she does the latter, the only possible result will be a war, a revolution, of the most bloody and terrible nature, by which she will be driven out of India, if not out of all Asia.

JT SUNDERLAND (President of the Indian Home Rule League of America and Editor of *Young India*). New York, 31 July.

In the wake of the Jallianwalla Bagh massacre at Amritsar on 13 April 1919, J T Sunderland once again summoned up the Indian situation in *India* on 24 September 1920:

THE INDIAN SITUATION IN A NUTSHELL

BY J T SUNDERLAND · PRESIDENT OF THE INDIA HOME RULE LEAGUE OF AMERICA · AND EDITOR OF 'YOUNG INDIA'

There is a famous saying of Macaulay concerning the British Tory Party in England of his day, which exactly describes the present British Government in India. Said Macaulay: 'It is the essence of the Tory spirit that instead of removing a grievance they try to put down an agitation.'

Here, in a nutshell, is the whole story of the Punjab troubles of last year. The people felt that they had very serious grievances. Rightly, they agitated for the removal of these. A wise, just and statesman-like government would have seen to it that all just causes for complaint were put away. Not so the Indian Government. Tory in spirit, Bourbon in spirit, bureaucratic, autocratic, militarist in spirit, it stopped its ears to the just cries of the people and 'instead of removing a grievance', it brutally, stupidly determined by methods of blood and iron 'put down an agitation'.

Unfortunately, the Punjab instance does not stand alone. It is only the latest, and a peculiarly shocking illustration of a general policy. Every student of the history of the British rule in India knows that from the beginning no class of persons have been so constantly frowned upon and persecuted by the government as the educated leaders who have dared to point out India's wrongs and agitate for their reform.

Sedition laws of the severest character have been kept constantly over the heads of the people, like a sword of Damocles. Because they have dared to express the nation's grievances and agitate for reform, hundreds of periodicals have been suppressed, and hundreds of the best and most honoured men in India have been thrown into prisons or banished to the inhumanities of the Andaman islands, often without trial or any opportunity for defending themselves.

It was hoped that when the war was over and India had shown such loyalty and had rendered to England such large and important services, that there would be a change in the spirit of the government. But all such hopes have been dashed. The spirit of suspicion, of repression, of tyranny, of arrogance, of downright brutality in dealing with the Indian people has never been so manifest as within the past two years. Is this spirit to continue? Much has been said about the great 'New Reform Scheme', about the 'New Government of India Act', by which India is to be put on the road to constitutional government, to Home Rule, to self-determination. Let nobody be deceived. Unless there is a complete change in the spirit of the British Government in India, the New Reform Scheme can prove nothing but camouflage. So long as the spirit of British rule in India is that of 'putting down agitation' instead of removing the cause or 'removing the grievance', India has nothing to hope for from Great Britain.

Will Britain radically and completely change her spirit and policy towards India? We shall see.

Public meetings, speeches, and now interviews of those involved in India's cause started being the regular features of journals. America was all eyes and ears for putting on record for national as well as international readers the full story, by carefully selecting dedicated freedom fighters to give vent to their views in their journals. Lala Lajpat Rai was their favoured Indian voice. A reporter of the *Christian Science Monitor* of San Francisco in July 1916, introduced Lala Lajpat Rai both as a man and his mission to rid India of the British imperial presence. He spoke on what India wanted; not as a revolutionary but as a rational politician at the height of the First World War. It was a carefully conducted interview. Lala Lajpat Rai was considered an ardent and uncompromising advocate of the nationalist cause who believed and promoted evolutionary and not revolutionary methods for dealing with the British. Bomb throwing was not his style, which he was at pains to express in this interview. He also spoke of the plight of the Indians living in the British colonies by demanding better treatment for Indians in the Colonies, with freedom of travel and emigration.

Often the journals published foreign news items regarding India – however short, as did the *Hind* on 24 March 1922. Under the headline 'The American Commission for Indian Swarajya', it reported: 'The American Commission to Promote Self-Government in India has issued a statement in which it charges Britain with having asked Japan for military aid in the event of a general uprising in India.' *Exchange.*

Yet another voice of dissent was heard from America. This time it was the expression of an Indian, Mr Syud Hossain, for the readers of the *NewYork Times*, which the *Hind* of 30 June 1922 reproduced.

The article was on the Indian struggle for Swaraj or self-rule. It was in reply to the claims put forward by the British propagandists in the USA that India was an inseparable and integral part of the British Empire by reasons of its historic association of 150 years.

'INDIA MUST BE FREE'

One thing is perfectly certain; India, with a population comprising one-fifth of the human race, cannot eternally remain the 'adjunct' – in Well's phrase – of a little island, 7,000 miles away from her shores. Neither any natural nor any economic ties bind her to the British Empire, and she can only form part of that system if it can be proved that such an arrangement would be of definite advantage to her. The onus of proof lies on Britain. On the other hand, there is every reason in the world why India should work out her own destiny, unfettered and uncoerced, and make her own contribution, as in the past, to the culture and civilisation of the world. Not only India, but the world is the poorer for her present compulsory emasculation and disorganisation. The British have fixed a stronghold on her creative genius and national growth. India must be free.

*   *   *

The First World War over and there was still no commitment from Britain to India. Four years later in 1922, the first work of one man slowly started being noticed – MK Gandhi. He was seen as a complex personality wanting to apply laws of religion to the political struggle. He puzzled observers everywhere, not least in America. A report in a Chicago paper, *Unity*, was reproduced by *Hind* on 16 June 1922.

MAHATMA GANDHI AND THE SAVIOUR

Will Gandhi succeed? The answer to this question is easy – Gandhi has already succeeded. In the short space of a year and a half he has organised a movement which numbers more adherents than any other movement in human history has ever gathered; he has disciplined his millions of followers to a rigour of life which obtains through spontaneous moral idealism what is ordinarily obtained only through dull obedience; he has released forces of social regeneration which mean the ultimate transformation of the Indian people. If Gandhi should die today and his movement as a distinct and separate organisation end tomorrow, his career would mark one of the supreme triumphs of all time. The trouble with our thought of Gandhi is that we picture his work exclusively in terms of nationalism. We imagine that he will succeed or fail, according as he secures or does not secure political independence for his native country. Such independence is, of course, central to his activities; it is the form in which his spirit now shapes itself. But to identify Gandhi's cause with any nationalistic movement, however noble, is to misunderstand the man completely. As well think of Jesus as a mere patriotic leader, and call his life a failure because he did not drive the Roman legions from Palestine! What we have in Gandhi is a religious prophet comparable to the few supreme historic incarnations of the divine spirit; and, in his movement, a religion comparable to Buddhism or Christianity. We believe that Gandhi will succeed in his political aims, and thus free India, but his achievement, great as it is, will be but an accident in his larger spiritual work.   *Unity*, Chicago.

In 1928/29 Mrs Sarojini Naidu was on a tour of America. The New York *Evening Post*, just as it interviewed Lala Lajpat Rai a quarter century earlier, once again sought the views of another of India's freedom fighters. Through Sarojini Naidu, first hand information on India's national leader was conveyed to the Americans. She also reviewed the hostile relationship with the British government, contrasting this with the friendship of the British people.

GANDHI – THE SOUL OF INDIA

'Gandhi is a man who represents the spiritual thought of India and one who is "looked up to" throughout the country. There is only one feeling about Gandhi – he represents the soul of India and symbolises all that is best in Indian culture. Our mysticism is a dynamic thing. It doesn't communicate with death but with life. Where you develop your muscles, we develop our mind, spirit and will.' When asked about the political destiny of India, Mrs Naidu remarked: 'In Lahore there is a statue of Baron Lawrence in the pose of asking India whether she wanted to be governed by the pen or sword? We now ask England: Will it make a settlement with us by pen or sword? If she chooses the pen, then we are ready and will treat on the basis of any great country that only asks for freedom. There are ways of doing things, and there is no reason for breaking every tie. But we must be friends with England as a free people; that is, free to be enemies too if we prefer. But if it is to be by the sword, then we shall be ready and we shall forge that sword from our bones, if need be. We don't ask pity or money. This is a straight issue between England and ourselves. And we must settle it ourselves. If we are unable to do it without help, we are not worthy of our freedom.'   *United India*, January 1929.

After the Salt march of 6 April 1930 and the Round Table Conference of 1931, Gandhi's activities and his own writings started making front page news in journals and newspapers. Britain could neither accept the demands of the man, nor could it ignore the national feelings he aroused, India's cause becoming synonymous with Gandhi's demands for freedom. Public meetings and organisations started adopting the name Gandhi to symbolise their peaceful mass agitation against Britain. Gandhi became a discussion point as it was at a meeting in Berlin in 1932. Peace, freedom and non-violence and passive resistance became part of the vocabulary of the era. The Berlin branch of the Women's League for Peace and Freedom held a meeting in Berlin on 12 December 1932. Among other subjects of a spiritual nature, the Indo-British relationship was also discussed. The meeting was described as a Gandhi Meeting for his constructive and peaceful approach to the British. The meeting was addressed by Mr Hector Walter Mann, an English Liberal Catholic priest, and Mr Acharya discussed Gandhi's opposition to the use of arms in favour of non-violent tactics, what an American writer described as a 'substitute for war'.

On 16 September 1933 there was a conference of the World Fellowship of Faith in Chicago. Reverend JT Sunderland, who had already spoken on India at Toronto twenty-seven years ago, gave an address to the delegates, asking the question 'Should India have freedom without delay?' It was a religious platform he spoke from, aimed at the conscience of the British Government to solve the political dilemma of India. India had as much right to its freedom as Britain. Britain was wrong in delaying it. *India Bulletin*, in its November 1933 isue gave a full transcription of the Reverend's thoughts on India:

SHOULD INDIA HAVE FREEDOM WITHOUT DELAY?

In this enlightened Twentieth Century ought any nation in the world to be in bondage? To have the rule of a foreign nation forced upon it? To be held in subjection to a foreign power by foreign bayonets?

If some nation possessing more modern arms and a larger army than England or France or Italy or Germany or the United States should conquer, disarm and reduce to subjection any of these nations, would not the whole world be shocked by the monstrous wrong? But is holding India in forced subjection a lesser wrong? Has any one of these nations a greater right to freedom and self-government than has India?

What is India? Is it a small and insignificant nation? It is the second largest nation in the world, containing a population greater than North America, Central America and South America all combined. Think of all the Americans held in forced bondage, then you have something like the bondage of India.

Is India a nation of semi-barbarians? On the contrary, India is a highly civilised nation – a nation which developed a rich culture much earlier than any nation of Europe, and has never lost it. India was the richest nation in the world until conquered and robbed of its wealth by Great Britain. India is a nation, a large part of whose people are Aryans in blood, that is, belong to the same great race as the Greeks, Romans, Germans, English and ourselves.

For twenty-five hundred years India was pre-eminently the intellectual and spiritual leader of Asia, which means half of the human race. For twenty-five hundred years before the British came on the scene and robbed her of her freedom, India was self-ruling and one of the most renowned nations of the world.

Such is India. Should such a nation be held in bondage? Has not such a nation a right to liberty, to self-government, and to a place once more, such as she occupied so long, among the great nations of mankind?

The world should know that the people of India feel the degradation and injustice of bondage exactly as Englishmen and Americans would do; and they claim as much right to freedom as do Americans or Englishmen.

The world ought also to know that the people of India would not remain a day under a foreign yoke were it not that they are disarmed, that forts and soldiers are at every strategic point ready for instant action, that hundreds of airplanes are ready to drop deadly bombs or poison gas on their villages, and the battleships are all in their harbours ready to raze to the ground their cities at the first sign of revolt.

Does this mean that the Indian people are a nation of weaklings and cowards? Let the British officer and soldiers who have witnessed their valour on a hundred battlefields answer.

India is under foreign rule today only because at a time of unusual political confusion and division, when the Mogul Empire was breaking up, Great Britain, with superior arms and with a persistent duplicity, which no reputable historian has dares to defend, conquered her territory, part by part, and disarmed her people; and has ever since determinedly prevented them from developing any independent military strength. Hence India's bondage, and consequent humiliation and degradation.

Today in India, after a century and a half of British rule, three hundred and fifty millions of human beings are held in bondage, one hundred millions of whom are actually worse housed, worse clothed, and worse fed than the slaves of America ever were.

Great Britain declares to the world that the Indian people are not fit to rule themselves, are not capable of self-government; that is the reason she is in

India, it is her duty. She must rule there because they are not able to rule themselves.

Does anybody doubt the ability of England or France or Russia or Japan to govern itself? Then why India, whose civilisation is far older than that of any of these nations.

Who is it that presumes to say that the Indian people are not capable of self-government? Is it the Indian people themselves? No! They declare the contrary. They say that they have proved by more than three thousand years of history their eminent ability to rule themselves.

Some years ago, the Reverend Doctor John Page Hopps, an eminent clergy-man of London, published an article in *The Modern Review* of Calcutta, answering the inquiry in a way that nobody has ever been able to refute. Wrote Mr Hopps: 'Who says the people of India are not fit for Home Rule? We, English, who profit by ruling them; we, who do not want to surrender power; we, who in our egotism think we are the best and ablest rulers in the world. But it is an old cry.'

The nation which declares the Indian people unfit to rule themselves is the one among all the nations of the world which is least capable of judging fairly and justly in the matter, because, as Mr Hopps points out, it is a deeply interested party. It is the nation which, some centuries ago, not by right, but by force of arms, and for selfish ends, conquered the Indian people, and ever since has been holding them in subjection, because thus she secured and continued to possess increased political power and prestige in the world, large commercial and industrial advantage, much financial profit, and high and lucrative official positions, with fat pensions, for her sons. It is this nation that tells the world that the Indian people are incapable of ruling themselves. But, pray, what else can she be expected to tell the world? How else can she justify herself for staying in India?

Why is there this delay in granting to India the freedom and self-rule which is her right, and which she is so eminently fitted for? If an additional period of forced subjection such as Britain insists upon would improve the Indian people, or make them in any way fit for self-rule, there might be some excuse for delay. But how can prolongation of bondage, with its humiliation and degrading influence, and with the irritation and feeling of injury, hostility and antagonism which it creates, fit men better for self-government? Gladstone, England's great statesman, long ago declared: 'Every year and every month that a subject people are kept under the administration of a despotic government, renders them less fit for free institutions'.

If such has been the terrible effect of British rule, how much longer ought it to continue? Can its continuance do anything else than inflict on India still further degradation? Dare any reasonable man declare that it ought to continue a single day longer than is necessary to turn over the country to its own great people?

In South Africa, it was Indian labour that cleaned the jungles, built railways and roads, cultivated sugar cane and helped construct cities like Johannesburg. Natal, Transvaal, Cape Colony and Orange Free State owed much to Indian labour and enterprise. Yet the Indians had to fight racism at local level and discrimination from the Union Government. *India Bulletin* of March 1934 reported that 'the Government of South Africa has tried to clear the Colony of Indians over and over again. But Gandhi's eight years' prolonged Satyagraha and the consequent Gandhi-Smuts agreement of 1914 has achieved for Indians the right to live in the land as sons of the soil. Since Gandhi went to India the Union Government has considerably whittled down the agreement and has made many inroads on some of its important provisions. The Indian community is bravely and doggedly fighting the battle.'

THE PRESS

Young India was published by the India Home Rule League of America in 1918 to inform the American public of the situation in India. It was the organ of the League and aimed at reporting its activities in India and Britain. It had a similar function to that of *India*, the journal of the British Committee of the Indian National Congress in London. The *Young India* editorial stated: 'Our work is open, perfectly constitutional and legitimate and we do not intend to meddle with American politics. Our work is for India and for humanity.' It was published in New York between January 1918 and December 1920 and edited by Lala Lajpat Rai who was in America in self-imposed exile for eight years. He was also the President and Treasurer. The Joint Secretaries were K D Shastri and N S Hardiker. The journal was the voice of the India Home Rule League of America with specific aims and objectives:

– To support the Home Rule movement in India;
– To co-operate with the political organisations in India and Britain;
– To further friendly relations between India and America.

It contained articles on Indian literature, art and science as well as reports of political and economic conditions in India.

*   *   *

The Voice of India was published in Washington by an organisation called the Committee for India's Freedom. It was presided over by Mr Syud Hossain, who taught at the University of Southern California and was appointed India's first Ambassador to Egypt after independence.

The India League was started in New York to publicise India's freedom movement in America. Its President was Mr J J Singh and there were numerous American members as supporters of India's cause.

A mass meeting to support India'a independence movement at Azad Maidan, Nairobi. The author is second from the left in the front row.

Sarojini Naidu

CHAPTER 8

Eyes and ears of the Raj: Indian political intelligence

Files on Indian political intelligence (ipi) between 1915 and 1945 have recently become accessible. These are extracts from Scotland Yard and Metropolitan Police reports, and the Colonial Information and the Intelligence Bureau. For the first time a number of new organisations and their India-associated activities in Britain and America have come to light: the language used to express dislike and distrust of some of the individuals and events by the police authorities can only be described as bizarre.

Sarojini Naidu, a frequent visitor to Britain and America, was shadowed between 1928 and 1944. Known for her politics as well as her poetry, she was never far from the watchful eye of the British authorities. The dossier on her politics was critical to the point of being abusive. During her speaking tour of America, she was described as 'a well-known agitator', who, 'while professing in her speeches over here that she has not come to fight or quarrel with Britain on American soil, never fails to make violent demands for Indian freedom'. In a despatch from Washington during her visit there in 1929, Mrs Naidu was criticised for her 'audacity' to speak to the Foreign Policy Association of the USA and go the 'whole hog' for India's cause. The words she used, according to the report, were, 'today we say to the great British power to readjust our relationship, one with a pool of ink and the other with a pool of blood...' She was also accused of promoting her poetry and publishers: the reports say that she was egotistical, with only two obsessions – her poetry and the House of Chatterjee (her family name).

There are files on Indian students at Oxford and Cambridge between 1936 and 1946, which included the years of the Second World War. The Cambridge University Majlis, addressed by Reginald Sorensen, passed a resolution demanding immediate independence for India. Another report dealt with the response to Gandhi's proclamation that Indian students should hold monthly demonstrations and meetings against the detention of political prisoners in India; still others mentioned the Indian Students' Hostel, 1935, in relation to the activities of various individuals; the report also referred to 'the *Daily Worker* being left at the hostel', but regretted that it was not possible to name the culprits responsible.

One of the most interesting items in the collection relates to the existence of the Indian Information Bureau, which was a non-official and non-commercial organisation. Its aim was to provide reliable news and information about Indian life and affairs in Britain to the vernacular press in India. Its membership included university faculties in Oxford and Cambridge; also bishops, Members of Parliament, lawyers, as well as Nehru and Tagore.

There was, of course, Gandhi, public enemy number one for the British authorities. They were convinced that, ironically, the great efforts made to oversee his personal safety and security also enabled him to continue with his fierce anti-British campaigns. Before his visit to London for the Round Table Conference in 1931, a telegram was sent from India to the Secretary of State for India stating that it was vitally important that nothing untoward should happen to him in England.

To avoid problems at Victoria station, London plans for his arrival there were cancelled. He was instead, brought from Folkestone straight to Friends House, in a car belonging to Dr CL Katial, an Indian medical general practitioner, who drove it himself.

Gandhi came to Europe in a wave of popularity in the wake of the Dandi Salt March the year before, an event that was widely covered in the cinema newsreels throughout Europe. He was an instantly recognisable celebrity, but not without his Indian critics in Britain. The British were not going to take any risks with his personal safety. Special police protection was given to him and all other Indian Round Table Conference delegates. Of Gandhi it was said that the authorities had definite information that Saklatvala had been talking of assassination in much the same way as the Indian Press and they thought it was quite possible that under the continued pressure of such propaganda, one of the more unbalanced Indian students might make an attempt on the Mahatma's life. A 25-page report in one file sees Gandhi as the principal reason for the widespread media coverage of the Conference. The report accepted the fact that his personality, 'to many, his semi-divinity, had no rival in India'. The report also provides information that 'an Indian millionaire' had placed a sum of £2,200 at Gandhi's disposal when he left India for his journey to Britain and Europe and back. Gandhi's expenses came to £450 and the balance was returned.

Outside his role as a delegate to the Round Table Conference Gandhi undertook numerous engagements. He attended a reception by the Indian Medical Association on 11 November 1931 at the Veeraswamy's Restaurant to raise funds for a hospital scheme. Privately it was believed that Gandhi's speech was so vague that it hadn't been a success. A sum of £493, however, was collected from the delegates to the Conference. A reception for Gandhi was also held by the Gandhi Reception Committee on the eve of his 62nd birthday and a gift of £612, collected by the Indian Chamber of Commerce and Indian students, was presented to him. Gandhi said that it would be to buy spinning wheels and to provide employment for peasants. Gandhi was given fifteen slips of questions at the meeting, chaired by Vithalbhai J Patel, to which he replied to only four. Heckling took place and there were shouts of 'Down with Gandhi', 'Kill Gandhi'.

Gandhi's movements during his return journey to India via Paris, Geneva and Rome were monitored just as closely as was his stay in Britain.

Playing the dual role of secret eye as well as critic, Gandhi's speeches were commented upon by the intelligence agency. At Geneva he was reported to have addressed an audience of 2,000 'adults', but 'he did not visit the League of Nations' which was described as a 'blunder'. He attended a prayer meeting in Rome, but made no speeches. He subsequently met Benito Mussolini, the Italian dictator, for half an hour and also visited his Fascist Headquarters and its branches in Rome.

Gandhi is said to have gone to Italy for the purpose also of meeting the Pope, but this never materialised. Officially, there was not enough time to prepare for an audience. But it was learnt later, 'that His Holiness vetoed a meeting on the ground that the scanty attire of the Mahatma did not meet Papal obligations'.

A New Scotland Yard report, dated 14 October 1931, referred to the following birthday greeting to Mahatma Gandhi from members of the Indian community in Britain:

Vande Mataram: 'On the occasion of your 63rd birthday, permit us to offer you our homage.

'We have followed with keen interest and unabated zeal and extended our unflinching moral support to the movement which under your leadership the people of India have carried on for the emancipation of our Motherland from political, economical and social thraldom. Whatever may be the immediate outcome of this gigantic experiment, one thing is certain. The standard which you have set up for the public work in India – of service, sacrifice and negation of self – will endure for eternity. You have thus not merely revolutionised the ethics of public life in India but have the whole world thinking. History will record your contribution to the corporate life of mankind of a new philosophy of warfare – that of truth and non-violence, to combat forces of evil, untruth and exploitation. The present world, weary, sick and tired of war, strife, confusion and chaos is looking to a new ideal to guide humanity and in their quest the gaze of the whole world is fixed on you. We are all proud that you, the most outstanding world figure today, are an Indian. We entirely endorse your view that the price of liberty is non-violence and we hope and trust that in no circumstances will India surrender to or compromise with the force for violence of the British Government. In conclusion, we wish you all success in your mission of peace and brotherhood.

Yours &c

MEMBERS OF THE INDIAN COMMUNITY IN GREAT BRITAIN

2 Beaufort Gardens, London SW3
2 October 1931

As if taking a cue from Sir Lepel Griffin, the authorities in London refused the Indian National Congress permission to fly a flag on 30 John Street, London, in 1930. The minutes of the meetings of the Congress on 14 May revealed that a book of slogans was sent for the use of a revolutionary campaign in India. The report said that there were 70 Indians who attended the meeting, several of whom had arrived and left in four motor-cars 'the numbers of which were noted. Some of the attendants were later kept under observation by police, with a view to possible identification'.

Prior to this meeting, a frantic urgent exchange of telegrams took place between London and India, marked 'secret'. The Secretary of State informed the Viceroy that the London branch of the Indian National Congress was arranging to send by the next mail a collection of slogans for use in the revolutionary campaign in India.

Four days later came the reply from India asking who the slogans were being sent to. The Secretary of State replied that, according to the latest information, the slogans were being forwarded to V J Kusha, a Congress publicity officer supposed to be in Bombay. A list of Congress members with their private addresses was filed by New Scotland Yard. There was a full list of names of delegates attending the Congress meetings, dates of their arrivals from India, where they stayed, and their occupations. A check was also kept on the movement of members after the meetings were over. With the increase in numbers and popularity of political and patriotic slogans, Indians had found a perfect weapon to hit the British Government where it hurt most – their image and ego. In turn, the authorities spared no effort or expense to see if the slogans could be neutralised.

According to a report of 28 August 1930, Horace Alexander, who was sent to India to study the political situation, was accused of collecting all Indian national songs, slogans and revolutionary songs, to make accurate translations of them and to take them back to Britain to the Quaker's Society of Friends, to which he belonged. They 'will be

Nellie Sen Gupta (1886–1973)
English. Married Sen Gupta, family friend and student in Britain; went to India and was well-received in his family. Involved herself in the Indian freedom struggle and was imprisoned in 1931. Chose to live in Pakistan after partition of India in 1947.

Gandhi at Muriel Lester's home.

used for propaganda and will also be placed at the disposal of The League Against Imperialism'.

A stray, comically audacious item in the files, is a letter from the Indian Freedom League founded in 1925, whose founder Mr Ally Khan, wrote thus to the Secretary of State for India, Viscount Peel, on 19 October 1928: 'requesting funds and financial help for the League's activities for the good of the teeming millions of Indians'. 'Not acknowledged' was the terse official comment.

Those considered dangerous enough to merit a file were: Subhash Chandra Bose (including his passport number), Vithalbhai Patel, Rangaswami Ayyangar, Lajpat Rai (not only were his motives questioned, but also those of his British friends such as Col. Wedgwood), Mohammed Ali Jinnah (who joined Annie Besant's Home Rule League in 1917), Madan Mohan Malaviya ('The taint of sedition and disloyalty which affects others, does not touch him'), Krishna Menon, Syed Hossain (under observation in the United States), Henry Polak, Gandhi, Horace Alexander, Vithalbhai Patel, Satyna Narayan Sinha, Agatha Harrison, Muriel Lester, Udham Singh, and Kamaladevi Chattopadhyaya.

Other files in the collection were devoted to: India Independence League of America (February 1930), Hindustan Association of America, India Freedom Foundation, India Society of America, Indian Students at Oxford and Cambridge (February 1936–April 1946), Indian Students' Union (August 1921–December 1941), Foreign Office 'Stop List' (February 1922–1925), Funds from the United States of America to India for political purposes (August 1923–December 1926), Correspondence/Interviews with Home Office – Prosecution/Sedition (1923–1926), Extracts from weekly reports (January 1925–August 1929), History sheets on Indian politicians (May 1921–December 1932), *Bharat*, quarterly issued by Oxford Indian Majlis, Indian Home Rule League (July 1925–December 1926), India Freedom Association (January 1929–December 1930), Commonwealth of India League [India League] (1928–1932), Indian National Congress [London]

(June–November 1928), India Swaraj League (January 1935–1940), National Union of Indian Students [Abroad] (October 1929–August 1930), Friends of India Association (October 1930–March 1942), India League (March–December 1932), International Committee for India (August 1932–1933), The London Mosque (July 1927–June 1946), and Federation of Indian Student Societies of Great Britain (December 1933–April 1947).

Entry to Britain was just as difficult in the 1920s as it is today. But the fact that the passports did not carry photographs meant that full descriptions of not only facial hair but also body characteristics had to be recorded. (Vithalbhai J Patel, entering the United Kingdom quite safely on his brother Vallabhbhai's passport, has become a legend in the Indo-British annals of immigration history). The Foreign Office had a 'Stop List' that had all the names of those not eligible for passport facilities without previous references to officials. Though the reasons given were the loss of passports, the authorities suspected that they were sold to others.

Some of the descriptions added to each name read like a CV of a cartoon character. Their height was often stated as 'perhaps' 5ft 9in (or often the age was recorded as between '30–50 years'. 'Very strong muscular looking Sikh: shaves and wears a small moustache: dresses well and slightly educated: age possibly 25; but not less than 5ft 8in; fairly good looking; hooked nose.'

Intelligence services down the ages, in every clime and continent, are prone to take each detail of their work with the utmost seriousness. Yet there is much of the surreal and the comic when such work is scrutinised in the cold light of history.

The Rt Hon. Clement Attlee, British Prime Minister at the
time of India's independence, August 1947.

CHAPTER 9

The changing of the guard: from British to Indian hands

A VAST COLLECTION OF DEPARTMENTAL PAPERS of successive Secretaries of State for India contain priceless files relating to the political situation in India between 1942 and 1947, and the eventual transfer of power. The ways to deal with Gandhi are especially interesting. Perhaps the most bizarre was the description of him as the 'villain of the peace'. 'Gandhi,' according to Sir A Hope (Madras) on 23 July 1942 said, 'still has a great influence among the ignorant masses and any mention of his name or state of health excites them. If the movement (Satyagraha) comes to anything, I would suggest arresting him at once and deporting him to Mauritius or Kenya and prohibit any reference to him in the Press. If he fasts, let it not be known: and if he dies, announce it six months later.'

Gandhi's fasts were always a cause of great concern for the British authorities. Not so much for his health but for the influence and interest

David Low's cartoon in the *Evening Standard*, 28 August 1942.

"HAVE EITHER OF THE PATIENTS REGAINED CONSCIOUSNESS?"

it generated in activating and accelerating political demands made by the Indians, and not only in India but also in Britain, East Africa, South Africa, America and Canada. The desperate British hope of killing the message of 'freedom' by way of killing its messenger was as short-sighted as it was unrealistic. In October 1942, a private and personal telegram from the Marquis of Linlithgow to Sir R Lumley (Bombay) said, 'Will you please let me have by letter or telegram your reaction to suggesting that if Gandhi should declare a fast at a moment of real military difficulty we should that very day fly him to Aden and hold him there whether he dies or lives?'

On 4 November 1942 Lumley replied, 'With regard to the suggestion that if he (Gandhi) should declare a fast at a moment of real military difficulty, we should at once fly him to Aden or Africa, I would not be in favour of this course if he had already started a fast. In that event, he would probably have to be carried out of the house and at the aerodrome. This would almost certainly become known, and I think the idea of flying a man of his age, who was fasting, would create a worse impression than if he were to die in custody where he is at present. On the other hand, the reactions to his death, through fasting while in detention, would be the same whether he died in Africa or in Poona.' 'With regard to the second question, I think it would be possible to conceal the fast from the public for three or four days. That would of course mean that no doctors would be allowed to visit him. I find it difficult to make up my mind whether this course would be expedient.'

A memo from Mr Amery, in November, to the Marquis of Linlithgow was quite forthright in his hopes, 'I confess I am still very sorry that it was not possible to deport Gandhi to Aden. My conclusion would be identical with Lumley's or even stronger: that is to say, I would let him fast to death'.

In a 'most immediate' telegram, on 13 February 1943, Churchill stated, 'I have heard that Gandhi usually has glucose in his water when going on his various fasting antics. Would it be possible to verify this. There seems to me to be no disposition in America to do otherwise than ridicule his conduct'. Back came a reply from the Marquis of Linlithgow.

This may be the case but those who have been in attendance on him, doubt it, and present Surgeon-General (European) says that on previous fasts Gandhi was particularly careful to guard against the possibility of glucose being used. I am told that his present medical attendants tried to persuade him to take glucose yesterday and today and that he refused absolutely.

I am delighted that American opinion is so sensible and reactions from home equally seem very good. There is a great deal of heat here at the centre and in political circles, but the country on the whole has taken the news well. Once he begins to go downhill, we may however have more trouble.

Thorn on the side of the pro-European lobby in Britain was the India League and the British intellectuals and academics who supported it. A secret and personal message from Mr Amery to Mr Churchill, on 23 May 1945 was quite irritated by the Labour Party's support for India.

Professor Lasky has already been making all the mischief he can at Blackpool, where the India League has been holding a session alongside the Labour Party conference. We are certain to be pressed for a statement on India as soon as the House meets, and only the announcement of an early day will prevent Attlee and Cripps, with their knowledge of the situation, probing the matter in the most embarrassing fashion in the House and if no statement is forthcoming then making all the trouble they can in the country afterwards.

The landslide Labour victory in the General Election in Britain after the Second World War in 1945 was regarded as 'non-plussed' in India. However, there was a general feeling in the Congress circles in India that by tradition the British Labour Party fully understood India's aspirations for self-government and it would now speed the matters up in that direction. In 1929, the leadership of Ramsey MacDonald had been a dependent character which the Indian Press used to describe as 'Labour being in office but not in power'. With majority in the House in 1945, the Congress felt that the Labour Party had no excuse for any 'delay' in implementing its pledges on Indian freedom.

The Second World War ended in 1945 with the Allied victory over the Axis. India's own battle for independence was gathering pace. India's fighting men had fought unflinchingly for the Allied cause but their loyalty to the British Empire was clearly under strain and the British read the signs. They got ready to leave rather than risk outstaying their welcome as the French were to do in Indochina.

The Times-Picayune of Washington, dated 10 June 1947, published a syndicated report by the famous American journalist Walter Lippmann, which was full of praise for Prime Minister Attlee.

Mahatma Gandhi pictured byDavid Low in the *Evening Standard* of 8 May 1944, as a spirit in front of No 10, Downing Street.

PASSING SHADOW

ANOTHER FINEST HOUR · TODAY AND TOMORROW
BY WALTER LIPPMANN

It will be said, I know, that it is too soon to say such things, that we must wait and see, and that the troubles of India are just beginning. All that is, I submit, beside the point. Mr Attlee does not profess to have solved the problems of India. He has, on the contrary, accepted wholly, without reservation or equivocation, the principle and the fact that the problems of India cannot be solved by British statesmen, that they must be solved by the Indians.

What Mr Attlee set himself to do was to solve the British problem in India, which was how to liquidate the Empire and transfer its authority to the Indians. As far as Britain is concerned, he has solved this problem. It is not, I think, premature to say that he has solved it. For having gotten the recognised leaders of India to agree on the time and the terms of transfer of authority, on when the British Empire in India is to end and who in India are to be its successors, the problems of India become the sole responsibility of the Indians. . .

He insisted not on the unity of India, or on the democratization of India, or on anything else but that the Indians who actually rule the various parts of India should severally and jointly accept independence from Great Britain. They have struggled for independence. Mr Attlee has not merely granted it. He has insisted that they accept it, so to speak unconditionally, in the sense that Britain is free of any commitment to give power to any Indian anywhere he does not in fact already possess.

Thus Mr Attlee has observed both the principles of national liberty and the realities of power, and has used them to reinforce each other. They are usually at odds in this world except at those rare moments in history when men have been able to rise to great statesmanship, and to resolve problems that to their lower natures and meaner minds are forever insoluble.

Perhaps Britain's finest hours are not in the past. Certainly this performance is not the work of a decadent people. This, on the contrary, is a work of political genius requiring the ripest wisdom and the freshest vigour, and it is done with an elegance and a style that will compel and will receive an instinctive respect throughout the civilized world.

(Copyright 1947, by the *New York Times*)

The following month, on 1 July 1947, Churchill wrote a letter to the Prime Minister openly showing his reluctance to let India have full independence:

My dear Prime Minister,
I am much concerned to hear from my colleagues whom you consulted yesterday that you propose to call the India Bill, 'The Indian Independence Bill'. This, I am assured, is entirely contrary to the text, which corresponds to what we have previously been told were your intentions. The essence of the Mountbatten proposals and the only reason why I gave support to them is because they establish the phase of Dominion status. Dominion status is not the same as Independence, although it may be freely used to establish independence. It is not true that a community is independent when its Ministers have in fact taken the Oath of Allegiance to the King. This is a measure of grave constitutional importance and a correct and formal procedure and nomenclature should be observed. The correct title would be, it seems to me, 'The Indian Dominion Bill'. I should, however, be quite willing to support it if it were called, 'The India Bill, 1947' or 'The India Self-Government Bill'.
I am glad to hear you are considering such alterations.
Believe me,
Yours sincerely,
WINSTON CHURCHILL

THE INDIAN INDEPENDENCE BILL

On 4 July the British Prime Minister introduced in the House of Commons the Indian Independence Bill, the main provisions of which were as follows:

The two independent Dominions, to be known as India and Pakistan, are to be set up from 15 August 1947.

India will consist of all the territories under the sovereignty of the King which are included in British India except those designated in the Bill as the territories of Pakistan.

Pakistan will consist of the territories which on 15 August are included in the Provinces of East Bengal and West Punjab, the territories included in the Province of Sind, and the Chief Commissioner's Province of British Baluchistan. If the referendum to be held in the North-West Frontier Province shows a majority of votes in favour of joining the Constituent Assembly of Pakistan, this Province, too, will be part of Pakistan.

If the referendum to be held in the Sylhet District of Assam shows a majority of votes in favour of joining the new Province of East Bengal this district will be a part of that Province and will be excluded from the Province of Assam.

As from 15 August the Province of the Punjab shall cease to exist and there shall be constituted two new Provinces to be called West Punjab and East Punjab. The Province of Bengal shall also cease to exist, and there shall be constituted two Provinces to be called East Bengal and West Bengal.

There is to be a Governor-General appointed by the King for each of the Dominions, but unless and until provision is made to the contrary by the Legislature of either of the Dominions the same person may be Governor-General of both.

The words 'Indiae Imperator' and the words 'Emperor of India' are to be omitted from the royal style and titles.

From the appointed day (15 August) his Majesty's Government in the United Kingdom will have no responsibility for the government of any of the territories which, before that day, were included in British India. The suzerainty of his Majesty over the States will also lapse from that date.

Temporary provisions are made for the government of each of the new Dominions. The powers of the Legislature of each Dominion, for the purpose of making provisions for its constitution, will be exercised in the first instance by the Constituent Assembly of that Dominion.

Except in so far as provision is made by a law made by the Constituent Assembly under the proviso above, each of the Dominions and all Provinces and other parts thereof shall be governed as nearly as may be in accordance with the Act of 1935; and the provisions of that Act and of the Orders in Council, rules, and other instruments made thereunder shall have effect accordingly.

The Legislature of each of the new Dominions shall have full power to make laws for that Dominion, including laws having extra-territorial operation; and no Act of Parliament of the United Kingdom passed on or after 15 August shall extend to either of the new Dominions unless it is extended thereto by a law of the Legislature of the Dominion.

Extensive powers are given to the present Viceroy and Governor-General to make such orders as seem to him necessary or expedient to bring the Act into force. He may make orders for dividing between the new Dominions the powers of the Governor-General in Council and for the division of the Indian armed forces. These transitional powers extend only to 31 March 1948, or such earlier date as may be determined by the Legislature of either Dominion.

[Under the Statute of Westminster it is necessary for the Parliaments of all the Dominions to give their assent to any change in the royal style and titles. Their Governments have already indicated that there will be no objection to the passing of the necessary legislation.]

Other consequences of the establishment of the new Dominions are set forth as follows:

As from the appointed day

(a) H M Government in the United Kingdom have no responsibility as respects the government of any of the territories which, immediately before that day, were included in British India;

(b) the suzerainty of his Majesty over the Indian States lapses, and with it, all treaties and agreements in force at the date of the passing of this Act between his Majesty and the rulers of Indian States, all functions exerciseable by his Majesty at that date with respect to Indian States, all obligations of his Majesty existing at that date towards Indian States or the rulers thereof, and all powers, rights, authority, or jurisdiction exercisable by his Majesty at that date in or in relation to Indian States by treaty, grant, usage, sufferance, or otherwise; and

(c) there lapse also any treaties or agreements in force at the date of the passing of this Act between his Majesty and any persons having authority in the tribal areas, any obligation of his Majesty existing at that date to any such persons or with respect to the tribal areas, and all powers, rights, authority, or jurisdiction exercisable at that date by his Majesty in or in relation to the tribal areas by treaty, grant, usage, sufferance, or otherwise.

There follows a proviso that notwithstanding anything in paragraphs (b) or (c), any agreements relating to Customs, transit, and communications, posts and telegraphs, or other like matters shall be continued until the agreements are denounced by the States or the tribal areas on the one hand or by the Dominions or Provinces, on the other, or are superseded by subsequent agreements.

Lord Mountbatten will become for a transitional period after the passing of the Act Governor-General of both Dominions. This transitional period will not continue beyond 31 March 1948, and may be terminated earlier at the instance of either Dominion. If it is so desired there will afterwards be a Governor-General for each.

The Governor-General will make such Orders as appear to him necessary or expedient for dividing between the new Dominions and the new Provinces to be constituted 'the powers, rights, property, duties, and liabilities of the Governor-General in council' or of the Provinces which are to cease to exist; for 'removing difficulties arising in connection with the transition to the provisions of this Act'; for authorising the carrying on of the business of the Governor-General in Council between the passing of this Act and the appointed day; for enabling agreements to be entered into and other acts done on behalf of either of the new Dominions before the appointed day; for authorising the carrying on for the time being on behalf of the new Dominions, or groups of Provinces, of services and activities previously carried on on behalf of British India as a whole; for regulating the monetary system and any matters relating to the Reserve Bank of India; and, for any of these purposes, for varying the constitution, powers, or jurisdiction of any legislature, court, or other authority in the new Dominions, and creating new legislatures, courts, or other authorities.

These powers are to be made retrospective to 3 June 1947. A special clause makes provision for the Indian armed forces, and stipulates that the Orders to be made by the Governor-General 'shall make provision for the division of the Indian armed forces of his Majesty between the two Dominions and for the command and governance of those forces until the division is completed'. Another clause lays it down that nothing in the Bill affects the jurisdiction or authority of the United Kingdom Government, or the Service departments, in relation to any of his Majesty's forces (not being Indian forces) 'which may, on or after the appointed day, be in either of the new Dominions' or elsewhere in the territories which are at present included in India.

The Bill recognises as the Constituent Assembly for India, with the necessary modifications, the Assembly which sat first on 9 December 1946. It also authorises the establishment for Muslim India of a Constituent Assembly of Pakistan to be set up under the authority of the Governor-General. The Indian States may accede to either of the two Dominions and their representatives may sit in either of the Assemblies.

King George VI,
the last Emperor of India.

When the Bill becomes law the functions of the Secretary for India and of the India Office will be ended, and all business relating to India and Pakistan will be dealt with by the Secretary of State for Commonwealth Relations.

*   *   *

The Indian Independence Bill was introduced in Parliament on 5 July 1947 and received with great delight in India. It signalled the termination of 200 years of British rule in the sub-continent. The Prime Minister, Clement Attlee saw the Bill as 'not the abdication but the fulfilment of Britain's mission in India, a sign of the strength and vitality of the British Commonwealth'. For Harold Macmillan, leader of the Opposition, it was a Bill that was to 'preserve, indeed to create, political and economic unity'. The Bill itself was passed without any vote, at any stage in both Houses of Parliament. Amid cheers, it was passed in the House of Lords, the day after it was read a third time in the Commons on 15 July. It received the Royal Assent on 18 July and became effective from 15 August 1947. King George VI, no longer the Emperor of India, sent a message of good will to the new Dominion, which was read out at the Independence Day ceremony in New Delhi on 15 August 1947.

" YOUR BABIES NOW "

18 JULY 1947

INDIAN INDEPENDENCE BILL RECEIVES ROYAL ASSENT

Be it enacted by the King's most Excellent Majesty, by and with the advice and consent of the Lords Spiritual and Temporal, and Commons, in the present Parliament assembly, and by the authority of the same as follows: As from the fifteenth day of the August nineteen hundred and forty seven, two independent Dominions shall be set up in India, to be known respectively as India and Pakistan.

*   *   *

In what must have been one of his last communiqués as Viceroy, Lord Mountbatten gave a personal report of the programme for Independence day celebrations in New Delhi on 15 August 1947. It appears also to be his last minute desperate effort to see that Britain did not leave India without leaving its footprints in the new emerging nation:

I have expressed a hope that I would be able to persuade the new Dominions to have the Union Jack in the upper canton of their flag, as do other members of the Commonwealth. This design has not been accepted. I have not pressed the leaders further.

The Viceroy's wish, thankfully, was not granted. For nearly a century India had battled and pleaded to be treated as the 'other members of the Commonwealth' in accordance with the Proclamation Act of 1858

David Low's very expressive cartoon, published in the *Evening Standard* of 18 July 1947 – the day the Indian Independence Bill received Royal Assent.

(and suddenly at the 11th hour India was perceived to be as good a Dominion as other nations of the British Empire.

This design has not been accepted by either party. Jinnah, in turning down the suggestion, explained that it would be repugnant to the religious feelings of the Muslims to have a flag with a Christian Cross alongside the Crescent. Nehru asked if I would mind if Congress rejected the design on the grounds that although Gandhi, Patel and others had originally expressed their willingness to accept it, they had now come to the conclusion that the general feeling among the Congress extremists was that the leaders were pandering far too much.

For the British this had reached a point at which it was inadvisable to press the design on them.

The new Indian tricolour, green, white and saffron, was designed by a Committee of the Constituent Assembly. It was originally the Indian National Congress flag, with the wheel from the Saranath Asokan capital replacing the old spinning wheel in the centre.

*   *   *

Krishna Menon's appointment as India's first High Commissioner in London was confirmed in July 1947. It was seen as a good idea to have someone of his experience of having lived in Britain as well as acquainted with the Indian National Congress, to be in charge of the High Commission in London.

With the official independence ceremony just ten days away, there was the problem of the mechanics of the actual flag hoisting at Indian missions abroad. The flag poles and the availability of the new flags posed a serious problem. It was left to Krishna Menon to sort out the problem. It has its human side.

An official circular of a minute of a meeting at the India Office, dated 8 August 1947, illustrates the problems:

When Mr Krishna Menon came to see me I mentioned to him, in order chiefly to make conversation and to say something which I hoped would be agreeable, that we were thinking of asking our Missions abroad to celebrate the great day in this manner; whereupon, despite my pointing out that I had no specific instructions to approach him on the subject, he insisted that he must telegraph to his Government to tell them this.

He rang me up to say that they would be getting flags ready for us, which we could send out to some of our principal Missions which could be reached in time!

This, I must confess, took me aback, since we had naturally assumed that our Ambassadors and Ministers would hoist what they always hoist, namely their diplomatic flag. Clearly, however, we cannot decline to hoist the Dominion flags without causing great offence and undoing all the goodwill we were hoping to create by our gesture on August 15th.

I have therefore consulted Mr Light of the Treaty Dept. who, though he does not like it, admits that it would be possible, failing additional flag poles, to fly the Dominion flag alongside the diplomatic flag on the same flag pole.

One snag is that Mr Menon is only busying himself with providing us with the Indian (Hindustan) flag and if we are to do the thing properly and not cause offence to the other side, we shall also have to have some Pakistan flags. If, however, we can get these, we should not perhaps let ourselves be too much put off by the rather unprecedented nature of the flag display which is contemplated. The great thing, I imagine is that the Indians shall feel happy on their Independence Day and realise that we are out to help them make an occasion of it. Presumably we shall have to send the flags out by bag as soon as possible to certain of our principal Missions in Europe with an informal letter of guidance, asking our Heads of Missions to do their best to get the Indian flags prominently displayed as well as their own, even if it means, in the extreme case, having the diplomatic flag flanked by those of India and Pakistan on the same flag post! (After all the latter are now official Dominion flags approved by the King.) Two additional flag posts would of course be much better.

...The Government of India are also being asked by the India Office to send to London at top speed by air, flags for the following posts (leaving them at such posts as they can on the way): (Cairo, Baghdad, Ankara, Beirut, Damascus, Jedda, Amman, Addis Ababa, Paris, Rome, Washington, Moscow. The Government of India also want to have flags sent on if possible through the proper channel, to Canada, Kenya and Tanganyika and will be sending some for this purpose also. If we receive enough, we might also possibly send them to Rabat, Algiers and Tunis.

Time is however very short and there is a serious risk these flags may not arrive quickly enough to be sent on in time. As it happens Mr Krishna Menon has volunteered to supply us with about fifteen India (Hindustan) flags here; so that we could get these off at once; and the India Office are hoping to get some Pakistan flags here from the London headquarters of the Moslem League.

When the day came, Gandhi was absent from the celebrations in New Delhi on 15 August 1947. The Viceroy's personal report of 8 August 1947 stated that:

Gandhi's absence from the celebrations in Delhi on the 15th August is, of course, intentional. He has never given the 3rd June plan his unqualified blessing and his position might be difficult. He also realises that it would not be possible to fit him into the programme in the way to which he would feel himself entitled. Arrangements for these celebrations are going well; and I think that they will be worthy of the occasion.

Gandhi has announced his decision to spend the rest of his life in Pakistan looking after minorities. This will infuriate Jinnah, but will be a great relief to Congress for, as I have said before, his influence is largely negative or even destructive and directed against the only man who has his feet firmly on the ground, Vallabhbhai Patel.

Sardar Vallabhbhai Patel, the strong man of India.

The astrologers are being rather tiresome since both the 13th and 15th have been declared inauspicious days, whereas the 14th is auspicious. I was not warned that I ought to consult the astrologers before fixing the day for the transfer of power, but luckily this has been got over by the Constituent Assembly deciding to meet before midnight on the auspicious 14th and take over power as midnight strikes which is apparently still an auspicious moment.

One or two of the more superstitious members of the Cabinet wished to have all the ceremony done at midnight in the Durbar Hall, but as, unfortunately, the older members of the Cabinet usually go to bed at 9 o'clock, sleep won the swearing-in battle over superstition; and we are now going to have the swearing-in ceremony in the presence of 500 people at 8.30 on the morning of the 15th, after which we will all proceed to the Constituent Assembly which I am to address in their new capacity as the Legislative Assembly for India.

In London *The Times* saw the independence as 'The end of an era', rather than the beginning of a new one, with the following editorial on 15 August 1947:

THE END OF AN ERA

Today sees the completion of a profound change in the relations of peoples whose institutions have been shaped for several generations under the authority of the British Crown. The Indian Empire disappears from the political map and the circle of the Dominions is enlarged in idea as well as in fact by the admission of two Asiatic States which, as the Viceroy truly said in his farewell speech yesterday, derive from their own ancient and lofty civilizations their title to the full sovereign privileges implicit in Dominion status. That this enlargement of the conceptions on which the Commonwealth rests should have been carried through smoothly and swiftly, with the manifestations of mutual good will which accompany the culmination of a natural process, is a tribute not only to the statesmanship which contrived it but to the confidence of the British Parliament and people in the strength and adaptability of the British tradition of political freedom. . .

Messages of good will came from all quarters of the world. President Truman sent the following message, on 14 August 1947, to the people of India. He also addressed the following messages to the Governors-General of the two new Dominions, India and Pakistan, on the occasion of their coming into being on 15 August 1947:

To Lord Louis Mountbatten, Governor General of the Dominion of India.
On this memorable occasion, I extend to you, to Prime Minister Jawaharlal Nehru, and to the people of the Dominion of India the sincere best wishes of the Government and the people of the United States of America. We welcome India's new and enhanced status in the world community of sovereign independent states, assure the new Dominion of our continued friendship and good will, and reaffirm our confidence that India, dedicated to the cause of peace and to the advancement of all peoples, will take its place at the forefront of the nations of the world in the struggle to fashion a world society founded in mutual trust and respect. India faces many grave problems, but its resources are vast, and I am confident that its people and leadership are equal to the tasks ahead. In the years to come the people of this great nation will find the United States a constant friend. I earnestly hope that our friendship will in future, as in the past, continue to be expressed in close and fruitful co-operation in international undertakings and in cordiality in our relations one with the other. *Signed:* HARRY S TRUMAN, *President of the United States of America.*

The following day, 16 August, *The Times* carried full details of the Independence ceremonies in London, New Delhi, Calcutta and in the capitals of other Commonwealth countries.

INDIA'S FIRST DAY OF INDEPENDENCE
JUBILANT SCENES IN DELHI
GOOD WILL TO BRITAIN
CHANGE OF SPIRIT
From Our Own Correspondent

Delhi, August 15. The Dominion of India was ushered in today with an elaborate ceremonial worthy of such a momentous occasion and amid scenes of intense popular enthusiasm. When Lord and Lady Mountbatten drove in state this morning to the Council House jubilant crowds broke through the police cordon, swarmed round the carriage, and amid shouting and cheering insisted on shaking them by the hand. Wherever Pandit Nehru and other leaders have made their appearance they have been accorded enthusiastic ovations. Their cars have been mobbed and movement for them has been difficult.

The Indians, no less than the British, love dignified pageantry, and all the ceremonies connected with the inauguration of the new State have been most impressive. They have been marked, from the Indian side, by gestures of great admiration for Lord Mountbatten, who has enjoyed a veritable personal triumph, and by expressions of unfeigned good will not only towards Great Britain but also to the west in general. For those who remember past periods of bitterness and hatred it marks a real transformation in the relations between the British and Indian peoples.

FAVOURABLE OMENS

Certain themes have run through all the speeches: an awareness of the greatness of the moment; sadness over the fact of partition, combined with good wishes to Pakistan and hopes for eventual reunion; and, most impressive of all, resolution on the part of the leaders to dedicate themselves with renewed energy to the service of the Indian people.

Although astrologers had declared that August 15 was an inauspicious day, favourable omens have not been lacking. Showers long overdue have come at last and freshened the green of Delhi's tree-lined avenues. The situation in the Punjab continues grave, but from Calcutta came reports of scenes of remarkable inter-communal fraternising in the streets, with people shouting 'Hindu-Muslim *ek ho*' (Hindus and Muslims are one), and last night in Old Delhi there were similar demonstrations.

As from midnight last night India has been a fully independent self-governing State within the British Commonwealth. Shortly before midnight there was a meeting of the Constituent Assembly in one of the great circular halls (formerly the library) of the great Council House designed by Sir Herbert Baker. The flags of the new Dominion hung in the frames which formerly contained the portraits of Viceroys.

The proceedings began with the singing of the first verse of *Vande Mataram*, India's national song, by the wife of the Congress President, accompanied by Indian lutes and zithers. The President of the Assembly, Dr Rajendra Prasad, spoke first in Hindi, then in English, his address being followed by two minutes' silence with all standing in memory of those who had died in the struggle for freedom in India and elsewhere. Pandit Nehru then moved that at the stroke of midnight all members of the Assembly present should take a solemn pledge of dedication to the service of India and her people.

'Long years ago,' he said 'we made a tryst with destiny, and now the time comes when we redeem our pledge, not wholly or in full measure, but very substantially. At the stroke of the midnight hour, when the world sleeps, India will awake to life and freedom. A moment comes, which comes but rarely in history, when we step out from the old to the new, when an age ends and when the soul of a nation long suppressed finds utterance.'

BRITISH SAGACITY

He was followed by the great philosopher and scholar Mr (he has dropped the title of Sir) S Radhakrishnan, who made a moving appeal for a spirit of tolerance and understanding, and declared, 'When we see what the Dutch and French are doing in Indonesia and Indo-China we cannot but admire the courage and political sagacity of the British people'.

The clock struck twelve and all members took the pledge, repeating it, sentence by sentence, after the President. The Assembly then authorised Pandit Nehru to go to Government House and formally request Lord Mountbatten to accept the office of Governor-General.

Only a few hours later, at 8.30, Lord Mountbatten was sworn in as Governor-General by the new Chief Justice of India, the Hon. Harilal Kania, in the marble-pillared Durbar Hall of Government House. Trumpets in the upper gallery blew a fanfare as Lord and Lady Mountbatten, preceded by ten Indian and British aides-de-camp, walked slowly to the dais. Having received the oath himself, the new constitutional head of the Indian Dominion then administered it to the twelve members of the new Cabinet, headed by Pandit Nehru, Sardar Patel, and Dr Prasad. Trumpets blew again as the procession left the Durbar Hall.

After an interval of one hour the Governor-General and Lady Mountbatten drove in an open carriage to the Council House. Before and after them rode the magnificent turbaned lancers of the Governor-General's Bodyguard, red and white pennons flying from their lances. As the procession approached the Council House the tumultuous scenes, already described, took place. The police failed completely to cope with the vast milling throng, but it was a remarkably good humoured and happy crowd.

Three chairs had been placed on the supreme dais of the Assembly Hall. The Governor-General sat in the centre, with Dr Prasad on his right hand and Lady Mountbatten on his left. In addition to members of the Assembly, all representatives of the Diplomatic Corps, senior British and Indian officers and many distinguished visitors were present.

THE KINGS MESSAGE

Less than 100 years after Queen Victoria assumed supreme power in India, her great-grandson stood before the elected representatives of the Indian people as the freely chosen constitutional head of their State. The Governor-General first delivered the following message from the King:

On this historic day when India takes her place as a free and independent Dominion in the British Commonwealth of Nations, I send you all my greetings and heartfelt wishes. Freedom-loving people everywhere will wish to share in your celebrations, for with this transfer of power by consent comes the fulfilment of a great democratic ideal, to which the British and Indian peoples alike are firmly dedicated. It is inspiring to think that all this has been achieved by means of peaceful change.

Heavy responsibilities lie ahead of you, but when I consider the statesmanship you have already shown and the great sacrifices you have already made, I am confident that you will be worthy of your destiny. I pray that the blessings of the Almighty may rest on you and that your leaders may continue to be guided in wisdom in the tasks before them. May the blessings of friendship, tolerance, and peace inspire you in your relations with the nations of the world. Be assured always of my sympathy in all your efforts to promote the prosperity of your people and the general welfare of mankind.

The Governor-General recalled that it was barely six months since Mr Attlee had invited him to accept the appointment of the last Viceroy. He described his discussions with the Indian leaders and paid tribute to them for the way in which they had faced up to difficult decisions. These leaders had placed him in their lasting debt by their sympathetic understanding of his position.

As for the position of the Indian States, said the Governor-General, after the formation of the States Department it had been possible for him, as the Crown representative, to tackle this great question. 'Thanks to that far-sighted states-man Sardar Vallabhbhai Patel, a scheme was produced which seemed to me to be equally in the interests of the States as of the Dominion of India.' Within less than three weeks nearly all the States had signed the instrument of accession and the standstill agreement, thus establishing a unified political structure covering over 300,000,000 people. Commenting on Hyderabad's unique position, the Governor-General said that negotiations were continuing and he was hopeful of a satisfactory solution.

ONE OF THEMSELVES

Loud applause greeted Lord Mountbatten's request to the Assembly that now, as the constitutional Governor-General, he be regarded as one of themselves. He announced, however, that he proposed to be released in April. 'It is not that I fail to appreciate the honour of being invited to stay on in your service, but I feel that as soon as possible India should be at liberty, if you so wish, to have one of her own people as Governor-General.'

Exactly two years ago he had been with 'that great friend of India, Mr Attlee in his Cabinet room when news of Japan's surrender was received. In India they had achieved a 'treaty of peace without a war', but India had suffered gravely from the effects of the war and recovery would require whole-hearted efforts. The emergence of a stable and prosperous India would be a factor of the greatest international importance for the peace of the world.

When the Governor-General referred to Mahatma Gandhi as the 'architect of India's freedom through non-violence,' there was again loud applause. Although he is taking no part in the celebrations and is spending the day fasting in Calcutta, many references have been made to the Mahatma in all these speeches and always there has been cheering.

This evening a vast crowd, which might have been anything from 100,000 to 200,000 strong, gathered to watch the ceremonial hoisting of the flag and the march-past in Princes Park, near the massive Victory Arch. Police arrangements broke down completely, but Lord and Lady Mountbatten were again welcomed enthusiastically by the people. Although it is not possible yet to know how this day was celebrated throughout the country, there can be no doubting the widespread spontaneous rejoicing in the capital. For Delhi's 1,000,000 inhabitants it has been a day they will long remember.

CROWDS IN CALCUTTA
From Our Correspondent

Calcutta, August 15. Calcutta celebrated Independence Day with an abandon not witnessed here since King George V's jubilee in 1935. Seldom has the city been so jubilant or so full of people.

For the first time since last year's communal riotings the city ceased to be a place of fear, and the flags of the two new Dominions flew over the battle-grounds of the past 12 months. The unexpected fraternization between Hindus and Muslims which was seen last night continued throughout today. Members of both communities tore past in lorries shouting Indian and Pakistan slogans. Europeans, Anglo-Indians, Chinese, and hillmen of Nepal and Tibet also joined in the celebrations. European business houses and homes flew both the Union Jack and the Indian flags.

Mr Gandhi, who is occupying an abandoned Muslim house in north Calcutta, fasted throughout Independence Day.

MR JINNAH SWORN IN

Karachi, August 15. Mr Jinnah, President of the Muslim League, today became the first Governor-General of the new Dominion of Pakistan.

Troops flanked the lawns of Government House, and a great assembly in glittering uniforms and brilliant costumes stood to greet Mr Jinnah as he took his seat on the dais. After Sir Abdur Rashid, Chief Justice of Lahore High Court, had administered the oath, the new Governor-General advanced to the steps overlooking the lawn, and the green and silver flag of Pakistan was broken from the flagstaff as a 31-gun salute was fired. *Reuter*

GATHERINGS IN SOUTH AFRICA

From Our Correspondent

Capetown, August 15. Indians throughout South Africa celebrated the birth of the new Dominions today by flying the respective flags. There were combined gatherings of Muslims, Hindus, and Christians, with, in many cases, European guest speakers. There was a message from the last Secretary of State for India, Lord Listowel: 'I have the utmost confidence in the future greatness of the two new Dominions, which will have a unique opportunity to contribute to the economic recovery of Asia and to enhance mutual understanding and promote friendly co-operation between the nations of the world. I send them both my heartfelt good wishes.'

INDEPENDENCE CEREMONIES
HISTORIC SCENES IN LONDON
NEW FLAGS UNFURLED

From Our Special Correspondent

The birth of the two new Dominions was celebrated yesterday in London by large gatherings of Indians. One scene of rejoicing was India House, Aldwych, headquarters of the High Commissioner for India; the second was Lancaster House, lent by the British Government for the occasion as a meeting-place for the adherents and well-wishers of Pakistan, which has not yet had time to set up its own offices in London.

Many non-Indians were present by invitation at both ceremonies. Among them were Mr Alexander, Minister of Defence, Mr Herbert Morrison, Lord Pethick-Lawrence, members of the Diplomatic Corps, and distinguished guests and representatives of organizations interested in Indian affairs. Great numbers of Indians not only attended and cheered the first unfurling of their own flag – and side by side with it the Union Jack – but also before or after their own celebration shared as guests in the other. The friendliness pervading both ceremonies was widely felt to be the happiest of auguries.

By mutual arrangement the events at India House began at 11 am and those at Lancaster House at 12.15 pm. Traffic in Aldwych was stopped, and crowds filled the pavements. Inside India House the principal guests were received in the domed library by the acting High Commissioner, Mr MK Vellodi. Mr V Krishna Menon, who was to succeed him as High Commissioner an hour later, was also present, with the High Commissioner for Pakistan, Habib Ibrahim Rahimtoola.

Behind the platform was a full-length painting of Mr Gandhi. The crowded scene was brightened by some white suits and the saris worn by many Indian women. Loud-speakers relayed the speeches to the people in Aldwych.

A PEACE-MAKER

MR VELLODI began his speech by welcoming the High Commissioner for Pakistan as an old friend, to whom he offered his hearty felicitations. As in the time of Asoka, he said, India proposed to function, as far as she could, as a peace-maker and peace-bringer.

It was a matter for deep thankfulness that her freedom had been effected by consent and in comparative peacefulness. In a speech punctuated by repeated applause, he paid homage to the leaders in the struggle for Indian independence, beginning with 'one whose name is imperishable, Mahatma Gandhi, the greatest Indian of all time, and one of the world's greatest men, who led us with unfaltering steps into the domain of independence'.

Mr Vellodi then read the King's message, which was also being given to the Indian Constituent Assembly, and a message from Mr Nehru.

MR ALEXANDER read a message from Lord Addison, Secretary of State for Commonwealth Relations, regretting that his departure for the Canberra conference prevented him from being present, and sending his congratulations. The hoisting of the flag of India, Mr Alexander said, was the symbol of so much ardent patriotism and meant the fulfilment of British rule and the attainment by India of her full political stature. It also meant the coming into existence of a new member of the British Commonwealth.

OPEN FUTURE

'The future now lies open before India,' Mr Alexander continued. 'For our part, we pledge ourselves to do all that lies in our power to ensure a happy and beneficial relationship between this country and our new associate in the British Commonwealth.

MR VELLODI led the company outside the building to the west corner, where a guard of honour of Indian sailors and airmen was drawn up, and he hoisted the flag of India beside a Union flag. Before and after the unfurling of the flag, two students, Miss Vijaya Patwardhan and Mr Pandya, sang the *Salutation to the Motherland* and the *Salutation to the Flag*.

The flag of Pakistan was unfurled inside Lancaster House from a flagstaff at one side of the landing of the great staircase. The assembly filled the hall, stairs, and gallery above, and many hundreds could not get into the building. A Muslim priest opened the ceremony by chanting a prayer from the Koran. Then the Pakistan flag was hoisted and, a moment later, amid renewed cheering, the Union flag on a second flagstaff. The King's message to the Constituent Assembly of Pakistan was read by the High Commissioner, Mr Rahimtoola.

MR ALEXANDER, after conveying Lord Addison's message, said: 'The Indian Empire dissolves – British Commonwealth of free nations welcomes two free peoples into their association'. Speaking in similar terms to those of his address at India House, he expressed the British Government's satisfaction that in a world much troubled by dissension their last Viceroy, Lord Mountbatten, had been able to work with such success with Mr Jinnah, Mr Nehru, and all their associates.

MR RAHIMTOOLA said that on the same day over 1,300 years ago the revelation of the Holy Koran was completed and Islam born, and it was providential that their new State should come into being on such an august day. There were great cheers when he said that they rejoiced in hailing Mr Jinnah as the first Governor-General of Pakistan.

When Mr Rahimtoola ended, the first to congratulate him on his speech and shake hands with him was Mr Krishna Menon.

STUDENTS' CEREMONY

In the afternoon a celebration was held at Friends House, Euston Road, by the Indian Conciliation Group, which was formed when Mr Gandhi was in London for the Round-Table Conference. The speakers were Mr Carl Heath, who presided, Lord Pethick-Lawrence, Mr Vellodi, Dr Maude Royden-Shaw and Dr Abdullah, of the Woking Mosque. Both new High Commissioners were present, and were warmly welcomed.

The flags of India and Pakistan were blessed by the Dean of Canterbury (Dr Hewlett Johnson) in the presence of 300 students of all nations at the International Club, Croydon. The two flags were unfurled to a fanfare of trumpets by the band of The East Surrey Regiment. Mr Krishna Menon was present.

The Independence Day celebrations at India House, London.

NEW ZEALAND HOPES

From Our Own Correspondent

Wellington (NZ) August 15. The New Zealand House of Representatives today passed a Bill assenting to the alteration in the royal title consequent on the assumption of Dominion status by India and Pakistan. Mr Fraser, the Prime Minster, said he hoped the settlement would be final, and that India and Pakistan would decide to be permanent Dominions and integral parts of the Commonwealth.

AUSTRALIAN GOOD WILL

From Our Correspondent

Canberra, August 15. Dr Evatt, Australian Minster for External Affairs, announced today that the Governments of Australia and Pakistan had agreed to exchange High Commissioners as soon as each Government could make the necessary arrangements. Sir Ivan Mackay would become High Commissioner for Australia in the Dominion of India.

INDIA · BRITISH-INDIAN CAMPAIGNS IN BRITAIN

MESSAGE FROM THE PRIME MINISTER

On this memorable day when His Majesty has signed the assent to the Indian Independence Bill, I send, on behalf of His Majesty's Government in the United Kingdom and of the British people, a message of goodwill and of heartfelt wishes for the future to all the peoples of the Indian Continent.

In a few days complete control of their affairs will have passed to the Indian people. I hope that the peoples of both the countries may enter into a new course of friendship and may join together with others in building a peaceful and prosperous world.   CR ATTLEE

THE INDIAN NATIONAL ANTHEM

The question of having a perfect national anthem tune to be played easily by orchestra and bands at home and abroad, became an urgent issue after the Independence in 1947. It was considered to be as important an issue as that of having a national flag. A decision had to be made between choosing *Bande Mataram* and *Jana Gana Mana*. *Bande Mataram* had a great historic attraction but was considered as not having enough movement in it. It was also thought to be too difficult for foreign orchestras to play.

After a Cabinet meeting, following consultation with Provincial Governors, the Indian Parliament was told on 26 August 1948 that *Jana Gana Mana* was to be the national anthem.

Biographies

Ahmed Shah Abdali

Afghan ruler, invaded India twelve times, on one occasion to fight the Marathas in 1761 at the battle of Panipat. Maratha power, dealt a grievous blow by Abdali's victory, never truly recovered from this defeat.

Horace Grundy Alexander (1889–1989)

Quaker, born in Croydon and educated at York and Cambridge; secretary of the Friends Peace Committee 1915; lecturer in international studies at Quaker College, Birmingham 1919–43; friend of CF Andrews who persuaded him to visit Gandhi at his *ashram* in India; became good friends with Gandhi, based on their shared commitment to the principles of non-violence; became involved with establishing civilised communication between the British Government and the Congress Party, scarcely on talking terms, first through the India Conciliation Group and later as a member of Gandhi's entourage; spent much time in India between 1946 and 1951; received the Padma Bhushan medal in 1984, in recognition of his services to the freedom movement, the highest civilian honour the Indian Government can give to a non-Indian.

Leopold Charles Maurice Amery (1873–1955)

Writer and statesman, born in India; studied at Harrow and Balliol College, Oxford. Worked for *The Times* 1899–1909; lived in South Africa 1899–1900. Committed to British imperialism. Tory Member for Parliament. Parliamentary Under-Secretary at Colonial Office 1919–21; Colonial Secretary 1922–9; founded Empire Marketing Board; Secretary of State for India 1940–5; founder of the Empire Parliamentary Association.

Lord Ampthill (1869–1935)

Educated at Eton and Oxford; Governor of Madras 1900–1906; acting Viceroy of India 1904; opposed India Bills of 1919 and 1935.

C F Andrews (1871–1940)

Charles Freer Andrews was a friend of India and was known as 'Deenabandhu' (friend of the poor) with great affection and respect. Went to India as a Christian missionary. Moved by the sufferings of the poor and the struggle for independence, he helped the 'Swaraj' movement in 1906. Met Rabindranath Tagore in England in 1912. His sense of justice for India was aroused by the humiliating conditions of Indians in South Africa, where he met Gandhi in 1914. The two struck a lasting friendship. He accompanied Gandhi to London for the Round Table Conference in 1931. He also finished

the job of abolishing indentured labour in Fiji, started by his friend Gopal Krishna Gokhale before his untimely and premature death.

Clement Attlee (1833–1967)

Educated at Haileybury and Oxford. British Labour politician and statesman. Became Ramsey MacDonald's Parliamentary Secretary 1922–4; Dominions Secretary, 1942–3; Deputy Prime Minister in the War Cabinet 1942–5. Prime Minster 1945–51; India attained Independence in 1947, during his premiership.

Surendra Nath Banerjee (1848–1925)

Distinguished Indian politician and enlightened educationalist. Appeared successfully for the Indian Civil Service Open Competitive Examination in London in 1869. His career in the ICS was shortlived on account of a conflict with the authorities, in which it was subsequently felt that he was unjustly treated. He later threw himself into public life and became a passionate and eloquent advocate of Indian rights and aspirations. He was a staunch member of the moderate camp in the Indian National Congress. He was the founder of the Indian Association in Calcutta (1876), one of the precursors to the Indian National Congress, of which he became President in 1894 and 1902. He was one of the earliest Indian National Congress delegates to Britain. He was knighted in 1921.

Mrs Annie Besant (1847–1933)

Active Fabian in early life, a theosophist, and Indian politician. President of the Indian National Congress 1917. Founder of the Central Hindu College, Benares (1899); started the Home Rule for India League 1916; imprisoned for her political activities

1917; organised the Home Rule movement for India 1917; changed the name to Commonwealth of India League (which later was to be the India League), 1922. Her whole life was dedicated to the cause of India. Also collaborated with another scholar for the translation of the *Bhagavat Gita* from Sanskrit into English.

Sir Mancherji Bhownagaree (1851–1933)

Judicial Counsellor, Bhavnagar; settled in London. Second and longest serving Indian Member of Parliament. Conservative MP 1895–1906; Committee Member for building of Imperial Institute, opened 1893. Sympathised with the injustices suffered by Indians in South Africa.

Karl Blind (1826–1907)

Writer and German political refugee, settled in Britain 1852; supported nationalist movements of all countries; wrote about Indian mythology.

W C Bonnerjee (1844–1906)

Studied Law at Middle Temple, London. Fourth Indian to be called to the Bar in England in 1867. Founder member of the Indian National Congress and its first President 1885. Successful lawyer; had chambers in Lincoln's Inn Fields. Settled in England in 1902 and continued to promote the cause of India until his death in London. With Dadabhai Naoroji started the London India Society in 1865.

Charles Bradlaugh (1833–91)

Social reformer and MP; refused, as an unbeliever, to take his oath of allegiance on the Bible; ejected from the House several times by force; published numerous leaflets ,and from 1874 to 1885 was a close associate of Mrs Annie Besant.

John Bright (1811–89)
Liberal politician, statesman and friend of India. Opposed capital punishment; chaired Select Committee for enquiring into problems on Cultivation of Cotton in India 1848; Advocated that Government of India be made a British Government department in 1853; favoured decentralisation in India 1858 and 1879; supported Indian Committee securing Parliamentary attention on Indian affairs 1883.

Baron Brockway (Fenner Archibald) (1888–1988)
Born in Calcutta and educated at Eltham College, England; influenced by Kier Hardie and converted to socialism; joined Independent Labour Party and became an ardent pacifist; imprisoned during the First World War; elected MP 1929–31 and again 1950–64; Chairman of Movement for Colonial Freedom and a vocal supporter of India's freedom struggle; made a life peer in 1964.

W S Caine (1842–1903)
Politician and temperance advocate. MP for Scarborough 1880–5; an able advocate of self-government in India and contributed to English journals, recording his views on Indian political and social matters. He said that 'the Congress movement contains everything that is serious, earnest and enterprising in Indian society. It can neither be ignored, depressed or suppressed'. Served on Royal Commission on administration of Indian expenditure (1895–6); was on the British Committee of the Indian National Congress.

Bhikaiji Cama (1861–1936)
Came to Britain and Europe in 1907 and met fellow Indian nationalists in London, Paris and Stuttgart. She spoke at the International Socialist Congress in Germany in the same year, putting before the world, in a fiery speech, the sufferings in India at the hands of the British and unfurled the Indian tricolour flag – green, yellow and red, with the words 'Vande Mataram' writ-

ten across it, the first time the Indian flag was so dramatically unfurled outside India. For her ceaseless nationalist activities in Europe, Cama was not allowed by the British authorities to return to India until 1935.

William Carey (1761–1834)
Missionary and orientalist; went to Calcutta in 1789; Professor of Sanskrit at Fort William College; preached in Bengali; Editor of *Ramayan* and compiled dictionaries of various Indian languages 1806–10; translated the Indian scriptures.

Kamladevi Chattopadhyay (1903–88)
Writer and social worker; involved with theatre and handicrafts of India; closely associated with Gandhi; Commander-in-Charge of Women's Volunteer Corps in the freedom movement; represented India at international conferences.

Winston Churchill (1874–1965)
Statesman and war leader, son of Randolph Churchill, Secretary of State for India, 1885–6. Served in his regiment in Bangalore in India, saw action in the North-West Frontier and wrote abut his experiences in the Boer War in South Africa. First Unionist MP 1900, and then Liberal MP 1906; Parliamentary Under-Secretary for the Colonies. Author of numerous historical books; Chancellor of Exchequer 1924–9; opposed India Bill of 1931. Prime Minister 1940–5.

Harvey Thomas Colebrooke (1765–1837)
Sanskrit scholar; studied Hindu law, judge at Calcutta 1801; returned to England 1814 and gave his Sanskrit manuscripts to India House; writer on Hindu mathematics and philosophy.

Sir Henry John Stedman Cotton (1845–1915)
Member of the Indian Civil Service; served in the Bengal Civil Service 1867; Chief Commissioner of Assam 1896–1906; President of Indian National Congress 1906; Member of Parliament 1906–10; Author of *New Indian or India in Transition* and *Indian and Home Memories*.

Professor Sir Reginald Coupland (1884–1952)
British Empire historian. Member of Royal Commission on Superior Civil Services in India 1923–4; travelled with Cripps mission to India 1942. Published *History of East Africa* and *Indian problems and politics*. Founder member of India Conciliation Group after meeting Gandhi in London 1931. Wrote numerous books on history: *History of East Africa* and *East Africa and its Invaders* (1938); *Exploitation of East Africa*. Visited India twice and devoted most of the years of the Second World War (1939–45) to study of India. Published *The Indian Problem* 1833–35 (1942); *Indian Politics 1936–42* (1943) in which there is to be found the first serious treatment in English of the idea of Pakistan; *The Future of India* (1943) and *India, a Restatement* (1945).

Sir Stafford Cripps (1889–1952)
Labour statesman and lawyer. Member of Parliament 1931–50. Member of Churchill's War Cabinet. Mission to India in 1942. He was Chancellor of the Exchequer from 1947–50 in the first post-war Labour Government of Clement Attlee.

Surendra Kumar Datta (1878–1942)
Biologist, educated at Lahore and Edinburgh. Welfare Officer in France with Indian Army in First World War. Member of Lytham Committee on the Education of Indian Students in Britain 1921–2; member of Indian Legislative Assembly 1929–36; member of the Round Table Conference 1931; visiting lecturer to USA 1935; Vice-President of the World Committee of YMCAs.

John Dickinson (1815–1876)
Educated at Eton; writer on Indian affairs; Founder of India Reform Society 1853, which pleaded for leniency after the Mutiny in 1857; Published *India, Its Government Under Bureaucracy*, 1852; and many other pamphlets.

William Digby CIE (1849–1904)
Editor of *Ceylon Hansard*; Editor of *Madras Times* 1877–9; Secretary of the National Liberal Club 1882–7; Member, British Committee of the Indian National Congress. Author *Prosperous British India* 1901.

Marquess of Dufferin and Ava (1826–1902)
Initiated establishment of the Indian National Congress. First Marquess of Dufferin and Ava. Under-Secretary of State for India 1864–6; Governor-General of India 1884; dealt with India's land questions; annexed upper Burma 1886; Returned from India 1888.

Reginald E H Dyer (1864–1927)
Born in India; educated at Sandhurst; responsible for massacre at Amritsar, at Jallianwallah Baag 1919.

King Edward VII (1841–1910)
King of Great Britain and Emperor of India. Prime Minister Gladstone unsuccessfully asked Queen Victoria to give the young prince a job in India; went to India 1875–6 on tour; organised Colonial and Indian Exhibition in London 1886; founded the Imperial Institute as a memorial to Queen Victoria's Golden Jubilee 1887.

Lord Ellenborough (1790–1871)
Governor-General of India, 1841; unpopular with the civilians; responsible for annexation of Sind 1843; recalled to England 1844.

Michael Foot (Born 1913)
Journalist, author and politician. President of Oxford Union 1933; Assistant editor of *Tribune* 1937–8; managing director of *Tribune* 1948–52 and 1955–6; Labour MP; supported Indian cause in Britain; Chairman of India League 1985–, President of Indian National Congress Centenary Celebrations Committee, UK, 1985.

Mohandas Karamchand Gandhi (1869–1948)

The architect of Indian Independence, moralist and social reformer. Studied Law at Inner Temple, London, 1887–91; returned to India, then went to South Africa 1893; opposed racial discrimination and set up Phoenix Settlement there. Returned to India during the First World War in 1914, via England. President, Indian National Congress 1924. Led Salt march to Dandi coast in 1930 in defiance of government's tax on salt; attended Round Table Conference in London 1931 and set up India Conciliation Group; chose civil disobedience, non-cooperation and fasting as weapons to fight British injustice. In and out of prisons for breaking law; failed to persuade M A Jinnah against partition. Assassinated in New Delhi by a fanatic on 30 January 1948 on his way to a regular evening prayer meeting.

King George V, Emperor of India (1865–1935)

Last Emperor to visit India. Inaugurated the First Round Table Conference in London 1930. Father of George VI. State visit to India 1911; Coronation Durbar at Delhi 1911. Removed seat of government in India from Calcutta to Delhi. Presented first Victoria Cross to Indian soldier in First World War. Visited wounded Indian soldiers at hospital in Brighton. Invited Gandhi, Sarojini Naidu and other Round Table Delegates to tea at Buckingham Palace 1931. Criticised Gandhi for his civil disobedience policy, to which Gandhi replied: 'Under no circumstance must I get involved into politics with His Majesty'.

King George VI, Emperor of India (1895–1952)

King of Great Britain, Ireland and British Dominions and the last Emperor of India. Created Duke of York 1920. Proclaimed King after abdication of elder brother, King Edward VIII. Opened Festival of Britain 1951.

Lal Mohan Ghosh (1849–1909)

Barrister, orator and politician; came to England to present a monster petition regarding the Civil Service; President Indian National Congress; first Indian to stand for Parliament in Britain 1896, but failed to win a seat.

William Ewart Gladstone (1809–98)

Liberal politician and Prime Minister 1868–74, 1880–5, 1886 and 1892–4, (when Naoroji was elected the first Indian Member of Parliament).

Gopal Krishna Gokhale (1866–1915)

Member of the Deccan Education Society, Poona; builder of the Fergusson College and editor of *Sarvajanik Sabha Quarterly* (1890); Founder of Servants of India Society, 1905, to train people to render services to the country; President, Indian National Congress 1905; went to South Africa at Gandhi's request. To Gandhi 'Gokhale was the image of truth, full of humanity, one who called nothing his

own'. Gokhale used to say, 'Love of one's country must so fill the heart that all else shall appear as of little moment by its side'.

George J. Goschen (1831–1907)

Liberal MP; declined Viceroyalty of India.

Lepel Henry Griffin (1838–1908)

Writer and Indian Civil Servant in Punjab 1860; Agent-General to Governor-General in Central India 1881–9; favoured use of vernacular in teaching in India; Co-founder of *Asiatic Quarterly Review* 1885.

Nellie Sen Gupta (1886–1973)

English. Married Sen Gupta, family friend and student in Britain; went to India and was well-received in his family. Involved herself in the Indian freedom struggle and was imprisoned in 1931. Chose to live in Pakistan after partition of India in 1947.

Agatha Harrison (1885–1954)

Quaker Society of Friends; University Welfare Tutor, London School of Economics 1917–20; visited India with Royal Commission on India 1929; invited by Gandhi to be his representative as mediator and conciliator in London in 1931; Secretary of the India Conciliation Group 1950; took interest in India League activities after the India Conciliation Group ceased operation in 1950.

Warren Hastings (1732–1818)

Went to India 1750; Governor of Bengal 1772; Governor-General of India 1773.

Lord William Hay (1826–1911)

Studied at Haileybury College. Entered Indian Civil Service 1845, returned to England 1862. Was Deputy Commissioner of Simla; a Liberal, first elected to Parliament in 1865.

Carl Heath (1869–1950)

Member of National Peace Council 1909; Chairman of Council for International

Service 1919; met Gandhi in London in 1931; became good friends; Chairman of the India Conciliation Group, liaised with Viceroys and the Secretaries of State for India; worked to win friends in Britain and to influence them regarding responsibility of policy on India.

James F Horrabin (1884–1962)

Left-wing socialist artist, cartoonist and lecturer; Art Editor of various English newspapers; Labour MP 1929–31; Vice-chairman of India League; Chairman of Fabian Colonial Bureau 1945–50.

Allan Octavian Hume ICS (1829–1912)

Educated at Haileybury. Went to India in 1860. Indian Civil Servant and ornithologist; joined Bengal Civil Service 1849; CB for services in Indian Mutiny 1860. Convinced that united action of responsible friends of India was necessary to counteract the dangerous current of opinions in the country and to turn them into positive channels of communication. Took initiative in organising and establishing the Indian National Congress in 1885, and its first and longest serving General Secretary. Prepared a scheme for the redemption of agricultural indebtedness and village Panchayats; declined offer of Lieutenant-Governorship; collaborated in standard work on Indian game birds. Helped maintain the Congress organ *India* in England.

Sir William Hunter (1840–1900)

Historian, Indian Civil Service 1861. Author of books on Bengal, Orissa and *Comparative Dictionary of Non-Aryan Languages of India and High Asia* 1868. Invited by the Viceroy to compile statistical survey of Indian Empire in 1869, that took him twelve years and 128 volumes, later condensed as *The Imperial Gazetteer of India*; author of *The Indian Empire; its people, history and products*; member of Governor-General's Council 1881–7; collected extensively for a history of India; wrote about the growth of British domination in India 1899.

Seth Alibhoy Mulla Jeevanjee

Prosperous contracting, shipping and trading merchant, in Mombasa, Kenya in the 1880s; employed by the Imperial British East Africa Company to import artisans and police from India; shared his wealth with the fellow Asians and became a politician; first Asian to be a member of the Legislative Council; founded a leading newspaper and was awarded the OBE.

Mohamed Ali Jinnah (1876–1948)

Studied Law in England. Barrister, Bombay High Court; Secretary to Dadabhai Naoroji when he was the President of the Indian National Congress. Joined Muslim League 1913; opposed Gandhi's support of the Khilafat movement and the non-cooperation policy of the Indian National Congress, resigning from it in 1920. Came to England for the Round Table Conference 1930–1 and stayed on till 1934; returned to India to devote time to the Muslim League. Prime mover behind the League's Pakistan resolution, 1940, which demanded a separate homeland for the subcontinent's Muslims. Governor-General of Pakistan (1947–8).

Atma Kamlani
One of the founder member of Friends of India and on Editorial Board of *India Bulletin*. Returned to India in 1934. A preacher and teacher – deeply religious. Campaigned for Indian freedom.

James Keir Hardie (1856–1915)
One of the founders of the Labour Party in Britain and the first Labour candidate for Parliament. He represented Merthyr Tydfil from 1900 to 1915.

Victor Kiernan
Emeritus Professor of Modern History, University of Edinburgh. Author of a number of major historical works, including *The Lords of Humankind*; also a translator of the Urdu poetry of Muhammad Iqbal and Faiz Ahmed Faiz.

Vengalil Krishnan Kunji Krishna Menon (1896–1974)
Indian politician. London School of Economics 1927, studying political science; University College 1930, studying psychology. Called to the Bar, Middle Temple, London 1934; Editor for publishers Bodley Head; Member of the Commonwealth of India League; Indian freedom fighter. Independent India's first High Commissioner in London.

Lala Lajpat Rai (1856–1928)
Took a leading part in organising relief of community distress of all kinds. Joined Indian National Congress in 1888. Member of the Congress deputation to England (1905). Deported to Burma for Sedition (1907); to escape political harassment he spent eight years in America where he ran a paper called *The Young India*, 1915. President of the special Congress Session in 1920 that adopted the programme of non-cooperation. Author of *Unhappy India, Arya Samaj*, etc. While leading a demonstration in Lahore in 1928 he was hit by a police baton and died from his injuries. Wrote foreword for Josiah C Wedgwood's book: *The Man and His Work*.

Lord Lansdowne (1845 – 1927)
Educated at Eton and Oxford. Under-Secretary of State for India 1880; Viceroy of India 1888–94.

Harold Laski (1893–1950)
Socialist and political scientist, in London School of Economics 1920–50. Chairman of Labour Party 1945. Friend of India.

Dr A D Lindsey (1879–1952)
An academic politician, born in Glasgow. Elected Fellow and classical tutor at Balliol College, Oxford 1922. Chairman of the National Council of Social Services. Trusted advisor to the Trade Union Congress and the Labour Party. Spent four months in India in 1930 to survey the work of Protestant colleges in India for the East-West Commission set up by the International Missionary Council. Struck up a friendship with Gandhi when he visited Balliol College during his visit for the Round Table Conference in 1931. Vice-Chancellor of the University of Oxford 1935–8.

Marquess of Linlithgow (1887–1952)
Educated at Eton; chairman, Royal Commission on Indian Agriculture 1926–8; Joint Select Committee on Indian Constitutional Reform 1933–4; Viceroy of India 1936–43; involved India in the Second World War, without consulting Indian leaders and politicians, by announcing in the *Gazette* that Britain was at war with Germany and that India was automatically at war with the Axis.

The Earl of Listowel (1906–97)
Supporter of the Indian National Congress, last Secretary of State for India; Under-Secretary to the India Office 1944; the influential figure in the Attlee government which ensured the smooth transfer of power in 1947.

Lord Lothian (1882–1940)
Journalist and statesman; Private Secretary to Lloyd George 1916–21; Under-Secretary of State for India 1931–2; Chairman of State for India 1931–2; Chairman, Indian Franchise Committee 1932. Met Gandhi in London 1931. Involved with India Conciliation Group foundation. Appointed Secretary of Transvaal Indigency Commission; its report represented the fundamental problems of the relations between white and black races; Under-Secretary of State for India and went to India in 1932 to report on the question of electoral franchise. Created an atmosphere of friendliness between India and the India Office.

Sir (David) Alexander Cecil Low (1891–1961)
Born in New Zealand. Political cartoonist; joined the *Daily Star* in 1919 and later the *Evening Standard*, both London publications. He attacked Fascism and was described as one of the 'greatest' of modern cartoonists.

Sir Lawrence Roger Lumley (1896–1969)
Educated at Eton, Sandhurst and Oxford. Governor of Bombay 1937–43; Parliamentary Under-Secretary of State for India 1945; President of the Royal Asiatic Society 1946–9, the East India Association 1946–61; Chairman of the School of Oriental and African Studies.

Emily Lutyens (1875–1964)
Daughter of Lord Lytton, Viceroy of India (1876–80); Married Edwin Lutyens (1869–1944), the architect of New Delhi, including the Rashtrapati Bhavan, the former Viceregal Lodge.

Thomas Babington Macaulay (1800–59)
First Baron; historian, writer, barrister, Liberal MP; member of the Supreme Council of India 1834–8; presided over the Commission for Composing a Criminal Code for India 1835.

Malcolm MacDonald (1901–81)
Son of Ramsey MacDonald. Member of Parliament 1929–35. Parliamentary Under-Secretary, Secretary of State for Dominions 1935–8, British High Commissioner in India 1955–1960; Governor-General of Kenya 1963–4; President, Royal Commonwealth Society from 1971.

Madan Mohan Malaviya (1861–1946)
Graduated from Calcutta University; President of Indian National Congress 1909 and 1918; High Court Vakil 1893; opposed the Press Act and the Seditious Meetings Act. Delegate to the Second Round Table Conference, London 1931. Always dressed in immaculate white which earned him the nickname of 'the spotless Pandit'.

Karl Marx (1817–83)
Political economist, philosopher and revolutionary socialist thinker; author of the massive *Das Kapital*. Wrote a number of articles on India for the *New York Daily Tribune*, including 'The Future Results of the British Rule in India' (1853).

Maria Montessori (1870–1952)
Born in Italy, first woman to graduate from Rome University, as Doctor of medicine and surgery. Spent ten years in India including a period during the Second World War, and was greatly admired by Gandhi, Tagore and others. Her name is synonymous with education of children of nursery age.

Lord Louis Mountbatten (1900–79)
Last Viceroy of India 1946; chose the date for Indian Independence 15 August 1947; India's first Governor-General after Independence; left India 1948.

Professor Gilbert Murray (1866–1957)
Internationalist, classical scholar, author of many books. Founder member of India Conciliation Group after meeting Gandhi in London 1931. A member of the Committee of Intellectual Co-operation from 1922–30.

Sarojini Naidu (1879–1949)
Poet and politician; sailed for England 1895, studied in King's College, London, and later at Girton College, Cambridge; returned to India after three years; published *The Golden Threshold* 1912; *The Bird of Time* and, in 1917, *The Broken Wing*. Involved in politics from 1921. Went to Kenya and South Africa on behalf of the Indian National Congress 1924–5, stating that 'let Congress be the voice of the people and not the voice of the politicians'. Gifted orator; went to America in 1928. Naidu met Gandhi in London for the first time in 1914 and joined him in his Dandi Salt March and for the Round Table Conference in London 1931. Repeated imprisonments damaged her health. Wrote to Gandhi in 1920 from abroad, 'the specialists think that my heart disease is in an advanced and dangerous state, but I cannot rest till I stir the heart of the world to repentance over the tragedy of Martyred India'. Her speech at the Albert Hall, London, on 7 November 1919, is one of the best made by any Indian in Britain.

Dadabhai Naoroji (1825–1917)
Founder of London Indian Society 1865, later to become East India Association; in 1882 launched in India the *Voice of India*; the only object was to present to the British

public a fair hearing and justice for India. Naoroji funded this monthly journal and bore losses until it was incorporated with *Indian Spectator* in 1890. This was an act of supreme dedication to secure India's voice in Britain in order to make the British understand and sympathise with the deep sense of injustice inflicted upon the people of India. Founder of Bombay Presidency Association 1885 'for the promotion and advocacy of the public interest of India'. Founder member of the Indian National Congress. President of the Indian National Congress 1886, 1893, 1906. Founder member of journal *India*, 1890; British Committee of the Indian National Congress 1890. First Indian member of British Parliament 1892; First Indian member of Welby Commission 1897; First Indian Professor at British university; author of *Poverty and Un-British Rule in India*.

Jawaharlal Nehru (1889–1964)
Politician and statesman. India's first Prime Minster, 1947–64. Educated at Harrow and Trinity College, Cambridge; read for the Bar at London's Inner Temple 1910–12.

Florence Nightingale (1820–1910)
Hospital nursing reformer; took nurses to the Crimean War in 1854; took interest in affairs of India and supported the formation of the Indian National Congress; supporter of Indian reform. Discussed Indian political situation in India with delegates from the Indian National Congress. On her death in 1910 Sir William Wedderburn received a legacy of £250 for 'some Indian object'.

Sir Michael Francis O'Dwyer (1864–1940)
Irish-born Indian Civil Service administrator 1885; Lieutenant-Governor of Punjab 1913–19, approved actions of General R E H Dyer in the massacre at Amritsar on 13 April 1919; favoured British control over India. Assassinated in London by Udham Singh, as a revenge for the Amritsar killings, at a meeting of the Royal Central Asian Society.

Vallabhbhai Patel (1875–1950)
Studied Law in Britain in 1910 and became a successful criminal lawyer. Met Mahatma Gandhi in 1917, and by 1924 had given up law to devote life to the Indian freedom movement that landed him in prison a number of times. After Independence, his greatest achievement was the integration of the Princely States and peaceful maintenance of unity of India. He was an extraordinary Indian statesman.

Sir Robert Peel (1788–1850)
British statesman and Conservative Prime Minister 1839–45 and 1841–5; reorganised police force in London whose members were known as 'Peelers' or 'Bobbies'.

Baron Pethick-Lawrence (1871–1961)
Politician and Socialist worker; called to the Bar 1899; edited and owned *Echo* and took up the cause of women's suffrage; edited *Votes for Women* (1907). Labour MP 1923–31. Financial Secretary to the Treasury. Re-elected MP 1935. Secretary of State for India

1945; led Cabinet Mission to India in 1946, failed to reach agreement with Congress and Muslim League. Influenced and supported legislation granting independence to India.

Henry Polak
Solicitor and theosophist. Friend of Gandhi from their South African days; joined Gandhi in establishing the Phoenix Settlement. Force behind the original Home Rule League in London; never forgave Krishna Menon for splitting the League.

Hodgson Pratt (1824–1907)
Peacemaker and journalist; joined East India Company in India 1847; helped establish the Vernacular Literature Society 1851; returned to Britain 1861; founder Editor of *Peace Association Journal* 1884.

Raja Rammohun Roy (1772–1833)
The inaugurator of the modern age in India, and considered 'the greatest Indian of his age'. The origin of all progressive and emancipation movements in India can be traced to Raja Rammohun Roy, the pioneer of modern education, promoter of freedom of speech and Press, possibly the first exponent of comparative religion.

Raja Rammohun Roy was the first Indian to come to England on an official visit. He arrived in 1831 on a mission of complaints to the British Government regarding the renewal of the East India Company's charter. He particularly wanted to be in Parliament for the debates on the Reform Bill, the Factory Act, the Act of Abolition of Slavery. Due to a mishap and misdirection of the hotel he was staying at, he was too late for the debates. Rammohun Roy had a select committee meeting at the House of Lords in March 1832 dealing with the issue of tax on salt in India. He died in Bristol where there is a monument where he was buried.

Dr Maude Royden-Shaw (1876–1956)
Educated at Cheltenham Ladies' College and Oxford; lectured for women's suffrage 1908–14; went on lecture tour to India.

Shapurji Saklatvala (1874–1936)
One of the earlier members of the Communist Party of Great Britain; third Indian Member of British Parliament, Labour Member 1922–3; Communist Member 1924–9; active in politics in England and India. Known for his fiery speeches in Parliament. A strong critic of Gandhi.

V S Srinivasa Sastri (1869–1946)
A Sanskrit scholar. Sastri, friend and follower of G K Gokhale, earned the sobriquet 'Silver-tongued orator of the British Empire' for his mastery of the English language. Came to Britain for the Imperial Conference in London in 1931. He proposed that the Dominion Governments of the British Commonwealth should give full citizenship rights to all Indians. He was later made a Privy Councillor. He also attended the First and Second Round Table Conferences in London; he asked for equal rights of citizenship for Indians in East Africa. He visited South Africa in 1927 and managed to get Indians admitted into White Trade Unions. He also founded a Teacher Training College – The Sastri College – in Durban; twice refused a knighthood.

Keshub Chandra Sen (1838–84)
Religious and social reformer; joined the Brahmo Samaj, started by Raja Rammohun Roy. Visited England in 1870 and gave more than 70 lectures and talks; was well received, among others, by Queen Victoria. One daughter married the Maharajah of Mayurbhanj and another married the Maharajah of Cooch Behar.

Nadir Shah
Persian adventurer and ruler, invaded India and sacked Delhi in 1739, massacring its inhabitants and carrying away enormous booty, including Mughal Shah Jehan's famous Peacock Throne.

Uday Shankar (1900–1977)
Dancer, choreographer; studied at J J School of Art, Bombay, and Royal College of Arts, London, 1920; teamed with Russian ballet dancer Anna Pavlova to play Krishna to her Radha; both toured Europe and America.

George Bernard Shaw (1856–1950)
Playwright born in Ireland.

Udham Singh (1899–1940)
Injured at Jallianwala Bagh massacre at Amritsar, 13 April 1919 when 1650 rounds were fired and 379 men, women and children killed and 1500 seriously injured; imprisoned for five years for a political offence. Studied in America and came to Britain in 1937, looking for an opportune moment to kill Michael O'Dwyer to avenge Amritsar massacre; succeeded by shooting him at a public meeting in London on 3 March 1940; committed to Old Bailey; sentenced to death and hanged at Penton-ville prison on 31 July 1940.

Lord Sinha of Raipur KC (1864–1928)
S P Sinha came to Britain in 1881. Called to the Bar 1881 (Lincoln's Inn, London). First

Indian Law member of Viceroy's Executive Council 1909–10. Knighted 1914. President, Indian National Congress 1915; Member, Imperial War Cabinet in London 1917, and member of the British delegation to the Peace Conference at Versailles in 1918; KC 1918; Under-Secretary of State for India 1919. First, and the only, Indian to be awarded hereditary peerage, 1919. First Indian to take silk.

Donald M Smeaton (1846–1910)
Indian Civil Servant from 1865; Liberal MP.

General Smuts (1870–1950)
South African statesman, politician and soldier. Prime Minister of South Africa 1919–24.

Cornelia Sorabji (1866–1954)
First Indian woman to study law in Britain, at Sommerville Hall, Oxford 1889; social reformer; campaigned for women's education; helped women in purdah; second Indian woman to be called to the Bar (Lincoln's Inn, London) 1923; against complete independence for India; favoured Dominion Status.

Reginald William Sorensen (1891–1971)
Labour politician. Member of Parliament 1934, 1935–50. Chairman of India League; Vice-President, Indo-British Forum; President, Indo-British Parlia-mentary Group; member of Parliamentary deputation to India 1946. Author of many publications including My Impressions of India. Created life peer 1964.

Rabindranath Tagore (1861–1941)
India's greatest renaissance man. First came to Britain in 1877. Poet, novelist, short story writer, essayist, dramatist, philosopher, educationalist, painter and founder of Shantiniketan (abode of peace), an institute of Indian Arts and Literature at Calcutta 1901, agricultural school, 1914 and International University, 1921; Nobel Prize for literature Gitanjali (Song Offering) 1913, the first Asian to be so honoured, Knighted in 1915, an honour which he resigned in 1919 as a protest after the Jallianwalla Bagh massacre

in Amritsar in 1919. Bestowed the title 'Mahatma' (Great Soul) on Gandhi; composed Indian national anthem – long before Independence in 1947, officially accepted in 1948 by the new Cabinet.

Balgangadhar Tilak (1856–1920)
A nationalist leader. Editor, The Maratta and Kesari 1890; Professor of mathematics at Poona; wanted nothing short of total independence for India. Imprisoned several times to prevent him from taking active part in the freedom movement. Visited England and spoke at various public meetings as delegate of the Indian National Congress. Never became its President, but inspired others by words and deeds, for support for freedom movement. Disliked the weak poli-

cy of the Indian National Congress; believed that 'political rights will have to be fought, not by persuasion but by strong pressure'.

Harry S Truman (1884–1972)
President of United States of America – Democrat, 33rd President 1945–53.

Victoria, Queen of the United Kingdom of Great Britain and Ireland and Empress of India (1819–1901)
Succeeded to the throne 1837; instituted Victoria Cross 1856; East India Company abolished and power transferred to the Crown; received the Royal Assent in 1858;

designation of Empress of India confirmed by Royal Title Bill 1876; her great interest in India led to the Colonial and Indian Exhibition in London 1886; laid foundation stone for Imperial Institute 1887 in her Golden Jubilee year celebrations; gifts for Golden Jubilee and Diamond Jubilee in 1897 displayed at the Durbar Hall in Osborne House, Isle of Wight. Employed Indian servants in Royal Household. Learnt little Hindustani and never visited India.

Swami Vivekananda (1863–1902)

Narendra Datta; later to become Swami Vivekananda, carried the message of India across the whole world; he attended the Chicago Parliament of Religions in 1893 where his speeches electrified the audience; he was made to speak last to keep the public from leaving the hall. Deeply impressed Max Muller during his visit to Europe; addressed the Congress of History of Religions in Paris in 1900.

Field Marshall Viscount Wavell (1883–1950)

First Earl Wavell. Educated at Winchester and Sandhurst. Served as a soldier in India 1903–10. Commander-in-Chief in India, July 1941, and Supreme Commander, South-West Pacific 1941–3. Viceroy of India 1943–7.

Alfred Webb (1834–1908)

Biographer and politician; visited India frequently and was the third British President of the Indian National Congress 1894.

Sir William Wedderburn Bt (1838–1918)

Judge, Bombay High Court (1885), Chairman, Governing Body of Deccan Education Society (1884–87), Member of Parliament (1893–1900). A distinguished member of the Indian Civil Service. After retirement from the ICS he took a leading part in the foundation of the Indian National Congress and attended its first session in 1885. President of the Congress in 1899 and 1910; helped maintain the Congress organ *India*; Chairman of the India Parliamentary Committee. Remained a steadfast supporter of the Indian National Congress until his death.

Josiah C Wedgwood (1872–1943)

Great-grandson of the famous founder of the Wedgwood pottery. Politician; naval architect; MP, Newcastle under Lyme 1906–42; responsible for the initiation of the History of Parliament; devoted to India's cause, and for a Jewish national home. Wrote foreword to *Young India* by Lala Lajpat Rai.

Charles Wilkins (C1749–1836)

Indophile writer in East India Company's Service 1770; the first Britisher to make a study of and master the Sanskrit inscriptions and to translate text into English including the *Bhagavat-Gita* 1785; helped set-up printing press for vernacular languages, co-founder of the Asiatic Society of Bengal.

Ellen Wilkinson (1891–1947)

Politician and trade unionist, MP; headed India League delegation to India 1932; led Jarrow march to London 1936.

Woodrow Wilson (1856–1924)

American statesman and Democrat politician, 28th President (1913–21) elected twice; champion of League of Nations, proposed peace plan, First World War.

Sir Francis Edward Younghusband (1863–1942)

Indian born; educated at Sandhurst; diplomat and soldier; Political Officer Chitral 1893; lived in Indore 1902–03; founder World Congress of Faiths 1936.

George Yule

The first Englishman to become the President of the Indian National Congress, in 1888. Member of the Committee of the British Committee of the Indian National Congress.

Sources

LIBRARIES AND ARCHIVES CONSULTED
National Archives of College Park, Maryland, USA
The Library of Congress, Washington DC, USA
The Religious Society of Friends in Britain
The British Library
The British Library, Oriental and India Office Collection
The British Library, Newspaper Library
The Daily Telegraph
University of Kent at Canterbury, Centre for Study of Cartoons
and Caricatures
House of Lords, Record Office
The Royal Archives, Windsor
National Portrait Gallery, London
Public Record Office, Kew
Getty Images

Bibliography

WRITERS' WORKSHOP BOOK: *Keshub Chandra Sen in England – Diaries, Sermons, Addresses and Epistles, 1871*, P Lal, Calcutta.

KUSOOM VADGAMA: *India in Britain*, London, 1984.

WILLIAM GOLANT: *The Long Afternoon – British India 1601–1947*, Hamish Hamilton, London, 1975.

GEORGE WOODCOCK: *Who Killed the British Empire?*, Jonathan Cape, London, 1974.

MARY LUTYENS: *Edwin Lutyens*, Black Swan, London, 1980, 1991.

LARRY COLLINS AND DOMINIQUE LAPIERRE: *Freedom at Midnight*, Book Club Associates, London, 1975.

DENNIS GRIFFITH, (Editor): *The Encyclopaedia of British Press*, Macmillan Press, London, 1922.

V D MAHAZAN: *India Since 1526*, S Chand, Ram Nagar, New Delhi.

I M CUMPSTON: *Indians Overseas In British Territories 1834–1954*, Oxford University Press, London, 1953.

PENDEREL MOON: *Strangers in Britain*, Faber and Faber, London, 1943.

ROBERT G GREGORY: *Quest for Equality*, Sangam Books, London, 1993.

ROBERT G GREGORY: *South Asians in East Africa*, Westview Press, Oxford, 1993.

K C ARORA: *Indian Nationalist Movement in Britain (1930–1949)*, Inter India Publications, New Delhi, 1992.

CATHERINE OWENS PEARCE: *Mahatma Gandhi: Father of Non-Violence*, Hawthorn Books, New York, 1969.

IVISON S MACADAM (Editor): *The Annual Register, A Review of Public Events*, Longman Green, London, 1948.

BRAJENDRANATH BANERJI: *Raja Rammohun Roy's Mission to England*, N M Raychowdhury, Calcutta, 1926.

MARIE SETON: *Panditji: A Portrait of Jawaharlal Nehru*, Dobson Books, London, 1967.

C F ANDREWS (Editor): *Mahatma Gandhi: His Own Story*, George Allen and Unwin, London, 1930.

DEMETRIUS BOULGER, (Editor); T FISHER: *Asiatic Quarterly Review*, Unwin, London, 1888.

MARY CARPENTER: *Last Days in England of Rajah Rammohun Roy*, Nabya Bharat Press, Calcutta, 1915.

R P MASANI: *Dadabhai Naoroji, the Grand Old Man of India*, George Allen and Unwin, London, 1939.

H H DODWELL AND R R SETHI (Editors): *The Cambridge History of India 1858 – 1947*, S Chand, Delhi.

Dadabhai Naoroji, A Study, Ganesh, Madras, 1907.

R P MASANI: *Dadabhai Naoroji*, The Publication Division, Ministry of Information and Broadcasting, Government of India, Delhi, 1959.

LAJPAT RAI (Foreword by JOSIAH C WEDGWOOD): *Young India*, Home Rule for India League (British Auxiliary), London, 1917.

LAJPAT RAI (Foreword by) *Josiah C Wedgwood: The Man and his Work*, S Ganesan, Madras, c.1920.

S K RATCLIFFE: *Sir William Wedderburn and the Indian Reform Movement*, George Allen and Unwin, London, 1923.

SADHONA BONNERJEE: *Life of W C Bonnerjee, first President of the Indian National Congress*, (Publisher's name not available). 1944.

East India Association Pamphlets, East India Association, London, 1909.

Indo-British Association Ltd, Indo-British Association, London, 1920.

Indian Worthies, Volume I, Manoranjak Grantha Prasarak Mandal, Bombay, 1906.

Audi Alteram Partem, being Two Letters on Certain Aspects of the Indian National Congress Movement, Simla, The Station Press, London, 1888.

Indian National Congress, Session at Allahabad, Impression of Two English Visitors, Indian Political Agency, London, 1889.

Indian National Congress, speeches delivered at Luncheon Given in Honour of Sir William Wedderburn , President-elect of the Congress Session to be held in Bombay, 26 December 1889 with Sundry Newspaper Comments thereon, Indian Political Agency, London, 1889.

London Indian Society, 10 December 1865 (booklet), Manchester Indian Association, *Discussion on Indian Affairs 11 December 1877 (booklet)*, Manchester Town Hall, *Speeches by the Rt Hon John Bright MP, Sir Arthur Cotton KCSI*, (Names of publishers not available)

SACHCHIDANADA BHATTACHARYA: *A Dictionary of Indian History*, Calcutta University Press, Calcutta, 1967.

VINCENT A SMITH: *Oxford History of India*, Oxford University Press, Oxford, 1919.

A O HUME: *A Speech on Indian National Congress, its Origins, Aims and Objectives, deliveried at Government Public Meeting, Allahabad and North West Provinces, 30 April 1888*. (Publisher's name not available)

India Today (Volume 1, Number 1), Published by The India League, London, 1934.

British Indian Association: Petition of the Indian Association to the House of Commons on various subjects of Indian Administration (booklet). (Publisher's name not available), 1859.

DADABHAI NAOROJI: *On Duties of Local Indian Associations in Connection with the London Association*, W Clowes and Son, London, 1868.

DADABHAI NAOROJI: *Poverty and Un-British Rule in India*, Swan Sonnenschein, London, 1901.

Who's Who of British Members of Parliament, The Harvester Press, Sussex, 1981.

Dictionary of National Biography, Institute of Historical Studies, Calcutta, 1972, 1990.

Who Was Who, Eminent Indians, 1900–1980, Durga Das Private Ltd, New Delhi, 1985.

Directory of Indian Women Today, India International Publications, New Delhi, 1976.

JAGDISH SARAN SHARMA: *Encyclopaedia of India's Struggle for Freedom*, S Chand. (Private) Ltd, New Delhi, 1971.

CECIL WOODHAM-SMITH: *Queen Victoria: Her Life and Times*, Vol.I, 1819–1861, Book Club Associates, London, 1973.

MAJUMDER, ROY CHOUDHURI AND DATTA: *An Advanced History of India*, Macmillan, London.

REGINALD CLEAVER, SYDNEY P HALL, PAUL RENOUARD, H W BREWER AND OTHER ARTISTS: *Parlimentary Pictures and Personalities: Graphic Sketches in Parliament 1890–1893*, Sampson Low, Marston & Company, London, 1893.

Illustration credits

Index